AN ADAPTIVE
NEURAL NETWORK

the cerebral cortex

AN ADAPTIVE NEURAL NETWORK

the cerebral cortex

YVES BURNOD

*INSERM Researcher
at the Institut Pasteur*

MASSON | 1990 | PRENTICE HALL
PARIS | | LONDON

The Masson edition of this book is published in the series *Biologie théorique* edited by G. Chauvet and H. Le Guyader.

Published in 1988 in France, Italy, Portugal, Spain, Switzerland and Belgium by Masson, and copublished 1990 by Prentice Hall International for distribution throughout the rest of the world.

© Masson, Paris, 1988, 1990

ISBN 0-13-019464-6

Library of Congress Cataloging-in-Publication Data
British Library Cataloguing in Publication Data
are available from the publisher.

Contents

Introduction

Tool-making and language: these capacities that have so dramatically multiplied the adaptiveness of the human species, issue in some poorly-understood way from the human brain.

It is generally recognized that the cerebral cortex, extensively developed in man, plays a crucially important role in the elaboration of these capacities. We are gradually acquiring an understanding of some of the fundamental aspects of cortical structure and function (Mountcastle 1978), and we can now attempt to relate these mechanisms to higher-level human capacities.

In the investigation of these complex phenomena, two general research strategies have greatly contributed to our understanding of cerebral mechanisms:

1. Experimental results from neurobiology and psychology. Powerful experimental methods, proceeding by testing verifiable hypotheses, confronting them with precise observations of concrete reality, have furnished a wealth of information. But this information has been gathered in heterogeneous experimental contexts and these facts need to be fitted into an overall theoretical structure in order to adequately explain the complexities of human adaptation.

2. Artificial intelligence has led to the construction of systems whose information processing capacities approach those of human beings. In particular, adaptive automata networks which perform parallel distributed processing have many analogies with mental processes like learning and generalizing from examples. But these artificial systems are still far from the adaptive wealth of the human brain.

The aim of this book is to propose a theoretical model of the cerebral cortex with an approach combining Neurobiology and Artificial Intelligence. This model defines a specific cortical function, based on the cellular organization of the cortex and shows how this cortical function can explain the principal adaptations and forms of learning possible to the human species: recognition of complex forms, visually-guided hand movements, execution of structured programs, language learning. The theory does not consider all possible aspects of the cortex but focuses on those adaptive functions which are already partially solved by Artificial Intelligence.

Real neural networks have inspired several theories of adaptive automata networks (see review in Rumelhart 1986). In these theories, every behavioural or cognitive process resulted from the coordination of a large number of cells or cell assemblies (Hebb 1949), each roughly localized in different regions of the brain, but all working together in dynamic interactions (Luria 1965).

These theories assume that information processing is parallel and distributed over wide sets of interacting elements - or automata- each sending excitatory or inhibitory signals to other units (Rumelhart 1986)).

The properties of the processing elements were inspired by the basic properties of the neural hardware. Biological neurons were modeled as logical decision elements described by all-or-none state variable (Mc Cullogh and Pitts, 1943). Adaptive properties of these networks were based on local "learning rules" for each automaton that can behave as single unit analogs of associative conditioning (Hebb 1949): this local learning mechanism adjusts the strength of connections between units based on information locally available at the connection, for example when input and output are simultaneously active ("Hebb rule"). Learning rules of processing units can be mathematically determined in order to produce a global adaptive function for the network (Widrow, 1960). In these models, behavioral learning is a result of tuning the connections: the memory and the knowledge is in the strength of connections.

These neural-like networks have many interesting properties. They can learn to associate representations, for example the association between the visual form of a word and its meaning . Although far from real neural networks, these parallel distributed models can account in detail for psychological data on the processes of pattern recognition, speech perception and generalization of learning from examples. As with human memory, the network tends to retrieve what is common to different input patterns. Such distributed mechanisms can learn rules from examples. For instance, a network can learn rules to construct the past tense of verbs from their root forms; in this case, the behaviour of the system follows the same learning stages as children, such as transient regularization of irregular verbs.

These automata networks can also precisely describe processes at the neurobiological level, like self organization of cortical maps (Kohonen 1984) or specific information processing performed by a cortical area; it is then possible to compare the behaviour of automata with the properties of cortical neurons experimentally analyzed in these areas (Zipser 1988).

A) We propose a model architecture for the four main organizational levels of the cortical system.

Our basic conception shares common features with these models which are neurally inspired: information processing is parallel and distributed, and learning is produced by changes in the connection strengths between elements.

But our approach is quite different: its originality is to start from the physical reality of the nervous system, with present available knowledge, to propose a network of automata specific to the cerebral cortex and capable of generating similar adaptive functions such as invariant recognition, manipulation and language.

Starting from the physical reality means taking into account the different levels of the cortical system: cells, columns, maps and areas; each level gives specific adaptive properties that are not presently included in models.

We focus on the constraints which arise from the physical reality at the different levels of the brain. We describe a biological system which has an adaptive efficiency that comes from a variety of means and levels more than a mathematical efficiency that comes from a single formula for a local rule resulting in a global function performed by the network.

This is because the adaptive properties of a biological system depend not on its organization at any one level, but rather at different hierarchical levels, each lower level being tightly articulated into the next highest level: an isolated cell can execute basic adaptations such as recognition and orientation towards a goal; cellular tissues and organs, by their three-dimensional geometry, facilitate certain exchanges with the outside world; at a higher level, the different organs co-operate to ensure a global energy balance for the whole organism.

In order to fully explain the adaptive characteristics of a biological system like the cortex, we are obliged to consider all these levels-- none can be omitted. It should be clear that one cannot arrive at explanations for behaviour by considering only the cellular level; even if it is possible to show that memorization is a general property of the nervous cells, behavioural learning capacities are not: learning in humans and in invertebrates is quite different. On the other hand, it is difficult to fully explain the adaptive capacities of the human brain by considering only the interactions between the different cortical areas, without knowing what the cortical cells are doing.

Our theory is original in that it proposes a model architecture and functioning rules as compatible as possible with experimental knowledge at the four main organizational levels of the cerebral cortex:

1. Cortical cells - pyramidal neurons and interneurons- share many common features with neurons in other structures but they have specific properties of integration and memorization of input information organized in layers.

2. Cortical "columns" are groups of cooperating cells. If we imagine the cortex as a two-dimensional tissue, with input and output at the bottom, a column forms a circuit running up and then down perpendicular to the surface of the tissue; the entire cortex itself is made up of billions of such columns. These columnar circuits perform transformation of the inputs, receiving and passing in the process signals from or to other such columns. This input-output processing - the "columnar function" - have adaptive and learning properties which do not exist at the single cell level.

3. Cortical "maps" are formed by contiguous sets of columns which have ordered topological input-output relations with sensory or motor areas, or with other nervous structures. At this "regional" level, the cortical network integrate columnar processes into behavioral adaptations such as positioning or recognition.

4. The network between cortical areas has an overall architecture which organizes the main information flows, such as relations between audition and phonation or between vision and manipulation. But this network can also integrate successive learning experiences in a coherent functional system such as language with its different components, auditory and phonetic, syntactic and semantic.

A number of observations will serve to orient the approach that we will undertake.

a) Cellular level: basic integrative properties of neurons.

Although the cortex has often been described as a general integration and learning system, these two capacities are not exclusively cortical in nature, but seem to be general neuronal properties since they exist in species such as invertebrates that have no cortex (Kandel, 1977b). The property of "memorization" seems to be generally found in a wide variety of nervous systems: this memorization has been studied at the cellular level in invertebrates (Kandel 1977b; Alkon 1982) and, in vertebrate nervous systems, in neural structures with a regular geometry, such as the hippocampus (Bliss 1973; Andersen 1977) or the cerebellum (Ito 1982).

b) Modular level: columnar processing.

The cortex has been subdivided into a number of specific areas, each of which has a functional specialization (Luria 1973), such as: motor sequence, spatial positioning, visual analysis, production and comprehension of language, abstraction, etc. But in spite of this functional diversity, detailed analysis at the cellular level has led researchers to formulate a structural and functional principle generalizable to the entire cortex: the "cortical column" (Mountcastle 1959; Szentagothai 1975).

The functional characteristics of this "column" have been detailed in the cortical receptive (Hubel 1977), motor (Evarts 1974), associative (Mountcastle 1975), and frontal (Fuster 1973) areas. It is therefore important to understand how such columns, functioning according to general principles of cellular interactions, accomplish the informational transformations typical of human learning.

This basic function is not a simple associative mechanism: for example language production demands the activation of a highly specialized mechanism that cannot be reduced to simple sensory-motor conditioning (Chomsky 1970). In order to define this specific operation, it is important to note that the internal structure of human cortical tissue is in direct evolutionary continuity with the cortex of mammals and the other primates (Cajal 1911). Consequently, it should be possible to find, in these species, a cortical capacity that is the functional precursor of the human cognitive capacities.

This basic cortical operation should be explained from its cellular components. In theory it is possible to deduce some properties of a neural tissue from neuronal shapes (Rall 1964), ionic channels (Traub) and long term changes of synaptic transmission (Hebb 1949). Such reconstructions have been attempted, for example for the cerebellum (Marr 1969, Pellionisz 1982) and the cerebral cortex (Marr 1970, Eccles 1981), but these models have not considered a specific columnar operation.

c) Regional or "tissular" level: construction of basic behavioural functions.

We now need to understand how the basic columnar function common to all the cortical areas, can generate extremely varied behavioural adaptations, depending upon the links of the cortical columns with sensory or motor organs and upon the cortical network which relates cortical maps. In order that we may understand the progressive learning of specific global behavioural functions, such as recognition, or positioning in space, we must find a model for this cortical network; its geometrical features may induce many combinatorial properties which determine learning capacities. For example visual guidance of arm movements is easier with a network which forms all possible combinations between command of muscles and regions of the visual field; verbal imitation of words is highly favoured by a network that links all positions of the vocal apparatus with auditory frequencies.

d) Global level: integrated learning.

The cognitive development in the child is an ordered process (Piaget 1968). Cortical maturation in the human species is slow, particularly in the frontal lobes which are much more extended than in other species. This neurobiological basis may be an important factor of the cognitive development. The construction of mental images and words should be highly dependent upon the growth and the resulting geometry of the cortical network: it is important to see how the semantic structure of words and the syntactic organization of language can be learned with this network.

B) We propose a "cortical mechanism" that can explain the adaptive capacities of the cortex.

In our model we focus on the behaviour of the columnar automaton that is the behaviour of a group of cells composed of pyramidal neurons and different types of interneurons tightly linked in a cylinder perpendicular to the cortical surface: we consider the columnar inputs as the combination of all inputs to each cell of the column which originate externally from the column, the columnar state to be the combination of the states of each cell and the columnar output, the combination of external outputs from each cell. Furthermore, just as it is possible to describe the process of memorization for a cell, by which it changes its behaviour, so this idea can be applied for columns, where, in learning situations, the columnar function may be altered.

Compared with a cellular automaton, a columnar automaton has more functional and learning capacities. To take an analogy with computers, we could imagine a cell to correspond to one computer memory location, and a column as an area of computer memory in which may be stored different computer programs to perform different subfunctions. The memorization of a subfunction by a cortical column can be compared with the development of a small computer program.

Furthermore, just as a large number of computer programs are integrated to provide a complex system, so cortical columns, each with its particular subfunction, are assembled by learning to provide a far more complex behavioral function. Learning of behaviour by a cortical region could be compared with the step by step integration of small programs to form a computer system. The major difference with computer programs is that columnar subfunctions possess their own intrinsic rules for building up larger structures.

In chapter II, we define this columnar automaton by an in-out table which determines the two outputs of a column (intra and extracortical) from its inputs (cortical and thalamic) and from its previous state. It is based on neuronal processing performed by the different cell types of the column and integrates known physiological properties such as gating by cortical inputs, lateral inhibition and vertical amplification. We define two learning rules that enable sets of columns to be assembled in integrated mechanism, one in the top-down direction from goals, and the other one in the bottom-up direction from the external information. We base these learning properties upon the memorizing properties of different cortical cells (pyramidal neurons and five interneuronal types) with a logic based upon cell position in the network.

This model of "columnar automaton" meets three essential requirements:

1. The ubiquity of the columnar architecture implies that the operational mechanism is the same in any region of the cortex. This columnar architecture provides a common framework upon which we can generalize; variations of cellular texture in different areas throughout the cortex ("cytoarchitectonics") are included in the variations of parameters of the columnar operations : they correspond to local adjustments of a common function.

2. The proposed mechanism is specific to the cerebral cortex in that it can only be deduced from the unique cellular structure of the column, but not from other brain textures such as the hippocampus or the cerebellum; this cortical process is basically an active "searching mechanism" that provides the possible pathways in order to reach a goal from any initial position. This mechanism which is compatible with experiments that relate cell activity and behaviour, can explain two main cortical properties, goal-directed behaviour and active self-driven learning.

3. This unique process can construct diverse behavioural functions depending upon the connectivity of each cortical area. It provides a unitary explanation for apparently diverse cortical functions such as visual guidance of hand movements, learning by imitation or the symbolic manipulation of language. In chapter IV, we examine the construction of these diverse functions depending upon the network of connections of each cortical area and upon its maturation. For this purpose, we propose in Chapter III an integrated model of the network between cortical regions, based on the present anatomical knowledge, in order to focus on its geometrical and combinatorial properties.

Each specialized region is formed by billions of columns which all represent possible actions, goals and subgoals; columnar automata construct the possible pathways in order to reach such goals from any initial position determined by environmental situations;

- In parietal areas, these call trees perform visual guidance of hand movements to reach a target, whatever the initial positions.

- In temporal areas they are algorithms that can recognize forms independently of their size or retinal position.

- In frontal regions which have short term memory properties call trees organize "structured sequences" with a variable number of internal levels such as sequences of words in language.

The network between columns and between cortical areas has a precise architecture that influences the learning capacities of the cerebral cortex. In the last chapter we will see how this architecture plays a key role in the cognitive development of the child: the external world will be represented in the child's brain in a coherent way.

C) The mechanism that we propose is compatible with the experimental results at all four levels of cortical organization.

Models of cortical function hitherto proposed are not equivalent when one accumulates constraints. We adopt a strategy that combines the neurobiological and artificial intelligence approaches and our model attempts to satisfy two criteria:

- functionality: the proposed mechanism produces behavioural functions and has adaptive capacities;

- compatibility: the model is consistent with what is known of the cellular structure of the cortex and the behavioural capacities attributed to it.

Many experimental approaches and techniques have been used to study the various levels of cortical organization, such as biochemistry, histology, anatomy, electrophysiology, neuropsychology, experimental psychology, and cognitive psychology.

The results are so extensive that it is impossible to take them all into account: our strategy has been to try to consider results from a variety of sources.

One of the cardinal requirements of the kind of experimental compatibility that we seek is that the model takes into account the different dimensions and the different levels of the cortical system. At each level we try to stick to general principles experimentally established in order to have a good representation of the immense amount of existing material that describes the path from cell function to language production. This work is not an attempt at a complete explanation for language, it is a description of a neuronal system that can generate language with its different syntactic and semantic components.

For our purposes it is necessary to show that the theory makes sense in terms of basic concepts before going into finer details. For example, autoproduction of language by children is a fundamental phenomenon which is not explained by simple associative models (Chomsky); furthermore, there are successive stages that are the same for all children and that do not depend on their specific environment as would be predicted by simple associationist schemes (Piaget). We do not want to examine supporting data in detail (other people have done this) and we do not wish to enter into discussions such as the precise description of stages of child development. We merely try to show that autoproduction of language in an ordered way is a direct consequence of cortical properties. The main difficulty is to discuss behaviour and language processes with concepts derived from biology. All the different concepts addressed in the last chapter on cognitive processes (cortical image, word, etc.) are related to a precise, imitable, neural process.

The different parameters of cortical organization are far from being completely known. The partial knowledge that we have of synaptic function and the action of neuro-mediators at the cortical level is the fruit of many experiments; we have tried to integrate the principle characteristics.

Different models of neuronal function have been elaborated from experiments performed on systems other than the cerebral cortex. We have chosen for study those that appeared to be best supported by experimental evidence, and from these models, considered to be general, we have derived rules that were subsequently applied to the parameters of the cortical network.

It is clear that the kind of mechanism attributed to the cortex here goes considerably beyond what is factually known, and enters the realm of the hypothetical. But this model makes predictions which are experimentally verifiable; for instance, electrophysiological techniques that permit the quantification of neuronal activity could confirm whether or not the cells follow the logic that we propose. Interactions of large populations of neurons cannot be directly analyzed as yet, but behavioural consequences of these interactions can be tested.

D) We adopt a systematic approach in order to focus on the coherence of the cortical system which is constructed from a single cell and produces a global adaptive behaviour.

Above all, the cerebral cortex is a part of a multi-level biological system which has a global coherence.

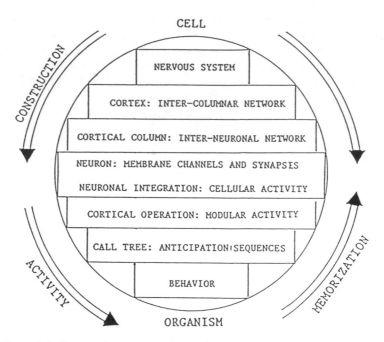

Figure 0-1 . From cell to behaviour: global coherence of the cortical system.

FIGURE 0-1 depicts the basic architecture of a multicellular organism and illustrates its fundamental property: the whole system is constructed from a single cell (upper part, downward arrows), and the results of its cellular interactions produce a globally adaptive behaviour (lower part, downward arrows).

Adaptive behaviour is possible thanks to two conditions:
- the cellular groups, such as organs, represent and amplify the different basic functions of the cell: energy, development, reproduction, communication.
- neural and hormonal communications coordinate the complementary functions of organs to ensure the energy balance of each individual cell, and therefore the survival of the organism in its environment.
The nervous system can be diversified within the limits of these two constraining conditions (fundamental programs and energy balance). Different parts of the nervous system (retina, spinal cord, cerebral cortex, etc.) are thus specialized to control various interactions with the environment, which contribute to the survival and the reproduction of the organism: for example recognition, oriented movement or communication.
Such adaptive processes can be described from their end result. This desired end result, we will call the "goal". For example, in homeostatic mechanisms, goals are constant physiological parameters regardless of external variation. In another example, placing the hand on an object is a spatial adaptation, the goal is the minimal distance between the object and the hand. More generally, a behavioural adaptation corresponds to a goal which is a minimal or a maximal value of a

parameter which represents an interaction with the environment. In visually guided hand movements, the parameter of the interaction would be the distance between the hand and the object. The goal is reached whatever the initial position by minimizing or "optimizing" this parameter by any combination of muscular contractions ; many different movements may have the same final result.

Whenever we refer in this text to the term "optimization", we mean the process of achieving an end result, which is defined as a maximal or a minimal value of a parameter, for example a minimal distance. Depending upon the parameter which is optimized, adaptations can be placing (minimal distances), recognitions (optimal matching to an external form), motor programs (optimal temporal patterns); communications and language correspond to more sophisticated forms of adaptations (optimization by social interaction) .

The cerebral cortex can generate all these specific forms of behavioural adaptations. Adaptive properties of a system like the cortex originate from three complementary factors: its structure, its function, and its learning capacities (shown by the three arrows of Figure 0-1).

a) STRUCTURE: Construction of a multilevel network of automata from a single cell.

The "structure" of a biological system is the organizational plan, the network of interactions between the cellular elements. Particularly important for a biological system is the progressive elaboration of complex structures from a single cell (ontogeny).

During embryogenesis, cellular divisions generate larger and larger groups of cells. Functional systems are genetically determined from the larger to the finer levels: organs, tissue, modules and cell types (downward arrow in Figure 0-1). The structure of the cortical network will not be described in an all-or-none manner, but as a result of a construction algorithm which determines connections between areas, between maps between columns and between neuronal types.

This construction is based upon the universal cycle of cellular division accompanied by diverse cellular actions controlled by the genes: cell migration forms layers of neurons, membrane extension forms axons and dendrites, intercellular communication forms synapses, etc. Simple genomic mutations can thus produce a great variety of neural networks (phylogeny) and the universal division-mutation process creates new adaptive networks by a simple "trial and error" method.

b) FUNCTION: From neuronal processing to adaptive behaviour.

Associated with each element or automaton is a property which is its internal state and this internal state we refer to as the "activity" of the automaton. An element in a particular state of activity, when receiving inputs from other elements may change its current state of activity as well as the output it produces. This input-output operation can be described in mathematical terms: for example it can produce an oscillation (rhythmic pattern generator) that is important for movement, or "filter" a patterned stimulus, that is important for recognition. More generally, we have described behavioral adaptations as "optimizations" of parameters which represent interactions with the environment; such optimizations can be obtained by two complementary neural operations:

- the comparison between the current state of the system and the desired goal;

- a modification of this "distance" by feedback actions until the optimal value is attained.

Throughout the text when we refer to an action, we mean the idea of the result of the neural activity on a parameter which measures a behavioural adaptation, such as a movement that changes a distance, a feature extraction that may increase matching of an image with a stored pattern, or even a word that modifies a social relation.

c) PLASTICITY, LEARNING AND MEMORY: from long term cellular changes to learning capacities.

Neural networks can learn and memorize new adaptations. Description of learning and memory is viewed as long term changes of the interactions between the automata: between two elements of the network, the presence of a physical connection in itself does not necessarily lead to communication. Associated with each physical connection, is the concept of a "coupling coefficient" which modifies any signal passing along the physical connection, either to strengthen the signal or possibly to inhibit it altogether.

This coupling coefficient can itself be modified on a long term basis so that an element reacts differently to particular inputs, and produces new types of outputs. This process is referred to as "memorization" when it depends upon activity in the network. "Learning rules" describe how "coupling coefficients" are modified in relation with activity; long term changes depend upon critical "activity patterns" which are particular combinations of inputs and internal states.

Two aspects of the network can be identified. The first, the physical substratum, comprises sets of neurons along with their interconnections; the second aspect, the "functional network", is the result of the superimposition, upon the physical substratum, of the results of memorization stored in coupling coefficients by elements of the network, by which information is actually processed.

Patterns of connectivity between neurons are modified by experience (learning rules), and they can internally represent the properties of the external world. Adaptive mechanisms are amplified by memorization processes. New adaptations can be learned by continual modification of the coupling coefficients with activity patterns which depend upon the result with respect to the goal.

Different types of neuronal tissues will have different learning capacities, from very simple forms (pavlovian conditioning) to very elaborate forms (language learning). We shall try to demonstrate that these more elaborate forms are due to the specific properties of the cortical tissue. The rules that we propose for columnar automata do not make the cortex into a simple associative system, but instead the material support for a general mechanism of adaptation that includes both an active searching mechanism and a highly structured learning process. We will show how this fundamental mechanism can assemble new functional networks which produce not only adaptations like form recognition and placing responses, but also basic linguistic functions, which are specific expressions of a more general adaptation of communication.

We shall use a systematic approach of the adaptive capacities of the cerebral cortex and we shall proceed on three distinct parallel pathways:

1. We shall describe with simple rules structure, function and memorization properties at the four levels of the cortical system : cells, columns, maps and organs.

2. We shall attempt to justify these rules on the basis of neurobiological and psychological data; we will try to preserve as much of the system's richness as possible, at each of the four levels.

3. These rules should, together, form a coherent system; the rules will be translated into a common formal language. We have defined a number of abstract concepts ie elements, connections, coupling coefficients, actions, optimization and goals which between them make up the structure and behaviour of an adaptive network. Specific instances of these concepts will be identified by associating the instance with the abstract term; for example we shall refer to "cortical actions" and "cortical goals" when describing the instance of the cortex. This formalism will be developed in the ANNEX.

This systematic approach may first appear both specialized and complex. It is not as specialized as experimental reports in the literature in each domain that it covers. For specialists, each part should have many more experimental references and it may appear oversimplified. The number of parameters that we use seems high, but is much less than in simple information-processing machines like microcomputers. A minimal precision is necessary for challenging simulations. The rules are simplified in order to facilitate their integration in higher levels: each rule is expressed in a semi-quantitative way, by a table, and not by an algebraic formula. The rules are not strictly deterministic, but are rather probabilistic and determine limits that are imposed on an activity that remains unpredictably variable.

We have relied heavily on schemes to shorten the explanations because they provide much more information, like maps versus guides.

Even if this approach is far from being complete- particularly given the present state of knowledge- we think it will allow progress beyond solutions that are currently proposed- because it provides a common framework within which these solutions may be integrated in a cumulative way, a framework which is coherent since it is inspired by the physical reality of the cortex which evidently has a very powerful internal coherence:

- in Neurobiology, this framework facilitates an integrated representation of a heterogeneous set of data; furthermore quantitative aspects allow simulations, for example at the columnar level, and can be compared quantitatively with experimental data;

- in Psychology, this biological framework, even though partial, can provide new insights into problems such as attention, learning capacities of children, stability of the visual environment or properties of the frontal lobe;

- in Artificial Intelligence: several aspects of knowledge are directly linked to the global coherence of the cortical system, as for example the internal semantic structure of words.

Structure, function and learning
at the four levels of the cortical system.

An overview of this discussion is provided by the analytical table, shown in FIGURE 0-2; the four organizational levels of the cortical system are represented on the vertical axis: cell, module (columns), tissue (maps) and global nervous system. For each level, we specify the structural, functional and learning properties of the neural network (horizontal axis of Figure 0-2). All these properties increase the adaptive capacities of the cortical system. The corresponding formalism which links them is developed in ANNEX I.

A) Chapter I: Cellular level.
Basic operations and memorization properties of neurons.

a) Structure of the intracellular molecular network: what are the adaptive capacities of each individual cell?

The basic elements of the nervous system are cells. Molecular interactions within each cell are becoming quite precisely understood from properties of genes, enzymes, channels and ions. At the cellular level, our job will be to simplify the wealth of information concerning the biology of the neuron, but conserve the adaptive logic of each cell.

We begin with a simple view of the basic molecular interactions responsible of the main adaptive capacities of cells, such as reproduction, recognition, goal-directed movement and intercellular communication. All these cellular adaptations are used to construct the neural network, with migration of cells and extension of neurites towards specific targets, and programs of communication resulting in the formation of new synapses.

b) Function of neurons: what is the basic information processing performed by neurons?

Neurons synthesize ionic channels that selectively control the movement of ions across their membrane. These ionic movements have a spatio-temporal form (action potentials and synaptic potentials) that represents a neural "information" . With different combinations of ionic channels, neurons can transmit, process, and memorize this information.

Via its synapses, each neuron receives information from several other "afferent" neurons; it combines these inputs into a unique axonal output. This basic combination is far from simple, and we have chosen to approximate it by logical operations such as "and", "or", etc. We relate these different operations to molecular and geometrical parameters of neurons. We use these relations in chapter II to characterize the basic operations performed by the different types of cortical neurons.

	STRUCTURATION	FUNCTIONING	MEMORIZATION
GENERAL	Main information flows Interstructural cooperation Geometrical properties of the cortical network	Specialized operations: Movements and placing Form recognition Structured sequences	Cognitive development: Manipulation; Imitation Mental images; categories Structured language
TISSUE	Cortical maps Relative extensions Recombination matrix Systematic connections	Call tree Functional redundancy Lateral subdivision Transversal couplings	Structured learning Integrated action bases Generalization Differentiation
MODULE	Cortical column Inter-neuronal network Connectivity by layers (De-)Coupling capacities	Mocular operation: Searching mechanism Progressive sequencing to reach a goal	Anticipation Oriented sequences Fixed sequences Selective inhibition
CELL	Synaptic network: receptors Membrane network: channels Specialized receptive zones Transmitter release zones	Spatial integration Combination of inputs Logical approximation: AND, OR, IF NOT, etc	Memorization processes 4 temporal levels 4 spatial levels Associative properties

Figure 0-2 . Analytical table: Structure, function and learning at the four organizational levels of the cortical system.

c) Memorization by neurons: what can a neuron learn?

Memorization at the cellular level appears to be a general process in the course of phylogeny. This process is the result of a cascade of events that occur in neurons with at least four temporal levels: (1) within a short time span (1 millisecond to 1 second) cell responses (channel opening, calcium flows) outlast the duration of input information. (2) Next, movements of calcium and activation of second messengers can modify transmission during minutes or even hours (facilitation or depression). (2) Critical patterns of activity can produce longer-term transformation of channels and synaptic receptors that last for hours and even days (long term potentiation). (4) Activity-dependant changes of gene regulations result in permanent modification of cell behaviour. During the "critical periods" in continuity with construction of the neural network, activation patterns can also result in a geometric re-shaping of the neural network with formation of new synapses. We focus on this progressive aspect of memorization and we formulate simple complementary rules for each of the four time spans .

Furthermore, we take into account the spatial parameters of these activity-dependent transformations: memorization can implicate widespread regions of neurons, or on the contrary, very restricted parts such as dendritic spines. This spatial extension is very important for the "associative" logic of the memorizing process.

We consider memorization as a basic cellular phenomenon, analogous to registration in computers, but more refined, with several spatial and temporal levels. Learning is a consequence of this cellular registration process but neuronal networks have different learning capacities which are highly dependent on their architecture: in chapter II we will analyze how the architecture of the cortical column gives specific learning properties to the cortical system.

B) Chapter II: Modular level.
Columnar processing and construction of new functional networks by learning.

In chapter II, we focus on the specific properties of the cerebral cortex. This way of proceeding, from the general to the specific, is essential for understanding what it is that distinguishes the cortex from the other neural structures.

a) Structure of the cortical column: What are the specific features which differentiate the cortex from other neural tissues?

In vertebrates, the basic organization of most neural tissues including the cerebral cortex is a cellular "texture": there are several cells types that form a local network repeated throughout the tissue. This basic circuit is often duplicated (as in the retina, the cerebellum, the hippocampus, the spinal cord) into two main layers (or transversal divisions) that correspond to two processing steps, one internal to the structure, and the other for the output. The cerebral cortex has six layers which can be grouped into two main divisions according to this general schema: the fourth layer (or granular layer) that receives the external thalamic inputs is intermediate between two subsets of pyramidal neurons, one in the supragranular layers (layers II and III) and the other one in the infragranular layers (V and VI): pyramidal neurons of these two divisions form the two principle output pathways, internal or external to the cortex.

Structural and functional properties of pyramidal neurons are linked to the depth of their cell body within the cortex. This positional parameter (layer) determines both their target structures, intra or extra cortical, and the specific operations that they perform on the principal inputs (reticular, thalamic and cortical) organized in layers.

The pyramidal cells are grouped in vertical columns, perpendicular to the surface, with strong interconnections: inside a column they share afferents that have the same sensory or motor significance. These connections are doubled by excitatory and inhibitory pathways formed by at least five main types of interneurons. These interneurons, when they are active, can couple or uncouple not only interconnected columns, but also the layers within each column. Furthermore, they participate in the memorizing process of the cortical column; thanks to their diversity, different functional pathways within and between columns can be reinforced depending upon patterns of activity. In order to detail all the possible long term changes of columnar function with learning, we propose a 3-dimensional model of the intrinsic and extrinsic connections of a column like a crystalline structure that allows repetitive associations in large assemblies : this model combines links between upper and lower layers, links between neighboring columns, links with columns in other areas, external links with other brain regions, and controls of all these pathways by excitatory and inhibitory interneurons.

b) Function: What is the computation performed by the cortical column?

Different nervous structures with specialized neural circuits effect different types of information processing: for example, they can filter the spatio-temporal pattern of their inputs (important for recognition) or generate oscillations and sequences (important for movements).

On this basis, we attack the problem of relating the cellular texture of the cortical tissue to the specific operation that each column effects upon its inputs. We synthesize known physiological properties of the cortical column, such as gating effects of cortical inputs, transversal amplification and lateral inhibition, by an in-out table that defines a "columnar automaton"; this table determines the two main outputs of a column (intra and extra cortical) from the two main inputs (cortical and thalamic) and the previous state of the column, with four properties: (1) the relation between two columns can be excitatory or inhibitory, depending upon the level of activity; (2) the activity can spread in the cortical network, even without significant output outside the cortex; (3) an amplifying effect is produced when cortical and thalamic inputs are simultaneously active; (4) the relative importance of these two inputs varies with cortical areas (cytoarchitectonic modulations).

This table which define columnar automata determines the configurations of columnar activities (parallel processing) and their sequences (sequential processing). This basic operation is an adaptive mechanism with two types of responses to external events:

- when a column is simultaneously activated by intra and extracortical inputs, it can effect a precise extra-cortical action, like a reflex.

- when this column is only partially activated, it does not produce an extra-cortical action, but it then signals to other cortical columns through the cortical network.

This intercolumnar signalling is termed a "call". Such calls to other columns may result in extra-cortical actions when they are in register with specific extracortical inputs (from the environment) or else calls to other columns. A "call" can remain in force until one of the "called" columns produces an extracortical action which results in an extracortical "feedback" input to the calling column. This column is then strongly active: it executes its own action and the call stops.

The action of each cortical column represents, in this sense, an equilibrium position, a kind of "goal" that organizes the activity of other columns that are connected by the cortical network. When a goal is not directly obtainable, the columnar automaton produces a call that results in an exploration, a search through the possible actions that the cortex can command in order to reach the goal.

c) Memorization: what are the learning capacities of the cortical column?

The very organization of the cortical column determines a mode of learning that is much more than a simple association; it is an active , structured process.

We define memorization rules at the columnar level from the registration processes of each of the cortical cell types - the pyramidal cells and the five types of interneurons. They give three learning capacities to the columnar automaton:

1. First, critical activity pattern can selectively reinforce either the excitatory or inhibitory aspects of connections between columns. Excitatory connections are strengthened when a called module produces an action outside the cortex that re-activates the calling module by an extracortical feedback loop (external causal link). Consequently, after learning, a column will selectively call other cortical columns that favour its own action. Thus, the columnar automaton organizes the permanent search for actions which can reach a goal (activation rules) followed by the progressive memorization of the efficient combinations (learning rules).

2. Second, activation patterns can affect the relations between layers within each column with two possible functional consequences: after learning, a cortical input can either "gate" the response of the column to other inputs (logical "AND" function), or it can directly trigger a columnar action (logical "OR" function). In the first case, learning "orients" a call towards possible actions which may be efficient to reach a goal but their execution depends upon external conditions (adjustment to environmental situations); in the second case a call produces fixed sequences of actions that are independent of external conditions.

3. Third, tuning of connections at the level of dendritic "spines" with simple Hebb rules, as described in other models, produces a more precise adaptation. After the qualitative learning which has defined the possible pathways in the top-down direction, this more precise quantitative learning determines the proportions between simultaneous or successive activities, in the bottom-up direction, in order to decrease the distance from the goal.

This progressive memorization adapts precisely to the regular features of the environment.

Learning properties of the columnar automaton causes new functional networks to be assembled; we have named these effective networks "call trees" because of their ramified hierarchical structure, formed by goal and subgoals. These "call trees" develop in space and in time, with a variable geometry depending upon external conditions. They have a top-down and a bottom-up activation. First in the top-down direction, "calls" emanate from possible goals and produce an anticipatory activation of a set of cortical modules which represent possible sub-goals and possible actions that could reduce the distance from the goal ; in this attentive state, specific external events are awaited which complete the call and thus satisfy the goal or subgoals. The call spreads until it is in register with activations from external inputs that represent "initial conditions".In the bottom-up direction, in response to these environmental conditions, a combination of actions are triggered both in parallel and in sequence, which bring about the attainment of subgoals and then ultimately the goal itself (in the reverse order to that in which the calls were issued).

These call trees provide the possible pathways in order to reach a goal from any initial position, by an appropriate combination (including sequences) of actions. We shall see that these call trees can not only organize motor programs and placement in space, they can also perform parallel, hierarchical, and dynamic processing of diverse sensory information (recognition algorithms).

This columnar mechanism can explain two main behavioural features of cortical processing:

1. The goal is very important in shaping neuronal activity and consequently behavioural acts. In this theory, any combination of columnar actions is a possible goal; there is a wide variety of possible goals and subgoals provided by the cortical maps. The equivalence between "goals" and "columnar actions" is a very powerful property of the cortical system: each action used to reach a goal becomes itself a possible subgoal.

2. Learning is rarely a passive process produced by external associations in the environment; it is an active process directed from the cortex. The mechanism that is described here is first a searching mechanism that "assimilates" external associations in direct relation with cortical goals. Active search and learning are permanent processes which depend upon disequilibria in the cortical network rather than upon rewards.

C) Chapter III: the regional or "tissular" level.
Geometrical and combinatorial properties of the cortical network.

a) Structure of the cortical network: What is the architecture of the network between cortical columns?

The surface of the cortex has been subdivided into different regions, each region having ordered connections with sensory or motor organs or with other brain regions; this subdivision has become more and more precise: hemispheres, cortical gyri, cortical areas and maps formed by sets of columns which have regular connective patterns (columnar bands or "stripes").

We propose an integrated model of the network between columns, focusing on its geometrical characteristics that will induce functional and learning properties. This model stresses the multi-level symmetries of the network between cortical areas: between left and right hemisphere, between frontal and associative regions, and symmetries across sulci (folds of the cortex). In this model, areas are delimited by six successive dichotomies of the whole cortical surface (that produce 2 to the sixth power cortical areas). Each subdivision is balanced by systematic connections between the two new subsets: consequently, every columnar zone in a cortical area has six standard cortico-cortical connections with six similar zones symmetrical with respect to the six dichotomies which formed this area. We show that this network has the optimal properties of an hypercube: each part of the cortex is linked to any other part with the optimal trade-off between the minimal number of relays which link them (6) and the maximal number of connections for each columnar zone (6). Furthermore, such symmetrical connections have important functional properties: they interrelate the different representations of the outside world in a systematic way, and they can induce isomorphic transfer of learning between them. For example, learning of new functional relations in the right hemisphere promotes learning of symmetrical relations in the left one.

This hypercube architecture forms several alternative pathways between two cortical areas. We show how these parallel pathways favour coherent combination of different sensorimotor information, not only correlations in maps formed by associative areas, but also more complex combinations; for example, combinations including the time dimension in the frontal cortex where regions are specified in functioning within particular time periods ("time" axis of the frontal cortex).

b) Function of a cortical zone: How can a large number of modules function in parallel?

The architecture of the intercolumnar network plays a key role in order to coordinate the parallel and sequential activity of a large number of modules.

It has been clearly demonstrated that the different afferent inputs of a cortical region are separated into parallel and alternating bands (or stripes) when they occupy the same layers, and they may cross each other when they arrive in different layers. This forms multiple combinations , like a table or a matrix, in the information flows between sensory inputs and motor outputs; multiple combinations are directly available for the columnar automata which can generate a variety of sequences using the same sensorimotor components in a non-competitive way.

Furthermore, these cortical combinations are redundant and formed by large groups of cells; the columnar mechanism can functionally subdivide such a cortical zone into a group of independent functional modules participating in different sequences. An important point is that every functional subdivision of a cortical zone creates new goals, new equilibrium positions for the cortical system: new modules will learn to call other cortical actions that increase the contrast of activity with their neighbouring modules. This parallel process continuously improves the recognition capacities of the cortex.

c) Memorization in a cortical zone: how can a cortical zone accumulate successive learning results?

In chapter II, we see how columnar automata learn combinations of actions in call trees in order to reach a goal. In chapter III, we examine the organization of successive learning experiences in a cortical zone and we analyze how the geometry of the cortical network can influence the construction of successive call trees.

In a particular learning situation, large cortical zones are concerned by the new sensorimotor combination and a large number of columnar automata can memorize in parallel the new functional links: for example memorization takes the form of new functional links between each column of one zone with each column of another. New networks are then constructed with a large cellular redundancy. Furthermore, this redundancy is amplified in "intermediate" cortical areas, such as associative and frontal areas. The consequence of widespread cellular changes is a process of generalization: each new learning is generalized to a category of situations, like examples which are generalized to become rules. The process of redundant learning creates a great number of identical functional networks, each one of which may later be tuned to a specific case: new resulting networks register several variants of the same learning scheme.

Alternate generalization and differentiation is a largely recursive process which leads to the formation of new functional networks of greater and greater functional precision, but considered together provides a coherent "family" of new integrated cortical actions: for example, sensorimotor adaptations, mental images, words, syntactic rules are such new integrated cortical actions. Thanks to the geometrical properties of the cortical network, this kind of learning is not only associative and active, it is also structured. We will see in chapter V, the importance of this process in language learning by a child.

D) Chapter IV: the global level. Learning of specialized behavioural functions in the main cortical regions.

a) Structure of the global neural network: What are the cooperative roles of the cortex and other structures of the nervous system, like the hippocampus or the cerebellum in producing behaviour?

The cortex never acts in isolation in controlling behaviour. The adaptive efficiency of the cortex depends upon its relations with other nervous structures specialized to some degree with respect to the major behavioural functions: recognition, placing, motor sequences and communication.

For example, the cortex is linked with the reticular formation which is a substructure of the neural network that can generate motor programs or basic vigilance cycles; the cortex has also direct links with the hypothalamus which controls the fundamental programs of the organism by hormonal actions.

We concentrate on three neural structures which are connected in parallel to the cortical regions, and favour the three major types of behavioural adaptation: the nigro-striatal system integrates the activities of a large number of cortical columns, combining many sensorimotor components to produce long sequences of motor actions; the hippocampus "correlates" cortical activities for recognition; the cerebellum makes quantitative adjustments to the links between sensory inputs and motor outputs.

b) Behavioural functions: How are complex behavioural functions constructed from local columnar processes in the cerebral cortex?

In chapter IV, we analyze the construction, by learning, of the major adaptive functions in the main cortical regions.

1. Motor areas precisely control hand muscles; we show how the cortical representation of the body in motor areas is well suited to construct manipulation movements, with a proximo-distal hierarchy. Columnar automata learn motor command algorithms which progressively integrate the sensory control of the movement being made and the signals which trigger it, by an active search which is much more effective than a simple associative mechanism.

2. Parietal areas form a large redundant pathway between vision and movements; parietal modules interrelate visual coordinates and motor coordinates by "matching" the somesthetic and the visual inputs: parietal automata will learn to call movements (actions of the motor cortex) that can match these two sensory activities (subgoal). These parietal automata will construct call trees that guide the hand toward a visually defined target, independently of its initial position, thanks to subgoals which are somato-visual correlations. We draw a parallel between the imitative function that positions the vocal apparatus to produce a sound, and that which guides the hand in the visual field. Thus, the phonemic sequence implicated in word production is constructed in a way fundamentally identical to that of any new movement. But this learning capacity is amplified in man by the richness of possible combinations afforded by the cortical network.

3. Receptive visual areas are subdivided in several visual maps, with a primary map which receives information from the retina, passing it on to secundary maps, each of which is specialized in a specific mode of processing the retinal image. Columnar automata can combine all these specialized actions in order to recognize forms and objects in the visual environment. In visual associative regions, we analyze how columnar automata can learn translations of visual information in order to fit together two aspects of the image, like an eye movement; but contrary to eye movements, these translations are internal to the cortex, and different translations can be effected in parallel on different parts of the image. Columnar automata memorize combinations of translations and rotations interrelate different features of the image. Resulting call trees are adjustable descriptors of environmental patterns, providing a skeletal representation of an object. Such cortical algorithms are important to recognize forms independently of their size or retinal positions, since they can match external inputs with expected patterns which have been previously learned, by transforming positions and sizes. Furthermore , thanks to a bidirectional cortical network, call trees from the somatic regions can integrate successive retinal images in body coordinates and stabilize the visual world even though the retina is swept with multiple images each time the eye moves.

4. The frontal cortex that is so spectacularly developed in the human species is implicated in temporal processing and "structured" learning. We concentrate on two properties of the frontal network: first, frontal regions can perform transient memorizations of information that comes from associative areas, with several temporal thanks to specific relations with other neural structures (striatum , reticular formation, hypothalamus etc.). Second, frontal areas can integrate in different ways this sensory and motor information over different period of time, thanks to the combinatorial properties of the cortical network; for example, it can wait for successive sensory information before triggering an appropriate movement.

We show how these two properties of the frontal lobe transform the columnar automaton into a stacking mechanism. This mechanism is used in computers to transform a tree structure into a multi-level sequence: transient memorization of a call is similar to stacking and reaching a partial goal is similar to unstacking. The frontal columnar automata are similar to stacks which can organize "structured sequences" with a variable number of nested levels, such as sentences formed with words. Different positions in the frontal lobe can organize different syntactic levels of the verbal sequence: each level corresponds to an increasing duration necessitated by greater integration of sensory information.

The specific capacities of the human frontal cortex are related mainly to its increased size and hence to the number of temporal and combinatorial levels that it contains.

E) Chapter V: the global level.
Cognitive development and langage learning as consequences of the basic properties of the cortical system.

What are the specific cortical properties responsible for the cognitive development of a child?

Cognitive development and language learning are specific to the human brain. The cortical maturation in the human species continues a long time after birth. Motor learning is at first very slow, but learning of language is relatively fast. As an example, we can consider the rapid learning of grammatical rules, given the limited exposure most children have to these rules.

In the last chapter, we analyze how the maturation of the cortical network can order the constructions effected by the columnar automata. Starting from sensori-motor adaptations (described in chapter IV), the columnar automata permanently form new functional relations between cortical areas; these new internal relations produce "mental images": in our perspective mental images are call trees that are constructed and function in exactly the same way as sensori-motor adaptations. The only difference is that they realize adaptations between the activities of cortical areas. They are distributed representations, but they are also call trees hierarchically organized around goals and sub-goals, with calls at a pre-conscious level (expectancies) and actions at a conscious level (active representations).

These mental images are constructed in a very progressive way beginning at childbirth, for example, the cortical representation of people is in fact a call tree which is constructed via the recognition algorithm of faces, but includes expectancies of possible social interactions. In the same way, we analyze how "images of relations", that is concepts, can be constructed with autonomous activity in the frontal part of the brain.

In our analysis, language is not produced by a new, specialized mechanism, but by columnar automata which form phonemic sequences in order to activate these "mental images" which are new subgoals. Learning of words by children is much more than a simple associative phenomenon, it is a dynamic process based upon the successive disequilibria produced by the development of cortical call trees. Reciprocally, words become subgoals which are powerful means to learn new mental images; for example, the assimilation of words representing new "categories" by the child is not a complex process in our perspective, since for us these categories correspond merely to components of existing call tree structures . The new word simply identifies the component, enabling it to be extracted.

Language learning is a general capacity due to the two complementary properties of the human cortical system: the columnar automaton acts as a driving force, and the cortical network is a coherent supporting substratum that induces many spatial and temporal relations.

The two levels of temporal organization of language- words and sentences-correspond to the two levels of columnar memorization that we developed in chapter II (fixed or oriented sequences): columnar automata form words by fixed sequences of phonemes related to a mental image; but columnar automata also produce variable combinations of cortical images: the corresponding combinations of words, or sentences, is "oriented" by syntactic rules. We show how the construction of call trees in the frontal areas underlies the learning of syntactic rules on the basis of just a few examples heard by the child.

We relate the various semantic and syntactic levels of language with the geometric features of the cortical network. Its symmetries are very important for systematic symbolic coding of images by words and of relations by sentences. We interpret in this way the hemispheric specialization of the brain since the left-right symmetry permits the construction of a linguistic world (in the left hemisphere) which is autonomous but isomorphic to the natural world represented by non-verbal mental images (in the right hemisphere).

Furthermore, there is a global correspondence between the basic components of a sentence (actions, actors, relations etc..) and the specialized regions of the cortex (motor, temporal, parietal, etc.). The cortical network forms a circular circuit between these regions and induces recurrent activations of the related cortical images. Frontal regions form another circular circuit which controls the successive syntactic levels of the sentence in accordance with the semantic relations which form the basis of the narrative.

Although the human being shares the columnar mechanism with several other species, the human cortex has a specific mode of maturation that considerably amplifies its capacity to communicate by a structured language; the result is a powerful cultural accumulation of individual adaptations.

CHAPTER I

Cellular level :
Basic function of neurons

The basic element of the cortical system is the cell; in this first chapter we consider general properties of neurons and groups of neurons. In the second chapter we shall focus on the neuronal organization of the cerebral cortex.

The first chapter is organized by four general questions:

1. What are the adaptive capacities of each individual cell and how can they lead to the information processing capacities of the neural network ?

2. How can we go from the cellular architecture of a nervous tissue to the behavioral function of that tissue?

3. What can a single neuron learn?

4. How can memorization processes at the cellular level produce behavioral learning capacities?

I. Single cell adaptations and neuronal programs.

We start from the general adaptive properties of individual cells, which are due do specific molecular associations: for example associations of DNA and enzymes can optimize cell reproduction, and associations of receptors, ionic channels, and contractible proteins can result in selective recognitions and directional movements toward other cells.

The intrinsic programs of nervous cells are in direct continuity with these general "adaptive" mechanisms: with programs of oriented growth and synaptogenesis, cells first construct a neural network. Cellular construction processes do not determine each individual synaptic contact, but rather configurations at higher spatial levels such as neural structures, layers of neurons, cell types, or dendritic zones. Outside these constraints the network is random.

Neurons synthesize ionic channels which selectively control ionic movements across their membrane. Resulting ionic concentrations have a spatio-temporal form that represents nervous "information" (action potentials and synaptic potentials). With different combinations of ionic channels, neurons ensure transmission, processing, and memorization of this information in the network.

Via its synapses, each neuron receives information from several other input neurons and integrates them in a common output. In order to simplify, we approximate this combination by semi-quantitative rules based on logical operations such as "and", "or", etc. and we relate these operations to molecular and geometrical parameters of the neurons. We use these relations in chapter II to characterize the basic operation performed by each cellular type in the cerebral cortex.

II. From neuronal to tissular function

We know that the basic organization of many neural tissues (including the cerebral cortex) is a cellular "texture" which forms a repetitive circuit perpendicular to the surface of the tissue: each local network is formed by principal neurons that establish connections with other structures, and excitatory or inhibitory interneurons which are connected in parallel. These basic circuits are often duplicated in two main layers that correspond to two processing steps , one organizing the internal relations within the structure, and the other layers the external ones.

Neural tissues transform the spatio-temporal patterns of neural information, and different cellular textures produce different types of information processing, such as oscillators and sequencers (important for movements), spatial filters (important for recognition), and "coding" of sensory information into motor patterns, important for sensory guiding of movements toward a target. We shall see in chapter II that the cortical texture produces an operation which is a general adaptive mechanism.

III. Cellular memorization: temporal integration

Memorization of nervous information is a general property of neurons. Furthermore, it is a progressive process, with at least four steps:

First, neuronal programs of transmission have their own duration which outlast the duration of input information (from 1 to 100 milliseconds).

Next, for longer durations (from seconds to minutes), phenomena such as calcium accumulation modify transmission as a function of the previous activity of the neuron (facilitation or depression) . For these time spans on the order of a minute, a neuron has several possible "functional modes": in the "integrative" mode, the effects of successive activities accumulate and can produce long term changes of transmission; in the "oscillating" mode, a transient information can be memorized over the short term by repetitive activity, but there is no long-term trace.

Longer-term memorization (a day or more) seems to be related to a transformation of ionic channels and membrane receptors. We insist on the spatial parameters of these long term changes for the adaptive logic of the registration process: memorization can implicate widespread regions of neurons, or on the contrary, very restricted parts of the membrane such as dendritic spines.

We underline the complementary aspect of these different cellular programs, which are all active in the cortical neurons. Their flexibility considerably increases the adaptive capacities of the nervous system.

IV. From cellular memorization to learning

We are particularly interested in the learning capacities of a nervous tissue as a function of the basic memorization processes of its different cell types. Three complementary aspects of the tissue architecture are important for learning: the transformation of activity which controls the cellular memorizing process, the "registration logic" of each neuronal type and the combinatorial properties of the network that interconnects different parts of the nervous tissue: we compare these architectures for different neural tissues such as cerebral cortex, cerebellar cortex, spinal cord and hippocampus.

I. Single cell adaptations and neuronal programs.

1. Single cell adaptations

The intracellular molecular network is structured in successive stages, each directly related to an adaptive capacity

Construction and functioning of the nervous system are due to the adaptive properties of cells.

Each cell is made up of a molecular interaction network, progressively structured in the course of phylogeny, thanks to new molecular combinations (enzymes, DNA, channels, etc.) which give each cell new adaptive capacities. Since cells are the fundamental components of the cortical system, we first give a simplified view of their internal organization, with special emphasis on the mechanisms responsible for adaptive capacities.

References

1. Any "active" adaptation first requires energy: each cell stores energy in the form of ATP (Krebs cycle, oxidative phosphorylation) that permits synthesis of many molecules by condensation of water (Lehninger, 1972).

2. The second precondition for adaptations is the capacity to control specific "actions": molecular reactions are "directed" by enzymatic proteins whose amino acids chains are coded by nucleotide sequences (mRNA) and "memorized" in the structure of the DNA. During cellular phylogeny, the transformation of enzymatic proteins by changes in the nucleotides sequences is responsible for the elaboration of increasingly varied adaptive mechanisms (Crick, 1968; Lorman, 1972; Wong, 1981).

3. Basic molecular programs controlled by proteins are common to most cells and permit their survival in a variety of environmental conditions. (Alberts 1983): thanks to their receptors, isolated cells can recognize specific environmental factors; with their secretory systems they can communicate with other cells to produce "cooperative" adaptations, and with their contractible proteins they can move toward a target to produce new interactions. For example, the chemotactism in bacteria (positional adaptation) is due to two cooperative properties (Koshland, 1979): cellular orientations randomly change but these fluctuations stop when membrane receptors recognize a factor emitted by the target. Receptor sensitivity then increases over a prolonged period and sustains the direction of the cell toward the target.

FIGURE 1-1 gives the most simplified description of the molecular network that is the basis of cellular adaptation: this network is typical of most cells, and therefore neural cells of the cerebral cortex.

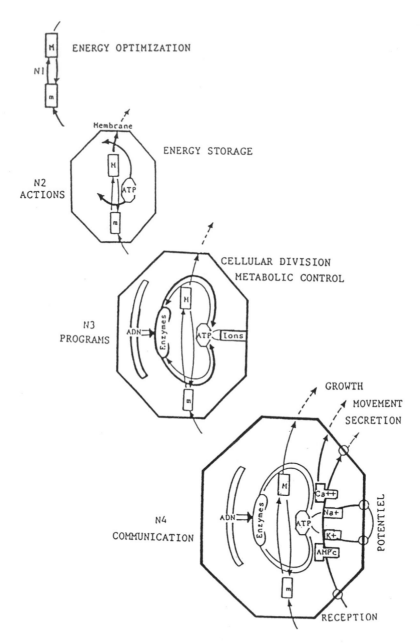

Figure 1-1 . Adaptive capacities of individual cells: progressive structuring of the intracellular molecular network.

Each "adaptation" can be defined as an active "optimization" of an interactive parameter between a cell and its environment (see ANNEX I-B and I-C, for further details). Figure 1-1 illustrates four molecular stages (N1-N4) which generate new optimizations:

N1: energy optimization is the general result of any molecular interaction;

N2: molecules that store energy, such as ATP, permits the execution of "actions" that are independent of this direct energy optimization;

N3: molecules that memorize the enzymatic "actions", such as DNA and RNA, optimize cellular reproduction in a given environment;

N4: molecules that control membrane permeability, such as receptors and ionic channels, permit adaptations of: recognition (response optimization); position (distance optimization); and communication (optimal cooperative actions between cells).

a) Energy optimization in any molecular system (N1).

Any simple, isolated molecular system evolves so as to minimize its free energy; it is this optimization that "generates" all molecular transformations, such as transfer of electrons, protons or radicals between molecules, or their linking in polymers. FIGURE 1-1 (N1) illustrates two molecular types ("m"-"M") linked by a reversible transformation: the ratio of their concentrations is directly determined by the minimal energy of the system. The molecules can "recognize" each other and mutually "position" themselves, but these operations are done passively and there is no action by the molecular system to modify its interactions with the environment, independently of minimization of free energy.

b) Performance of independent actions with the association polymer-ATP (N2).

The cell differs from any other molecular system in that it is able to perform adaptations. The cell's capacity to perform molecular "actions" independently of immediately available energy is the driving force behind all adaptations.

"Actions" are mostly accomplished via molecules such as ATP with phosphate groups; for example reproduction of a polymeric molecule is produced by two alternate actions: linking by the phosphate groups (polymeric growth) and unlinking by water molecules (monomeric separations). These polymeres have a tridimensional form with an "internal" spaces where energy can be stored as ATP. These primitive cells can produce molecular transformations to optimize different parameters besides energy: a form or a distance for example.

c) Optimization of reproduction by the association proteines-polynucleotides (N3).

The next stage of cell adaptation is the phylogenetic capacity to "memorize" the "actions" that favor its reproduction.

Enzymatic proteins, by their combination of amino acids, have a double capacity: by their specific structure, they can "recognize" specific molecules with a complementary form, and then by their catalytic "action" they can direct the transformation of these molecules. The amino acids sequence of a protein is coded by a sequence of nucleotides (mRNA) and "memorized" in a coded form by the DNA whose essential activity is autodivision and autoreplication:

- replication of DNA (longitudinal unlinking) potentially reproduces the cellular programs;
- transcription of DNA into RNA (transversal unlinking) activates one program.

Transformation of DNA (by mutation or combination with external DNA) "proposes" new enzymes, and therefore new possible adaptive actions. If a new combination of DNA produces a new action that facilitates reproduction, this DNA reproduces itself more quickly and populations of cells therefore "memorize" these new actions. For example, enzymes better adjusted to their substratum are reproduced more quickly. These phylogenetic "memorizations" are cumulative: the new actions do not destroy the old ones, but supplement them in cases of variations in the environment.

d) Intrinsic programs, recognition and positioning thanks to receptors and ionic channels (N4).

The DNA memorizes various types of adaptive mechanisms: intrinsic programs of molecular reactions (optimization of a combination or a sequence), recognition (optimization of a form), positioning (optimization of a distance), and social adaptations (optimal cooperation by communication processes).

1. Cellular programs: optimization of an intrinsic sequence.

Cell homeostasis is due feedback loops: the control sequence "DNA -) RNA -) enzymes -) molecule" is completed by the reciprocal control "molecule -) enzyme -) DNA".

These loops can produce not only homeostasis but also "calibrated" actions at the cellular level and consequently cellular "programs": for instance the synthesis of a molecule, its transport, and its secretion in discrete quantities, is the basis of cellular communication. In the same way, the control relation "enzyme -) channels -) ions" is completed by reciprocal controls: the relation "ions -) channels" can produce standard neural information (action potentials) and by the relation "ions -) enzymes", this information can control the cellular "programs".

2. Recognition: optimization of interaction with an external form.

Associations between receptor molecules and ionic channels transform "molecular recognitions" into processes of "cellular recognitions" that can trigger specialized programs. By modifying the sensitivity of membrane receptors, the cell can optimize its response to an environmental factor.

3. Positioning: optimization of directions and distances.

Cells can move toward a target. Contractible proteins can deform the cellular membrane: reversible deformations produce a movement, and irreversible ones result in a polarized growth. Random changes in the direction of movement may be adaptive since energy expended during movement is compensated by an increased probability of encountering an energy source. Orientation of cells toward molecular sources (chemotaxy) minimizes the energy expenditure.

4. Social adaptations: optimal cooperation by communication processes.

Cells can communicate with each other , thanks to the parallel development of specialized secretory systems in a group of cells and complementary receptor systems in another group: the programs of two different cells can thus interact and merge together in order to accomplish new cooperative adaptations. All these types of "individual" adaptations are used by cells for the construction of multicellular organisms. For instance, cells begin with programs of "recognition" and "positioning" to construct a neural network, then continue with programs of "communication" which transfer, transform, and memorize the information in this network.

2. Neuronal programs for information processing

References

I. Network construction

The cellular programs of migration, membrane extension and synaptogenesis construct specific neural networks. Polarized membranary extensions (axons and dendrites) are elaborated from growth cones that divide and thus provoke cellular bifurcations (Cajal 1911). Several factors guide the axon terminals toward their targets (Cowan 1979): network formation depends upon the "memory" of each cell line (Weisblat 1983); growing axons adhere specifically to linear supports , due to specific "adhesion molecules" (Edelman 1983) and form ordered groups (Martin 1983); directional change is accomplished by binary choices at each crossing (Goodman 1983). Polarization of cellular extension is due to "growth factors" emitted by the target cells (Levi-Montalcini 1964, Henderson 1983).

Synaptogenesis is the construction of a specialized apparatus for information transmission between two cells. Synapse formation depends upon a molecular "affinity" between the transmitter secreted by the growth cone and the receptor synthesized by the target cell. Synaptogenesis is in fact dependant upon a triple adjustment: the transmitter may be specified as a function of the target (Patterson 1978); the growth cone moves toward the target cell, and the receptors within the target cell membrane move toward the arrival point of the growth cone (Fishbach 1976).

II. Transmission and processing.

Transmission and processing of neural information is performed by four complementary programs in four regions of the neuron:

a) Transmission: Action potential.

The variations of electrical potential between the interior and the exterior of the cell constitute a type of "universal" information in the neural network. The action potential, which is fixed in duration and amplitude, is produced by the successive opening of two types of channels (sodium and potassium) which are themselves sensitive to membrane potential (Hodgkin 1952).

b) Transmitter release.

This action potential is then transmitted without change along the axon. When it reaches the synapse, it provokes an influx of calcium that in turn controls the release of the neurotransmitter (Katz 1969) in the form of all-or-nothing "quanta" (Katz 1972). The number of quanta released by an action potential is a probabilistic variable (binomial law) whose maximal value is related to the number of releasing sites (Korn 1981); its average value also depends upon the functional state of the terminals (probability of release).

c) Post-synaptic receptors and ionic flows.

The neurotransmitter molecules released become attached to post-synaptic receptors that in turn control the opening of ionic channels; these channel receptors are specific for a particular ion (Na+, K+, CL-). Consequently, when the ion channel is opened, the neuronal potential move toward the equilibrium potential for that ion (Eccles 1964, Kuffler 1976, Takeuchi 1977); if this equilibrium potential is superior to the threshold for the action potential, the synapse is called "excitatory" (can produce an EPSP). Otherwise, the synapse is "inhibitory" (IPSP).

The functional specialization of the synapse, excitatory or inhibitory, is related to its anatomical form (Gray 1959). In the cerebral cortex, two major transmitters are glutamate and GABA (Jasper 1965, Krnjevic 1965, Curtis 1971, Emson 1981):

*   - Glutamate is an excitatory transmitter between pyramidal cells (Stone 1976, Baughman 1981);*

*   - GABA is an inhibitory transmitter, activating chloride or potassium channels, in is released by a large class of interneurons which project on pyramidal cells (Ribak 1978).*

d) Dendritic integration

Transmission of the synaptic potential along the dendrites toward the soma depends upon the geometrical characteristics of the neuron (Rall 1967, Jack 1975; Barret 1974, Turner 1980 for hippocampal pyramidal cells)): the effects of synaptic activities upon somatic potential is modelled by first order differential equations with respect to time (time constant T) and by second order equations with respect to distance (length constant X). These relations can be applied for each portion of the membrane which has homogeneous types of channels (Traub 1979).

The duration and amplitude of the post synaptic potential in the soma depends upon geometrical factors such as the size of the cell and the relative distance between synapses and soma.

Duration (slowing) increases as the distance between synapses and soma increases and also for larger cells because of the capacitance of the membrane (Tsukahara 1981, Jack 1975) : Amplitude decreases with distant synapses and with small diameters of dendrites but this diminution is often weak as for example in hippocampal pyramidal cells (Andersen 1983). Amplitude decreases with the overall conductance of the neuron that is correlated with its size. There is a "scale principle" : length constant, that defines the attenuation of the synaptic potential, seems to be adjusted to the size of the cell (for example, Turner 1984 for hippocampal neurons; Levtov 1983, Luschei 1983).

When several excitatory inputs are combined, the amplitude of the neuronal response increases with the number of afferent cells that are simultaneously activated (Andersen 1983, MacNaughton 1978, for hippocampal neurons). When inhibitory and excitatory inputs are combined, the effect of inhibitory synapses upon transmission of excitatory signals is mostly a "shunting effect" proportionately greater when the inhibitory afference is close to the soma (Rall 1969, Jack 1975).

III. Memorization

Neuronal activity has long term effects on transmission parameters, with several time constants:

a) In the range from milliseconds to seconds, channels have different intrinsic time constants (1-500 ms) and postsynaptic potentials outlast the durations of afferent impulses (Neher, 1983). Potassium channels regulate the firing frequency of the neuron, for example by imposing a minimal refractory period (Stevens 1980, Llinas 1984). On the other hand, sodium current can maintain a continuous firing frequency (Llinas 1983) after a single transient synaptic input: such channels are found in pyramidal neurons of layer V in the cerebral cortex (Stafstrom, 1986).

The postsynaptic potentials produced by GABA and Glutamate (important transmitters in the cortex), have a duration that outlasts the effect of an action potential by a factor of 10, and even more with long-lasting potassium conductances (Alger 1982, Connors 1982).

b) In the range from seconds to minutes, channel properties can produce oscillations of membrane potential and the generation of repetitive "bursts": this oscillation is due to alternate opening of the voltage-dependant calcium channels, followed by opening of the calcium-dependant potassium channels, (Meech 1979).

High frequencies of action potentials result in prolonged changes of transmission (Kuno 1964). Fast repetitive activation of the cell produces a cumulative increase of internal calcium that facilitates transmitter release; this accumulation increases with the frequency of the action potentials, and is more marked for smaller cells (Rasmussen 1984, Morris 1985). Conversely, other activity patterns may result in a decreased transmission (habituation) for example when there is no significant variation in action potential frequency; this habituation is partly due to a decreased probability of transmitter release (Castellucci 1976).

c) In the range from minutes to hours, long term activity-dependant changes of neuronal transmission have been observed in invertebrates during learning. The memorization effect at the cellular level is a prolonged closing of potassium channels: it produces an increasing calcium flow for each action potential that result in a increase of presynaptic transmitter release (Klein 1978); it can also produce an increase in cellular response because of a decrease in the global conductance of the cell (Alkon 1982). These long term changes in cell excitability can be produced by neuromodulators (such as dopamine, norepinephrine, serotonin and acetylcholine) which activate second messenger systems which in turn can phosphorylate channels and then stabilize an open or a close state during long periods (Klein 1978, Kandel 1981).

Long term changes of neuronal transmission has been well studied in the hippocampus, a structure which has pyramidal cell types similar to those of cerebral cortex (Bliss 1972). A high frequency input produces first a post-tetanic potentiation (from seconds to minutes) and then a long term potentiation of the transmission (from minutes to hours).

The post-tetanic potentiation is significantly increased by the voltage properties of receptors: for example, the channels linked to NMDA-type Glutamate receptors become more and more efficient when the membrane depolarizes (Nowak 1983); such receptors exist in the hippocampus (Collinridge 1983) and in the cortex (Thomson 1986).

The long term aspect of potentiation seems to be due to several changes of transmission parameters that act in a cooperative way: presynaptic increase of transmitter release, increased sensitivity of glutamate receptors (Lynch 1984), diminution of potassium conductance as in invertebrates (Disterhoft 1985), etc.. For the pyramidal cells of the cortex, high frequencies of action potentials provoke a prolonged increase of the cell's response to its inputs: this process could be due to a similar decrease of the global cellular conductance (Woody 1976, Bindmann 1979).

A) Cellular programs construct a neural network at four spatial levels

The construction of a neural network can be viewed as a series of adaptations, of successive adjustments that are increasingly precise. This pattern of construction does not produce precisely determined connections for each neuron considered individually, but rather a four-level architecture from the whole nervous system to the subcellular level :

1. At the larger level, the anatomical network between neural structures organizes the main information flows between sensory or motor organs. For example the visual information goes from the retina to the thalamus and then to the cortex. We shall describe the main features of this network in chapter III (we shall call it "general" network).

2. At the tissue level, the network between two regions of the same structure "recombines" information and is very important for learning. For example, the network between cortical areas combines information from visual and somesthetic area in the parietal associative area. We shall describe a "geometrical model" of the network between cortical areas in chapter III (we shall call it "recombination" network).

3. At the modular level, the network between adjacent neurons and interneurons determines the local processing performed by each nervous structure. We shall describe the modular cortical network in chapter II, to explain the basic operation performed by the cortex (we shall call it "interneuronal" network).

4. At the cellular and subcellular levels, synapses and parts of membrane form local synaptic networks that do not concern the whole cell. For example, the "triads" in the thalamic nuclei, is formed by three closed synapses: an input makes two excitatory synapses on two neurons connected by an inhibitory synapse (local "synaptic" network).

Successive steps of construction produce more and more precise connectivity at these four levels and place increasingly strict limits upon the possible values of functional parameters.

The construction process of a neural network from cellular programs is formalized with further details in ANNEX 2-B where Figure A-5 depict the progressive determination of its four-level architecture .

B) After network construction, neuronal programs perform three functions: transmission, combination and memorization of information.

In order to explain the functional properties of the cerebral cortex on a cellular basis, we give an integrated view of neuronal programs and transmission parameters.

FIGURE 1-2 illustrates the molecular interactions that generate neuronal programs in the same way as Figure 1-1 illustrates the adaptive programs of every cell. FIGURE 1-3 represent these neuronal programs on three functional axes:

1. Transmission and transformation of information through the neural network.
2. Combination of several input information (spatial integration).
3. Memorization of this information (temporal integration).

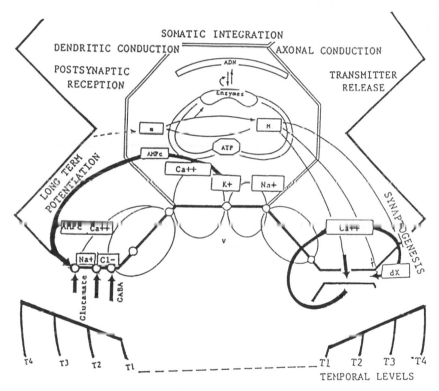

Figure 1-2 . Neuronal programs: construction of a network, information processing and memorization.

a) Transmission: the four specialization of the neuronal membrane.

Neurons use four transmission modes with four types of membrane specialization, as illustrated on the vertical axis of FIGURE 1-3:

1. The "synaptic receptors" recognize only specific molecules.
2. Dendritic zones with homogeneous types of synapses and channels, transform the molecular messages into ionic flows.

3. The soma and the axonal initial segment of neurons, transforms the different ionic currents into a single output, all or nothing, that can be transmitted over large distances.

4. The axon terminals which release transmitter transform this universal signal into a specific molecular message.

These functional specializations are due to specific molecular associations: ionic channels and active pumps, membrane receptors and neurotransmitter secretory systems. These molecular associations control movements of ions and transmitters on each side of the membrane, according to general laws of ionic currents (Goldman's law, Ohm's law), and produce elementary "actions" of communication: post-synaptic potential (EPSP), action potentials, transmitter release, etc.

b) Spatial integration.

Neuronal programs are organized on a second functional axis (Figure 1-3) which represents the molecular and spatial diversity of neuronal membranes: for example, a membrane area specialized for GABA receptors linked to chloride channels, can coexist with a neighboring zone specialized with Glutamate receptors linked to sodium and calcium channels. Integration of several inputs depends upon their relative positions and their extensions on the neuronal surface.

c) Temporal integration: "memorization" at four "temporal levels".

Neuronal programs have effects of very variable duration, ranging from a millisecond to several years. A third axis in Figure 1-3 order these programs on four temporal levels, from "T1" to "T4"; these levels are also illustrated in FIGURE 1-2 where neuronal programs have shorter time-constants from inner (nucleus) to outer (membrane) parts of the cell:

1. Temporal level "T4" (a day to a year) corresponds to structural differentiation of the molecular network, for instance changes in gene expression that lead to new types of receptors and channels; it's also the temporal level of membrane extension and synaptogenesis. We shall place permanent memory at this level.

2. Temporal level "T3" (hour-day) is that of molecular synthesis ; it corresponds to long-term modifications of ionic channels and receptors. We will place the processes of long-term memory at this temporal level.

3. Temporal level "T2" (second-minute) is that of the cell's energy regulation, variations in the concentration of calcium and second messengers (cAMP, etc), and different "activation states" of receptors and channels. It is the temporal level of short-term memory.

4. Temporal level "T1" (1 millisecond - 100 millisecond) is that of the transmission and transformation of the basic neural information (membrane action potential and synaptic currents).

d) Neuronal programs are complementary.

1. The construction programs (division, polarized membrane growth, and synaptogenesis), controlled by the genetic code, determines the "structural parameters" of the neural network (number of cells, surfaces or receptor zones , etc), at the temporal level T4.

2. Once the network is in place, the cooperative programs of reception, action potential, and secretion, produce recursive transmission of neural information in this network, at the temporal level T1.

3. Neuronal geometry determines the integrative function of simultaneous input activities.

4. Four programs produce progressive memorization of the activities at four temporal levels, from T1 (activity) to T4 (permanent memorization) with intermediate periods at temporal levels T2 (short term memory) and T3 (long-term memory).

C) Transmission of neural information is controlled by a set of coefficients defined in a space-time matrix.

As depicted in Figure 1-3, the output information of a neuron combines the inputs with the intrinsic parameters of four specialized regions of the neuron (pre and post synaptic, dendritic, axonal).

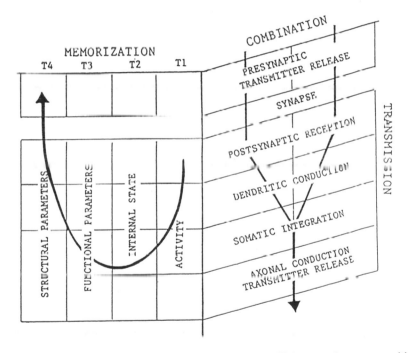

Figure 1-3 . Functional axes of neurons: transmission coefficients at four temporal levels (T1-T4).

These "transmission coefficients" are stable within more or less extended time domain. "Long term" coefficients (for example the number of channels) limit the value of short-term coefficients (for example the conductance due to the open state of the channels). The largest limits will thus be directly related to the structure of the neurons (their "morphology"). We shall use this progressive structure-function relationship, in the following chapter, to interpret the diversity of neuronal types in the cortex and the layered pattern of inputs. These relations are formalized with further details in ANNEX III-A and III-B where Figure A-8 details the whole set of transmission coefficients in a 4x4 space-time matrix.

a) Axon terminals: control of the random all-or-non synaptic transmission.

The quantic and probabilistic nature of transmitter release gives a randomly-varying aspect to transmission, but this variability is controlled at upper temporal levels:

- the maximum number of quanta that could be released by an afferent action potential depends upon the number of synapses per afferent neuron (morphological parameter at temporal level T4);

- the transmitter content of each quantum is constant and can vary only over a relatively long period (temporal level T3);

- the number of quanta actually released per action potential has an average value that is constant during a stable repetitive activity (temporal level T2).

b) Post-synaptic receptors: control of the influence of each type of input.

Post-synaptic coefficients limit the influence of each input:

- equilibrium potentials of post-synaptic channels represent the limiting value toward which the membrane potential moves following afferent activity; they determine the absolute limit of the influence of an input's type (temporal level T4). For the cortex, the equilibrium potentials will be mostly due to glutamate ("G+") which opens sodium and calcium channels ("excitation"), and due to GABA ("G-"), which opens chloride and potassium channels ("inhibition").

- Within each synapse, only a part of the receptors is "available", since another part may be closed by internal factors during a long period . The number of available receptors limits the influence of each afferent cell and activity dependant changes of this number provides a basis for long-term memorization (temporal level T3)

- At a shorter time span, states of receptors depend also upon the internal state of the neuron; for example receptors can be "modulated" by calcium or second messenger concentration (temporal level T2).

c) Dendritic zones: influence of an homogeneous group of afferent neurons.

The influence of synchronized inputs on the somatic membrane potential is dependant upon a ratio: it increases with the conductance activated by the afferent group but decreases with the global membrane conductance of the neuron:

- Influence of a group of afferent cells is thus limited by the "maximal proportion of conductance" activable by these afferences (temporal level T3);

- This maximal influence is controlled by a structural parameter which is the morphological ratio between the surface of the afferent synapses on the receptive membrane and the total surface of the neuron (temporal level T4).

- This influence may also depend upon the distance of the inputs from the cell body; attenuation and especially slowing are more pronounced when the afferent group is farther from the soma.

In a very simplified way, we can thus use geometric criteria to distinguish the structural weight of afferent groups of cells: "strong" afferences, which influence a high proportion of the post synaptic membrane and "weak" afferences which influence a small proportion. The strength of an afference may also depend upon its distance to the soma.

For the cortex, the maximal conductance activable by each afferent type will be strongly influenced by the layered cortical organization.

d) Soma and initial segment of the axon: combination of two different groups of afferent cells.

When two different groups of afferent cells are coactivated , the global output is an all-or-non action potential which is triggered in the initial segment when the somatic potential exceed a threshold (voltage-dependant channels); it is propagated in an unmodified way down the axon and gives a functional image of the soma over all the axon terminals. The frequency of action potentials is regulated by somatic potassium channels.

There are several ways to express the rules which describe the global combination of two inputs, from a qualitative description to a precise spatio-temporal function. We shall use a semi-quantitative description with approximations by logical rules. In this first approximation the global neuronal activity of homogeneous group of cells is considered all-or-nothing and the processing done by the neuron is expressed by logical functions such as "and", "or", etc.. We give examples of these functions in the next paragraph.

D) Combinations of two inputs: the neuronal integration is first approximated by logical operations.

FIGURE 1-4 shows the logical operation that most closely approximates the combinatorial function of a particular neuron, depending upon its structural parameters.

The upper part illustrates a receptor neuron ("K") with two dendritic zones ("a" and "b") postsynaptic for two homogeneous groups of afferent cells ("I" and "J").

The TABLE (lower part) shows how logical operations may be related to two structural parameters:

- on the vertical axis, the molecular type of transmitter and receptor and therefore the equilibrium potential (Va,Vb) of the response which determine the "excitatory" or "inhibitory" nature of the synapse ,

- on the horizontal axis, the "strength" of the afference which is determined by the "maximum proportion of membrane activated" by the afference (a/K, b/K), and by the position with respect to the cell body (xa,xb).

Symbols used are explained in more details in ANNEX II and III.

For two excitatory inputs (upper row), three types of logical operations are possible with respect to the geometrical parameters of the neuronal network, which determine the "strong" or "weak" influence of the two afferences:

1. Neuronal function resembles the logical function "and" if the two afferences are "weak" and arrive on the same dendritic tree: their coactivation is necessary to influence the output activity of the cell (symmetric gating effect).

2. The neuronal function resembles the logical function "or" if the two afferences

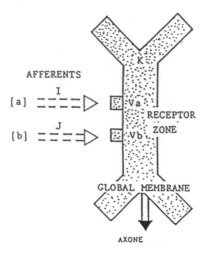

AFFERENTS

[a] ====▷ ☐ Va

[b] ====▷ ☐ Vb   RECEPTOR ZONE

GLOBAL MEMBRANE

AXONE

AFFERENTS	2 WEAK	2 STRONG	1 WEAK 1 STRONG
Proportion of activable membrane Relative distance from the soma	a/K 〈 k1 b/K 〈 k1 xa 〉 x0 xb 〉 x0	a/K 〉 k1 b/K 〉 k1 xa 〈 x0 xb 〈 x0	a/K 〈 k1 b/K 〉 k1 xa 〉 x0 xb 〈 x0
2 EXCITATORY Va 〉 V1 Vb 〉 V1	AND	OR	IF
1 EXCITATORY 1 INHIBITORY Va 〉 V1 Vb 〈 V1	MINUS	EXCLUSIVE OR	IF NOT

(left vertical label: Equilibrium potential)

Figure 1-4 . Spatial integration of two inputs by neurons: approximation by logical operations.

are "strong" and arrive on different dendritic trees: either input is sufficient to trigger the output activity of the cell (convergent transmission).

3. The neuronal function resembles the logical function "if" when one of the afferences is "strong" and the other is "weak": the "weak" afference has an impact on the output only if the "strong" input is previously activated so that the membrane potential approaches the threshold for the action potential (asymmetric gating effect).

When excitatory and inhibitory inputs interact (lower row), the neuronal operation also depends upon the geometrical parameters of the neuronal network. When the inhibitory afference is "strong" (numerous inhibitory synapses on the cell body), it can completely block the output activity: neuronal function resembles the logical function "if not". When the inhibitory afference is "weak", it exerts a quantitative negative modulation of the excitatory influence.

We shall use these logical approximations in chapter II to explicit the operations performed by neurons of the cerebral cortex. This type of "coarse grained" analysis does not prevent from applying more precise quantitative methods later.

E) The specific operation performed by neurons is shaped by the construction process of the neural network.

The neuronal operation performed on two inputs (and, or, if, etc..) is specific for each cellular type in each nervous tissue. This operation is shaped by the sequence of construction of the neural network. We give three examples that will be useful later, in FIGURE 1-5 : the Purkinje cells of the cerebellum, the relay cells of the thalamus, and especially the cortical pyramidal cells whose operation differs according to whether the soma is in the supragranular or infragranular layers.

The two sets of diagrams (left "N1" and right "N2") represent in two steps the sequential arrivals of the two afferences ("I" then "J") that will be combined by the neuron. The different construction patterns induce different integrative properties.

- For the Purkinje cells of the cerebellum, a single climbing fiber ("I") forms a large number of synapses, while a great number of parallel fibers ("J") each makes only one synapse: the influence of the parallel fibers on the Purkinje cells is entirely conditioned by the activity of the climbing fiber : the integrative function may be approximated by a logical "if" (asymmetric gating).

- For the principal cells of the thalamus, the first afferent that comes from the sensory organs is strong ("I") while the second afferent group that comes from the cortex is weaker ("J"). The neuronal operation may also be approximated by an asymmetric gating.

- For the cortical pyramidal cells, their two inputs from thalamus ("I") and from other cortical areas ("J") are organized in distinct layers. This layered pattern gives a more balanced importance to the two inputs. The integrative operations performed by the pyramidal cells will be modulated by the thickness of layers (depending upon the cortical area) and by the transversal extensions of dendrites across layers.

Thalamic inputs occupy the intermediate layer IV between the two main types of pyramidal neurons, supra and infragranular . Thanks to this architecture, the two pyramidal types execute two different operations on their two common inputs (cortical and thalamic). These structure-function relationships are detailed in ANNEX 3.

In a standard "associative" area, the pyramidal cells of the upper layers execute an operation that is closer to an "or" gate while the lower pyramidals perform an operation that is closer to an "and" gate. This difference is important for cortical function: when only cortical afferences are active, this activity can spread across the cortical network ("or" gate of supra-granular layers) but not in the network outside the cortex ("and" gate of infragranular layers).

We shall use these logical approximations in chapter II to differentiate the integrative modes of the pyramidal cells of the cerebral cortex. This type of "coarse grained" analysis does not prevent from applying more precise quantitative methods later.

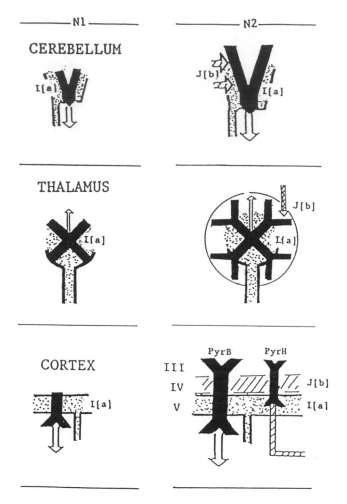

Figure 1-5 . Specific combination of 2 inputs (I[a], J[b]) shaped by 2 steps of construction (N1,N2) of the neural network.

II. From neuronal
to tissular function.

1. Interneurons: functional coupling or uncoupling.

During construction of a neural tissue, several neuronal types differentiate locally in the same tissue and form repetitive local circuits, like repetitive molecular associations in a crystal, as illustrated in Figure 1-6. This figure shows a standard

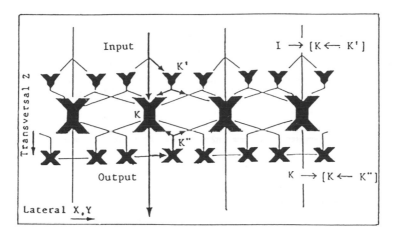

Figure 1-6 . Repetitive interneuronal network in a neural structure: coupling and uncoupling properties.

repetitive cellular pattern which is common to many neural structures; this common pattern is due to constraints of construction by distributed cellular processes, such as successive guiding of neurites by molecular affinities. The standard circuit is established on the "transversal axis" of a neuronal tissue, perpendicular to the surface, and then repeated on the "lateral axes", parallel to the surface.

The principal neurons ("K") form the basic input-output network: their dendrites receive external afferences and their axons project to other neural structures. They perform basic operations on inputs, as described in the previous section.

The interneuronal system develops in relation to this general input-output pattern: the interneurons are connected in parallel and project to the the principal neurons (affinity between their transmitters and the receptors of the principal neurons). Consequently, when they are active, interneurons can couple (or uncouple) principal input-output circuits; they shape the spatial extension of the activity in the neural tissue.

Interneurons are specialized according to three types of actions: coupling or uncoupling, input or output, lateral or transversal.

a) Coupling or uncoupling.

Depending upon the transmitter-receptor systems (that control the ionic equilibrium potential), interneurons will be either inhibitory (uncoupling) or excitatory (coupling). If their transmission coefficients change (memorization), the coupling and uncoupling can become permanently consolidated: several interneuronal types in the same tissue can shape different types of input-output functions.

b) "Input" or "output" action.

If the interneurons have receptors for transmitters of external inputs (K') their coupling action will depend upon input activity, before processing by the principal neurons.

If they have receptors for the transmitter of principal neurons (K") their coupling action will depend upon output activity, after processing by the principal neurons.

c) "Transversal" or "lateral" action.

If the interneurons extend on the transversal axis, they modulate the relation between external inputs and principal neurons. If they are inhibitory, the external input has both an excitatory and an inhibitory action on the principal neurons: the overall effect (excitation or inhibition) will depend upon the intensity and the temporal form of the external input. This interneuronal network is essentially a temporal processor: for example it can limit the firing frequency of principal neurons.

If the interneurons extend on the lateral axis, they modulate the relations between principal circuits: excitatory interneurons can reinforce the coupling between two coactivated principal circuits; inhibitory interneurons can reinforce uncoupling between two neighboring principal circuits when their activities are different (contrast amplification). This "lateral network" is mostly a spatial processor: it can filter the spatial form of the input activity.

2. Tissular patterns of activity.

References

Neurons have specific temporal patterns of activity due to temporal properties of their ionic channels (Neher, 1983) like potassium channels that limit the firing frequency of the neurons (Stevens 1980, Llinas 1984), or sodium current that maintain a continuous firing frequency (Llinas 1983) after a transient synaptic input ; such channels are found in pyramidal neurons of layer V in the cerebral cortex (Stafstrom, 1986).

In the cortex the postsynaptic potentials produced by Glutamate and the feed forward inhibitory pathways that release GABA activate prolonged potassium conductances which increase with the intensity of the stimulation and thus limit the effects of intense afferent activities (Connors 1984).

The general result of potassium channels opening is a regularization of action potential frequency: they impose limits to neuronal activity . The input exerts its effects precisely within these limits. The firing frequency of cortical neurons can attain 100 Hertz, but these intense activities usually have a limited duration (Spencer 1977). The regular aspect of firing frequencies in cortical neurons can be modelled by simple "trapezoidal" functions (Burnod, 1982).

A) Activity of a nervous tissue can be represented by a spatio-temporal "trapezoidal" form.

FIGURE 1-7 (upper part) illustrates in a simplified way the activity of a tissue, which is a spatio-temporal pattern of action potential frequencies:

- On the temporal axis, the activity of each neuron, the action potentials, are illustrated by vertical bars. The output activity of the tissue is that of the principal neurons.

- The spatial axes are the lateral axes of the tissue, as illustrated in Figure 1-6. Each position corresponds to a principal neuron.

- Intensity (action potential frequency) is represented on the vertical axis.

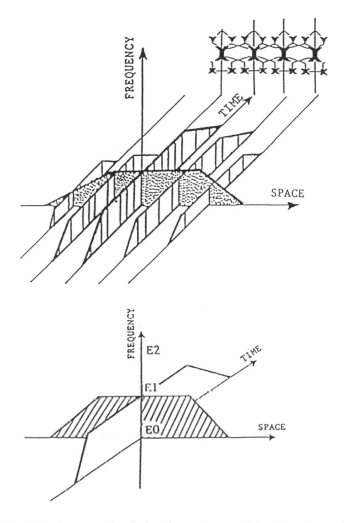

Figure 1-7 . Activity of a group of cells in a tissue: trapezoidal spatio - temporal patterns.

The spatio-temporal form, that represents the activity of an homogeneous group of neurons, is limited in time by the "transversal" inhibitory circuits, and is also limited in space by the "lateral" ones . Intensity is relatively constant over a certain time span and spatial region.

We can represent the temporal pattern of activity by a simple regular, "trapezoidal" form: this form is characterized by three linear parts: an ascending ramp, a plateau, and a descending ramp.

From the activity patterns of individual neurons, we can then describe the activities of neuronal groups of neurons which have similar behaviours. Activities of a group of cells form, at any given moment, a spatial function that can be also represented by a trapezoid on the lateral axis of the tissue.

We represent the spatio-temporal form of activity of a group of neurons by a "double trapezoid", on both the spatial and temporal axes, as illustrated in FIGURE 1-7 (lower part). This spatio-temporal form is completely determined by eight parameters: two ramps, two plateaus (intensities), two extensions, and two positions on temporal and spatial axes. The input output functions of a neural tissue can be summarized by transformations of the parameters of this trapezoidal function, for instance an increase in the maximal frequency of the plateau, or changes in the slope of the ascending ramp.

The plateau of this double trapezoid represents the frequency of action potentials in a homogeneous group of neurons. In chapter II, we shall approximate this intensity by 3 possible levels: "EO" corresponds to an inhibited state, "E1" is a low frequency, and "E2" a high frequency of action potentials. These intensity levels will be used to formulate simple functioning and memorization rules of the cortical column.

B) The dimension of a "module" is determined by the functional homogeneity of its component cells.

Trapezoids are spatially and temporally discontinuous: the boundaries define the functional "modules" of the tissue.
A module is a spatial zone ([A]) of a neural structure ("K"), which has not only a structural homogeneity but also a functional unity.
The lateral extension of a functional module does not have fixed anatomical limits, but is defined according to the criterion of functional homogeneity of the cells. In this way, there is a direct correspondence between the spatial dimensions of a module and the "trapezoid" representing the neuronal group's activity.
Once the dimensions of a module are determined (zone [A]), we can precise the other parameters of tissular activity: functional mode of the neurons, intensity of the output neurons, activity levels of excitatory or inhibitory interneurons, etc.

3. Behavioral function of a neural tissue.

References

The causal relations between the cellular structure of a tissue and its function have been well studied in invertebrates and in the neural structures of vertebrates linked with sensory or motor organs:
- Temporal processing: multicellular oscillations and sequencing interneurons organize motor function (Stent 1978, Miller 1982).
- Spatial processing: nervous tissue effects spatial filtering and reorganizes the spatial form of sensory activations. For example, amplification of contrasts by retina (Dowling 1979) is the first step of image recognition.
- Neural tissues can transform a spatial or a temporal parameter of the activity into an intensity; this processing is important for the sensory control of motor function (Kirshfield 1979): for instance recruitment of motoneurons as a function of their size

(Henneman 1980) transform a position parameter into intensity of muscular contraction; in the vestibulo-ocular reflex, a temporal integration translates a sensory activity into a muscular contraction (Robinson 1975).

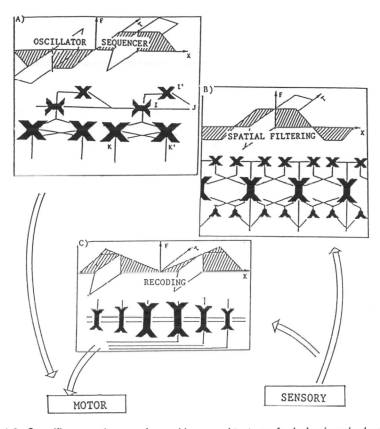

Figure 1-8 . Specific operations performed by neural textures for behavioural adaptations.

Each neural tissue operates primarily on the spatial and temporal form of the input activity and produces another spatio-temporal pattern. This operation is part of an adaptive mechanism, and is not necessarily completely deterministic: to some extent, random fluctuations can be an intrinsic characteristic of the system. Thus, several types of functions can describe the spatio-temporal shaping of the activity by the neural tissue, from an "all or nothing" qualitative description, up to and including a complete, quantitative description.

FIGURE 1-8 gives three examples of structure-function relationships for three nervous tissues that can effect three types of sensori-motor adaptations:

- "Oscillators" and "sequencers" (temporal processing) organize motor programs (1-8A);

- "Spatial filters" are critical for recognition (1-8B);

- "Re-coding" between activity parameters (for instance the transformation of a position into an intensity) is critical for sensory guidance of motor adaptations (1-8C).

Each box in FIGURE 1-8 represents a neural texture and its processing summarized by a "transfer function": this function is illustrated by a trapezoid, on both the spatial (X) and temporal (T) axes. These basic operations participates in behavioral adaptations by external relations to sensory or motor organs.

Analysis of examples of such adaptive processes performed by different types of neural tissues, will bring out the uniqueness of cortical function, described in the next chapter.

a) Temporal processing: oscillators and sequencers for movements (Figure 1-8A).

Specific oscillation modes of individual neurons are due to different types of ionic channels. Reciprocal inhibition (K-K') between neurons stabilizes these oscillations. The transmission coefficients create delays and phase differences between oscillations of different cells. The input activity level ("I") can trigger and accelerate these oscillations while preserving the phase differences. Depending upon the local interactions (transmitters and modulators) these oscillators can have quite varied periods, from a few milliseconds to a circadian rhythm, and can be associated to produce various temporal patterns. Such networks can produce cyclic and ordered activation of different muscles and generate intrinsic "motor programs" (flight, swimming, walking...).

When several motor actions participate in the execution of the same behavioral program, overall efficiency is critically dependant upon an appropriate sequence of responses to the external environment; this is particularly true for positioning movements that optimize the distance between the organism and an object in the environment.

Sequential triggering of different actions is made dependant upon external conditions; the sequence is made longer when the external situation is less favorable and more distant from the goal; for example, the behavioral program "eat", can be obtained by activating oscillations in more and more distal parts of the muscular map (for instance, chew - bite - put into mouth - catch - move toward).

This adaptive mechanism can be obtained by a group of inhibitions which establishes a conditional hierarchy among the different motor actions; inhibitory interneurons (I'), are connected in parallel to the command network (J-I). Progressive sequencing is then ordered by the level of the global command that adjusts the balance between the excitatory (J-I) and inhibitory (J-I'-I) effects:

- if the motor action closest to the goal (for instance "eat") can be executed, the command level inhibits the other actions;

- otherwise, the command is excitatory and the other motor actions ("catch", "move towards") are activated in a progressive way.

- Each motor action has an effect which favors execution of other actions closer to the goal; for example "move toward" allow to "catch" and then to "put in the mouth".

We will see that this progressive sequencing mechanism that moves a system toward a goal, regardless of initial positions, will be generalized by the cortical system.

b) Spatial processing for recognition (Figure 1-8B).

The basic operation performed on the spatial form of input activity by nervous structures is an operation of "filtering", with a transfer function which is determined by intrinsic connectivity (Figure 1-8B): different types of interneurons, excitatory and inhibitory, shape respectively the positive and negative parts of the transfer function: for example, this operation can amplify contrasts or oriented lines. Spatial filtering is important to extract features from the activity of sensory organs.

c) Spatio-temporal processing for sensory control of motricity (Figure 1-8C).

More generally, specialized neural tissue can effect operations that we call "coding" (Figure 1-8C).

The spatiotemporal form of afferent activity, represented by a trapezoid, is coded by eight different parameters (position, intensity, etc, as shown in figure 1-7). The tissue can "code" one of the parameters via one of the others: for example, in FIGURE 1-8C we have illustrated a tissue that can translate a position into an intensity, thanks to recruitment of neurons with size. A neuronal tissue can translate a spatial parameter of the input (like the extension of the afferent activity) by an output intensity (firing frequency); likewise, by temporal summation, neurons can translate the duration of an activity into an intensity. Several transformations can be combined sequentially to effect all the possible codes of activity parameters (eight in the trapezoidal form). Intermediate intensity coding can be pivotal to these various codes.

Processing that directly relates spatial and temporal parameters of the activity is very important for sensori-motor coordinations and placing adaptations: for instance, a position on the receptor map is transformed into an intensity of muscular contraction. Generally speaking, a limb codes a spatial parameter (muscle group activated) into an intensity (amplitude of movement). Neural tissues that effect inverse coding are important for an efficient control of movement.

III. Cellular memorization : temporal integration.

a) Causes and consequences of memorization.

We call "memorization" or "registration" all prolonged changes of transmission parameters which are activity-dependant. Memorization at the neuronal level has three related aspects:

1. Memorization capacities of a neuron: they can be described by the set of neuronal transmission coefficients that change with activity, for example the conductance of a dendritic zone, or the probability of transmitter release. This set can be arranged in a space-time matrix as illustrated in paragraph I of this chapter (Figure 1-3), and detailed in ANNEX 3-B.

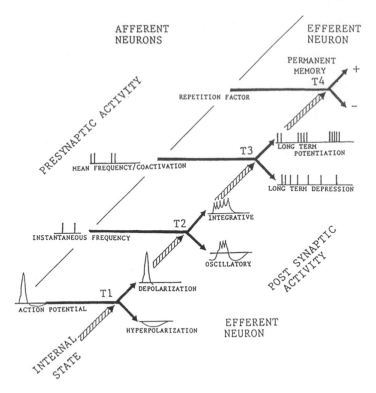

Figure 1-9 . Progressive memorization by a neuron at four temporal levels (T1-T4) depends upon its presynaptic activity and its internal state.

2. Critical parameters for memorization: the memorizing process depends both upon input activity (discharge frequency, number of active synapses) and upon the "internal state" of the neuron (such as internal calcium). There are critical conditions for each time span, as illustrated in Figure 1-9. These conditions are formalized and detailed in ANNEX 4-A and 4-B.

3. Consequences of memorization upon the neuronal functions of information processing: long term changes of the neuronal transmission coefficients modify the input-output relations and the operation performed by a neuron: for example , if a "weak" coefficient increases, an approximate "AND" gate can be changed in an "OR" gate. For the cerebral cortex, these consequences will be exposed in chapter II (Figures 2-15 to 2-18); more details are given in ANNEX 4-D .

b) Temporal levels of memorization.
Here we shall insist on the progressive aspect of memorization, (both spatial and temporal), that corresponds to very precise regulations of the neuronal function and is very important for the adaptive consequence of memorization processes. FIGURE 1-9 illustrates this progressive process, from the shorter to the longer time spans, from bottom to top:

1. Afferent action potential is in the millisecond range (T1); in response the cell produces its own temporal pattern of activity , that can multiply this time by ten or hundreds, thanks to channel properties (T1).

2. In the range of minutes (T2), memorization depends upon two basic functional modes of the neuron, linked to internal calcium and second messengers systems: in the "integrative" mode, the cell can cumulate successive inputs; in the "oscillatory mode" , the cell can repeat a transient information and ignore other inputs.

3. In the integrative mode, the cell can cumulate successive input activities with a long term trace (T3); we shall insist on the spatial aspect of this memorization and we shall distinguish two possible processes: either a local memorization with associative Hebbian rules at the cellular level, or a more global, all-or-none memorization.

4. Memory can become permanent (temporal level "T4"). This stabilization depends upon two factors: the long term pattern of activations, but also the intrinsic maturation program of the cell; permanent memorization can be faster during the critical period of development.

1. Functional mode and short term memorization (T2)

References

1. Neurons can respond to transient synaptic inputs by a continuous activity, thanks to their sodium and calcium channels. Motoneurons in the spinal cord (Hounsgaard, 1986), and pyramidal neurons in the cerebral cortex (Stafstrom, 1985) may thus have bistable properties : each transient excitatory input triggers the "active" state and each transient inhibitory input triggers the "inactive" state.

2. Neurons have several functional modes. For example long-term oscillations of membrane potential and the generation of repetitive "bursts" are produced in different cell types under specific conditions: in the pyramidal cells of hippocampus, repetitive bursts occur after a synaptic stimulation, when the cell is depolarized (Schwartzkroin 1980, Hotson 1980); but in the thalamus, oscillation is triggered by synaptic inputs when the neuron is hyperpolarized, as for instance during slow-wave sleep (Hirsch 1983). In the cerebral cortex, intrinsic bursting neurons seem limited to a cortical layer (Connors 1982); but most cortical neurons follow the 5-10 cycle rhythm generated in the thalamus (Purpura 1964) at the onset of sleep. The same cell can thus respond in two different ways to an afferent activity (Traub 1979): without bursts, the output frequency depends directly upon the input frequency; but burst generation produces output information that is independent of the input frequency.

3. When the cell is not bursting, high frequencies of action potentials can result in a prolonged periods of synaptic facilitation; this phenomenon of post-tetanic potentiation is due to a cumulative increase of internal calcium that facilitates transmitter release (Kuno 1984). In the hippocampus or in the cerebral cortex , the potentiating effect is amplified by the NMDA-type Glutamate receptors whose conductance increases when the membrane depolarizes (Nowak 1983; Collinridge 1983; Thomson 1986). Conversely, other activity patterns result in a decreased transmission (habituation), for example when there is no significant variation in action potential frequency.

4. Short term changes in cell excitability can also be due produced by neuromodulators such as dopamine, norepinephrine, serotonin and acetylcholine (Hotson, 1983; Dingledine 1984, Ropert 1984); cells have several functional programs due to their different types of channels and each type of neuromodulator can favour one of the possible modes (Hounsgaard, 1986). Such neuromodulators, originating in specific nuclei of the reticular formation, are extensively secreted in the cerebral cortex (Hokfelt 1972, Ungerstedt & Henderson 1981, McKinney 1983); they influence the responsiveness of cortical cells to their inputs (Taylor 1981), with quite varied effects depending upon the activated receptors.

A) Neurons have several functional modes which correspond to different types of memorization.

Neurons can memorize transient synaptic inputs for short durations (T1 and T2) when they have bistable properties given by their ionic channels: these channels can maintain an active state (continuous firing frequency) after a single excitatory input (channel opening by depolarization); this activity stops after a single inhibitory input and the cell remains in this inactive state until the next excitatory input. Thanks to this flip-flop property, cells "register" the past input information until the next one, and can maintain a continous output activity. Furthermore, neurons have two possible functional modes at temporal level T2, the "oscillation" and the "integration" modes.

a) "Oscillation" mode
This state is due to the activation of a feed-back loop between two types of channels (voltage dependant calcium channels and calcium-dependant potassium channels); the intracellular calcium concentration and the membrane potential oscillate and produce bursts of neuronal activity.

When these oscillations are triggered by a synaptic input, the repetitive burst is therefore a form of sequential short term memory. During the bursts, the neuron becomes relatively insensitive to other input activities, in a state of functional isolation. Oscillation permits both short-term memorization of transient information and functional isolation from succeeding input activities. These two functions are activated in two different ways in two neural structures directly connected to the cerebral cortex, the hippocampus and the thalamus:
- For hippocampal neurons, oscillation is triggered by input activity, when the cell is depolarized. The afferent information (from the cortex) is memorized by a repetitive bursting , and can be recombined with another information occurring later in time.
- For thalamic neurons, oscillation is triggered when the neurons are hyperpolarized. Since the thalamus is the principal input structure to cortex, thalamic oscillation isolates the cortex from sensory inputs and induces oscillation of cortical activity. Rhythmic, synchronized thalamic and cortical activity does not correspond to memorization of any particular message, but rather to a state of global isolation that leads to sleep.

b) "Integration" mode.

When there is no oscillation, if the inputs are sufficiently close in time, they change the internal state of the neuron by accumulation of intracellular calcium; there is then a double relationship between input and output-- a direct effect of each input, and a cumulative effect which is proportionately stronger as the inputs are more closely grouped in time. The critical parameter that produces a prolonged period of facilitation is the intensity of activity (frequency of action potentials). For the cortex, in the next chapter, we will distinguish three activity levels in the cortical neurons; the higher level will produce a short-term facilitatory effect.

This potentiating effect is mainly due to phasic increases of action potential frequency, since an unvarying frequency may have an opposite effect (habituation).

The two functional modes, "Oscillation" and "Integration" correspond to two different mechanisms of short-term memorization:

- In the oscillating mode, repetitive bursts can be triggered by a single synaptic activation; this "memorization" isolates the cell from other inputs and produces a repetitive activation of target cells..

- In the integrative mode, the neuron performs a temporal integration of successive information and become more receptive to other inputs. Memorization of afferent information is cumulative.

B) Neuromodulators condition functional modes of neurons.

We shall not go into the detailed action of neuromodulators , but we shall consider that these neuromodulators produced by the neurons of different reticular nuclei, change the functional state of the cortical neurons and their responsiveness to other inputs.

- Noradrenaline is important for maintaining the integrative mode of the cortical neurons during the whole period of active waking; it conditions the summation of successive activities and favor the memorizing process.

- Dopamine is important to maintain cortical activity in motor or frontal regions of cortex during prolonged behavioral activities (chapter IV).

- Acetylcholine can favor neuronal bursting and therefore the short-term memorization of transient input information; in the septo hippocampal system, it may represent significant situations related to the expression of fundamental programs of the organisms (eating for example).

2. Long term memorization

References

Long-term memory processes at the cellular level are phylogenetically universal (Kandel 1981). In the nervous system of vertebrates, cellular changes related with learning are not limited to isolated neurons but they occur in parallel in several neural structures (Olds, 1954; Cohen 1982; Woody 1982). Long term changes of cellular transmission involve either the whole cell, such as a global increase of excitability (Woody 1976, Bindmann 1979), or a restricted number of synapses in relation with the active pathways (Tsukahara, 1981).

Long term potentiation (LTP) is an activity-dependant increase of neuronal transmission produced by direct stimulation of afferent pathways (Bliss 1972). This long term memorizing process has associative properties at the cellular level. Only synaptic activity can produce this potentiation (Dunwiddle 1978), and the phenomenon is limited to the inducing afference: response to other afferences is only slightly modified (Andersen 1977)..

Furthermore, temporal association of a "weak" input with a "strong", potentiating input, results in a increased transmission for the "weak" input (Levy 1979, Barruonuevo 1983): potentiation occurs only for those weak inputs temporally associated with another strong input. The effect of the potentiating input seems to be attributable to the post synaptic depolarization produced by this strong input (Wigstrom 1985). The associative effect that require conjunction of pre and post-synaptic activity can be explained by glutamate receptor of the NMDA type which function as AND gates between presynaptic input activity and post-synaptic output depolarization (Dingledine, 1982) . Similar associative properties at the cellular level is also observed in the Purkinje cells of the cerebellum (Ito 1982): coupling of a "weak" mossy fiber input and a "strong" climbing fiber input produces a long-term change for the long term change of the "weak" afference (here a depression).

Associative properties highlight the differential memorization capacities of restricted regions within the membrane of a single cell . Dendritic spines can favor this spatial isolation, and modification of their shape can be an important factor to selectively increase the weight of a single afference (Diamond 1970, Rall 1971, Crick 1982). Memorization can also be due to synaptic destruction in less active circuits and, on the contrary, to formation of new synapses in more active circuits by axonal sprouting (Tsukahara 1981); selective sprouting of active terminals in response to a post-synaptic factor is also an "associative" process at the cellular level.

Long term memorization involves either the whole cell or local subcellular zones

Activity can modify over a long term period (temporal level T3) the transmission coefficients of a neuron, under two conditions :

- An intense input (high frequency of action potential) produces at first a short-term potentiation (T2) of its own transmission ("post tetanic potentiation). Duration of short term memorization produced by post tetanic potentiation decreases exponentially with time.

- A long-term potentiation (temporal level T3) develops from the short-term facilitation if the post synaptic cell is depolarized by a "strong" input (that activates a high proportion of the membrane). Passage from short term to long term memorization is dependant upon the spatial extension of the intense input activity on the cell membrane. These conditions are detailed in ANNEX 4 and Figure A-11.

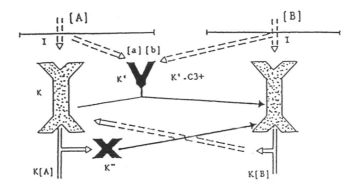

GLOBAL MODIFICATION OF CELLULAR TRANSMISSION

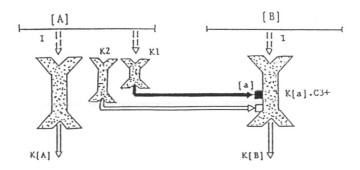

DIFFERENTIAL MODIFICATION OF MEMBRANE ZONES

Figure 1-10 . Global and local memorization by neurons: associative effects for groups of cells.

Long term memorization may involve several transmission coefficients, from the synaptic level (mediator release, receptor activation), up to the level of the entire neuron (global change in membrane conductance). Functional consequences are different depending upon the spatial extension of the changes. We shall now compare the two main possibilities, which are depicted in Figure 1-10: global cell changes are illustrated in the upper part and local changes in the lower diagram. In the two diagrams, the cellular regions involved by long term changes are accented in black.

a) Global changes (upper diagram).

Some transmission coefficients involve the whole cell: for example somatic conductance, threshold for the action potential, or the amount of available transmitter. In this case all the inputs have an increased impact upon the neuron. In the next chapter, we shall suppose that these "global changes" are possible for all cortical neurons, including interneurons, when their activity is very high.

Global changes of cellular transmission are unspecific with respect to the inducing afference, and is therefore not "associative" at the cellular level. But it can be associative at the level of a cellular group. Thus, in figure 1-10 (upper diagram), the combined activity of two independent cellular groups ([A] and [B]) on the interneuron ("K'") provokes its global transformation. But because of the articulation of this interneuron in the network, this global change produces an associative and selective coupling between the two cell groups ([A] and [B]).

b) Local changes (lower diagram).

Local specializations of the membrane such as spines permit the stable and selective conservation of memory traces involving only parts of the cell. For the cerebral cortex, we will suppose that local memorization processes are possible for those neurons possessing spines.

The general model that we will adopt is that of "associative" long term potentiation (LTP) at the cellular level. A neuron receives two types of afferences that have different influences, the first type is "strong" and the other is "weak" (as defined in paragraph II, Figure 1-4, by the proportion of activated membrane).

The transmission coefficients for specific inputs are increased when these inputs are active (short term facilitation) and when the post synaptic cell is depolarized (i.e when the proportion of activated membrane is high). Coefficients change only in the synaptically activated membrane: this memorization is selective and involves only previously activated afferences.

Activation of "weak" input alone cannot produce these long-term changes. But influence of the weak input can increase if and only if it is time locked with other inputs and the global effect is obviously that of a "strong" potentiating input.

The two long term cellular memorization processes, cellular and subcellular, are not competitive and can be activated in a progressive way. They correspond to increasingly precise adjustments of the function of a neural tissue:

- simultaneous activations of all inputs produce a strong response that can increase the whole transmission (for example by a decreased membrane conductance or increase in neurotransmitter release); these global changes can be associative at the level of cellular groups;

- temporal association between "weak" and "strong" inputs on a single neuron selectively modify the coefficients of the "weak" afference (for example, local conductance changes); this property is particularly important for membrane zones that can be functionally isolated (for example dendritic spines).

A whole range of coefficient values between cells or groups of cells is thus possible.

3. Permanent memory

References

There are many forms of learning in the various animal species; as a general rule, learning becomes more complex with the phylogenetic development of nervous structures.

The simplest form of learning, seen in most species, is classical conditioning (Pavlov 1949): essentially, this is an "external program" which repetitively produces a conditional stimulus ("CS") time locked with an unconditional stimulus ("US") triggering a reflex response ("UR"); after such pairings,conditional stimulus alone can trigger the reflex response.

- The temporal linking is precise: only stimuli that regularly precede the unconditional stimulus can trigger the response; irrelevant stimuli are inhibited.

- The number of repetitions necessary for learning depends upon a certain adaptive hierarchy: an aversive alimentary conditioning can occur in a single trial.

- Probability of response to the conditional stimulus approaches that to the unconditional stimulus. The conditional stimulus thus becomes a functional equivalent of the unconditional stimulus. Additional stimuli can then be linked to the conditional stimulus, but learning speed depends upon response probability, and learning can become impossible if the response demanded is too unusual for the animal.

- Learning of a new movement (operant conditioning) depends upon that movement's "proximity" to a natural movement.

During classical conditioning, the cells that participate in the reinforcement of the link between the conditional stimulus and the reflex circuit show a characteristic change in their activity during the period of conditioning (Olds 1954, Woody 1982):

1. Before conditioning, the conditional stimulus has a weak influence on a group of cells that can control the reflex.

2. When the conditional and unconditional stimuli are first paired, these cells show a weak response to the conditional stimulus, and then a stronger response to the unconditional stimulus.

3. During repetition of stimulus pairing, the intense activity of these "coupling" cells becomes more clearly time-related to the conditional stimulus.

During differential conditioning to two stimuli, the cellular response to the conditional stimulus increases while responses to the irrelevant stimulus show a marked decrease (inhibition).

Speed of memorization and permanence of the transformations is strongly dependant upon maturity, and particularly upon critical periods at the end of construction of the neural network. Memorization depends then on correlative activation of pre and post synaptic activities (Singer, 1983; Fregnac, 1983)

Generalization of the associative process is the basis of models of "associative memory" (Hebb 1949, Marr 1969, Kohonen 1975, Cooper 1981): the transmission coefficients ("internal" couplings) are modified as a function of correlations between neuronal inputs and outputs ("external" couplings).

Permanent memory depends upon repetition of critical patterns of activity and upon maturation of the neural network.

a) Repetition factor

Cellular memorization occurs at successive temporal levels:

- Short term memory (passage from temporal level T1 to T2) depends upon the input frequency; it decreases exponentially in time.

- Long term memory (passage from T2 to T3) depends upon the spatial extent of the activity: transmission coefficients are modified during hours or even days, but can come back to their initial value.

- Permanent memory (passage from T3 to T4) is irreversible. It will depends upon the long term activity patterns, and in fact upon the repetition of the "strong" activations that underlie long-term memory. Repetition of this critical pattern of activity produces a cumulative effect toward a threshold where the coefficients are stabilized permanently at their new values.

We will consider like many authors that permanent, irreversible memorization at the cellular level depends upon repetition of temporally contingent input and output activities, i.e. their correlations. But we shall consider that this effect is only produced after the two steps that we have described:

1. The neuron is in the "integrative mode" (temporal level T2), and the strong short term correlations induced by synchronous oscillations are thus excluded;

2. The spatial extension of input activity on the cell membrane is a critical factor for long term memory (temporal level T3) : strong coactivations, even if relatively rare, are more effective than repetitive high frequency inputs. The number of co-activations necessary for the production of irreversible memory will be strongly dependant upon the geometry of the neural network.

We measure the effective correlations between pre and post synaptic activities by a "repetition factor": this factor counts the occurrences of the critical pattern of co-activations. In the next chapter, we shall use a semi-quantitative description: the cells may be "always", "sometimes" or "never" co-activated with this critical pattern.

When one considers a neural tissue and its input and output activities, the repetition factor needed to reach a permanent memorization will be dependant upon each neuronal type. In Chapter II we will see how several patterns of cortical afferent activities will act selectively on different cell types in the cortical column and will produce different transformations of the cortical function .

b) Maturation factor

The "maturation" factor is also important: during the last stages of neuronal growth, irreversible changes can occur more rapidly. There is a critical period during which exaggerated variations of activity can affect the factors governing stabilization of synapses or other structural parameters.

Construction of pre- or post-synaptic structures can depend upon the activities of "emitting" or "receiving" cells. In the case of double dependency, formation and stabilization of contact between two cells will be dependant upon the temporal conjunction of their activities. Since synapses stabilize membrane extensions (axonal branches, dendritic spines), the neural network can be remodelled as a function of activity .

We saw that structural parameters impose limits to functional changes of transmission coefficient (see paragraph II). Changes in the structure of the neural network extend these limits. In the last chapter, we will analyze the functional structuring of the cortical system. Late maturation of cortical regions in the early childhood can lead to the shaping of the neuronal network with activity; these structural changes have the same logic as the other forms of memorization but they have a stronger quantitative effect on transmission parameters. This plasticity will be an important element for the cognitive constructions.

IV. From cellular memorization to learning.

Long term activity-dependant changes is a very general property of neurons and in a behavioral context, these memorizations are effected in parallel in different neural structures. But each type of neural tissue, by the transformations and combinations that it effects, selectively facilitates certain memorizations and learning: one can speak of "learning capacities" of a specific neural tissue based on a general cellular memorization process. At this point, two questions arise:

- What is the relation between cellular memorization and its effect upon the function of the tissue?

- What type of learning is favored by each neural tissue?

In this paragraph, we shall discuss general aspects of these two questions. They are treated more precisely in Annex 4. They are developed for the cortical tissue in chapter II.

A) Different forms of learning depend upon the structures of the neuronal networks.

"Pavlovian" conditioning is the simplest expression of the memorization capacities of a neuronal network. An external program presents a temporal association (repetition) between a sensory activation (conditional stimulus) and the activation of a natural "reflex" circuit (unconditional stimulus and response).

FIGURE 1-10 shows a simple network that can be related to an external conditioning program. Conditioning can occur when an "alternative" circuit ([B] linked to the conditional stimulus) has access (via a "coupling" circuit "K'") to the "principal" circuit ([A]) that produces the response to the unconditional stimulus. In general, in a behavioural situation, these circuits are not unique, and memorizations can be produced in parallel in several neural structures.

Behavioral modification follows the cellular transformations. The neural network "translates" the sensori-motor pattern in a critical co-activation pattern for "coupling cells" (cell "K'" in FIGURE 1-10). Activities of the coupling neurons are illustrated in Figure 1-11 by temporal trapezoidal forms (as defined in paragraph II), before and after conditioning, for the two types of stimuli, conditional (CS) and unconditional (US). During each external association of CS and US, coupling cells have a double activity-- weak and random for the CS, strong for the US. This critical co-activation changes the transmission coefficient for the weaker pathway, and the .

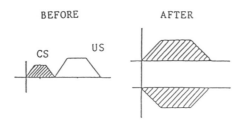

Figure 1-11 . Trapezoidal activity of a neuron in the circuit coupling CS and US before and after learning.

activity of the coupling cell becomes stronger in response to the CS: the motor response (UR) is increasingly linked to the CS which becomes the functional equivalent of the US. Learning speed is linked with the probability that the US triggers the response: conditioning can occur in one trial, but conditioning of a response that is too unusual for the animal can be impossible.

Inhibition of irrelevant activities by the unconditioned reflex (US-UR) is critically important because it introduces an implicit causal relation: only activities that "anticipate" this reflex are taken into account by the nervous system.

The network illustrated in FIGURE 1-10 allow different kinds of conditioning, for example a differential conditioning between two stimuli: in this case transmission coefficients of inhibitory interneurons increase as a function of differences in activity in the two cell groups.

The network can also produce "instrumental" conditioning, of a new movement, with the same cellular logic as Pavlovian conditioning. A new movement (for example commanded by [B]) can be learned because of its "proximity" with a natural movement (for example [A] is the movement that catches a "reward"). The transmission coefficient of the coupling interneuron increases when the new movement favors the triggering of the natural movement, by any external causal link.

B) Memorization programs of different neuronal types can modify different aspects of tissular function.

Memorization rules are specific to each neural tissue:

- All the information processing performed by the neural structures are very important for learning because they condition the behavioral significance of critical activity that leads to memorization. We saw in a previous section that some neuronal tissue can code a spatial or a temporal parameter of activity as "intensity" (frequency of action potential) . Since intensity is a critical parameter for learning, coding permits the learning of the different parameters of a spatiotemporal function: the neural network can learn a position, an extension, a duration, a delay, a speed (derivative of time), a contrast (spatial derivative), or an orientation (spatial derivative on two dimensions).

- A neuronal texture regulates the relative weight of inputs on each neuronal type, and thus determines the critical conditions for long term memorizations. For example one of the inputs can be indispensable for memorization (like the climbing fibers for the Purkinje cells of the cerebellum).

- Cellular memorization modifies the tissue activity in different ways, depending upon the position of the cell in the network (principal neuron or interneuron, coupling or uncoupling, lateral or transversal, etc..

C) Learning depends upon combinatorial properties of neural structures.

In learning, the role of each neural tissue is first to "propose" combinations in relation to sensory and motor organs. The neural network forms circuits that constitute the "behavioral repertoire": reflexes, "fundamental programs" (basic acts like eating).

But the neural network forms also alternative circuits that are connected in parallel with the circuits of fundamental programs. This organization is important for learning: memorization never replaces an existing circuit, but rather modifies it in a progressive and quantitative way.

This progressive link (parallel alternative pathway) exists at several levels; for example, a whole neural structure can be connected "in parallel" to the circuits that effect fundamental program. But each neural tissue can also form a specific "recombination" network between its different parts already connected with different sensory and motor maps.

FIGURE 1 12 illustrates several types of recombination networks, formed by various vertebrate neural structures such as spinal cord, cerebellar and cerebral cortex, or hippocampus. They share common features due to similar constraints in their cellular construction processes. For example, the recombination network is usually formed by differentiation of the tissue into two functional layers along the tissue's transversal axis. These two layers form two distinct networks:

The "output layer" ("Kb") projects towards other neural structures ,The extrinsic inputs ("I" and "J") and outputs interrelate each region of the structure (lateral zone [A]) with specific regions of sensory and motor maps.

- The "recombination layer" ("Kh") forms an internal network between two regions of the same structure. A neuron of the recombination layer ("Kh" in zone [A]) projects toward the output neuron ("Kb" in zone [B]) of another region of the same structure having a different sensory or motor significance.

The architecture of the internal recombination network conditions the learning capacities of a neural tissue:

a) Peripheral neural tissues.
In peripheral neural tissues (for example, in the retina) there are two functional layers, but they organize a very precise transmission of the sensory map : position information is preserved between the input and the output, and no changes are expected with learning;

b) Hippocampus.
The recombination network can form a matrix, organizing systematic connections between two groups of neurons. For example, in the hippocampus, the recombination layer (dentate gyrus) has a transversal axis that is perpendicular to the

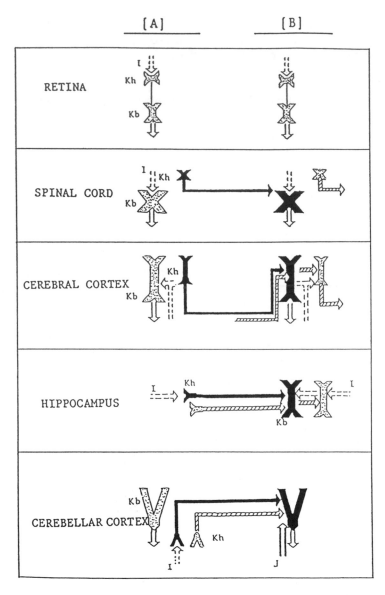

Figure 1-12 . Different types of combinations between two sensory or motor components ([A],[B]) performed by 5 neural structures.

transversal axis of the output layer (CA1-CA3): consequently each combination neuron ("Kh") can form "matrix" connections with a large number of neurons of the output layer ("Kb") . The two divisions receive the same type of external inputs (from the temporal cortex); therefore each neuron of the output division combine two messages (direct and recombined) which may have close sensory-motor meanings but which are temporally separated; this architecture favors the recognition and learning of the temporal structure of input information.

c) Cerebellum.

In the cerebellar cortex, axons of the combination layer (granular cells "Kh") form systematic connections with dendrites of neurons of the output layer (Purkinje cells "Kb"): the axons and dendrites form a large matrix thanks to their relative perpendicular orientations. The two functional layers receive two different inputs , a "general" sensorimotor information on the recombination layer (mossy fibers in a [A] zone), and a specific proprioceptive information on the output layer (climbing fibers "J" in a "B" position): the matrix will learn to recognize general sensory-motor situations linked with precise proprioceptive activations.

d) Spinal cord.

The recombination network can relate distant zones in a recursive way when it projects not only on the output layer, but also on the recombination layer : these recursive projections favor learning of sequences. For instance, the recombination network of the spinal cord forms recursive links between motoneurons that participate in the same motor sequence.

e) Cerebral cortex.

In the cerebral cortex, the recombination network has two main properties:

1. The network is recursive, as in the spinal cord. Furthermore, it links regions that have very different sensorimotor "meanings" . This recursive property favors learning of precise sensory-motor sequences including very heterogeneous behavioral elements.

2. The network organizes a recombination matrix as in the cerebellar cortex or the hippocampus. But this matrix is not organized at the cellular level, but at the level of larger groups of cells where each combination is repeated in a redundant way . We shall see in chapter III how this cortical architecture multiplies learning capacities.

The basic mechanism of the cortical column.

Having examined in chapter I the general properties of neuronal groups, we will now focus more specifically on the properties of the cerebral cortex. This way of proceeding, from the general to the specific, is essential for understanding what it is that distinguishes the cortex from other neural structures.

In this chapter we analyze the properties of the repetitive cellular arrangements in the cerebral cortex which form the CORTICAL COLUMNS. Continuing the general perspective developed in chapter I, chapter II is organized around five questions:

1 - What are the cellular combinations that are specific to cerebral cortex ?

2 - What is the basic operation performed by the cortical column?

3 - What can a column learn ?

4 - What are the behavioral significance and the adaptive consequences of the cortical process?

5 - What are the properties of the new "functional networks" constructed by learning within the cortex?

I. Architecture of the cortical column

Starting from the general architecture of neural tissue analyzed in chapter I, we will focus on the cellular texture of the cortical tissue that form the cortical columns; the main feature of its cellular architecture is a 6-layered laminar organization of cell bodies and afferences, with vertical extension of pyramidal neurons perpendicular to these layers. The cortical texture is due to its specific mode of ontogenetic construction: an important element is the fact that the maturation of the pyramidal neurons is linked to the position of the cell body on the transversal (vertical) axis of the cortex.This positional parameter determines both the target structures of pyramidal neurons and the specific operations that they perform on their inputs.

At first, we will differentiate the two main divisions of the cortical sheet, the supragranular layers (layers I to III) and the infragranular layers (V and VI), separated by the cortical layer IV that receives the thalamic input: they form the two principle cortical outputs (internal and external to the cortex), and perform two different operations, both on the three principal inputs (reticular, thalamic, and cortical).

Next we analyze the connectivity of the main types of cortical interneurons, in order to understand their role in the control of intracortical communication channels, either between two columns or between two layers. We analyze how each of these interneurons can participate in the learning process.

II. The basic operation performed by a cortical column

Within this framework, we then attack the problem of passing from the cellular texture of the cortical tissue to the specific operation performed on the input information.

Groups of neurons in the same "column" perpendicular to the cortical surface are tightly connected and share common sensori-motor properties. It is thus possible to consider in a global way input and output activities of columns whose cells of the same type have an homogeneous activity in each layer.

We summarize the basic operation of a column by an in-out table that defines a "columnar automaton": it combines two major different inputs, a thalamic input in layer IV and a cortical input from other columns in layers II and III; it has two major different outputs, one from the supragranular layers that project to other columns, and one from the infragranular layers that projects outside the cortex.

We describe this columnar automaton by semi-quantitative rules, with three levels of activity: the levels of activity of the two main outputs of the column are determined by the activities of the two main inputs (cortical and thalamic) and by the previous activity of the column.

For each combination of activities (two inputs and an internal state) the behavior of the automaton is determined by a rule that we justify from experimental results.

1. When the two inputs are co-activated there is an amplification of activity within the column. The cortical inputs, when they have a low intensity, have an excitatory effect which is a "gating" effect on thalamic inputs.

2. The response to low cortical inputs alone is not the same for the two main divisions of the column: the supragranular layers can transmit this low activity on the cortical network, even if the infragranular layers produce no significant output outside the cortex.

3. If columns are strongly activated, their influence on others columns can be excitatory or inhibitory depending upon the difference in their activity, since direct excitatory connections are doubled by inhibitory interneurons. When they arrive in upper layers (as in "feedback" connections), strong cortical inputs may have an inhibitory effect if the receptive columns have a low activity.

III. Learning properties of a cortical column

The very organization of the cortical column determines a mode of learning that is much more than a simple association; it is an active and structured process.

The essential property of the cortical memorization process is its ability to progressively modify the columnar automaton defined by the in/out table. Several changes are possible and depend upon the long range patterns of coactivation between a column and its cortical inputs; they may be "never", "sometimes", or "always" co-activated. We justify these effects by the registration processes of each of the cortical cellular types-- the pyramidal cells and the main types of interneurons. Different long term cellular changes are produced by different critical patterns of coactivations and they can amplify or decease functional connections between two different modules or between two layers of the same module.

After learning the low cortical inputs may have three very different effects: they can become inhibitory; they can have a "gating" effect for other inputs; they can alone "trigger" the outputs of the column.

IV. Columnar automata: goal-directed behaviour and active learning

Taken together, the columnar operation and the learning rules determine a precise mechanism which has very important adaptive consequences.

We call "functional modules" the set of columns which have an homogeneous activity. The columnar automaton controls the dimensions of the functional modules (parallel processing) and the sequences of their activities, with two possible modes:

1. Each cortical module can effect a precise "action" upon the other organs, when it is simultaneously activated by its two main inputs (thalamic and cortical);

2. But if it is only activated by its cortical inputs, a module cannot execute an action outside the cortex, but it can "call" other modules through the cortical network and gate other modular actions: cortical actions are triggered in modules where this cortical call is in register with thalamic activations produced by environmental situations. The "call" continues until such modular actions can re-activate the other inputs of the calling module, via an external feedback loop produced by any external causal link; in this case, the calling module is strongly activated, its action is triggered and the call stops.

The "action" of each module represents, in this sense, an equilibrium position, a kind of "goal" that organizes the activity of other modules that are connected within the cortical network. A partial cortical activation defines a possible goal; the cortical automaton produces an exploration, a search through the other possible cortical actions until the full reactivation of the calling module by an external feedback loop. The behaviour is adjusted to the environment since actions are triggered only when the call is in register with thalamic inputs.

Each cortical modular action is a possible goal, and the activities of the other modules can be combined by the columnar automaton to accomplish this goal. Given the logic of cellular memorization in this context, a module will selectively "call" after learning those other modules that can favor its own action. The columnar automaton thus constructs combinations and sequences of "cortical actions" that are likely to accomplish "cortical goals". But because of differential memorizations of cortical neurons, this modular mechanism can generate three kinds of sequences: (1) It can produce random actions that search a solution by the trial and error method. (2) It can remember actions which were efficient and "orient" its call toward these actions, but the final choice will depend upon environmental conditions. (3) It can execute fixed combinations and sequences of actions that are independent of external conditions. These three strategies result in a precise behavioral adaptation to the regular features of the environment.

V. Functional networks between columns: call trees

The equivalence between "goal" and "modular action" is a very powerful property of the cortical system. The cortical mechanism constructs new functional networks, having a variable geometry, that we have named "call trees" because of their ramified hierarchical structure around goals and partial goals. These "call trees" are elaborated in space and in time: first a "call", emanating from a possible goal, produces an anticipatory activation: it gates the possible actions that can be efficient to reach a goal. The call spreads until it is in register with activations produced by the environmental conditions. In response to this external situation ("initial conditions"), the call tree then produces an appropriate combination and sequence of actions which bring in cascade the cortical system close to the goal; sequence of actions are triggered in reverse order from that of the call.

These call trees combine cortical actions in order to reach a goal, whatever the initial conditions. They can organize motor programs and placement in space, whatever the initial positions; they can also perform parallel and dynamic processing of diverse sensory information, whatever their initial forms on the receptive maps (recognition algorithms). These different behavioral functions will be developed in the next chapters.

I. Architecture of the cortical column.

The principal characteristics of intrinsic cortical organization are depicted in Figure 2-1 to 2-5. We shall first examine the structural properties of the principal cells, the pyramidal neurons, following which we will analyze the properties of the different types of interneurons.

1. Pyramidal neurons and afferences

References

A. *Layers and columns*

Though we are still far from an exhaustive knowledge of the cortical structure, it has been known for some time that this tissue has a typical morphological and functional organizational pattern, the "cortical column" (Szentagothai 1975, Mountcastle 1978, Hubel 1977, Gilbert 1981). The characteristic structure of cerebral cortex is a 6-layered laminar organization. The layers have relative dimensions that vary according to the cortical region (cytoarchitectonics).

The principal cellular type, the pyramidal neuron, is characterized by the vertical extension of "apical" dendrites that attain the cortical surface, regardless of the vertical depth of the cell body, thus giving an orientation perpendicular to that of the laminar structure.

The cortical tissue is formed by repetitive "columns", with several embedded patterns as seen from the cortical surface:

1. The "minicolumn" has a width of about 30 to 50 microns and correspond to a small group of pyramidal neurons closely related with apical dendrites often grouped in bundles (Mountcastle 1979); 30 micron is a minimal dimension since it corresponds to the largest diameter of the soma of pyramidal cells in infragranular layers. The number of neurons in a minicolumn is constant, about one hundred, regardless of animal species and cortical zone (Rockell 1974,1980).

2. The "maxicolumn" has a width of about 300-500 microns and corresponds to a functional unit in sensory-motor maps (Mountcastle 1979); it also corresponds to the lateral extension of "basal" dendrites of pyramidal cells (Cajal 1911, Von Economo 1929).

3. "Stripes" or modular bands" group several maxicolumns in an elongated zone with a width of around 500 microns and a variable length of several millimeters (Hubel 1977); the larger dimension corresponds to the horizontal projection of axons of pyramidal neurons.

B. In-out connections of cortical neurons.

Synapses and spines are arranged in a relatively regular fashion on the membrane surface, spaced at intervals of about a micron: the number of synapses on a pyramidal cell could therefore be on the order of 10 to the fifth power (Booth 1979, Colonnier 1981).

Three principal types of "extrinsic" inputs are organized within the layered structure, and form synapses with the pyramidal cells: they come from the thalamus, from the other cortical regions and from nuclei of the reticular formation.

a) Thalamic inputs.
Thalamic afferences are limited mostly to layer IV intermediate between the two divisions of the cortical sheet which contain the cell bodies of supra and infragranular pyramidal neurons. Thalamic inputs connect the basal dendrites of supragranular pyramidal cells, and the apical dendrites of the infragranular pyramidal cells (White 1981, Feldman 1984). The transmitter is unknown, but the direct action of these inputs is excitatory.

b) Output division of the cortical column.
Within the 6-layered cortical lamination, we focus on the two divisions of pyramidal neurons, separated by the "granular" layer IV; each division has specialized outputs (Lorente de No 1938, Jones 1981):

1. The "infragranular" pyramidal neurons (layers V and VI) project outside the cortex toward other neural structures. Furthermore the target structure varies as a function of the depth of the cell bodies of pyramidal neurons. For example in the somato-motor regions (Jones, 1982) targets of progressively deeper pyramidal neurons project toward more distant neural structures: the striatum, then the red nucleus, the medulla and the spinal cord; pyramidal cells of layer VI project to the thalamus which is the principal input structure of the cortex. Infra-granular neurons can also project to other cortical regions; for example they participate in the "feed-back" cortico-cortical connections from associative toward receptive areas (Van Essen, 1983).

2. "Supragranular" pyramidal cells (layers II and III) project mainly toward other cortical regions: from layer II toward adjacent cortical zones; from layer III, toward more distant cortical areas, first ipsilateral and then contralateral, for deeper neurons.

This connective subdivision is linked to the maturation process of the cortical tissue. Cortical neurons migrate from the ventricular zone and follows the transversal axis, perpendicular to the surface: new migrating cells cross layers of cells that arrived before and settle into place above them closer to the surface. Consequently, the infra-granular pyramidal cell arrive and mature first, and the supragranular pyramidal neurons arrive and mature in a second wave (Rakic 1971, 1974, 1981).

c) Laminar pattern of cortico-cortical connections.

The transmitter of pyramidal neurons is glutamate, which has an excitatory effect through different types of receptors. Both locally and long-range, inter-pyramidal interactions seem to be essentially excitatory (review in Gilbert 1981, Krnjevic 1984).

For each column, cortical afferences which are axons of pyramidal cells arrive from directly adjacent columns or from more distant columns in other areas. The supra-granular pyramidal cells that form the long-range intracortical network project toward the supragranular layers of other columns, thus forming a recursive corticocortical network (Jones 1981, Feldman 1984). Corticocortical connections between two distant zones are reciprocal, but the laminar pattern may be different. For example, the cortical connections from "primary" sensory maps toward "secondary" associative maps ("feed-forward" connections) arise from supragranular layers and project to layer IV (and not to layers II and III); but the reciprocal connections from secondary areas to primary maps ("feed-back" connections) arise from both infra and supra-granular layers and project mostly to the supragranular layers II and III (Van Essen 1983, Jones 1977, 1978).

Besides these distant cortical connections, pyramidal cells are locally interconnected:

- The pyramidal cells are directly connected to each other, laterally, in the same cortical layer.

- Higher pyramidal cells send collateral axons toward lower pyramidal cells in the same column: layers II and III toward layer V, from layer V to layer VI, and recurrent collaterals from layer VI project toward layer IV (Lund 1975, Gilbert 1981). These collaterals can extend for several millimeters, and may be clearly oriented on axes parallel to the cortical surface (Szenthagothai 1979).

d) Cytoarchitectonics variations.

The laminar pattern is modulated as a function of cortical area and varies between a "granular" pole, with layer IV highly developed in sensory areas, and an "agranular" pole in the primary motor area; intermediate patterns are seen in associative and frontal areas (Brodmann, Van Economo 1929).

In the primary visual cortex (area 17), the layer IV is thick and is subdivided into sublayers (IVa, IVb, IVc) which receive different types of inputs from the thalamus ("X" or "Y" for instance) (Gilbert 1981). The thickness of layer IV in this region is consistent with the functional importance of sensory reception: in visual (Hubel 1962) and somatosensory (Mountcastle 1958) cortex, thalamic inputs are very efficient and produce a strong activation of pyramidal neurons.

By contrast, in the motor area (area 4), thalamic inputs are less important and less efficient. Areas which are intermediate between the agranular motor area and the granular receptive area (for example area 2), are characterized by more equal influence of thalamic afferences compared to other cortical inputs (Jones 1981).

A) Pyramidal neurons effect several integrative functions upon layered inputs with specific outputs on the transversal axis

Our functional model is based upon the main architectural features of the cortical column, and more precisely upon those features which are direct consequences of simple principles of ontogenetic construction of the cortical tissue.

Figure 2-1 illustrates this progressive construction, with two parallel diagrams on the time axis (horizontal):

1. The upper diagram shows the shaping of spatial relations organized by layers: cell types and their extrinsic connectivity are ordered by successive cellular migrations perpendicular to the surface.

2. The lower diagram shows the successive molecular affinities between transmitters and receptors which direct the interneuronal pattern of connectivity; two affinities seem very important: Glutamate which is excitatory (G+) and GABA which is inhibitory (G-).

The effects of these two combined factors - transversal migrations and molecular affinities- upon the structural parameters of the column are detailed in ANNEX 2.

a) The laminar architecture and the apical dendrites.

The cortex has three main axis:

- two lateral axes, parallel to the cortical surface;
- a transversal (or vertical) axis, perpendicular to the surface : this transversal axis is subdivided in 6 layers.

During the successive waves of cellular migrations on the transversal axis, new migrating cells cross cell layers already present, and form new layers above them. Consequently, maturation of each pyramidal cell, its structural parameters (size, diameter) and related functional parameters (such as conductance) depend directly upon the transversal position of that cell's soma.

Dendritic growth is parallel to the thickening cortex: apical dendrites extend all the way to the cortical surface . Extension of the apical dendrites, and consequently the integrative properties of pyramidal neurons are linked with the transversal position of the cell body.

b) Layered organization of inputs and outputs: the two main cortical divisions.

The position of the cell body on the transversal axis which represents an ontogenetic clock is also linked with the time of axonal growth which differentiate the targets of the pyramidal cells. The axons of pyramidal neurons of the two main transversal divisions, infra-granular and supra-granular, form two output networks:

1. Pyramidal neurons of the "lower" infragranular layers V and VI form the general network with the other neural structures.

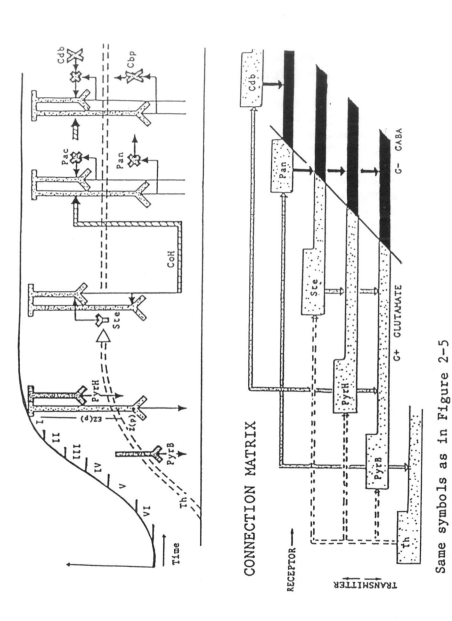

Figure 2-1. Ontogenetic structuring of the cortical network : spatial organization by layers (upper) and connections by molecular affinities (lower).

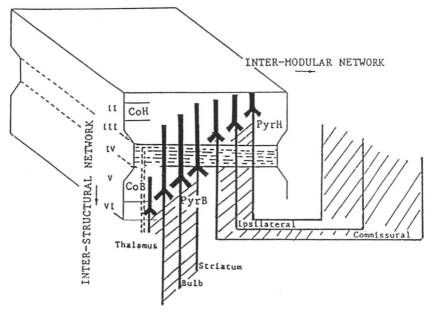

Figure 2-2 . Intra and extracortical targets of pyramidal neurons organized by layers.

2. Pyramidal neurons of the "upper" supragranular layers II and III form the intracortical network between columns.

Infragranular layers also participate in the cortico-cortical network, as in the feed-back connections from associative to primary receptive areas.

The two major types of cortical inputs, from thalamus and from the other cortical regions are also organized by layers: they connect the different dendrites inside their layers and thus connect both upper and lower pyramidal neurons. Thalamic inputs which occupy the intermediate layer IV (granular layer) are thus differentially connected to upper and lower pyramidal neurons: they project to the basal dendrites of the upper pyramidal cells, and to the apical dendrites of the lower pyramidal cells.

The main functional consequence is that upper and lower pyramidal cells integrate the same inputs (thalamic and cortical), but with quantitatively different parameters.

The architectural "framework" that form a columnar automaton is constituted of the two main divisions of the pyramidal neurons (upper and lower layers) that form two outputs, and that both combine two types of external inputs (thalamic and cortical) separated in different layers on the transversal axis.

c) Multiplicity of pyramidal targets and subsets of input-output functions.

Although the columnar automaton is based upon these two main input/output relations, several sub-functions could be defined in a more precise way, with new subdivisions in sub-layers of the transversal position of the soma of the output neuron. This is illustrated in Figure 2-2. Thanks to their differential maturation on the transversal axis, pyramidal neurons can connect different targets and integrate external inputs with slightly different quantitative parameters. For lower pyramidal cells of infragranular layers V, the first to migrate in the Cortex have more distant targets: they first project to spinal cord, then medulla, red nucleus, and striatum. For the "upper" pyramidal neurons that form connections with other cortical regions, the first to migrate have also more distant targets: they first project to contralateral cortical areas, then ipsilateral cortical areas, then adjacent areas, and then columns in the same area. This more detailed architecture will be used in chapter III to propose a combinatorial model of the different corticocortical connections.

B) The cortico cortical network is reciprocal, symmetric on the lateral axes and recursive.

The pyramidal cells are directly interconnected (thanks to their glutamate affinity), with four important functional consequences:

1. The two main divisions of a column are directly inter-connected: the lateral branches of upper pyramidal neurons project toward pyramidal cells of lower layers, and reciprocally lower pyramidal axons have upward collaterals. We will see in the next sections the functional importance of this pattern for the vertical integrative properties of the columnar automaton.

2. The upper pyramidal cells that form the long-range intracortical network project not only to lower, but also to upper pyramidal cells, thus forming a recursive cortico-cortical network: we will see in chapter III how this pattern favours learning of multiple sensori-motor combinations and sequences.

3. The cortico-cortical connections between two distant columns in two different areas are reciprocal, but their layered organization is not: we will see in chapter IV how this pattern is important for the progressive integration of sensory information.

4. The cortico-cortical connections are organized in symmetrical "mirror" fashion with respect to linear features of the cortical surface such as sulci and convexities. In chapter V we will examine the functional importance of these symmetrical connections for structured learning.

C) Functional modules have variable dimensions, from mini to maxi-columns.

In the preceding chapter, we saw that a functional "module" is a group of cells which have similar activities. In the cerebral cortex, a functional module is formed by a set of minicolumns which are grouped in a lateral zone of the cortical surface; lateral extension of a cortical module depends upon behavioral situations; furthermore its limits will change with learning. Modular zones have variable extensions which are intermediate between two anatomical units, minicolumns and maxicolumns, as shown in Figure 2-3:

- The minicolumn limits the minimal size of the smallest modules (30-50 microns diameter): it correspond to the thickness of bundles of apical dendrites and to the diameter of the larger soma of pyramidal cells; such minicolums form minimal functional units, with at least a possible inhibitory circuit toward other units.

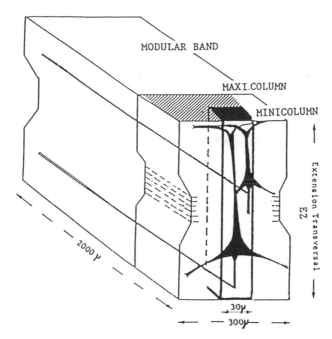

Figure 2-3 . Possible dimensions of a functional module; from mini to maxi - columns.

- The maxicolumn (300-500 microns) correspond to the length of basal dendrites in the "lateral" directions, and to the smallest size of "axonal" bands that come from the thalamus or from other cortical regions; these connective patterns induce a functional homogeneity for the neurons in register with the afferent axons. But several combinations of inputs can coexist and induce several functional modules inside a single maxicolumn. Since maximal lateral projection of axons collaterals can continue for several millimeters, "modular bands" with a width of around 500 microns and a length of several millimeters, correspond to the maximal extension of modules.

2. Neuronal types of the cerebral cortex

References

Different classes of cortical interneurons have been described (Jones 1981,1984; Lund 1981), with their excitatory or inhibitory nature based upon the form of their synaptic terminals (Gray 1959, Colonnier 1968), or their molecular contents, such as GABA which is inhibitory; a general model of synaptic relations within the cortical column has been proposed (Szentagothai 1975,1979).
    - "Spiny stellate" cells of layer IV receive primarily thalamic excitatory inputs (Lund 1984, White 1981). They send an excitatory projection vertically, toward the supragranular pyramidal neurons. The density of these layer IV stellate cells which

form the "granular layer" is very high especially in sensory areas, and is low in motor cortex.

- "Smooth stellate" cells, mainly in layer IV, are inhibitory (Jones 1975, Shepherd 1979) and GABA-ergic; they have reciprocal relations with stellate interneurons of the same layer (IV). They are far less numerous (Lund 1984), existing mostly in visual sensory areas.

- "Basket" cells have axons that form dense nets around pyramidal cell bodies (Cajal 1911, Marin-Padilla 1984); they are inhibitory and their transmitter is GABA (Ribak 1981, Freund 1983). Their soma are in layers III or V and they project horizontally through several layers (Jones 1984). Their dendritic trees (moderately spiny) receive collateral pyramidal axons. The density of "basket cells" is high in the cortical motor regions.

- "Chandelier" cells have an extremely dense axonic branching structure that projects specifically to the initial segment of the pyramidal cell axon; they form axo-axonal inhibitory synapses (GABA) (Somogyi 1977, Peters 1984). Their soma are in layer II (descending axon) or in layers V (ascending axon). They have been studied in sensory areas.

- "Double Bouquet" cells have their soma in the supragranular layers and their axons form dense vertical curtains in the upper (II) and lower (V) layers (Somogyi 1984). They are inhibitory (GABA) on other neurons that are themselves inhibitory; thus their overall function is a "disinhibition" (Jones 1983).

- "Bipolar" cells (soma in layers II to V) have a shape similar to that of "Double bouquet" cells, with a preferentially vertical orientation of axonal and dendritic branching patterns (Peters 1984). They are excitatory, and receive information from supragranular pyramidal cells.

There are other interneuronal types such as Martinotti cells which are found specifically in layer VI (Braitenberg 1978), and horizontal cells of Cajal in layer I.

Interneuronal connectivity is determined by layers (Garey 1976, Lund 1981); thalamic axons arriving in layer IV connect all the cells of that layer, regardless of cell types (White 1978, 1981). Vertical axonal and dendritic extensions of cortical neurons are often related to the vertical extension of a layer (Lund 1981).

Membranary regions of pyramidal cells are specialized according to their different input types: inhibitory "basket cells" on the soma, inhibitory "chandelier" cells on the axonal initial segment, thalamic excitatory afferences on the apical dendrites and spines.

A) Cortical interneurons: coupling or uncoupling between columns and between layers.

FIGURE 2-4 depicts the simplified wiring diagram of a cortical column (a "mini-column"), that is the basis of our functional model.

The different types of cortical interneurons under study are depicted in FIGURE 2-4 by a characteristic form and symbolized with a group of three letters. Symbols are explained in FIGURE 2-5 (vertical axis).

The cortical column has two principal types of output neurons,
   - "lower", infragranular pyramidal cells ("PyrB"),
   - "upper", supragranular pyramidal cells ("PyrH"),

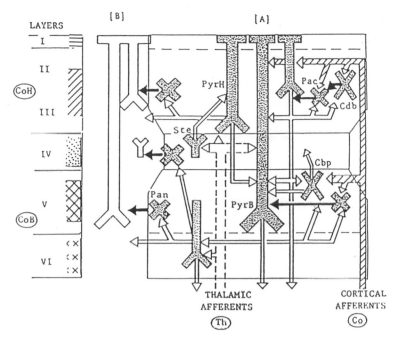

Figure 2-4 . Cortical column with its interneuronal network, its 2 outputs (supra and infra granular) and 2 major inputs (thalamic and cortical).

The column has several interneuronal types that we have classed in five functional groups:
- "stellate" cells of layer IV ("Stc"),
- "basket" cells ("Pan"),
- "chandelier" cells ("Pac"),
- "bipolar" interneurons ("Cbp"),
- "double bouquet" cells ("Cdb").

The column has two main external inputs (symbolized by two letters):
- thalamic inputs ("Th"),
- cortical inputs originating from pyramidal cells in other cortical regions ("Co").

The main functional characteristics of the different neuronal types are detailed by a table in Figure 1-5:

1. The first characteristics is cellular action ; neuronal types are specialized by their excitatory (+) or inhibitory (-) action, from their transmitter, Glutamate (G+) or GABA (G-); these actions are detailed in the second column of Figure 2-5.

2. The second characteristics is the position in the columnar network. The very way in which neural tissue is generated (see ANNEX 2) arranges different interneural types "parallel" to other circuit previously formed with pyramidal neurons: each interneuronal type modulates a specific circuit within the cortex, as detailed in the third column of Figure 2-5.

	TYPE	ACTION	CONNECTION UPON	MAIN AXIS T:TRANSVERSAL L:LATERAL	SPINES
	PYRB: LOWER PYRAMIDAL	G+	I-J	T,L	S
	PYRH: UPPER PYRAMIDAL	G+	TH-PYRB	T,L	S
	STE: SPINY STELLATE	+	TH-PYRH	T	S
	PAN: BASKET	G-	PYRB-PYRB PYRH-PYRH	L	
	PAC: CHANDELIER	G-	PYRH-PYRB PYRB-PYRH	T	
	CBP: BIPOLAR	G+	PYRH-PYRB	T	
	CDB: DOUBLE BOUQUET	G-	PAC-PYRB	T	
	TH: THALAMIC	+		L	
	CO: CORTICAL	+		L,T	

Figure 2-5 . *Different neuronal types in a cortical column with coupling or uncoupling properties.*

3. The third characteristics is the preferential orientation of dendrites and axons of interneurons along the cortical axes:
- when dendrites and axons are elongated on the transversal axis (symbolized by "T" in the table), interneurons couple (or uncouple) the upper and lower layers of a column;
- when the elongation is on the lateral axis (symbolized by "L"), interneurons couple or uncouple two neighboring columns.
4. The fourth characteristics is the registration capacity of each neuronal type. The presence of spines ("S") on a neuronal type permits a local memorization (see chapter I), and thus affects the "finesse" of learning.

B) Intrinsic connectivity of the column forms four levels of coupling or uncoupling circuits.

In this model, we view the interneuronal connections in the column as a multilevel system of coupling and uncoupling circuits:

1. At the first level, the lower infragranular pyramidal cells form the extrinsic network with the other neural structures.

2. At the second level, the upper supragranular pyramidal cells couple different parts of this extrinsic network by an intracortical network between columns.

3. At the third level, two types of inhibitory interneurons counterbalance these coupling circuits by uncoupling ones:
- "Basket" cells are inhibitory interneurons that can uncouple two neighbouring columns; this uncoupling will be mostly dependant upon output activities of the two columns. "Smooth" stellate cells in layer IV can also uncouple neighbouring columns by acting on their inputs .
- "Chandelier" cells are interneurons that can uncouple the upper and lower divisions of a column: they control the output of the upper division, by inhibiting the initial segment of upper pyramidal cells. This uncoupling depends upon activity in the cortical network.

At this same third level of coupling, we can find two types of interneurons that supplement selectively the excitatory action of the two external inputs, thalamic or cortical:
- Stellate neurons of layer IV are excitatory interneurons, connected in parallel to the connection between thalamic inputs and pyramidal neurons (especially of the upper division).
- Bipolar interneurons are characterized by the preferentially vertical orientation of their dendrites and axons: these are transversally coupling neurons, connected in parallel to the connections between upper and lower divisions. This coupling depends upon co-activations of the two main divisions of the column.

4. At the fourth level, interneurons can act upon other interneurons. For example, "double bouquet" cells inhibit the inhibitory interneurons that uncouple the upper and lower columnar divisions; since their axonic and dendritic branching patterns have a preferential transversal orientation they can couple upper and lower divisions, when these two divisions are co-active.

The interneuronal system form parallel pathways which are both excitatory and inhibitory:
- Thalamic afferences project to both upper and lower pyramidal cells: either directly or via the excitatory stellate cells ("Ste") or the inhibitory ("Pan") cells of layer IV.
- Cortical afferences also project to both upper and lower pyramidal cells: either directly, or via vertically integrating interneurons (excitatory"Cbp" or disinhibitory "Cdb").
- Pyramidal cells in the same layer are interconnected: either directly, or via inhibitory ("Pan") cells.

- Pyramidal cells in upper and lower layers are connected directly by pyramidal axon collaterals, and indirectly by inhibitory ("Pac") and excitatory ("Cbp") cells.

Intercolumnar connections (and connections between layers) are both excitatory and inhibitory: the global nature of the relation between the two columns (or the two layers) will depend essentially upon their activities. Connections between two distant columns are generally reciprocal, and the cortical afferents have the same kind of connection to the column as do the upper pyramidal cells: long-range relations are functionally similar to relations between neighboring columns, with a balance between an excitatory and an inhibitory influence.

C) Integrative functions of interneurons are also organized by layers.

Interneurons command coupling (or uncoupling) effects depending upon a combination performed by their dendrites on their inputs. Intrinsic connections (interneurons- principal cells) as well as extrinsic (external afferences- interneurons), are determined layer by layer: for example, thalamic inputs connect all the cells of layer IV, regardless of neuronal type.

As in the case of the pyramidal neurons, the operation performed by interneurons depends upon the extension of their dendrites with respect to the cortical layers, since axonal extension on the transversal axis is often related to the dimensions of a layer: for example thalamic axons in layer IV, axons of upper pyramidal cells in layers II and V, axons of lower pyramidal cell in layer VI. Collateral axons of lateral inhibitory interneurons are also localized within a cortical layer. Consequently interneurons are specialized by their dendritic extensions in cortical layers. For instance, dendrites of "stellate" cells are found in the layer of thalamic input (layer IV), and are specialized for this input.

Actions of interneurons on pyramidal cells is controlled by the membranary specializations of pyramidal neurons . For example inhibitory interneurons have a privileged position with respect to the soma of pyramidal cells or to their initial axonal segment: they mainly control the output activities of the columnar efferent pathways.

II. The basic operation
performed by a cortical column.

In order to go from the cellular texture of the cerebral cortex to its function, we apply the general rules developed in chapter I : we define a "modular" activity, and we determine how it changes with inputs thanks to the integrative properties of the different cell types.

As illustrated in Figure 2-4, the cortical column effects temporal and spatial processing on two main inputs (thalamic and cortical), with a layered connectivity, and combines them to produce two main outputs, intra and extra cortical, from upper and lower layers.

We analyze the columnar operation in four steps that correspond to four activation rules of a columnar automaton:

1. Operation upon thalamic inputs (or more generally, on "layer IV" inputs): the cortex filters the spatio-temporal form of the thalamic input and transforms a continuous form into local modular activations

2. Operation upon moderate cortical inputs: the cortex transforms them into "gating signal" for thalamic inputs. Furthermore the cortex can transmit these signals in the cortical network (by upper layers), without significant output in the extrinsic network (by lower layers).

3. Operation upon synchronous thalamic and cortical inputs: the cortical column produces an amplification effect that result in a higher level of activity when the two major inputs are coactivated.

4. Operation upon strong cortical inputs: a strong cortical input may have an excitatory effect (transmission) but also an inhibitory one, depending upon the laminar pattern of cortical connections and the previous activities of the columns. When connections arrive in upper layers, this operation is equivalent to the comparison between two columnar activities: important differences of activity between columns will be amplified.

The basic columnar operation is performed by layers and does not depend upon origin of inputs in each layer : for instance, the inputs to layer IV, generally thalamic, may also originate from other cortical areas. In this case, the basic columnar operation combines two cortical inputs, with similar rules.

Two important factors modulate the basic cortical operation:
  - the cytoarchitectonics variations from the sensory to the motor poles;
  - the memorization processes, that will change the strength of cortical inputs: in the next section of this chapter, we will show how learning modifies the columnar operation.

1. Transversal amplification: activity levels.

References

During appropriate stimulation discharge frequency of pyramidal cells in receptive sensory areas is commonly around 50/sec, up to 100/s (Hubel 1962, Mountcastle 1975); about the same frequency range is seen before and during voluntary movement (Evarts 1965, Mountcastle 1975).

Direct cortical stimulation produces a weak response of neurons but the response is amplified by repetitive stimulation of afferents (Takahashi 1967, Creutzfeld 1966). This process is due to recruitment of excitatory vertical circuits that amplify the response by an "avalanche phenomenon" (Lorente de No 1937).

During a behavioral task, the spatio-temporal pattern of cortical activities can be modelled with simple mathematical functions, such as "trapezoidal" temporal forms (Burnod 1982); several levels in the intensity of firing frequency are distinguished: for example two distinct levels are observed during learning of a new movement.

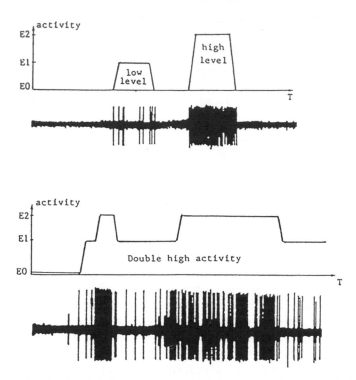

Figure 2-6 . 2 levels of activity (low E1 and high E2) in a pyramidal neuron during a single movement (upper diagrams) or a sequence (lower).

A) Homogeneous activities of output neurons define functional modules.

a) Integrative mode of cortical neurons.

The cortical neurons have several "functional modes", as described in chapter I.

These modes are influenced by reticular inputs which secrete modulators (dopamine, noradrenaline, serotonin): for example, noradrenaline can maintain the cortical neurons in an "integrative state", during long periods of active waking phases; dopamine can change cell excitability during periods of organized behaviors.

Consequently we consider the basic cortical operations in a state where the reticular inputs have a constant level of activity; this reticular activity corresponds to an organized behavior in the active waking state, with cortical neurons in the cellular "integrative" mode (as described in chapter I).

b) Spatio-temporal form and intensity level of cortical activity.

As already discussed in chapter I (figure 1-7), the temporal pattern of a neuronal activity (frequency of action potential) is approximated by a "trapezoidal" form, comprising a positive slope, a plateau, and a negative slope. In this way, a "double trapezoid" linearly represents the most important variations of the cellular activity, on both temporal and spatial axes.

Figure 2-6 represents activity of a cortical pyramidal neuron in different behavioral situations: within each schema, the lower row shows the action potentials directly recorded from the neuron; the upper diagram depicts the trapezoidal approximation of the neuronal activity.

Modules are groups of minicolumns with an homogeneous activity; the lateral extension of a cortical module corresponds to the plateau of the spatial "trapezoid" which represents the homogeneous activity of a neuronal group. Modular activity is first approximated by the activity of the output neurons, that is the upper ("CoH") and lower ("CoB") pyramidal cells of the component columns. The "intensity" of modular activity is the frequency of action potentials during the plateau of the trapezoid.

B) Transversal excitatory circuits give a column three distinct levels of activity

Activities of pyramidal neurons in a column are amplified if they are synchronized. This amplification is due to the transversal excitatory connections in columns:

- direct connections between pyramidal cells of upper and lower layers, grouped in vertical bundles;

- "transversal" coupling effected between upper and lower layers by excitatory interneurons which are sensitive to the co-activation of these two divisions ("CdB" and "Cbp" in Figure 2-4).

Increase of activity in a column recruits excitatory transversal circuits, thus producing an "avalanche" phenomenon up to an high level of activity .

In first approximation, we can thus distinguish three intensity levels for the trapezoid that represents cell activities, and therefore three activity levels of the cortical module:

1. Inhibited level "E0" represents very weak activity, with zero or very low action potential frequency, unmodulated; it is mainly the consequence of an inhibition.

2. Low level "E1" represents small variations of relatively low frequencies (5/sec or 10/sec). This type of activity is shown in the upper left schema of Figure 2-6.

3. High level "E2" represents a much higher frequency (50/sec or 100/sec), more phasic, when the columnar amplification effect is triggered ; it is shown in the right upper schema of Figure 2-6.

These three activity levels are not arbitrary, but correspond to three zones of activity in which the modular operation can be defined by a simple mathematical mapping.

The differences between the activity levels "E0" and "E1" are non-linearities due to action potential thresholds for each cell.

The differences between the levels "E1" and "E2", are non linearities produced by the amplifying effect of the transversal excitatory connections of the cortical columns.

The two upper diagrams of Figure 2-6 illustrate two levels of activities of the same neuron in the motor area, just before the onset of a movement.

Differences between levels of modular activity correspond to differences in the functional states of the component neurons:

- Level "E1" corresponds to a state of greater neuronal receptivity than level "E0", which is mostly an "inhibited" state.

- Level "E2" corresponds to a possibility of short term memorization (see Chapter I): the neurons are in the "integrative" mode, and the persistence of an activity level "E2" produces an accumulation of intracellular calcium which can result in a potentiation effect (short term memory at temporal level "T2"). This pattern of activity is shown in the lower schema of Figure 2-6, where neuronal activity is recorded during learning of a movement, in the motor region that controls the new movement (same neuron as in upper diagrams). The neuron has two successive phases with the higher level of activity: the first peak occur just before the learned movement, and the second peak occur during the reward (and its motor aspect). We will see in next sections how these two successive activations correspond to a critical pattern which induces memorization processes at the cellular level.

C) Coactivation of inputs produces the higher level of modular activity.

a) Input activities.
Activities of columnar inputs (thalamic and cortical) can also be described by intensity levels:

- Afferences from cortical origin are the outputs of other columns and have, correspondingly, the three intensity levels "E0", "E1", and "E2".

- Variations of thalamic activity can be simply represented by two levels, "E0" and "E1": the level "E1" represents an afferent information from periphery, for instance from the retina. These two levels apply only to waking state, since during drowsiness, thalamic neuron produce oscillating bursts of action potentials, that induce the "oscillating" mode in cortical neuronal populations and block sensory inputs.

b) Coactivation and amplifying effect
Thus, when the two inputs, cortical and thalamic, are both active at level E1, the upper and lower pyramidal cells become active and this simultaneous activity triggers a vertical amplifying effect: the whole column then passes to higher level E2. Simultaneous coactivation of moderate thalamic and cortical inputs (level E1) produces an intense activity (level E2) in all the pyramidal neurons.

2. Cortical operation on thalamic inputs

References

The "operation" performed by the cortex upon the thalamic inputs has been well studied in receptive cortical areas, with precise sensory stimuli: in the somatosensory area (Mountcastle 1958), in the visual area (Hubel and Wiesel 1962) and in the auditory (Abeles 1970, Miller 1974, Goldstein 1982).

Three properties characterize the cortical operation upon thalamic inputs:

1. Spatial selectivity: all neurons within a "column" respond to the same position of the stimulus on the sensory map (Mountcastle 1958). This selectivity is reinforced by a strong lateral inhibition.

2. Orientation selectivity: the cortical columns amplify stimuli which are oriented in the sensory map; all the cells in a column respond with a high level of activity for the same orientation of the stimulus in the sensory map: this property has been particularly well demonstrated for the visual areas (Hubel & Wiesel 1962), as well in somatosensory areas (Mountcastle 1958, Whitsel 1972).

This orientation selectivity has been attributed to a polarization of the intracortical connectivity: orientation of the pyramidal cell axonal fields (Gilbert 1981) and oriented lateral inhibition by GABA-ergic cells of layer IV, that receive collaterals from the pyramidal cells of layer VI (Sillito 1975, Tsumoto 1979).

This tuning of columnar responses for preferential orientation is stabilized during the "critical periods" of cortical development and is sensible to strong biasing of thalamic inputs during these periods (Hubel 1977). Columns that amplify the same orientation are grouped together (Hubel 1977; Blasdel 1986). Zones of clear tuning alternate with less specialized zones (Livingstone 1982; Blasdel 1986).

3. Layer specificity: Stimulation of thalamic afferences produces an activation of all the pyramidal cells within the column. But the quantitative effect depends upon layers. The sequence of cortical activation with a thalamic input has been traced from layer IV to upper and lower layers (Bullier, 1979, Ferster 1984, Toyama 1984); the specific characteristics of the cortical operation, for example the size of the receptive field or its "complexity", depend upon the cortical layer. The functional characteristics of each cortical layer seem to be adjusted as a function of their target structures (Gilbert 1981, Poggio 1977). For instance , in the visual areas, the lower pyramidal cells (layer V) are very sensitive to orientation and direction of the stimulus, and they project to the superior colliculus which commands ocular movements toward a moving stimulus.

A) The cortical column transforms a continuous thalamic form into a precise pattern of modular activation

Thalamic activity is often a continuous spatial form generated in a sensory organ, for example by visual information in the retina. The cortical operation upon the thalamic inputs can be approximated by a spatial filtering that is mathematically a "convolution" of the spatial form of the input activity by an intrinsic cortical "transfer function". The spatial form of this transfer function can be approximated, like an activity, by a "trapezoid" on the two lateral axes of the cortical surface, as shown in Figure 2-7 (lower part): it has a central positive part and a peripheral negative part, and has an elongated shape oriented relative to the lateral axes of the cortical surface .

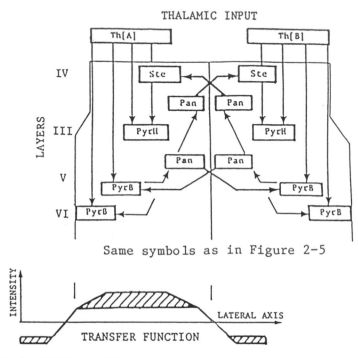

Figure 2-7 . Spatial filtering of thalamic inputs by the columnar network (upper diagram) with its transfer function (lower).

Characteristics of this cortical transfer function are shaped by the connections between the different cellular types of the column, as illustrated in a schematic way in FIGURE 2-7. Connectivity is shown in the upper part with an information flow that arrive in layer IV; cell types are represented with the same symbols as in Figure 2-5 . Thanks to the strong transversal connections between layers, the preferential orientation will be the same for all the pyramidal cells which belong to the same column:

- Thalamic axons and their direct connections to pyramidal neurons determine the lateral dimensions of the intrinsic transfer function.

- Stellate cells ("Ste") increase the positive part;

- Inhibitory cells of layer IV ("Pan") receive recurrent collaterals of pyramidal neurons of layer VI and inhibits the stellate cells of layer IV; consequently they uncouple thalamic inputs and stellate cells which are out of register; they can contribute to the negative part of the transfer function.

- Axonal branching patterns of pyramidal cells and inhibitory cells may be oriented on the two lateral axes of the cortical surface ; in consequence, the transfer function is polarized with respect to the lateral axes and amplifies similarly oriented thalamic inputs.

The orientation specificity is common to all cortical receptive areas, visual (stimulus orientation on the retina), somatosensory (stimulus orientation on the skin), and auditory (frequency variation). The result of this spatial filtering is an homogeneous level of activity in predifined cortical zones which represent the different orientations of stimuli.

B) The quantitative effects of thalamic inputs depend upon cytoarchitectonics

The maximal intensity of activity produced by thalamic inputs alone depends upon the thickness of layer IV and the density of stellate cells ("Ste"): this "granular layer" is thicker in receptive areas than in associative areas and very weak in motor areas ("agranular" areas).

Consequently, in the "granular" pole (sensory areas), thalamic inputs can activate the entire column to the higher activity level (E2), regardless of the cortical inputs, when their forms are in register with the cortical transfer function (orientation specificity). Interneurons of layer IV can functionally couple ("Ste") or uncouple ("Pan") thalamic inputs and increase the selective amplification of sensory information.

In the associative areas and frontal areas, the thalamic inputs are weaker: all these areas will respond to thalamic input with a weaker activity level E1. The minimum effect is produced in the "agranular" pole (primary motor area).

3. Operation upon moderate cortical inputs

References

The responses of cortical columns to their different inputs have been studied by direct stimulation of afferent cells: reticular (Oshima 1971), thalamic (Creutzfeldt 1966), and cortical (Asanuma 1975).

Cortical stimulation is by itself insufficient for activating the whole column with an high level of activity; however it can augment the columnar response to thalamic stimulation. This "gating" effect is more significant when the thalamic input is anatomically sparser, as in the motor cortex (Asanuma 1973, 1982); more generally, the gating effect is a function of density of cortico-cortical synapses (Vogt 1982). It exists in the visual receptive area since most of striate cells become less responsive to visual stimulations , mainly in infragranular layers, when activity of cortical inputs is suppressed by cooling (Sandell, 1982).

This "gating" effect can explain the large variations in cellular activation generated by a peripheral stimulation, as a function of behavioral "expectancies", probably induced by activities of cortical inputs (Mountcastle 1984).

The gating effect varies quantitatively with layers and cell types. For example before execution of a movement the smallest cells in motor' areas have a longer anticipatory activity (Shinoda 1984); lower pyramidal cells are progressively recruited as a function of their size: the largest are the last to be activated (Evarts 1984).

A) Moderate cortical inputs have a gating effect.

The response of a column to different inputs is determined by their relative strengths, due to direct interactions with dendrites of output pyramidal neurons and to indirect influences via the coupling interneurons.

A moderate cortical input alone cannot activate the whole column to the higher level "E2", but it produces a moderate activation (E1) which has a "gating effect" for other inputs; a thalamic input in register with this cortical gate will produce a strong activation of the column.

The "gating effect" is modulated according to the laminar pattern of the cortical region implicated: it is more marked in the associative areas, and in "agranular" motor areas, since strength ot thalamic input diminishes from receptive to associative areas and becomes quite weak in motor cortex. Inversely, the relative strength of cortical inputs increases as one moves from sensory to associative and then to motor cortex. In motor areas, the high density of upper pyramidal cells multiplies the possibilities of gating the same cortical output (a muscular command) by different cortical sources.

The response to a cortical input depends not only upon synaptic strength of cortico-cortical connections but also upon interneuronal parallel pathways: in our model all these connections are plastic and their strength can increase (or decrease) with experience . These long term changes will be described in section III of this chapter.

B) Cortico-cortical activity can spread without any output outside the cortex

We now analyze more precisely the responses to cortical inputs in upper and lower layers of the column.

Although the two pyramidal cell types, upper and lower, have qualitatively homogeneous behavior within a module, there are important quantitative differences. We have already mentioned these differences in Chapter I and their functional effects are detailed in Annex 3-D (Figure A-10).

FIGURE 2-8 depicts the different inputs that arrive in layers and the two main types of pyramidal cells, with their apical dendrites perpendicular to these layers:
    - thalamic inputs (dashed lines) arrive in the intermediate layer IV; in this case, we consider a weak thalamic input (associative, frontal or motor area);
    - cortical inputs from other columns (oblique dashes) arrive in the other layers, with a high density in the upper layers II and III;
    - the upper layers project toward the lower layers (layer V).

Because of the position of their cell bodies and the different extension of their apical dendrites, upper and lower pyramidal cells effect two different combinatorial operations upon thalamic and cortical inputs.

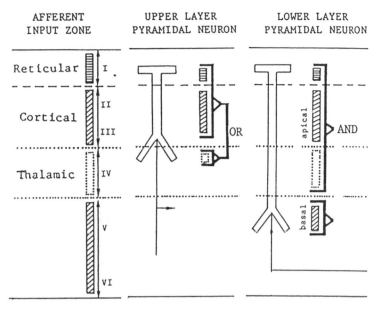

Figure 2-8a . Integration of cortical and thalamic inputs by upper and lower pyramidal neurons.

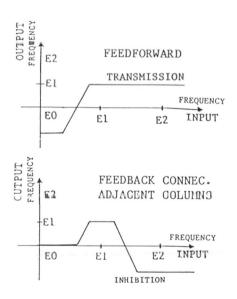

Figure 2-8b . Effects of feedforward and feedback cortical inputs when the previous state of the column is low (E0,E1).

a) The upper pyramidal cells perform an "or" function on the thalamic and cortical inputs.

As explained in chapter I, strengths of inputs depend upon the proportion of membrane that they can activate. Upper pyramidal cells receive cortical inputs on their apical dendrites and thalamic inputs on their basal dendrites: the "proportion of membrane" activated by one or the other of input is sufficient to activate the cell (dendritic trees of comparable size). Stellate interneurons of layer IV ("Ste") that project toward layers II and III, increase the sensitivity of upper pyramidal cells for thalamic inputs.

Thus, upper pyramidal neurons perform an "or" function on the two inputs, cortical and thalamic. The upper layer will be activated to the "E1" level if the thalamic OR the cortical inputs are activated to the "E1" level.

b) The lower pyramidal cells perform an "and" function upon the thalamic and cortical inputs.

The apical dendrites of the lower pyramidal cells traverse the layer of thalamic inputs (IV) and the layer of cortical inputs (II and III) which can activate a restricted proportion of the cell membrane: consequently cortical and thalamic inputs have to be simultaneously active in order to activate these neurons. Lower pyramidal cells perform mostly an "and" operation on the cortical and thalamic inputs, as opposed to the "or" operation of the upper pyramidal cells. However in receptive areas , layer IV is wide, and thalamic input is strong enough and can alone produce an output.

Differential sensitivity of upper and lower pyramidal neurons is amplified by differences of membrane surface: smaller neurons have a lower membrane conductance and are activated at a lower threshold. Consequently, when intensity of cortical inputs increases, the interneurons of the upper layers are first active, then the upper pyramidal neurons, then the lower pyramidal neurons.

Cortico-cortical information can thus be transmitted in the cortical network by the upper layers of the cortex ("E1") even without thalamic activation; This information (E1) is transmitted through the cortical network (upper layer), even in the absence of activity in the extrinsic network (lower layer).

4. Columnar operation on strong cortical inputs

References

Connections between pyramidal cells of neighboring modules are excitatory, but there is a parallel inhibitory pathway via Basket interneurons:
    - in sensory cortical areas, columns activated by a precise peripheral stimulus will strongly inhibit neighboring columns (Mountcastle 1958); the same type of lateral inhibition is also produced by direct cortical stimulation (Stephanis 1954); for example, microstimulation of the motor area provokes limited muscular contractions (Asanuma 1973, Jankowska 1975);
    - depending on the behavioral situation, two neighboring columns can be either strongly co-activated or in strong opposition (one activated and one inhibited). This is particularly evident in motor areas during execution of simple movements (Evarts 1965, Fetz 1950, Lamarre 1978).

A) Reciprocal lateral inhibition accentuates the differences of activity in neighbouring columns.

The influence of a cortical column upon its neighbors depends upon the reciprocal excitatory and inhibitory interconnections. Inhibitory ("Pan") cells are activated by the pyramidal cells of a column and project upon the pyramidal cell bodies of other columns. Inhibition will decrease the activity of other columns and thus decrease the inhibitory feedback: the more a column inhibits, the less it is inhibited. In consequence, the strength of the lateral inhibition between two columns is proportional to the difference of their activities.

The overall effect of lateral connections between two columns is to amplify differences of activity which exceed a certain threshold: we consider that the threshold is reached when only one of the two columns has an high activity level "E2" while the other has a weaker level "E1" or "E0".

This activity-dependant lateral inhibition increases the non-linear behavior of the cortico-cortical relations. A significant inter-columnar difference of activity increases lateral inhibition, thus amplifying the difference up to a maximal level "E2-E0".

The functional relation between two neighboring columns can be expressed by two rules:

1) If the two columns have a low activity "E0" or "E1", the excitatory connections are active and the columns will not inhibit their neighbors; similarly, if both columns are at the higher activity level "E2", the inhibitory cells will be ineffective and the two columns will remain with the same high activity "E2".

2) By contrast, if only one of the two columns has an high activity level "E2", it will inhibit neighboring columns that have a lower activity "E1". The difference "E2-E1" is amplified into a difference "E2-E0".

B) Distant columns: strong cortical inputs may have excitatory or inhibitory effects

Connections between distant columns are reciprocal on the lateral axes (surface axes) but their laminar pattern may be different, as in the feedback vs feedforward connections.

These long connections are excitatory, since they are the axons of pyramidal neurons which release glutamate, but the global relation is both excitatory and inhibitory:

- direct connections between pyramidal neurons are excitatory;

- these direct relations are complemented by local parallel inhibitory connections.

Consequently, inhibition or excitation depend upon differences of activity between columns, as for neighboring columns. But the corresponding rules are modulated by the laminar pattern of cortico-cortical connections.

a) The laminar pattern of cortical connections is similar for the two related columns.

In this case, the rules governing interactions between distant columns are thus similar to those for neighboring columns, since long-range cortico-cortical connections are similar to connections that link neighboring columns. In fact, the distance simply implies an additional excitatory synapse: the distant columns is "represented" locally by afferences which are both excitatory (direct connections) and inhibitory (parallel connection via interneurons).

If activities of the two related columns are similar (two low or two strong activities), reciprocal connections maintain these previous activities; but if the pattern is contrasted, cortical connections increase this contrast: columns with higher activities inhibit the columns with lower activities.

b) The two columns are related by feedforward/feedback connections.

The laminar pattern is different and induces quantitative differences in the response of a column to its cortical inputs, when this column has a previous weak activity: the two types of responses are illustrated in the two diagrams of Figure 2-8B.

In the feedforward connections (upper diagram), the corticocortical outputs of the primary sensory maps project to layer IV of the secondary areas. In this case, the functional rules for cortical inputs in layer IV are similar to functional rules for thalamic inputs, since these rules only depend upon the organization of layer IV: the strong feedforward cortical inputs are mostly excitatory when the receptor column is centered on the afferent axons, and inhibitory when it is out of register.

The feedback connections are more similar to connections between neighboring columns: they arise from lower and upper layers and project to upper layers of receptor columns. In this case, the cortical input has an inhibitory effect when it is much higher than the receptor column (lower diagram of Figure 2-8B).

This connection pattern between primary and secondary areas introduces a sequence of successive operations in the sensory information flow: on the feedforward connections, each area receives a sensory information in its layer IV, transforms it, and re-projects this information toward layer IV of the next area on this processing pathway. On the feedback connections, cortical activity controls this sensory information flow in the reverse direction:

- when they are low, cortical inputs in the upper layers have a gating effect upon the sensory information flow;

- when they are high, they may become inhibitory on receptor columns which have a weaker activity.

We will in section III of this chapter that inhibitory influence between columns can increase (or decrease) with learning.

5. Columnar automaton: equivalent circuit

A) The basic operation of the cortical column can be defined by an input-output table

Columnar function can be summarized by compiling the preceding rules in an "input-output" table (TABLE 2-9). This table gives the modular outputs (right columns of the table) for each possible combination of thalamic and cortical inputs (left columns).

| INPUTS | | COLUMN | OUTPUTS | | |
LAYER II-III CORTICAL	LAYER IV THALAMIC	PRIOR STATE	UPPER LAYERS COH	LOWER LAYERS COB	
E0	E0	E0,E1	E0	E0	
E0	E1	E0,E1	E2 E1 E0	E2 E0 E0	DEPEND ON AREAS - GRANULAR - ASSOCIATIVE - AGRANULAR
E0	E2	E0,E1	E1	E0	FEEDFORWARD
E1	E0	E0,E1	E0 E1 E2	E0 E0 E2	DEP. ON LEARNING - INHIBITION - GATING - TRIGGERING
E1	E1	E0,E1	E2	E2	AMPLIFICATION
E2	E0,E1	E0,E1	E0 E1	E0 E0	CONDITIONAL INHIBITION FEEDBACK CONNEC. ADJACENT COLUMNS
E2	E0,E1	E2	E2	E2	REACTIVATION MEMORIZING CONDITIONS

E2: High level of activity
E1: Low level of activity
E0: Inactive

Figure 2-9 . Input/ output table of a columnar automaton ; dependence upon learning and cytoarchitectonics.

There are two outputs:

1. The activity of the upper layers ("CoH") is defined by the action potential frequency of the pyramidal cells of layers II and III, with three possible values, E0/E1/E2;

2. The activity of the lower layers ("CoB") is defined by the action potential frequency of the pyramidal cells of layers V and VI ("PyrB"), with three possible levels E0/E1/E2.

As shown in TABLE 2-9, the two outputs (CoH and CoB) depend upon combinations of three activities:

- the prior activity of the module (central column of the table);

- the thalamic input has two possible levels: "E0" (weak or zero activity) and "E1" (afferent information). More generally, the input that arrives in layer IV may have a cortical origin with three activity levels.

- the cortical input, that arrives in layers II-III from another cortical column, and thus has three possible levels, E0/E1/E2.

The table is ordered from top to bottom by the intensity level of cortical inputs that arrive in layer III:

1. When there is no cortical input, effects of thalamic inputs (E1) depend upon the thickness of layer IV (cytoarchitectonic modulation), that decreases from receptive (granular) to motor areas.

First of all, the cortical texture transforms thalamic input by a spatial filtering that amplifies afferent activity in register with an intrinsic transfer function.

2. When cortical inputs are moderate (E1), their effects depend upon previous experience.

Before learning, these inputs can moderately activate the upper layers, but they cannot alone produce a strong activation of the whole column.

If thalamic inputs are inactive (E0), the cortical input can activate the cortical network via the upper layers independently of output activities in lower layers.

When thalamic and cortical inputs are both active, the amplifying effect results in the higher level "E2" in the whole column.

The transmission coefficients of cortical inputs change with learning (as detailed in section III of this chapter) with three possible effects : (1) the cortical input can become inhibitory; (2) it can gate the thalamic input; or (3) it can even trigger the higher level of activity E2 when there is no thalamic input. When several cortical inputs from different origins project on the same column, their influences can become different with learning, for example one inhibitory and the other one excitatory.

3. When activities of cortical inputs in layer III are strong, there is a conditional lateral inhibition which amplifies contrasted activities.

Strength of lateral inhibition depends upon activity differences between columns.

When a column is much less active than its cortical afference (difference E2-E1), inhibition augments, and the difference of activity increases to a maximum "E2-E0".

But if the column has the same activity level as its cortical inputs (E1 or E2), cortical relations stabilize these activities.

Functional rules are not changed by the fact that the layer IV input has a cortical, rather than thalamic origin (as in feedforward connections). The basic cortical combination deals with layers and not with the significance of inputs: the column in secondary areas can combine two different cortical inputs, one in layer III (from feedback connections) and the other one in layer IV (from feedforward connections).

But these two cortical inputs are not equivalent. The cortical input that arrives in layer III (first column of the table) may have an inhibitory effect when it is much more active (E2) than the column (E1). But the cortical input that arrives in layer IV (second column of the table) has mostly an excitatory effect (like a thalamic input), even if the column has a low activity .

If we consider all the possibilities of corticocortical connections, the input can originate in one of the two main cortical divisions (CoH and CoB) or in the intermediate layer IV, and can project upon one of these three subdivisions (upper, lower or intermediate layer IV). There are thus nine possibilities for the significance of the afferent excitation in each layer, but the functional process between layers which is expressed in the table does not vary.

Obviously, this description of columnar function in terms of layers and levels of activity is only approximate. Within levels "E1" and "E2" there are more precise activity modulations and fine-grain adjustments of activity within the levels are possible. For example, several activation modes of the upper layers ("CoH") within the moderate level (E1) could be discussed, for example depending upon the activity of inhibitory neurons which control the output of upper-layer neurons.

C) The basic cortical operation can be represented by an equivalent 3-D functional circuit

In order to take into account the spatial dimensions of connections between columns, we summarize the structure-function relationship of the cortical column in an functional equivalent circuit: this circuit is a simplified representation of the different neuronal types and their connectivity; its global function corresponds to the input-output table summarized in Figure 2-9.

In FIGURE 2-10, we represent this columnar circuit in three dimensions, with a "crystal" form that can be repeated in space: the upper schema shows the circuit projected on the transversal axis (Z axis), and the lower schema represents the same neuronal network projected on the two lateral axes parallel to the surface (Y and X axes).

The integrative functions of the different neuronal types are depicted in a simplified way, with circles and lines which represent their transmission coefficients that can change during learning (as described in annex III , figures A-6 and A-7); Symbols are the same as in Figure 2-5.

The projection on the transversal axis (upper diagram) is directly derived from the connection schema of the cortical column shown in Figure 2-4. We have depicted two types of pyramidal neurons, upper and lower, and the principal interneuronal types, distinguished by their lateral or transversal coupling and uncoupling roles.

The projection on the lateral axes (lower diagram), depicts a cellular pattern that can be repeated in space, with five interconnected elements:

1. A "central neuron" depicts the lower pyramidal cells; the thalamic inputs will be centered around this position.

2. A crown of eight neurons (in black) represents the upper pyramidal cells; four cortical inputs from different origin arrive on the four corners, each directly connected to two upper pyramidal cells. This pattern accents the double functional role of the upper pyramidal cells: they can reinforce the coupling between cortical inputs and lower pyramidal cells, and they can also increase the coupling between two neighboring columns.

3. Four "lateral" inhibitory interneurons (open circles with crosses), are located on the same external crown. Their connections represent their two functional properties:

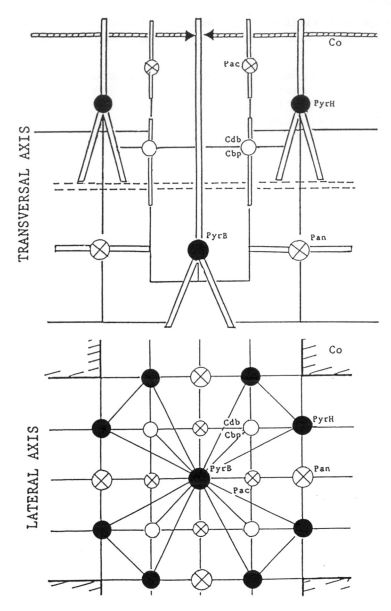

Figure 2-10 . Simplified 3-D functional circuit of the cortical column on transversal (upper) and lateral axes (lower).

they can uncouple two neighboring columns (lower layer), but they can also uncouple a column from a set of cortical inputs.

    4. Four "transversal" inhibitory interneurons (open circles with crosses) are located on an intermediate crown halfway between the upper and lower pyramidal

neurons. Their connections depict their functional role: they can uncouple the upper and lower layers of the column.

5. Four "transversal" coupling neurons (open circles) are located on this same intermediate crown: they can produce an active coupling between the upper and lower layers, either directly, or by inhibiting the uncoupling interneurons.

Figure 2-11 illustrates how this basic pattern can be repeated in space: a modular zone is composed by a set of such elementary circuits and may have varying dimensions.

We will use this "equivalent" circuit in the following section to illustrate the different possibilities of functional reorganization of the cortical network by learning.

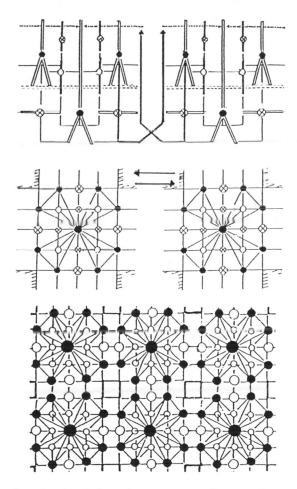

Figure 2-11a . Functional relations between two distant columns (upper,middle diagrams) or neighbouring ones (lower).

Figure 2-11b . Modular zone formed by a group of adjacent columns

III. Learning properties
of a cortical column.

References

*1. Several studies have demonstrated the plasticity of sensory maps in the cortex.
For example, during critical developmental periods, the dimensions of ocular*

dominance columns can change with activity (Hubel 1977): asymmetrical activation of the two eyes provokes a corresponding asymmetry in the geometry of ocular dominance columns involving diminution of the inactive regions and expansion of the active region. A similar phenomenon occurs for orientation selective columns in animals deprived of contoured stimulation: many cells do not develop selective orientation, or this selectivity is restrained to orientations that the animal is allowed to see (Hubel, 1977; Blakemore 1980)

2. The effects of deprivation are reversible during a critical period (Fregnac 1984). Active movement or proprioceptive stimulation, is more effective for this recovery than passive stimulations (Buisseret 1983). Consequently it has been proposed that plasticity at the cellular level depends upon the correlation between a presynaptic activity due to sensory stimuli and a postsynaptic depolarization due to another cortical activation (Singer 1981).

3. In adults, maps are not rigid and their plasticity may be very important , for example in the somesthetic receptive areas (Merzenich 1984). Somatosensory maps in the adult monkey are remodeled after peripheral changes such as preferential use of restrained parts of the hand, when animals perform a repetitive task demanding sustained attention: cortical representation of the active fingers extend ; however this lateral extension is limited to the anatomical dimensions of the afferent thalamic axons in the cortex. This plasticity can also be explained by cellular memorizations due to coactivations of neuronal groups. Similar changes are observed in the auditory maps for stimuli that acquire significance in a conditioning task.

4. Pyramidal cortical neurons have been directly observed during pavlovian conditioning: cortical cells in the pathway between the conditioned stimulus and the unconditioned response have an increased excitability that parallel the conditioned response (Woody 1973). At the cellular level, an elevated frequency of action potentials can produce a prolonged augmentation of the cell's response to afferent stimulation, probably due to a decrease of membrane conductance (Woody 1976, Dinalmann 1979). Discharge frequency of a single cortical neuron can be used as a conditioned response: the rewarded pattern of activity will occur more often (Fetz 1973).

5. During motor learning, the critical pattern of cellular activity that could lead to memorization occur when a single cell has two successive intense activations, first before the conditioned movement, and secondly during reward (Burnod 1982).

1. Modular transmission coefficients

A) Several types of cellular memorization are possible in the cortical column

We start from the "general" memorization properties of neurons as they are developed in chapter I (and detailed in annex 4-B):

1. Cellular memorization is a general phenomenon: every cell type can register information according to its own logic that depend upon the relative strength of its inputs. The specific registrations by different cell types within a neural tissue give great finesse to the learning process.

2. Cellular memorization is a progressive phenomenon that occurs across four temporal levels: the neuron has to be in the integrative state (T1); high frequency is an important factor for short term memory (T2); large activations of the cell membrane and large depolarizations are important for longer term effects (T3); specific long range activation patterns are needed for permanent memory (T4).

3. Several transmission coefficients can change in the same cell: membrane conductance, probability of transmitter release, local conductance of spines. FIGURE 2-12 illustrates in two diagrams two types of neuronal registration in the cortex:
  - interneurons can change in a global way (Figure 2-12, upper schema): for example a bipolar cell ("Cbp") can increase its whole transmission if its main inputs (pyramidal neurons and cortical afferences) are strongly coactivated.
  - in spiny neurons, such as pyramidal cells, transmission can change in a restricted part of membrane (Figure 2-2, lower schema); if the cortical inputs arriving on a spine are activated just prior to a strong cellular depolarization, the influence of this cortical afferent upon the pyramidal cell increases selectively.

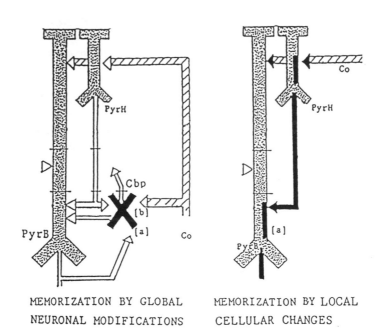

MEMORIZATION BY GLOBAL   MEMORIZATION BY LOCAL
NEURONAL MODIFICATIONS   CELLULAR CHANGES

Figure 2-12 . Two types of memorization within a column, by an interneuron (upper diagram), or by dendritic spines of pyramidal cells (lower).

The different cellular parameters of the cortical column that can change according to activity are explicitly depicted in FIGURE 2-13 (reinforced). But these cellular coefficients do not change in the same conditions: for each cell type, registrations will depend upon specific activation patterns and upon the past history of the column.

B) Cellular transmission coefficients within a column are integrated into global "modular" transmission coefficients

We can integrate all the "cellular" coefficients in a column into "modular coefficients": these global coefficients represent the transmission states between two cortical modules.

FIGURE 2-14 depicts the transmission between two modules, a "receptor" that receives cortical inputs from an "transmitter" module. We shall analyze the modular coefficients at the level of the "receptor" module.

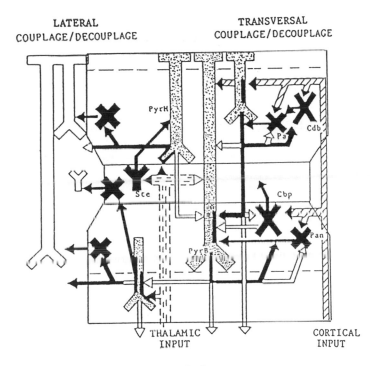

Same symbols as in Figure 2-3

Figure 2-13 . Possible cellular sites of memorization within a column (in black).

Modular coefficients can be first approximated by "conditional probabilities": as we have defined the modular activity in terms of intensity levels (E0, E1, E2), the coefficient values are the conditional probabilities "Pi" of triggering an output level of activity (in the receptor module), for each activity level of the cortical inputs (from the transmitter module). Appropriate formalism is developed in Annex 4, mainly in figure A-12 and 13.

Since activity levels can be different for the upper and lower layers, we shall

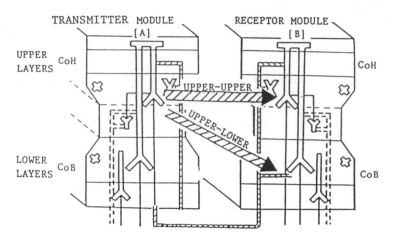

Figure 2-14 . Modular transmission coefficients between two columns integrate a set of cellular transmission coefficients.

distinguish two probabilistic coefficients that summarize intermodular relations (Figure 2-14):

1. The "upper-upper" coefficient ("Ph") represents transmission between the cortical inputs and the upper layers of the receptor module: this coefficient represents the probability that moderate cortical inputs activates these upper layers (at the level "E1").

This modular coefficient integrates several cellular transmission parameters (figure 2-13):

- the probability of transmitter release of cortico-cortical afferent cells (pyramidal neurons of the transmitter module);
- the membrane conductances of upper pyramidal cells (of the receptor module);
- the membrane conductances of interneurons that form a parallel pathway between the cortical inputs and the upper pyramidal cells.

2. The "upper-lower" coefficient ("Pb") represents the transmission states between the cortical inputs and the lower layers of the receptor column: it is defined by the probability that moderate cortical inputs activates the lower layers of the module; in this case the upper and the lower layers will be coactivated and the whole column will go to the higher intensity level (E2).

This coefficient includes, at the cellular level, the same coefficients as the "upper-upper" coefficient, and in addition:

- the probabilities of transmitter release by the upper pyramidal cells of the receptor module;
- the membrane conductances of lower pyramidal cells;
- the membrane conductances of interneurons that form a parallel pathway between upper and lower pyramidal cells.

C) Probabilistic transmission coefficients between activity levels can be refined by continuous coefficients

Modification of the modular transmission coefficients, measured by conditional probabilities, is primarily due to "global" registrations of cortical cells: but "local" registrations (for example by dendritic spines of pyramidal cells) also occur, and they produce more precise modulations of transmission coefficients. Consequently the two probabilistic coefficients can be complemented by more "continuous" coefficients that represent the quantitative ratios between input and output activities within activity levels (see annex 4-C and table A-13 for more details).

The probabilistic coefficient "upper-upper" (Ph) can thus be complemented by a continuous coefficient ("Ch") that quantitatively represents the output/input ratio of action potential frequencies between upper layers of the receptor module and its cortical inputs. This coefficient includes the conductances of dendritic spines of the upper pyramidal cells.

The "upper-lower" coefficient (Pb) can be complemented in a similar way by a continuous coefficient ("Cb") that represents the output/input ratio of activities between lower layers of the receptor module and its cortical inputs.

2. Activity-dependant changes of modular coefficients

A) Several activity patterns act upon different cell types of the cortical column

a) Activity patterns that produce short term memorization.

Activation of a cortical column at a high level (E2) is an important factor for cellular memorization (see chapter I). Short term memorization can be provoked by two consecutive activations at the higher level "E2": this pattern result in calcium accumulation and short term post potentiation, increased by voltage properties of NMDA receptors.

Two contrasting forms of modular activation can both result in cellular registration:

1. For excitatory neurons: cortical inputs are strongly activated (E2) just after high (E2) activity in the column. This condition potentiates the transmission between cortical inputs and pyramidal neurons. For a receptor module "B" that receive cortical input from an transmitter module "A", we call this conditional activation "B2/A2" (see annex 4 for further details). The reverse condition (A2/B2) is not efficient: when cortical inputs are first highly active , they inhibit the receptor column.

2. For inhibitory neurons: cortical inputs are strongly activated (E2) immediately following inhibition of the column (E0). In this situation, the inhibitory cells are highly activated (E2) during inhibition and then reactivated by cortical inputs: they are in critical condition for registration. We call this conditional inhibition "B0/A2" (receptor module "B" inhibited, followed by a strong activation of transmitter module A).

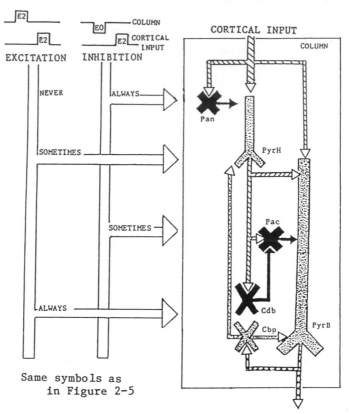

Figure 2-15 . Effect of activation patterns upon memorization by different neuronal types and consequences on the cortical information flow.

b) Long term activity pattern

Long term memory depends upon repetition of these potentiating conditions. As explained in chapter I, a "repetition factor" describes the long-range pattern of co-activations between a column and its cortical inputs:

1. The repetition factor that measures the recurrence of the conditional activation "B2/A2" is called the activation pattern "P2";

2. The recurrence of the conditional inhibition "B0/A2" is called the inhibition pattern "P0".

These patterns are conditional probabilities which vary between 0 and 1 (see Annex 4, figure A-13 for further details) . They measure the recurrence of an event that may occur "always" (P2=1), "sometimes" (P2)0), or "never" (P2=0). The two types of long term patterns (activation or inhibition) are not independent: if a module is always activated before high activity of cortical inputs (P2=1), it is never inhibited (P0=0) .

c) Differential effect of long range activity patterns.

FIGURE 2-15 illustrates the effect of these different patterns (arrows in the left part) on the main information flow in the receptor column (diagram in the right part): from cortical inputs (from top) to outputs of the lower layers (to bottom).

The different cell types are depicted with same symbols as in table 2-5 and previous figures (PyrH, PyrB, PanH, PanB, Pac, Cdb, Cbp).

Because of the competitive aspect of excitatory and inhibitory influences of cortical inputs, long term changes of cellular coefficients depend upon both repetition factors (inhibition P0 and activation P2). Each activity pattern (vertical arrows) preferentially modifies a type of neuron and thus favors an information pathway in the cortical column. Successive cellular registrations have a cumulative effect upon the modular coefficients: each neuronal registration increases the cellular output and therefore the possibilities for registration by other cellular types forward in the circuit. Passage from cellular memorizations to modular modifications is developed in ANNEX 4 (see Figure A-14).

B) Intracolumnar pathways can memorize different types of functional relations between two interconnected cortical modules.

FIGURE 2-16 shows the changes of the modular coefficients (upper-upper Ph and and upper-lower Pb, vertical axis) for the different long-range activity patterns (inhibition P0 or excitation P2, horizontal axis).

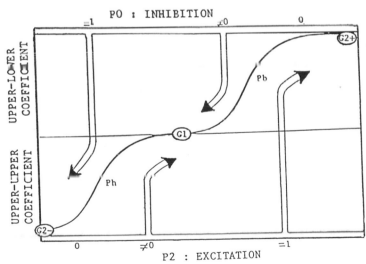

Figure 2-16 . Changes of modular coefficients (upper-upper and upper-lower) as a function of activation patterns.

FIGURE 2-17A illustrates the changes in the intra-columnar pathways and the consequences on intercolumnar relations: two connected modules are represented by their functional equivalent circuit, as described in the previous section (in Figure 2-10). New functional relations that are favored by cellular registrations are shown by accented lines; these diagrams show how activity patterns reorganize the functional networks in the cortical columns.

INHIBITION

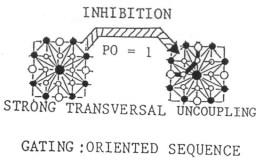

STRONG TRANSVERSAL UNCOUPLING

GATING :ORIENTED SEQUENCE

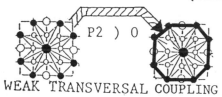

WEAK TRANSVERSAL COUPLING

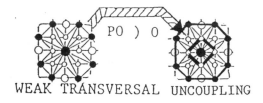

WEAK TRANSVERSAL UNCOUPLING

TRIGGERING : FIXED SEQUENCE

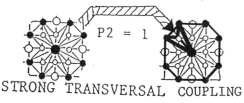

STRONG TRANSVERSAL COUPLING

Figure 2-17a . Long-term changes of intercolumnar relations by cellular memorizations depending upon activation patterns (P0, P2).

Four long range activation patterns will produce four limit values of the modular coefficients ("upper-upper Ph" and "upper-lower Pb"). They correspond to new stable relations, excitatory or inhibitory, between columns and between layers.

a) Inhibition: strong transversal uncoupling.
It occurs when the module is "always" inhibited before intense activation of its

cortical inputs (P0=1). This pattern reinforces the inhibitory cells and thus decreases the two probabilistic transmission coefficients, "upper-upper" (Ph) and "upper-lower" (Pb). When these coefficients approach zero, the cortical inputs inhibit the module.

b) Gating: weak transversal coupling.
It occurs when the module is "sometimes" activated in an important way before intense activation of its cortical inputs (P2)0). This pattern particularly reinforces transmission coefficients of cortico-cortical inputs, then upper pyramidal cells and parallel interneurons ("Cbp"), since they receive two consecutive intense activations.

These cellular changes have cumulative effects on the "upper-upper" (Ph) modular coefficient. When this coefficient reaches its maximal value (Ph=1), the cortical inputs cannot activate the whole column but can gate the external inputs: furthermore, activity can be transmitted in the cortical network (between upper layers) even if there is no activity in the external network.

c) Gating: weak transversal uncoupling.
Another activation pattern is entirely compatible with the preceding one: the module is "sometimes" inhibited before intense activation of its cortical inputs (P0)0). This condition particularly reinforces inhibitory cells ("Pac") between the upper and lower layers of the module, and therefore increases uncoupling between the cortical inputs and the lower layers. This condition, then, decreases the upper-lower coefficient toward a minimum value (Pb=0), but it does not affect the "upper-upper" coefficient that maintains a maximal value (Ph=1).

In this stable registration state, the cortical inputs activate the upper layers, but do not activate the lower layers: cortical afferences cannot trigger a strong response, but can "gate" thalamic inputs; they condition the efficiency of the "external" inputs which come from sensory organs to the cortex via the thalamus. Modular activation by cortical inputs is thus mainly a preparation or an anticipation that "orients" cortical activity toward possible actions: the concrete production of a behavioral sequence will depend upon environmental conditions (that is upon thalamic inputs).

d) Triggering: strong transversal coupling.
This occurs when the receptor module is always strongly activated (level E2) before activation of cortical inputs (P2=1). This activation pattern produces an increase in the transmission coefficients of upper pyramidal cells, and especially a strong increase in the transmission of vertically integrating excitatory (Cbp), and disinhibitory (Cdb) interneurons. These disinhibitory cells suppress the "upper-lower" uncoupling that may have previously occurred. All these cellular registrations act in a cooperative way on the "upper-lower" coefficient that increases toward its maximal value (Pb=1).

The overall effect is a strong increase in the coupling between cortical inputs and lower layer of the receptor module. The module will be strongly activated by a moderate activity of its cortical inputs, even if thalamic inputs are not active. The activation is maximal and does not depend upon extracortical conditions: this state of registration produces fixed sequences of cortical activities that are independent of environmental conditions.

C) Differentiation of two neighbouring modules: modular dimensions depend upon activation patterns.

FIGURE 2-17B illustrates adjacent cortical columns. These neighboring columns have some inputs in common but not all. Their activation patterns may change their relations with two possible consequences: the columns can merge into one single module with an homogeneous activity, or they can form two independent modules:

a) Merging of two columns in a single module.
If two adjacent columns are strongly coactivated in a repetitive way (P2=1), transmission of the upper pyramidal cells increases. Because of the axon collaterals of these cells, coupling between the columns increases as well: the two columns merge to become a single, larger module.

PO = 1

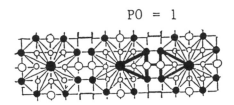

FUNCTIONAL SUBDIVISION OF MODULAR ZONES

P2 = 1

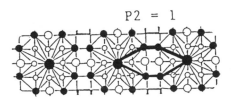

FUNCTIONAL MERGING OF TWO MODULES

Figure 2-17b . *Changes of dimensions of functional modules depending upon correlations of activities of components columns.*

b) Subdivision of a modular zone.
On the other hand, great differences of activity between two adjacent cortical columns result in an increase of the transmission coefficients of inhibitory cells ("Pan") that produces an irreversible lateral uncoupling: a cortical zone can be subdivided in two modules that have a more limited lateral extension.

Cellular registrations can thus modify the lateral extension of a module. The first effect will be a change in the geometry of the functional maps on the cortical surface; the same sensory stimulus that produces the same thalamic input will have a larger influence (merged modules) or a smaller influence (subdivided modules) on the cortical surface.

The stability of these transmission coefficients is strongly dependant upon a "maturation factor" (Chapter I): the coefficients are particularly unstable during the "critical" periods at the end of cortical growth: "a few" coactivations can produce stable cellular registrations and then shape the cortical maps.

3. Effect of memorization on input-output functions of columnar automata

A) After learning, a low cortical input has three possible effects on a column: inhibitory, gating or triggering cortical actions.

a) Changes of input-output rules by learning.

FIGURE 2-18, illustrates the changes of input-output rules when the transmission between cortical modules changes.

The left part of the table represents the critical long-range activation patterns that measure co-activations of a receptor module and its cortical inputs (P2 and P0).

The central part shows the differential effects upon the modular transmission coefficients (Ph and Pb).

The right part of the table illustrates the resulting changes of the in-out relations for upper and lower layers, when the prior activity of the module is low (E0,E1), the thalamic input is zero (Th=E0) and cortical input is moderate (Co=E1). The other combinations have less changes with learning.

The first row in the table represents the "naive" state, before learning, and the three other rows represents three possible stable states of intermodular transmission after learning:

1. The moderate cortical inputs can have an inhibitory effect ("G2-"); this occurs when the receptor module was always inhibited before strong activities in the transmitter module.

2. The moderate cortical inputs can have a gating effect ("G1+"or "G1-"); this occurs when the receptor module was sometimes inhibited and sometimes active before strong activities in the transmitter module;

3. The moderate cortical inputs can have a triggering effect and produce directly an high activation in the receptor module (G2+); this occurs when the receptor module was always active before strong activities in the transmitter module.

b) Differences of activities produced by learning.

FIGURE 2-19 underlines the differences in modular activities before learning (upper diagram) and two stable states after learning , weak ("gating" , middle diagram) or strong ("triggering" , lower diagram).

The four columns in each diagram represent the average responses (mean discharge frequency) of the pyramidal neurons for four types of in-out combinations, which are defined in the lower table of the figure. The mean activities of upper and the lower layers are quantitatively different: the activities of upper layers are illustrated in dashed lines, those of lower layers with continuous lines. Since coefficients are

MEMORIZING CONDITIONS			PARAMETER CHANGES		MODIFICATION OF FUNCTIONAL RULES			
REPETITION FACTOR	ACTIVATION PATTERN P2	INHIBITION PATTERN PO	TRANSMISSION COEFFICIENT		FUNCTION WHEN INPUTS CO = E1 TH = EO PRIOR STATE = EO,E1			
			UPPER UPPER PH	UPPER LOWER PB	UPPER LAYER	LOWER LAYER		
-	-	-	(1	((1	EO , E1	EO	RANDOM	G0
	0	1	0	0	EO	EO	INHIBITING	G2-
	)0	(1	1	0	E1	EO	GATING	G1
	1	0	1	1	E2	E2	TRIGGERING	G2+

E2: High level of activity
E1: Low level of activity
EO: Inactive

Figure 2-18 . Learning rules of the cortical column: critical activation patterns change transmission coefficients and consequently input-output rules.

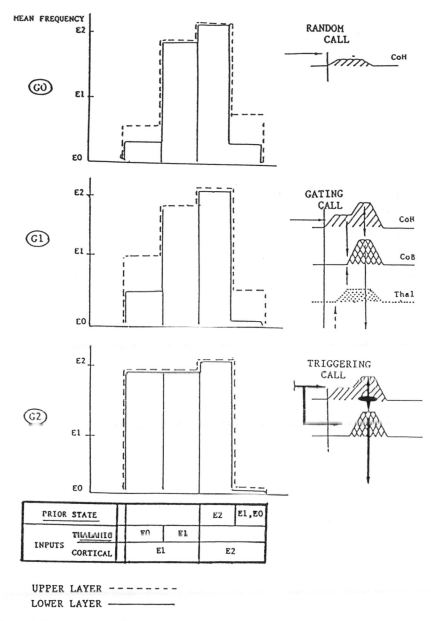

UPPER LAYER – – – – – – – –
LOWER LAYER ——————

Figure 2-19 . Average activities of upper and lower layers in three possible memorizing states (diagrams G0,G1,G2) and in four functional situations (columns).

probabilistic, these mean activities are intermediate with respect to activity levels (E0, E1, and E2).

We can see that the two conditions depicted by the central columns produce the

same type of activity, whatever the registration state, i.e the previous memorizations of the column:
- when cortical and thalamic inputs are co-activated (left central column) they produce a strong modular activity, whatever the registration state;
- when the module has an high activity (prior state E2) and then is reactivated by a strong cortical input (right central column), its activity stays at the high level: this is the condition of new memorizations, whatever the previous registration state.

By contrast, the two conditions depicted by the left and right columns have effects that depend upon the "history" of the module:
- when cortical inputs alone are active with a moderate level (left column), upper layers respond more than lower layers, in the weak memorization state (gating state); but in the strong memorization state (triggering state), both divisions are highly active;
- when cortical inputs are strong, they have an inhibitory effect when the receptor module has a prior weak activity; this inhibition can increase with learning.

B) Refinement of learning is produced by adjustments of "continuous" coefficients.

Within the stable registration states defined by probabilistic coefficients (Ph and Pb), the "continuous coefficients (Ch and Cb) can be modified by learning: they effect a precise quantitative adjustment of the transmission between columns and between layers.
These continuous coefficients correspond to local registrations at a subcellular level (dendritic spines). This memorization is "associative" at the level of each individual cell (chapter I): a precondition of registration is the activation of a synaptic input (E1) upon a dendritic spine just before intense depolarization of the receptive cell (E2).
This condition occurs repeatedly when the probabilistic coefficients have maximal values (Ph and/or Pb close to 1). When the "upper-upper" probabilistic coefficient is maximal (Ph=1), cortical inputs increase their influence upon the upper layers; consequently they are often active (E1) before strong activities in the upper pyramidal cells of the receptive module (E2): this pattern will modify the transmission in specific spines and will increase the continuous "upper-upper" (Ch) coefficient in a precise way. Similar configuration occurs for "upper-lower" coefficients and correspond to changes for spines of the lower pyramidal neurons. These fine memorization processes are detailed in Annex 4-E (Figure A-14).

There is an important difference between large registrations by probabilistic coefficients and finer registrations by continuous coefficients:
- Registrations by probabilistic coefficients occur especially when the receptor module has a high activity and is reactivated in an intense way by its cortical inputs; this registration occurs by level, with stable states.
- Registrations by continuous coefficients occur when the module is activated only once in an intense way, and they are related to inputs that anticipate these strong activations. In contrast with probabilistic coefficients, the continuous coefficients do not tend to approach a maximum or a minimum. There is an equilibrium point : no more

continuous registration occurs when high activity in the receptor module is always followed by intense activation of its cortical inputs.

This continuous registration process is thus a quantitative adjustment of intermodular relations: the output/input ratio between a receptor module and its cortical afferences will change in such a way as to favor (as much as possible) strong reactivation of these cortical inputs.

IV. Columnar automata : goal-directed behaviour and active learning.

We describe in this section the general behavioral consequences of the columnar mechanism. The functional and memorization rules define a columnar automaton which controls the extent of modules and the sequence of modular activation. We shall see that contrasted activities (strong excitations or inhibitions) represent an equilibrium position, a "goal" for cortical activities:

- partial modular activation produces a disequilibrium in the cortical network, that is manifested behaviourally by an active search that continues until goal attainment;

- because of the logic of cellular registrations in the column, each module which is partially activated "calls" selectively the modules that can favor its goal, that is its own re-activation with the higher intensity level.

Learning by columnar automata is much more than a simple "associative" memorization, and is instead an active, structured process. Columnar automata constructs new functional networks relating cortical modules, the "call trees" organized by goals and subgoals. These networks have a characteristic overall activity:

- first, a potential goal "calls" all possible actions and this call produces anticipation and attention;

- then cortical actions, gated by this call, are triggered as a function of environmental conditions, in a sequence inverse to that of the calls.

A call tree effects a global function that brings the cortical system close to the goal, whatever the initial conditions. We shall see in chapter IV that these call trees can organize motor programs and spatial positioning of the hand toward a target; they can also effect parallel, hierarchical and dynamic processing of sensory information (recognition algorithms).

References

Neural activity that is recorded in cortex of behaving animals during stereotyped behavioral tasks point out important properties of the cortical mechanisms:

1. Cortical neurons are specialized: the activity of a column is related to a specific aspect of stimuli or movements; different aspects can coexist in the same cortical regions. Each neuron has a specific pattern of activity during behavior: for example a tonic anticipation that is followed by an intense phasic activity, etc. (Mountcastle 1984, Fetz 1984).

2. Cortical neurons are also particularly active during periods of "directed attention" (Jasper 1958, Hyvarinen 1974, Mountcastle 1975): learning is directly dependant upon this pre-existing attentive activity (Jasper 1958). Each cortical region produces a specific type of attention (Wurtz 1984): movement initiation in motor areas, visuospatial attention in parietal areas, visual discrimination in temporal areas, etc.

3. Excitability or activity of cortical neurons increases in relation with the intensity of expectancy (Mountcastle 1974). In motor areas, during the preparatory period before a movement, the cell activity increase in the modules that will command the muscular contractions (Evarts 1975, Kubota 1980). In associative regions, the effect of a peripheral stimulation on cortical activity is directly dependant upon the logic of the behavior occurring ("significance" of the stimulus): for example, in the parietal areas (Hyvarinen 1974, Mountcastle 1981), or auditory areas (Goldstein 1978, Kitzes 1982). This effect is extensive and is not limited to cortical modules activated by the target stimuli (Mountcastle 1984).

4. Goals are represented in cortical activities. In motor areas, the activity of neurons is a direct function of distance from the goal (Phillips 1972, Evarts 1974, Tanji 1976). At the moment of motor performance, there is a strong inhibition of irrelevant cells (Evarts 1964). In associative areas, neuronal activity is linked both with the sensory result of a motor action and the command of this action: action and sensory goal of this action have a common representation. Neurons have a sensory aspect and can be activated via sensory stimulation, and they have a motor aspect and can be active just before a movement; the important fact is that they are active before the movement that induces this very sensory stimulation. For example, a cell which can be strongly activated by contact of two parts of the body (sensory activation), is also active just before the specific movement that precisely brings these two body parts closer together (motor command activation) (Hyvarinen 1974, Robinson 1975, Rizzolati 1981).

1. Modular outputs: action or call

The behavioral significance of the cortical mechanism can be deduced from the basic functional in-out rules of the columnar automaton (as shown in Figure 2-9), and from its memorization properties (as shown in Figure 2-18).

a) The network.

FIGURES 2-20 and 2-21 illustrate, on the upper diagram, two modules ([A] and [B]), with their reciprocal relations and their connections to sensory and motor organs; their lateral extension is determined by their functional homogeneity. The behavioral significance of their operations depends upon their three relations:

- modular inputs: thalamic inputs represent an "external situation" extracted from the environment by sensory organ, or an "internal state" extracted by hypothalamus or information processed by other neural structures; the variety of specific input information will be detailed in the next chapters;

- modular outputs: a module which has an intense activity (E2) performs an "action" upon efferent nervous structures. For instance, a cortical module in motor areas acts upon motoneurons and commands a muscular contraction. These cortical actions can also effect more "internal" actions by activating other neural structures, such as the hypothalamus, the hippocampus or the cerebellum; the variety of effects of cortical actions will be examined in the next chapters;

- intermodular connections: cortical modules (here [A] and [B]) are interconnected, either directly, if they are adjacent, or by the network that inter-connects cortical areas .

b) The neural activities.

In Figures 2-20 and 2-21, the lower frames illustrate the parallel activities of the upper and lower layers of the two modules ([A] and [B]).

These activities are depicted by "trapezoidal" temporal functions, with three possible intensity levels on the vertical axis: "strong" activation (E2), "moderate" activation (E1) and inhibition (E0).

Time is on the horizontal axis: the starting point at the left of each trace represents the same time (t0). Activities of the two layers of a given module ([A] for example), are vertically aligned; the activities of the upper layers of the two modules are horizontally aligned.Arrows between the traces indicate causal relations between variations in activity.

Each module is an automaton which determines causal chains between events. These causal chains are detailed in Annex 5-A (Figure A-15) with the formalism that we have previously developed.

A) An active cortical module "calls" other modules if and only if its own action is not possible.

When a module (for instance [A]) is activated by its cortical inputs in a prolonged way (moderate activation E1), the consequences depend upon the extent to which its thalamic inputs are also activated. The two possible situations are illustrated in the two lower frames of FIGURE 2-20: in these two configuration, the left module [A] is activated by its cortical inputs.

1. If the thalamic inputs are also activated (middle frame of Figure 2-20), the resulting coactivation produces an intense modular activity (at level E2) that has two results:
- a specific action on an efferent structure, for instance a muscular contraction;
- an inhibition of neighboring columns (and those linked by the cortical recombination network, such as [B]) having a lower activity level (E0 or E1).

The activity is then limited to one module ([A]) and the mechanism resembles a reflex arc: a thalamic activity ("external situation") produces an isolated cortical action (level E2). The action of a module [A] is depicted by A!.

2. If the thalamic inputs of module [A] are inactive (lower frame of figure 2-20), the module cannot produce a cortical action; however, the upper layers (activated to

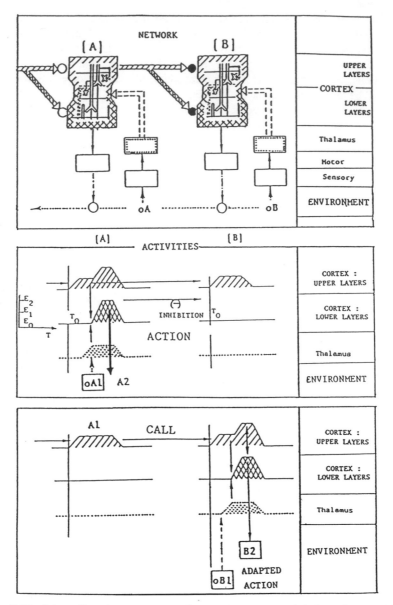

Figure 2-20 . Interactions between two columnar automata and their environment (upper diagram) resulting either in an action (middle) or a call (lower).

E1), transmit their moderate activity to the nearest neighboring modules (for instance to [B]). The activity spreads in the cortical network.

This moderate activation of other modules (at E1 level) in the cortical network is a "call" effected by a module when its own activation is insufficient. The call from module [A] toward module [B] is depicted by B?.

B) Among possible modular actions which are called, only those adapted to environmental situations will be executed.

After a "call" (B?), the result will depend upon the external situation which controls thalamic activation of the called module ([B]):
1. If the called module ([B]) is also activated by its thalamic inputs, the coactivation effect triggers a specific action (B!).
2. Otherwise, the call continues to spread through the cortical network.

C) The call process continues until effects of cortical actions modify the thalamic input of the module originating the call.

Two causal chains become possible following execution of the specific action of the called module (B!):
1. The action of the called module (B!) activates, by an external feedback loop produced by any causal link, the thalamic input of the calling module ([A]). This situation is illustrated in the middle frame of figure 2-21. The calling module is then coactivated by thalamic and cortical inputs and the resulting high activity (E2) has two consequences: it executes its own specific action (A!), and inhibits other, less active modules, thus dissipating the excitation of the "call".
2. The action of the called module (B!) does not activate the thalamic input of the calling module ([A]) via an external loop: the "call" activity continues to spread along the cortical network. The call stops only if the possible actions that are "called" modify, by any external causal chain, the thalamic activation of the calling module ([A]), at which time its action will be executed, inhibiting the call.

In both of these causal chains, the strong activation of the called module (B!) can momentarily inhibit the calling module ([A]), but not in an efficient way, because of the prolonged activation of the calling module by its cortical inputs.

2. Behavioural consequences before learning

A) The columnar mechanisms produce active explorations.

Let us consider the example of two modules ([A] and [B]) in sensorimotor cortex (without the intervention of visual inputs):
- The first module ([A]) can command an elbow-flexing response (action A!) when the fingers touch an object (thalamic activation of [A]);
- This module may be continuously activated by other cortical modules, for example from modules of the "limbic" cortex, that represent an internal state of "hunger";
- If the fingers touch an object, the module commands the flexing movement (A!) that brings the hand (and therefore the food) toward the mouth.

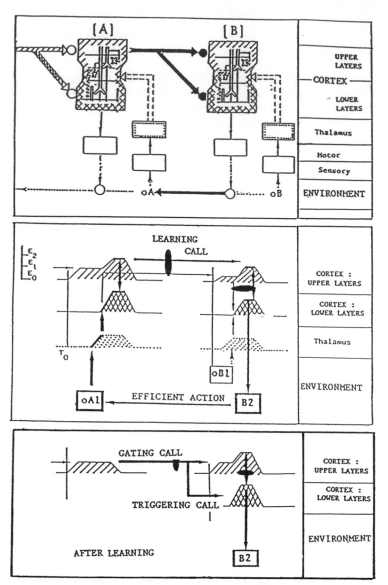

Figure 2-21 . Learning of sequences by 2 columnar automata (upper) when a call results in an external feedback loop (middle) with two possible functional consequences (lower).

   - If the fingers touch nothing, this cortical action (A!) and thus the corresponding motor response cannot occur; the module "calls" other modules in the network.
   - The call activates other parts of the motor cortex; neighboring modules ([B]) can command other types of arm movement, for instance arm extension, which produce exploration of environmental space.

- The call and therefore the exploration continue until the fingers touch an object: the calling module ([A]) can then command the flexing movement and inhibit the other exploratory movements.

B) Modular action is an equilibrium position, a goal.

As soon as a module (such as [A]) is persistently activated by its cortical inputs, it can in turn activate other modules (if it is at moderate level E1), or inhibit them (if it reaches strong level E2). We will call it a "pilot module":
- realization of its action (E2) becomes a goal, an equilibrium position for the cortical system;
- as long as the goal is not reached, the pilot module activates (in E1) the other modules of the network; this activation is a "call", and extension of the call on the cortical network produces a disequilibrium;
- if the action of the "called" modules renders possible the goal (A!), via some external feedback loop (extrinsic causal chain), the pilot module ([A]) becomes inhibitory and the disequilibrium provoked by the call disappears.

The persistent activation of a module by its cortical inputs, at the origin of the disequilibrium, can be produced initially by continuous thalamic activation of another cortical module: the hypothalamic nuclei activate the thalamic inputs of limbic cortex in a prolonged manner. Modules of the limbic regions are prototypical "pilot modules" that represent "fundamental programs" of the organism.

On the other hand, cortical images of sensory activations from the environment are too short for creating a disequilibrium, since persistent activities are eliminated by habituation. Sensory activation may have different cortical effects depending upon the previous calls: when the stimulation corresponds to a behavior already in progress, the receptive modules are already activated by the cortical calls and the stimulation's effect will be much greater (E2).

The disequilibrium of the call produces a subliminal activation that is selectively extended through the cortical tissue: this selective configuration of the "call" pattern, related to the accomplishment of a particular behavioral goal, is thus the material basis of selective "attention". This call "gates" the cortical effects of external stimuli and thus amplifies different stimuli, as a function of their relevance for goal-attainment.

3. Learning of oriented and fixed sequences

A) A columnar automaton learns to selectively call other modules which favour its own action.

A priori before learning, a module ([A]) will call randomly other modules connected in the cortico-cortical network; the spread of the call depends upon anatomical connectivity: for two modules that are not directly connected, the strength of the transmission is inversely proportional to the number of intermediate modules linking them in the chain.

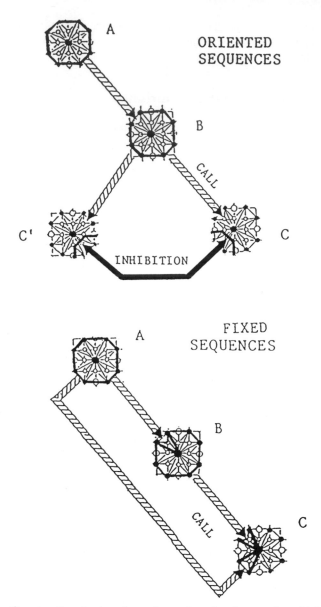

Figure 2-22 . Construction, by learning, of new functional networks which can produce either oriented or fixed sequences.

Let us consider again the situation described in Figure 2-21, in the middle frame: the called module ([B]), effects a specific action (B!) that reactivates the thalamic input of the calling module ([A]) via an external feedback loop. The probability of such a causal chain depends upon a certain behavioral logic in the cortico-cortical connections. We shall give many examples of such properties in the next chapters.

In this situation, the goal-action (A!) is then triggered; this action inhibits the other cortical modules that are weakly active, but reactivates (in E2) the modules that were just effecting an action (such as [B]). The strong reactivation (by [A]) of the module already active at an intense level ([B]), is precisely the learning condition that changes the transmission coefficient between modules ("upper-upper" coefficient "Ph" between [A] and [B]).

The pattern of activity that produces memorization (action B! followed by action A!) is possible only if a double condition is present:

1. A disequilibrium condition: the action of the called module (B!) is possible only if the pilot module ([A]) is not directly activated by its thalamic inputs, because in that case the strongly activated pilot module would directly inhibit other modules.

2. A condition of "apparent causality": the action of the called module (B!) has a global effect that favours the action of the pilot module (A!) via an external feedback loop. In that case, the called module is not inhibited by the action of the pilot module because it has already a strong activity.

Because of the activity sequence (action B! followed by action A!), the transmission coefficient between the upper layers increases and may become maximal ("upper-upper" transmission coefficient Ph from [A] to [B] changes from a value close to 0 to a value close to 1). After learning, the cortical input (from A) has a strong gating effect on the receptor module . This registration state selectively orients the call towards possible efficient actions: when the action of a pilot module cannot be directly triggered (disequilibrium), this module selectively calls (Ph=1) those modules whose actions in the past have proved effective for goal attainment (action of the pilot module).

This registration is thus a patterned extension of the cortical call network: the "efficient" modules (for instance [B]) become functionally linked to the call network of the pilot module ([A]).

FIGURE 2-22 illustrates two call networks constructed by learning. The modules are depicted by their "functional equivalent circuits" (as in Figure 2-10). The cortico-cortical connections which are reinforced are symbolized by striped arrows. As shown in the upper schema, a module can call several other modules in parallel. If the called modules are competitive, they will reinforce their inhibitory connections (black arrows): in this case, the choice will be effected by external inputs.

The property of patterned extension of the cortical call network is recursive because the registration rules depend only upon the activities of the cortical modules and not upon their external connections. As soon as a module is linked to the call network of a pilot module, it can itself activate in turn other modules when it is partially activated (E1); its action (E2) becomes a new goal for cortical activity.

A new functional network can be constructed around this new "partial goal". After learning, it will selectively call all the modules whose actions favour this "partial goal". Attainment of the partial goal will permit in turn the attainment of the "final goal" (initial call).

Modules that are not linked to such a call network will not be able to construct new call networks around themselves since they have a low probability of strong activation.

B) Cortical automata can construct fixed sequences of actions independent of external conditions.

a) Two levels of learning.

After learning that has resulted in construction of a call network (upper-upper coefficient Ph close to 1), two situations can arise and are illustrated in the lower frame of Figure 2-21:

1. One possibility is that several actions permit goal attainment, and selection is thus dependant upon external conditions. The called modules (for instance [B], or [C]) are sometimes strongly activated, but sometimes inhibited before the action of the pilot module: the "upper-upper" coefficient becomes maximal (Ph=1), but the "upper-lower" coefficient is minimal (Pb=0). The new functional network is shown in figure 2-22, in the upper part. The two modules are called in parallel and the external inputs make a choice if their two actions are competitive (inhibitory connections shown by dark arrows)

2. Another possibility is that the same specific action, (for instance B!) is always necessary before a strong activation of the pilot module; in this case the sequential action of these two modules is always produced for goal attainment, and the called module ([B]) is "always" strongly active before the action of the pilot module [A]. This activity pattern (always coactivated) is the learning condition that changes the transmission coefficient from cortical inputs toward the lower layers: the "upper-lower" coefficient becomes maximal (Pb=1). After learning, a moderate cortical input triggers an action of the receptor module, at the higher activity level. In this stronger registration state, a cortical call produce "fixed" sequences of actions that are sequences which do not depend upon external conditions.

b) Progressive learning of a sequence.

The call network can extend from each new component of the sequence, as shown in Figure 2-22, in the lower part. The columnar automaton can construct longer and longer fixed sequences of actions, like sequences of phonemes that form the "words" of a language.

The cortical process produces a recursive behavioral pattern of "repetition" and "differentiation" of new components in the sequence:

1. Repetition of the new component: the initial call (A!) produces a fixed sequence of two actions (B!-A!). When a two-step sequence (B!-A!) is established, either it becomes stable if the goal is always attained, or a new disequilibrium produces a call originating from the new component ([B]). Because of the spatial redundancy of cortical modules, the call will produce the repetition of the new component that is the first one of the behavioral sequence: the call A-B-B? produces the sequence B!-B!-A!.

2. Differentiation of the new component: the extension of the call on the cortical network then produces new actions which differentiate the first component of the sequence : the call A-B-B? becomes A-B-C? and transforms the sequence of actions B!-B!-A! into a new sequence C!-B!-A!.

3. Stabilization of the new component: the new call is oriented toward an action that permits goal attainment via the three-steps sequence (C!-B!-A!). The behavioral sequence of action C!-B!-A! is thus the reverse of the call sequence A-B-C?. The intermediate action B! is called first but is not triggered first since there is a competitive

aspect between the calls to other modules (towards C) and its own direct action : it is not the case with the new component (C) that will be triggered first.

The process continues and generates longer and longer differentiated sequences. These sequences of actions are triggered in proper order by the call from the pilot module.

C) Construction of behavioural sequences can include "attentive" states directed towards triggering signals.

a) Attentive state

The cortical call produces an anticipatory activity in the called modules (E1). But a module has several different cortical inputs, and these inputs can have competitive effects, one having acquired an excitatory influence and another having acquired an inhibitory influence. Such a functional network is shown in Figure 2-23: after learning a module [B] has two cortical inputs with opposite effects, an excitatory from [A], and an inhibitory from [W] (black arrows).

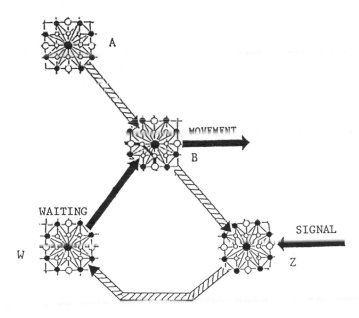

Figure 2-23 . Construction of a new functional network including an attentive state towards a signal triggering a movement.

Simultaneous activation of two competitive cortical inputs produces an equilibrium. Upper layer activity remains low, and there is no long-range information transfer by the upper and lower modular outputs. But sensitivity to other inputs is still present (gating effect) and another input, either cortical or thalamic (E1) can now trigger a strong modular activation (E2): the module is in an "attentive" state. The corresponding patterns of cortical activations are detailed in Annex 5-C and the causal chains are exposed in Figure A-16.

b) Sensory signals which trigger motor actions.

Some motor actions are internally-directed, "self-paced", while for others, effectiveness is directly dependant upon a "triggering signal". Furthermore, this signal can be indispensable for the completion of the motor sequence. FIGURE 2-23 illustrates a cortical configuration that can learn to command the proper response when the signal occurs: one module ([B]) commands motor actions; another module ([Z]) in receptive or associative areas can selectively amplify the signal; and a third module ([W]) has an intermediate position.

In the absence of the signal, the action of the "motor command" module ([B]), is inefficient to reach the goal; after learning it will selectively call other modules potentially favorable to sequence effectiveness, that is modules that increase the "signal reception" ([Z]). But precipitate motor action (by [B]) is not only ineffective but can also disturb signal reception. The receptor module ([Z]) will, in turn, call a new, "suspending" module (for instance [W]), whose activity inhibits motor action when there is no signal. We will see that these "suspending" modules, activated by sensory modules ([Z]) , and inhibiting motor modules ([B]) in a long-term way, actually exist in frontal cortex.

Motor command modules ([B]), both activated by a goal (from [A]) and inhibited by the "suspending" module ([W]), shifts into the "attentive" state. When the triggering signal arrives, the receptor module ([Z]) effects a cortical action that has two correlated effects: direct activation of motor module ([B]) and dishinibition, that is suppression of the call towards the "waiting" module ([W]) that inhibited the motor module ([B]). These two cooperative effects trigger the motor action (from [B]).

This call network produces an "active" waiting for the signal necessary for the proper unfolding of the sequence.

This mode of triggering enlarges the possibilities of sensory-motor interactions in the cortex: the relation between the external signal and the motor action is not performed by the direct "sensory" thalamic input of a motor module: this relation can be learned, and each step is stabilized by a cortical action. The functional network can extend far beyond the "genetic" logic of the anatomical system.

In this way, the cortical mechanism select appropriate "internal signals" that can represent a wide variety of external stimuli, after processing and selection by the cortex.

Furthermore, any cortical modular action can serve as a triggering signal for another sequence of cortical actions: as long as this internal signal is not perceived, the other actions are blocked and the corresponding modules are inactive, but remain in a state of increased receptivity. Adaptation of behavioral sequences to the environment can be much more varied.

V. Functional networks
between columns : call trees.

A) Columnar automata construct call trees with three dimensions: set of possible actions, goal distance and sequence order.

In a new situation, cortical automata produce random actions within a system of cortical "proximity": spread of activity on the cortical network (call) first results in a repetition of actions of the behavioral repertoire, and then their progressive differentiation. Each effective adaptation is memorized.

Successive memorizations result in the progressive construction of new functional networks; we turn now to the properties of these networks, defined by strong coupling coefficients on the anatomical pathways.

Columnar automata progressively construct call networks around "goals"; these goals are cortical actions, i.e strong and contrasted activations of cortical modules; each called module can in turn organize its own call network, and its action will become a partial goal.

Call networks have a tree-like structure, and new branches can "sprout" from any given module.

- FIGURE 2-24 represents a call tree with its component modules which are called and their functional relations: each participating module is illustrated as a cortical column with its upper and lower layers (as in Figure 2-4).

- FIGURE 2-25 focus on the principal functional relations between modules in a call tree; this simplified representation will be used in the next chapters to depict the sensori-motor algorithms constructed by the cortical mechanism.

Two modules are functionally linked in the call network when their transmission coefficients are strong (probabilistic coefficient close to 1):

Each module in the call network has three types of functional relations, depicted by arrows:

- "calls" (arrows with stripes) are moderate activations of cortical inputs (level E1);

- thalamic activations (upward dashed arrows) are due to sensory stimulations;

- modular "actions" (downward black arrows) command movements.

These modular actions are triggered when cortical inputs (calls) and thalamic inputs (external situations) are in register. The strong resulting activity inhibits other modules which were also called at the same level or lower levels (lateral black arrows).

a) The two types of sequences

Transmission coefficients between upper layers of cortical modules participating in the call tree define the set of possible actions that can contribute to the attainment of

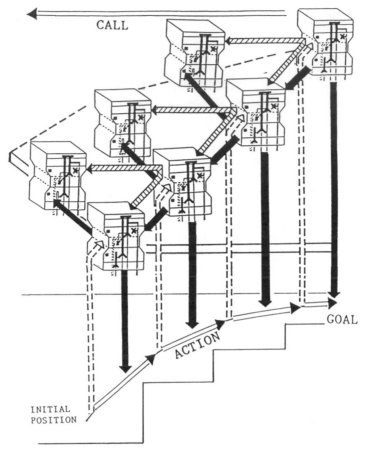

Figure 2-24 . Call tree which links columns after learning: search of appropriate actions
(call) and actual sequence in order to reach the goal.

a goal; the precise combination of actions that will be executed depends upon external condition (thalamic inputs). When several possible actions are competitive, the one bringing the system toward the goal the quickest has priority (inhibitory relations): only the possible actions that are closer to the goal are executed.

But call trees can also generate "fixed sequences" of actions thanks to increased transmission coefficients between upper and lower layers of component modules; these new relations define both the actions to be performed and their order of performance (fixed combination). This stronger stage of memorization is possible when the external situation is very stable or neutral: the "external" combination is then replaced by an "internal" combination. Triggering of modular actions is done directly by cortico-cortical connections, regardless of external conditions.

b) The three dimensions of the call tree.

As illustrated in FIGURE 2-24 and 2-25, a call tree can be depicted by a "prism" having three dimensions:

1. Possible actions : one of the horizontal axes of the prism represents the various actions that can be called by the same goal (for instance , in Figure 2-24 and 2-25, the pilot module [D] calls [C] and [C'], which then call [B], [B'], then [A], [A'], etc). The upper face of the prism represents the parallel call of different possible cortical actions.

2. Effective sequence: the other horizontal axis represents the temporal sequence of the effective modular actions. Modules that effect cortical actions (extracortical output) are those where call and thalamic inputs are in register (sequence of actions A!-B!- C!- D!).

3. Goal distance: the vertical axis represents the successive levels of construction of the call tree and the distance from the goal: the summit represents the final goal and the other levels represent the successive subgoals.

c) The two directions of functioning

Functioning occurs in two successively opposed directions:

1. First, the call activates an increasingly large number of modules. On the prism, this call corresponds to a downward movement from right to left on the upper face (the call sequence is "D?-C?-B?-A?" in figure 2-25).

2. Then, execution of modular actions moves the system toward the goal (in the order "A!-B!-C!-D!" in figure 2-25) on the horizontal axis from left to right. The performance of each modular action contributes to the thalamic activation of the next module in the sequence. The system progressively approaches its goal, with an upward movement on the vertical axis of the prism.

d) The call levels.

Construction of a call tree proceeds by progressive extension from modules whose actions are final goals; this construction corresponds to an extension on the vertical axis of the prism, from the top down. This growth represents the learning of longer and longer sequences with larger and larger calls. The most direct actions for goal attainment are learned first; if these actions are not always effective, they become in their turn partial goals and organize new branches of the call tree.

Several levels of functional relations are formed, each level corresponding to a partial goal. The highest level is that of the final goal: by convention it is considered level 0, and successively called partial goals are given decreasing values: -1, -2, -3, etc.

Attainment of a partial goal of level "k" (for example B! at level -2), modifies the thalamic inputs of modules at level "k+1" ([C] at level -1): the system progressively approaches the final goal at level 0 (action D!). When a partial goal is accomplished, it inhibits partial goals at inferior call levels, but not those at superior levels.

B) Call trees are adaptive functions that can guide a sensori-motor system toward a goal, whatever the initial conditions.

Generally speaking, the columnar automaton is an adaptive mechanism: it generates a sequence of actions adapted to external conditions in order to attain a certain goal:

- The representational equivalence, in cortex, of an "action" and a "goal" renders modular action, of whatever kind, a possible "goal" and thus an equilibrium position for the cortical system.

- If this action is not directly possible, the columnar automaton produces a systematic search for other cortical actions that can move the organism closer to the goal.

- Among the different possible actions called on the cortical network, only those adapted to the external situation will be executed.

- A possible "action" is not called unless other, more directly effective actions , are not possible. For example, only one action can be called and executed to reach the goal if it is sufficient.

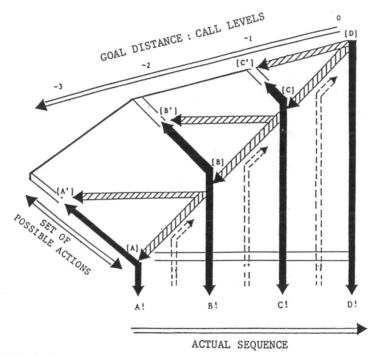

Figure 2-25 . 3 dimensions of call trees: the set of possible actions, the actual sequence of actions and the distance to the goal.

The call tree is a global "function" that brings the sensori-motor system toward an equilibrium position , whatever the initial conditions, by an appropriate sequence of actions. Within a specified external context , this function continually re-orients the cortical actions towards a goal. We shall see that these functions not only effect spatial positioning, they also constitute "recognition algorithms".

As illustrated in Figure 2-24, the call levels represent the different possible initial conditions, as determined by their distance from the equilibrium position. Only the sequence necessary to reach the goal is executed; more actions are called when the starting point is more distant.

Each action brings the system toward a position closer to the goal; consequently, each initial position does not imply a new independent learning. The cortical call tree assimilates progressively all the implicit relations that exist between all the possible initial conditions.

C) The laminar pattern of cortico-cortical connections favours the construction of call trees from internal goals towards sensori-motor actions.

a) Priority of fundamental programs.

In the cortical system, the goal that is the equilibrium position is not permanent, but functionally determined by the activity in the cortical network: for example, inputs from hypothalamus can produce a prolonged activation of the cortical network which represent needs for fundamental programs of the organism. In another example , in placing the hand upon a visually perceived object, the final position of the hand is not fixed but functionally determined by the position of the target object.

In other neural structures, the equilibrium positions are determined by the anatomical pathway , and are for the most part linked to reflexes and fundamental programs, such as feeding behavior. In the cortical system, each modular action can become a goal, an equilibrium position; a circuit-produced hierarchy is replaced by a a a set of functional hierarchies, built by learning regularities in the external environment.

However, the priority of fundamental programs is ensured by the great influence of hypothalamic inputs to the limbic areas of the cortex and by the persistent character of these inputs.

b) Anticipatory calls in feedback connections.

Furthermore the feedforward/feedback laminar pattern of cortical connections between sensory and associative areas introduces a natural hierarchy on the sensory information flows: the call trees will be naturally constructed from the associative toward the primary receptive areas on the feedback connections and they will control the succession of actions in the feedforward connections:

- the direction of actions correspond to the feedforward directions, since these connections are mostly excitatory and transmit sensory information.

- the direction of the call correspond to the feedback direction; these connections arrive in the upper layers and control the afferent information flows depending upon cortical goals. Feedback connections also arise from lower layers whose strong activity represents a modular action and consequently the realization of a subgoal: this strong activity is inhibitory on the feedback connections toward the columns at a lower level in the call tree.

It is important to note that anticipatory activity (call) in "feedback" connections precedes sensory information flows (actions) in feedforward connections.

D) Continuous transmission coefficients permit precise behavioural adjustments to the environment.

Each module has several input-output connections in the cortical network, and each one can memorize a functional relation: an oriented call, a fixed sequence, or an inhibition. These types of relations depend mostly upon the intermodular "probabilistic" coefficients which define a call tree in a qualitative way (what is the set of possible actions in order to accomplish a specific goal).

But we have seen that more precise relations can be memorized by "continuous" coefficients: they define quantitative rations between calls and between actions . These continuous coefficients permit precise adjustments which optimize the speed with which equilibrium is reached.

As illustrated in Figure 2-26, each module in a call tree has four continuous coefficients, two in the direction of the call, and two in the direction of actions.

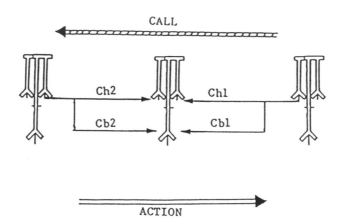

Figure 2-26 . Continuous transmission coefficients between columns within a call tree in the two functional directions.

1. In the direction of the call , the "upper-upper" continuous coefficient ("Ch1") determines activities of upper layers of a module in response to a call. This coefficient tends to decrease with the successive extensions of the call when the distance from the final goal increases. In consequence, actions closer to the goal have priority.

2. The "upper-lower" coefficient in the direction of the call ("Cb1"), is the weight of the call toward the lower layers. When the distance from the goal increases, this upper-lower coefficient can increase since less upper pyramidal cells are specialized to call other modules. In consequence intensity of actions can increase and the system will return faster to its equilibrium position.

In the construction of a fixed sequence of actions, each module calls only one "antecedent" module. The call is maximal for the last module called, and the action of this module is the first of the sequence executed.

3. In the direction of the sequence of actions , the upper-upper coefficients (Ch2) represent in a way the "recall" force produced by actions. Execution of an action suppresses calls at inferior levels but reinforces the call toward partial goals at superior levels. The call is enhanced, as the system approaches the goal, on all those branches "confirmed" by actions in fact executed. Reciprocally, if no action reinforces a call on a branch, this call is progressively extinguished.

4. The "upper-lower" continuous coefficient, in the direction of the sequence of actions ("Cb2") can register the optimal ratio between intensities of two successive actions that brings the cortical system toward the goal in the most effective way. These coefficients do not register intensities of actions, but rather the proportions between related activations. This kind of learning permits the recognition of forms in the environment, independently of their sizes.

The properties of the different continuous coefficients inside a call are analyzed in Annex 7 (Figure A-18 and A-19).

E) Call trees effect parallel distributed processing in hierarchical sequences

Movements or images of objects are represented in the cortex by a pattern of activity distributed over a wide set of cortical modules, with each module encoding a feature of the global entity.

In a real call tree, each step does not correspond to the action of a single module, but a whole combination of actions can be called in parallel or triggered together. In the same way, the goal is not the action of a single column, but the coordinated action of a set of columns.

At each instant, the behavioral effect is due to a combined activity distributed on a population of columns which cooperate in a global effect. These columns are not necessarily contiguous; their unity is due to the fact that they can be coactivated simultaneously with a high level of activity (E2) while inhibiting other sets of columns. So call trees relate "multi-modules" which are subsets of cooperating columns, even if they are not contiguous.

All columns within a multi-module have the same probabilistic coefficients, but the continuous coefficients can be varied. Consequently, columns within a multi-module have similar levels of activity, but with quantitative modulations distributed over the population.

Call trees (as illustrated in Figure 2-24 and 2-25) are both sequential and parallel processes:

1. Each step (probabilistic coefficients) correspond to the qualitative choice of "efficient" actions; they define a subset of features or primitives to be used for representing a sensorimotor entity.

2. When this qualitative representation is chosen, each step in the call tree is quantitatively defined by a set of continuous coefficients; this set corresponds to the matrix of weights in Parallel Distributed Processing models. Each arrow in Figures 2-24 and 2-25 represents a parallel process.

For example, a movement has a global qualitative aspect (probabilistic coefficients), and each step has quantitative characteristics which can be represented by a vector whose components are command of local muscular contractions (continuous coefficients).

Call trees are interactive processes with both top-down and bottom up connections between multi-modules which are subsets of cooperative cortical columns:

- In the direction of the call (top-down), all subsets are activated in parallel, with a hierarchy depending upon the goal.

- In the direction of actions (bottom up), a subset of cooperative actions is triggered, depending upon the environment.

Precise intensity of each action inside this subset depends upon specific continuous coefficients and external inputs. The combination of actions distributed over this population determines behavior.

F) Cortical neuronal activity recorded during behavioural sequences can be explained by the properties of columnar automata.

Dynamic aspects of the call trees described by this model are consistent with the experimental results that relate cortical neuronal activity and behavior:

a) Goal-directed activities.
1. Goals organize cortical activities: for example activities in motor areas are functions of the distance to the goal.
2. Many different sequences can be effected to reach a goal; the actual sequence depend upon initial conditions.
3. There is a wide variety of goals and subgoals that depend upon the past experiences.

b) Anticipation and attention.
1. A patterned call augments the response to thalamic inputs: consequently, the cortical effect of a stimulation is dependant upon the logic of ongoing behavior.
2. Patterned call corresponds to a "preparatory" activation: columns in motor areas have an anticipatory activation before triggering of a movement. In associative areas, modules activated by sensory stimuli will have an anticipatory activity for every stimulus that usually precedes this "target" stimulus.
3. "Attention" is due to a general call that is more or less selective: neuronal activation is more or less widespread.
4. The "attentive" state can correspond to an increase in neuronal excitability with no increase in activity.

c) Distributed but contrasted activity.
1. Neuronal activity is distributed over a wide set of neurons.
2. This distributed activity shows contrasted spatio-temporal patterns: several subsets are sequentially activated (probabilistic coefficients)
3. Inside each subset, there are quantitative modulations (continuous coefficients).

d) Active learning.
1. Learning is more effective during a call and therefore during an attentive state. New patterned calls that anticipate cortical actions appear after a small number of repetitions.
2. Performance of an effective motor action corresponds to a position of equilibrium (inhibition of competing modules). On the contrary, ineffectiveness produces a general call and a "cortical disequilibrium": the cortex commands several

actions, beginning with the nearest actions in the network and searching the effective ones. This disequilibrium is the main source of new learning.

3. Any strong cortical activity is a possible partial goal from which cortical automata can construct new networks. For example, in associative areas, a module intensively activated by sensory stimuli will call the actions of other modules that favor these stimuli: after learning the call network will be selectively patterned towards motor command modules whose associated movements provoke the sensory stimulation. In this case, the partial goal that organizes a motor sequence is the final sensory stimulation (to touch, for example).

CHAPTER III

Cortex within the nervous system and organization of the cortical network.

The adaptive effectiveness of the columnar automata (chapter II) depends upon the external relations of the cortex with other neural structures, and upon the internal relations between cortical areas.

We focus on the functional properties of these two networks and orient this chapter around three questions:

1. What is the place of the cortex within the nervous system?

2. What are the sensori-motor combinations favored by the network connecting cortical areas?

3. What are the functional reorganization of the cortical space produced by learning?

I. Place of the cerebral cortex within the nervous system

We place the cortical mechanism into the general context of global brain function. The cortex participates in the elaboration of behavior in cooperation with other neural structures which effect specialized operations in order to perform the main behavioral adaptations: recognition, positioning, intrinsic programs and communication.

We can sharpen our understanding of the specific nature of the cortical contribution by comparing it with other operations performed by other nervous structures which cooperate with the cortical function and condition its adaptive efficiency: the reticular formation, the thalamus, the striatum, the hippocampus and the cerebellum:

- the reticular formation generate intrinsic rhythms and command basic sensori-motor programs; furthermore, the reticular formation controls the long term rhythms of cortical functioning;

- the thalamus projects a large variety of "external" information onto the cortex; each thalamic nucleus sends specific sensory-motor information or results of processing performed by other neural structures such as the nigro-striatal system or the cerebellum.

- the nigro-striatal system can integrate cortical activities in the spatial and temporal dimensions: it favors the construction of intrinsic cortical programs;

- the hippocampus performs spatial and temporal correlations between sensory information already treated by the cortex: it contributes to cortical recognition algorithms;

- the cerebellum makes a quantitative adjustment of the motor output of the cerebral cortex. The cerebral and cerebellar cortical structures cooperate in the learning of placing movements.

These cooperative functions will be more fully studied in section IV of this chapter..

II. The network between cortical areas and its geometrical properties.

The inputs and outputs of each cortical area orient the construction of specific adaptive functions by learning. Learning capacities depends upon combinatorial possibilities that are "wired into" the cortical network.

The network between cortical areas is complex: we propose a simplified model in order to focus on its main functional properties. Following the classical schema of "cortical areas", we delimit 24 functionally homogeneous regions and we represent the interareal network from two perspectives: one places the accent upon the main information flows and the other underlines the geometric properties of this network, such as symmetries; these symmetries are functionally important because they induce isomorphic links between the different representations of the external world.

In this model, cortical regions correspond to successive dichotomies of the cortical surface; the cortical network form systematic connections between two equal parts, symmetric with respect to their border. After six dichotomies each area is linked with six other areas, in a parallel and systematic way. This global architecture is close to an hypercube with six dimensions; hypercube geometry is an optimal trade-off between the number of connections of each module and the number of intermediate relays in the pathway between any two modules of the cortical surface. In our model, every cortical zone has six standard cortico-cortical relations and the maximal number of relays between two cortical modules is also six. These six relations are stratified and inter-related locally by the columnar automaton. Furthermore, the cortical network form several parallel pathways between a sensory input and a motor output: we will see in chapter V that this organization has important properties in the context of structured learning (cognitive development, language production) that involves successive associations between different cortical areas.

We stress the combinatorial properties of the cortical network which form systematic and ordered connections between various cortical maps-- not only sensory and motor, but also a "temporal" (time) map, in the frontal cortex. A systematic "combination matrix" is formed by alternation and crossing of modular bands; this matrix considerably accelerates learning of new sensori-motor sequences.

In chapter IV, we shall focus on the behavioral consequences of the cortical architecture; in chapter V, important properties will be deduced for the cognitive development in the child.

III. Functional reorganization of the cortical space.

The columnar automata constructs new functional networks which form both parallel combinations and hierarchical sequences. This learning reorganizes the cortical anatomical space. The thalamo-cortical and cortico-cortical networks have a large redundancy and each cortical representation of a sensory-motor pattern involves a large group of minicolumns: they can register different combinations with different transmission coefficients and consequently a cortical action can participate in different sequences. New functional networks are constructed with the maximal cellular redundancy by two complementary processes:

- "Uncoupling" mechanisms (Chapter II) subdivide a cortical zone into a group of independent modules.

- "Coupling" mechanisms construct new sequences from these differentiated modules.

These two processes alternate: components of sequences can be again differentiated, since they are redundantly learned; reciprocally, differentiation creates new goals that in turn call sequences of actions.

In learning situations, the mechanism functions throughout the cortex; not only in the direct pathways but also in the "parallel" pathways formed by associative and frontal areas. In these intermediate areas, the learning space is amplified and a single sensori-motor association will be "generalized" to many similar situations; this general pattern will then be differentiated in many subsets which represent different variations of a common property.

We examine the learning capacities of the cortex from the cellular redundancy of cortical areas, maps and columns. Cortical learning is not only associative, it is also structured by the geometry of the cortical network and the successive reorganizations of the cortical space. In Chapter V we shall focus on the consequences of these cortical processes in cognitive development and language learning.

I. Place of the cerebral cortex within the nervous system.

References

The cortex is an integral part of a group of neural structures that appear together in the course of phylogeny, and become differentiated and developed in a coordinated way (Ariens-Kappers 1936, Diamond 1969, Posser 1973): reticular formation, colliculus, cerebellum, hippocampus; these neural structures receive inputs from cortical regions and send back their outputs to specific cortical areas (Crosby 1962, Brodal 1969). Each neural structure is characterized by its cellular architecture which results in a specific function.

1. General network between nervous structures

In the course of phylogeny, the nervous system undergoes transformation at the four organizational levels that guide our analysis - cellular, modular, regional and global:

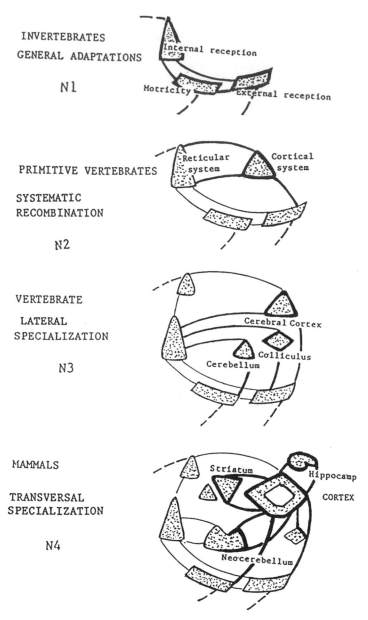

Figure 3-1 . Phylogenetic differentiation of neural structures and parallel construction of the network which links them.

1. At the cellular level ("S1"): new types of channels and receptor molecules provide new capacities to transmit and memorize basic neural information. Each cell type acquires specific functional properties: for example, new channel types can generate an oscillating mode of neuronal functioning (see chapter I) either to generate

motor programs (reticular formation), or produce short term memory (hippocampus) or block input transmission (thalamus).

2. At the modular (or columnar) level, ("S2"): new interneuronal circuits produce new operations, more appropriate for new types of sensory and motor organs: for example spatial and temporal filtering (for example in the retina), or temporal integration (for example in the vestibulo-ocular system).

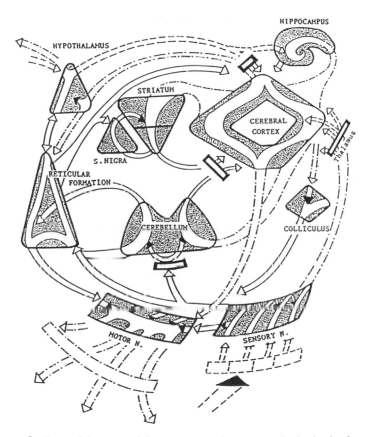

Figure 3-2 . Outlines of the network between neural structures in the brain of mammals.

3. At the regional (or regional) level ("S3"): the network that connects different parts of a neural structure (for example the network between cortical areas) effects behavioral combinations between sensory and motor activities: these combinations can be more appropriately related to the structure of the body and to the external world (for example, relation between audition and phonation). They induce new learning capacities.

4. At the general level ("S4"), each neural structure is placed in a general information flow and participates to a behavioral adaptation, such as recognition or positioning. Some structures are highly specialized for specific operations (like the

retina), while others effect all types of adaptations (like the cerebral cortex or the reticular formation).

FIGURE 3-1 illustrates the phylogenetic transformations of the nervous system in a very global way, in four successive stages (N1 to N4) in relation with new adaptive capacities. When new neural structures differentiate they form parallel alternative pathways on the circuits which perform the main behavioral adaptations: the global neural network conserves the property to effect coherent behavioral adaptations, and new structures produce new operations and new combinations.

FIGURE 3-2 illustrates the network which is the end result of the phylogenetic development depicted in Figure 3-1: it gives the outlines of the mammalian nervous

NEURAL STRUCTURE	INPUT	OPERATION	OUTPUT
SENSORY RETINA COCHLEA	VISUAL AUDITIVE	FILTERING	RETICULAR F. CORTEX
SPINAL CORD	SOMESTHESIS	RECODING POSITION INTENSITY	MUSCLES
HYPOTHALAMUS RETICULAR F.	INTERNAL SENSORY	OSCILLATORS TEMPORO-SPATIAL LEVELS	HYPOTHALAMUS MOTOR N. CORTEX
CEREBELLUM	RETICULAR VESTIBULAR CORTEX	RECODING INTENSITY	RETICULAR VESTIBULAR CORTEX
NIGROSTRIATAL	CORTEX	SLOW FILTERING	CORTEX
HIPPOCAMPUS	CORTEX	CORRELATION	CORTEX

Figure 3-3 . Functional specializations of the main neural structures which cooperate with the cerebral cortex.

system. This network is highly simplified, in order to clearly illustrate the main features of its functional architecture. This general anatomical network organizes the main information flows and coordinates the various operations of information processing performed by the different neural structures.

FIGURE 3-3 is a table that indicates, for the main neural structures shown in Figure 3-2, the origin of inputs, the specific operation effected on these inputs, and the output target.

FIGURE 3-4 is a similar table for the main cortical regions. In this case the specialized operations are constructed by columnar automata, as described in the previous chapter.

We now give an overview of the adaptive structuring of the nervous system in order to focus on the specific role of the cortical system.

A) The three main types of behavioural adaptations are first effected by specialized neural structures (N1).

Although invertebrates do not have the structural equivalent of the cerebral cortex, their nervous systems effect the principal types of information processing and behavioral adaptations (a minimal network is shown in schema N1 of Figure 3-1). We have seen in Chapter I (figure 1-8) some basic neural tissues that can produce such behavioral adaptations: recognition, positioning, intrinsic programs.

The vertebrate nervous system has such neural structures specialized for each basic behavioral adaptation:

1. Recognition is performed by a neural network that interrelates external stimuli and internal molecular reception which gives significance to them. A specialized structure is associated with each sensory modality ("sensory nuclei" in Figure 3-2): retina for vision, olfactory lobe, and cochlear nuclei for audition. These structures can perform spatial processing and feature extractions from the receptor maps (spatial filtering, contrast enhancement, etc.). For "internal" molecular reception a specific structure, the hypothalamus, translates hormonal activity into a neural activity; it can recognize (and control) fundamental programs of the organism.

2. Positioning ("move toward") is effected by coding operations in the neural network between sensory parameters (as position, size, speed of stimuli) and muscle commands:
- The spinal cord "codes" positional tactile and proprioceptive information (dorsal layers) into an "intensity" of muscle command (motor nuclei), in order to produce local somatic adaptations (spinal reflexes);
- The superior and inferior colliculi "code" visual and auditory positions into intensities of muscle commands in order to orient receptors toward stimuli;
- the vestibular nuclei "code" temporal variations of vestibular stimuli into intensities of muscle commands, in order to maintain the global equilibrium of the body.

3. Intrinsic programs (such as eating, or locomotion) are produced by neural structures that interrelate internal reception (fundamental programs) and motor nuclei.

The reticular formation (left part of Figure 3-2) commands such motor programs thanks to two properties:
- The reticular network can produce oscillations for the basic rhythms of motor patterns. Different oscillations with several temporal levels (from a minute to an entire day), are produced by different reticular nuclei using specific transmitters : Raphe nuclei with serotonin, locus coeruleus with noradrenaline, etc.

- The reticular formation link these rhythms to different spatial levels of sensory-motor activities. On the sensory side, the various regions of reticular formation effect increasingly large convergencies upon sensory inputs; on the motor side, these regions command larger and larger muscle groups: antagonistic groups, proximal and distal groups, anterior and posterior, left and right parts of the body.

B) The three main types of adaptations are also effected by a "cortical system" more efficient for learning (N2).

The reticular system performs basic adaptations in direct relation with fundamental programs represented by activities of the hypothalamus.

Around this reticular core system, the genetic program produces another network that will form the cortical system (at right in Figure 3-2). These two systems are formed like two concentric cylinders and the sensorimotor maps can be represented in parallel on these two "neural tubes". The reticular and the cortical system are on the three pathways between sensory information, internal state and motor actions, and they can effect the three major behavioral adaptations (positioning, recognition and intrinsic programs) .

But the two systems operate in a different way:

- the reticular system generates oscillations with different temporal levels and links them with various combinations of sensory and motor maps with different spatial levels;

- the cortex precisely recombines their sensorimotor information in a goal-directed manner, and columnar automata construct new adaptive functions by learning.

The two systems , reticular and cortical, are interrelated (Figure 3-2): the cortex can command reticular programs (from its frontal regions); reciprocally, the reticular formation controls the whole cortical processing, since reticular oscillators project to the cortex and command the functional modes of cortical neurons (see chapter I); these modes are responsible for states of vigilance:

- during active waking, the cortical neurons are in the "integrative mode", and columnar automata can produce adaptive mechanisms;

- during drowsiness and sleep, the neurons are in the oscillatory mode in the thalamo-cortical system, and they disconnect the cortical adaptive processing.

C) The cortical processing is generalized to all sensori-motor systems thanks to cooperative operations performed by specialized neural structures (N3, N4).

Phylogenetically, the different types of behavioral adaptations are first effected by different structures (stage N3 in Figure 3-1): the telencephalon (the primitive cerebral cortex) interrelates external and internal molecular reception (olfaction and hypothalamus), the tectum (colliculus) interrelates visual reception and the command of ocular movement; and the cerebellum links proprioceptive and vestibular inputs with motor commands.

But the cerebral cortex has two adaptive properties which are very general and independent of sensorimotor modalities: the columnar automaton that learns appropriate combinations to reach a goal, and the recursive properties of the cortical recombination network. During phylogenesis the cerebral cortex will progressively integrate all the different sensorimotor modalities to effect all types of adaptations.

The adaptive mechanisms of the cerebral cortex can be generalized to all sensorimotor modalities thanks to the parallel development of other neural structures that supplement the cortex in cooperative processing (Figures 3-1 and 3-2). For example, the thalamus effects a "regularization" of the input activity, whatever its sensory significance; consequently, the cortex can receive afferences from all the sensory organs as well as from all the other neural structures (input generalization).

Furthermore, three "cooperative" neural structures - cerebellum, striatum and hippocampus - receive information from large cortical regions, transform this cortical information and send back the result to the cortex. These supplementary operations are indispensable for effective cortical functioning:

1. The nigro-striatal system effects a slow spatio-temporal filtering of cortical activities and sends the result to the frontal regions of the cortex. This process helps for the construction of intrinsic programs that integrate information having very different spatial and temporal dimensions. The cortical adaptive mechanism can be generalized to environmental "situations" represented on several sensory modalities (universal thalamic coding), and of varying extension and duration (nigrostriatal transformations).

2. The cerebellum forms parallel pathways on motor command systems - reticular formation, vestibular nuclei and cortical network. The cerebellum performs a quantitative adjustment between sensory and motor information, as a function of proprioceptive feedbacks (olivary nucleus), in order to maintain an overall body equilibrium. Thanks to the cerebellum, the cortical mechanism becomes more efficient in the learning of placing movements.

3. The hippocampus effects correlations upon the cortical information involving fundamental programs; thanks to the hippocampus, the cortical mechanism becomes more efficient to recognize regular information in the external world.

These cooperative operations are detailed in section IV of this chapter.

2. Input-output specialization of cortical regions

The columnar automaton (Chap II) is the same in all cortical regions, but the behavioral expression of the cortical mechanism will depend upon the inputs and outputs of each cortical area; each area will learn specific adaptive functions.

The regional specialization of behavioral functions is detailed in Figure 3- 4: this table represents the main cortical regions, the origin of their main thalamic inputs and their main extracortical outputs, and in the intermediate column, their specific functions. These functions will be detailed in chapter IV. We will now stress the input-output properties of the cortical system.

CORTICAL AREA	THALAMIC NUCLEI	INPUT	OPERATION: FUNCTION	OUTPUT
LIMBIC FRONTAL	CM	HYPOTHALAMUS RETICULAR	DYNAMIC MEMORIZATION ⟶ STRUCTURED SEQUENCE	HYPOTHALAMUS RETICULAR F.
MOTOR	VL	STRIATUM CEREBELLUM	COMMAND SEQUENCES ⟶ MOUVEMENT	MOTOR NUCLEI CEREBELLUM
PARIETAL	PULVINAR	CORTEX	MATCHING TEST ⟶ POSITIONNING	CORTEX PULVINAR
TEMPORAL	PULVINAR	CORTEX	INTERNAL MATCHING ⟶ RECOGNITION	CORTEX PULVINAR
RECEPTOR	CGL CGM	VISUAL AUDITIVE	DIFFERENTIATION ACTION ⟶ RECOGNITION	COLLICULUS THALAMUS

Figure 3-4 . Functional specializations of the main cortical regions depending upon their positions on the general network.

A) Cortical outputs: the cortex can act upon all possible interactions in order to adapt the organism with its environment

Cortical outputs have a specific distribution in the three cortical dimensions:
- Connections with sensory and motor organs are specific for each cortical area ; they are specialized on the cortical lateral axes. Cortical modules act in a specific way upon a precise part of the peripheral sensory and motor organs.
- Each column have several targets depending upon the layer of the output pyramidal neuron (specialization on the cortical transversal axis). A single cortical column acts simultaneously upon several neural structures. For example, the same column of the motor area produces simultaneous actions upon the thalamus, the nigro-striatal system, the pontine nuclei, and several groups of motoneurons that command the contractions of muscles.
Cortical outputs produce parallel independent actions (on the lateral axes), but also simultaneous actions (on the transversal axis) in order to adapt the internal state of the organism to the external environment.

FIGURE 3-5 depicts in a global way this variety of cortical actions (by black arrows): the cortex controls all possible interactions between its most internal parts (the cortical system) and the external environment:
1. Control of thalamic inputs: every cortical region filters its own inputs by the cortico-thalamic connections.
2. Control of other neural processes: large areas of the cortex project to the "cooperative" neural structures: frontal regions towards the striatum, parietal regions towards the cerebellum, and the temporal region towards the hippocampus.
3. Control of sensory inputs : receptive cortical areas control the entry of sensory information, for example by orienting sensory receptors toward external stimuli (stimulus enhancement).

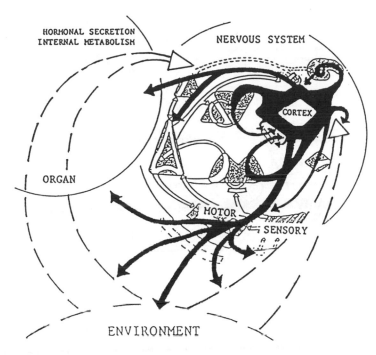

Figure 3-5 . Outputs of the cortex control all possible levels of interactions with the environment.

4. Control of the internal state: the limbic cortical area can command the secretion of peptides that in turn control activation of fundamental programs, by modulating hormonal secretion.

5. Control of positions: the motor cortex can command gamma motoneurons that regulate lengths of muscles and positions of limbs.

6. Control of distances: the cortex project toward reticular regions that command motor programs such as walking.

7. Control of the external world: the motor cortex projects on motoneurons of the hands and these commands can transform the environment.

B) Cortical inputs: thalamic afferences project a large variety of internal and external information upon the cortex.

Cortical inputs are also distributed in the three cortical dimensions:

- inputs from different cell types (reticular, thalamic, cortical) project to different cortical layers (specialization on transversal axis); thalamic inputs are restricted within layer IV.

- inputs from different thalamic nuclei project to different cortical areas (lateral partition of layer IV). Specialization of the thalamic nuclei is reproduced on the cortical areas.

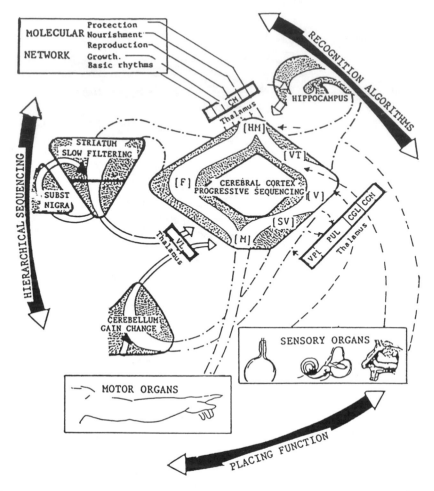

Figure 3-6 . Input-output relations of the main cortical regions correspond to the main behavioural adaptations.

FIGURE 3-5 focuses on the main information flows in the cortex (with same symbols as in Figure 3-2). This figure illustrates the lateral specialization of thalamic inputs, that represent four types of "situations" in distinct cortical areas:

1. External world: one part of the thalamic nuclei (VPL, CGM, CGL) reproduces the various external sensory maps.

2. Internal world: A second part ("CM") represents the internal molecular map of the hypothalamus, that is related to the activation state of fundamental programs.

3. Cooperative structures: A third group of thalamic nuclei represents the results of processing by "cooperative" neural structures, such as the cerebellum (part of the VL), the nigrostriatal loop (another part of the VL), the amygdala (part of the MD) and certain reticular nuclei (another part of the MD). Inputs from the cerebellum represent the possible corrective movements for a gravitational disequilibrium and inputs from

the nigro-striatal system represent the possible corrective programs for a "cortical" disequilibrium.

4. Cortex: a fourth group of thalamic nuclei (pulvinar) represents the activities of the associative cortical regions , parietal and temporal, and sends it back to the cortex.

No matter how different their significance, the different inputs enter the cortex with the same "thalamic" cellular organization. Cortical inputs, "remodeled" by the thalamus according to a common mode, represent on different areas the external and internal environments, but also the result of processing by various neural structures, including the cortex itself.

Each thalamic projection is more or less redundant (lateral extension of the thalamic axonal branching patterns). The cortical extension of these maps is directly related to their functional importance.

C) The cortex has five sensori-motor poles that form maps with intrinsic axes

FIGURE 3-7 illustrates the sensory and motor maps projected on the cortical surface.

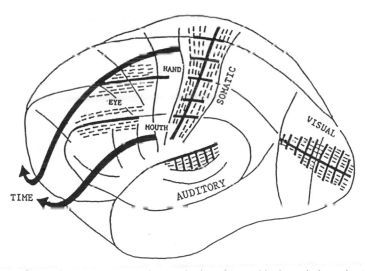

Figure 3-7 . Sensorimotor maps on the cortical surface with the relative orientations of
   their main axes.

The cortical network has five sensorimotor "poles" (auditory, visual, somatomotor, olfactory, and internal molecular); each one is a two-dimensional map whose main axes are parallel to the principal sulci (Figure 3-7):

1. The somatic map (VP and VL nuclei) represent the anterior-posterior corporal axis (motor and somesthetic) on a cortical axis parallel to the central sulcus (Rolando).

2. The visual map (thalamic nucleus CGL) represents increasingly peripheral spatial positions on a cortical axis parallel to the calcarine sulcus (in the occipital region);

3. The auditory map (thalamic nucleus CGM) represents the different auditory frequencies on a cortical axis parallel to the temporal sulcus (Sylvius).

4. The olfactory map (MD nucleus) represents the different types of molecular receptors from the outside world on a cortical axis parallel to the temporal sulcus (in the median cortical face, not shown).

5. The "internal molecular" map (CM nucleus) represents the different types of molecular receptors from the internal media on a cortical axis parallel to the cingulate sulcus (median cortical face). This area can command hormonal secretion by its projections toward the hypothalamus.

D) The frontal areas form a "time" axis

The frontal areas are arranged between the somatomotor pole and the internal "molecular" pole (limbic cortex), along a cortical antero-posterior axis oriented perpendicular to the frontal sulci. This cortical axis is shown by black arrows in Figure 3-7.

We interpret this axis as a "time" axis because the different frontal areas are connected with neural structures that have longer and longer activities as one advances along this axis from the somato-motor pole toward the "internal molecular" pole; these relations will induce increasing durations of activity in the different frontal areas ordered by this axis:

1. Activity in motor areas related to the muscle map have durations proportional to those of muscular contractions.

2. Activity in frontal areas connected with the striatum have longer durations, proportional to those of longer, repeated movements.

3. Activity in frontal areas connected to the amygdala have long durations that correspond to global behavior directed toward other organisms (move toward, move away from).

4. Finally, activity in the frontal areas that are connected to the reticular and hypothalamic nuclei have very long durations related to fundamental programs of the organism.

The second axis of the frontal region is a "sensori-motor" axis due to the cortico-cortical network: the frontal areas are connected with associative areas which have precise relations with sensory and motor maps:

1. The more medial regions of the frontal lobe are related with general motricity and somesthesia.

2. The intermediate frontal regions are related with hand movements and with vision.

3. The more lateral frontal regions are related with audition and speech.

In the next chapter (IV) we will stress the importance of these two cortical axes ("time" and "sensori-motor") for the functional properties of the frontal cortex.

II. The network between cortical areas and its geometrical properties.

1. The global architecture of the cortico-cortical network

We propose a model of the network between cortical areas: a number of functional properties will be deduced from the geometrical characteristics of this network (Chapters IV and V).

References

1. Cortical areas are defined by both their cytoarchitectonic specialization and by their relations with other neural structures (Brodmann).

2. The cortico-cortical network is characterized by precise connections which are usually reciprocal (Yakovlev 1949, Krieg 1948).

3. Furthermore, these connections are usually symmetrical with respect to the sulci and gyri of the cortical surface (Nauta 1962;Jones 1970): symmetry between left and right hemisphere; symmetry between somatosensory areas and motor areas, and symmetry between parietal and frontal areas, with respect to the central sulcus ; symmetry between parietal and temporal areas, around the Sylvian sulcus; and finally symmetry within each cortical region, with respect to the different sulci and border between areas .

A) The cortical network has geometrical and combinatorial properties

Following the classical schema of "cortical areas", we divide the cortical surface into 24 functionally homogeneous regions per hemisphere defined by their input-output connections and their cytoarchitectonic texture; within each one, the columnar automaton will construct the same type of function.

FIGURE 3-8 illustrates these different areas on the cortical surface. Theses functional regions represent not only externally visible surface areas, but also regions "folded" within the sulci. Dashed lines demarcate changes in the cyto-architecture.

To label these areas, we use a combinatorial nomenclature, that gives an idea of their respective positions on the cortical network with respect to the sensory and motor maps. TABLE 3-9 gives a plausible correspondence between these functional cortical regions defined with a combinatorial nomenclature and the areas of Brodmann. These cortical regions can be further subdivided into several "maps", for example the multiple

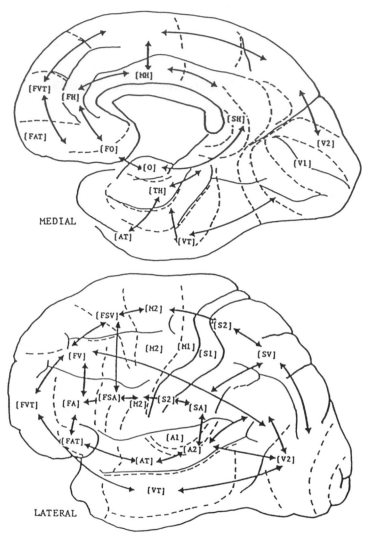

Figure 3-8 . Network between cortical areas: combinatorial properties (symbols in relation with function as in table 3-9).

maps in the "visual areas": for these maps, not shown here, we shall use the same type of combinatorial naming (for example in chapter IV).

   There are multiple connections between these main 24 functional regions, and they are also shown in Figure 3-8. In order to outline the general design of this cortico-cortical network, we propose a model that focuses on its specific geometrical properties; in next sections we shall analyze the consequences of this geometry upon functional and learning properties of the cortical system.

   The model of cortico-cortical network is illustrated in Figure 3-10 and 3-11: the main functional regions are individualized and depicted by dark rectangles; the cortico-cortical connections between areas (depicted by lines) are reciprocal and correspond to the anatomical connections shown by arrows in FIGURE 3-8; external relations with sensory and motor organs are depicted by dotted arrows.

| | RECEPTIVE ASSOCIATIVE | | MOTOR FRONTAL | |
	FUNCTIONAL AREA	BRODMANN AREA	BRODMANN AREA	FUNCTIONAL AREA
Somesthetic: receptive	S1	1,2,3	4	M1
Somesthetic: secundary	S2	5	6	M2
Somato-Visual (parietal)	SV	7	8	FSV
Visual : receptive	V1	17		
Visual : secondary	V2	18,19	9	FV
Visual : Temporal	VT	21	10	FVT
Hypothalamic reception	SH	23	24	MH
Olfactive: receptive	O	34	25	FO
Temporal : Hippocampic	TH	38	32	FH
Visual – Auditive	VA	39		
Somato-Auditive (pariet.	SA	40	44	FSA
Auditive: receptive	A1	41		
Auditive: secondary	A2	42	45	FA
Auditive: Temporal	AT	22	47	FAT

Figure 3-9 . Associative areas are named according to the sensorimotor combinations that they form, and frontal areas according to their symmetrical positions with respect to associative areas.

FIGURE 3-10 and 3-11 shows two aspects of the model: Figure 3-10 shows the "closed form" that focuses on the main information flows and the adaptive properties; Figure 3-11 shows the "open form" that focuses on the geometrical properties important for learning:

1. The model has a "closed" form, shown in Figure 3-10, that lays particular stress on the connections that favor the major types of behavioral adaptation (recognition, positioning, intrinsic programs and communication). The two rings correspond to two major sensorimotor coordinations: the outer ring represents the link between vision ([V2]) and manipulation ([M2]), and the inner ring between audition ([A2]) and phonation ([M2]); the connections between these two rings will be very important in language learning. These two rings are linked to the limbic region, that represent "fundamental programs" of the organism.

The whole circuit has a clear symmetry between the "associative" areas (right half) and the "frontal" areas (left half). The different frontal areas have privileged relations, each with an associative area: we give them a denomination from the name of this associative area (for instance, [FSV] for the frontal area in direct relation with the parietal area [SV]). The motor area ([M]) can itself be considered the frontal correspondence of the somesthetic sensory area ([S]). Furthermore the network between frontal areas is symmetrical of the network between associative areas. This model remembers that the human frontal cortex has a global surface equivalent to the whole sets of associative and receptive areas.

2. The model has an "open" form, shown in FIGURE 3-11, that puts the accent on geometrical properties of the network mostly the "symmetries" between the cortical regions and the "alternative pathways" between the sensory and motor information . We will insist on the importance of these "geometrical" features for structured learning in the child (chapter V).

The two representations ("closed form"--"open form") are two planar projections of the same three-dimensional network and are of course equivalent. The "open" network model is obtained by unfolding the two rings of the closed form, beginning at the upper pole. The two main types of external information, auditory and visual, form two symmetrical "arms" that converges toward the motor outputs. The frontal network (at left) is again symmetrical of the associative network (at right). With this representation, we can give a symmetrical aspect to the relations with the limbic regions ("medial" part of the model).

The internal organization of the frontal cortex is particularly underlined in the model. We will stress the combinatorial properties of this network, not only sensory and motor, but also "temporal", between the different representations of the external world.

B) The cortical network organizes the main sensori-motor information flows upon which columnar automata produce the main behavioural adaptations.

The cortical network (figure 3-10) form three large pathways between the motor system, the internal state and the perception of the outside world (as illustrated in Figure 3-6):

1. The parietal regions (SA,SV) interrelate the outside world (A2,V2) with the motor system (SH,MH).

2. The temporal regions (AT,VT) relate the outside world with the internal state (SH,MH).

3. The frontal regions relate the internal state and the motor system.

Columnar automata will construct on these information flows the three main types of adaptations:

a) Parietal regions: adaptations of positioning.

Parietal areas combine sensory information and muscle activities: they link somatosensory activities with visual (SV) or auditory inputs (SA).

Modules of these areas are activated by visual-somesthetic correlations, and they control, via the cortical network, motor command areas: in these areas, the columnar automaton can command movements that match two sensory activations. This process is developed to construct "positioning" functions that bring a part of the body toward an equilibrium position which is defined by a visuo-somatic sensory matching: for example, a function that guides the hand toward the visual fixation point, etc.

The cortical relation between sensory and motor information is supplemented by the quantitative adjustment of the cerebellum.

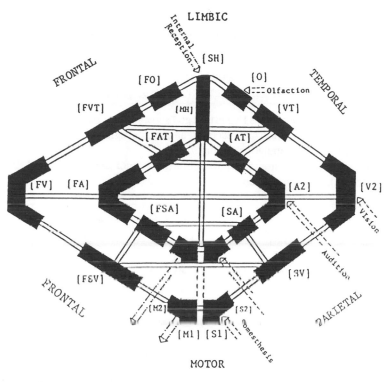

Same symbols as in Figure 3-9

Figure 3-10 . Model of the network between cortical areas: closed form.

b) Temporal and occipital areas: adaptations of recognition.

Temporal associative areas (AT,VT) combine external sensory information (A,V) and fundamental programs (internal receptors represented in the limbic area SH). We will show that modules in these areas can effect internal matching of two sensory inputs (internal exploration). In these areas, the cortical mechanism explores the regular elements of the external world which are "significant" for the fundamental programs of the organism , and then constructs recognition algorithms.

The temporal areas (AT and VT) are also related to the hippocampus that effects recognition of sensory activities separated in time.

c) Frontal areas: construction of structured sequences.

The frontal areas link fundamental programs (in the limbic area SH, MH) and motor actions (M).

Their thalamic inputs consist of slow activities (striatal filtering and reticular oscillators) , with several spatial and temporal levels. In turn, frontal modules can act on long-lasting activities, such as motor programs produced by the reticular formation. Consequently, the frontal network can produce prolonged activities which memorize transient input information.

In these frontal areas, the columnar automaton construct intrinsic programs with sequences involving several organizational and temporal levels. We will see that this capacity is important for language acquisition: the frontal mechanism can effect coding and decoding of structured symbolic sequences, such as sentences.

C) The cortical network forms privileged circuits for production and recognition of sensori-motor patterns.

The cortical network forms two privileged sensorimotor pathways:

1. A pathway between visual reception and motor regions which command hand movements forms the "manipulation circuit".

2. A pathway between auditory reception and motor areas implicated in speech production forms the "phonation circuit".

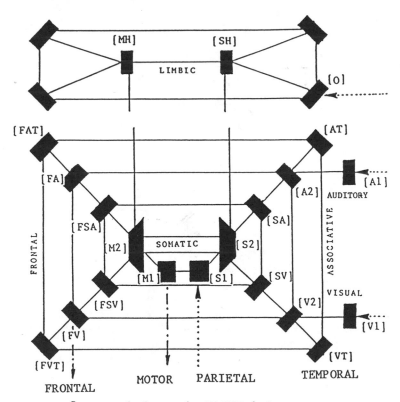

Same symbols as in FIGURE 3-9.

Figure 3-11 . Model of the network between cortical areas : open form.

These two circuits are stressed in the network model by two circles (closed form in Figure 3-10) or by two diagonal arms (open form in Figure 3-11) and they are illustrated in Figure 3-12 (lower part).

Each circuit is formed by several cortical areas which are reciprocally connected:
- in one direction, call trees can produce a motor sequence in relation with a sensory input;
- in the other direction, call trees can recognize a sensory pattern in corporal coordinates.

The two sensorimotor circuits have a symmetrical representation in the frontal region. Thanks to frontal areas, sensorimotor coordinations can include different spatial and temporal levels. We shall give several examples in the production and recognition of language (in chapter V).

Within these "privileged" sensory motor circuits, the three main types of adaptations are coupled: the cortical mechanism can construct algorithms that include recognitions in the temporal part, positioning in the parietal part, and intrinsic programs in the frontal part.

These "privileged circuits" are formed with redundant parallel connections: within intermediate "associative areas", these large redundant connections form systematic combinations between sensory and motor maps: for example a part of the body will have connections with all parts of the visual field.

D) The cortical network proposes several alternative pathways between sensory inputs and motor outputs.

In the network between cortical areas, several parallel pathways are possible between a sensory input and a motor output. Figure 3-12 (upper part) illustrates these pathways in the "open form" of the model: the cortical network form four concentric rectangles around the somato-motor regions. These four rectangles form four alternative pathways between sensory inputs and motor outputs with an ordered relation between space and time, like a system of spatial scanning; as the spaces become larger and larger in associative areas, the times become longer and longer in corresponding frontal areas (from inner to outer rectangles in Figure 3-12):

1. The somato-motor circuit: somatosensory information and muscle commands are directly linked: this connection favors direct and fast, limited reflex-like activities.

2. The parieto-frontal circuit: vision and audition are combined with body space perception in the parietal area to control a movement; symmetrical frontal regions control positioning sequences from these somatosensory combinations.

3. The receptor-frontal circuit: visual combinations are linked to frontal regions that control sequences of visual explorations.

4.The temporo-frontal circuit : larger visual (or auditory) combinations are related to fundamental programs and favour purely sensory recognition; they are linked to the most anterior frontal areas and correspond to a more global motor control.

The two subsets of cortical circuits shown in Figure 3-12 (in upper and lower diagrams respectively) connect the cortical areas in two ways like concentric circles (or rectangles) and radii (or diagonals) ; these two groupings correspond to a behavioral logic:

1. Privileged sensorimotor circuits ("convergent" circuits in the lower schema) represent natural relations between sensory and motor: for example they link audition with phonation. Each circuit organizes a cortical information flow which has a feed-back in the outside world: for example, phonation produces an auditory feed-back.

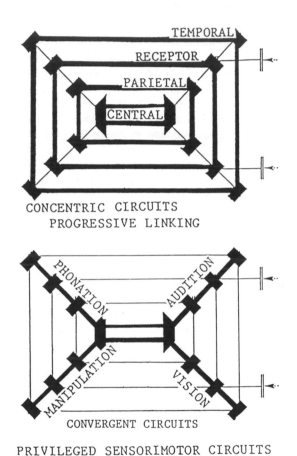

CONCENTRIC CIRCUITS
PROGRESSIVE LINKING

CONVERGENT CIRCUITS

PRIVILEGED SENSORIMOTOR CIRCUITS

Figure 3-12 . 2 complementary sets of circuits formed by the cortical network: concentric (upper) and convergent (lower).

2. Parallel alternative pathways (that form "concentric" circuits, in the upper schema) correspond to a combinatorial logic. For instance, visual and auditory information are combined with somatosensory inputs before triggering of a motor act (in the parieto-frontal circuit).

These two subsets, convergent and concentric circuits, are also illustrated in Figure 3-13, where they form the lines and columns of a table that represent the different cortical areas. We will see in chapter V that these two subsets of cortical circuits are important organizational factors which relate the different components of language in a coherent way.

| CONCENTRIC CIRCUITS PARALLEL PATHWAYS: PROGRESSIVE LINKING | | | | PRIVILEGED CIRCUITS CONVERGENT CIRCUITS |
TEMPORAL	RECEPTOR	PARIETAL	SOM.-MOTOR	
VT	V2	SV	S2m	VISION-MANIPULATION
AT	A2	SA	S2b	AUDITION-PHONATION
FAT	FA2	FSA	M2b	VISUOMOTOR EXPLORATION
FVT	FV2	FSV	M2m	SYNTACTIC ORGANIZATION

Same symbols as in Figure 3-9

Figure 3-13 . 2 complementary sets of circuits between cortical areas: each area is a node between two circuits.

E) The cortical network has four symmetries that favour transfer of learning between different sensori-motor systems.

The cortical network forms connections that are generally symmetrical about a surface feature such as a gyrus or a sulcus: these symmetries induce a functional isomorphism between circuits in the regions that are thus connected. New relations learned in a cortical region guide the construction of similar relations in the symmetrical areas. There is a rapid transfer of learning between two symmetrical regions.

There are four major symmetries in the network model presented in Figure 3-11. They are illustrated in FIGURE 3-14. Three of them correspond to the main axes of the body (internal-external, anterior-posterior, and left-right) and the fourth is the symmetry between the two main sensori-motor systems (audition- phonation and vision-manipulation).

1. Inter-hemispheric symmetry: symmetry between the left and right part of the body.

Symmetric areas of the two hemispheres are interconnected. These systematic connections produce priveleged functional relations between symmetrical parts of the body; but we shall see that this symmetry is also implicated in the symbolic "coding" of sensori-motor representations in language.

2. Anterior-posterior symmetry (around the central sulcus): symmetry between frontal and associative processing.

The symmetry between the sensory associative areas and the frontal areas results in the reproduction, in frontal cortex, of the interconnections between the associative regions: not only is each associative area related to a corresponding frontal area, but also the interconnections within the frontal area are symmetrical to the interconnections between the associative cortex. This symmetry induces an isomorphism between space (sensory associative area) and time (frontal area); it will be very important for structured learning.

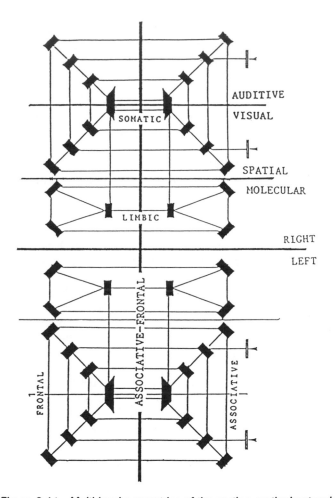

Figure 3-14 . Multi-level symmetries of the cortico-cortical network.

3. Symmetry between the medial and lateral faces of the cortex: symmetry between molecular and spatial information.

The lateral and medial faces of the cortex are symmetrically connected with respect to the superior cortical convexity.

These symmetrical connections produces functional relations between a molecular reception-action system (hypothalamic and olfactory, on the medial face) and a spatial reception-action system (visual, auditory, and somatic on the lateral face). This symmetry will give significance to sensory patterns in relation with fundamental programs: parents/children, prey/predator, sexual partners, etc..

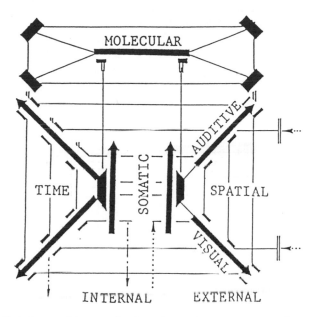

Figure 3-15   Relative positions and orientations of the main sensorimotor maps in the cortico-cortical network.

4. Symmetry between the two privileged sensorimotor circuits (manipulation and phonation).

The two privileged sensorimotor circuits are connected in a symmetrical way with respect to the Sylvian sulcus. Thanks to this symmetry, the cortical mechanism will construct, in the systematic way, algorithms that code cortical images by sequences of phonemes. We shall develop this aspect in chapter V.

The major types of representation (molecular, spatial, auditory, visual, and time), are thus systematically connected on the basis of four major axes of symmetry.

2. Hybercube geometry of the cortical network

A) Systematic connections compensate successive subdivisions of the cortical surface: every cortical zone has six standard connections with other areas.

Cortical areas are produced by cell divisions and they can be viewed as the end product of successive dichotomies of the cortical sheet. In each dichotomy, a cortical zone produces two new zones of about equal size. The main important aspect of cortical connectivity is that new connections are systematically formed between the two new cellular subsets and these connections are symmetrical about their border line: they link symmetrical columns in a parallel, systematic way.

In our model of cortical network (Figure 3-11), the whole cortical surface is subdivided in functional areas by six successive dichotomies: six sets of systematic and symmetrical connections will correspond to these six subdivisions; this fundamental relation is illustrated in the upper part of Figure 3-16. Every cortical column is linked

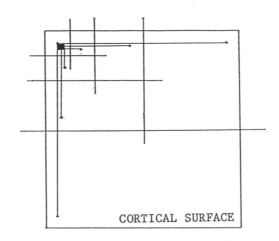

CORTICAL SURFACE

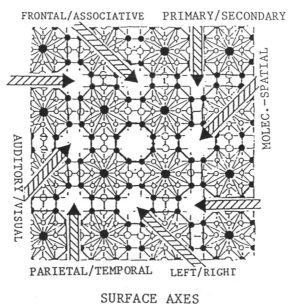

FRONTAL/ASSOCIATIVE   PRIMARY/SECONDARY

MOLEC.-SPATIAL

AUDITORY/VISUAL

PARIETAL/TEMPORAL   LEFT/RIGHT

SURFACE AXES

Figure 3-16 . Standard connections of columns (lower diagram) in correspondence with the multi-level symmetries of the cortical network (upper).

with six other columns in six other areas ; these six connected columns are symmetrical with respect to one of the six subdivisions of the cortical sheet.

Figure 3-16 (lower part) shows how these six standard connections can be integrated in the functional equivalent circuit that we proposed for the cortical column, projected on the lateral axes of the cortical surface (chap II, Figure 2-10 and 2-11). A column is a cortical zone which is depicted by the repetition of the equivalent circuit that represents a mini-column (for example , with four mini-columns in Figure 3-16); this simple cortical zone can send and receive the six standard cortical links (illustrated by arrows) with a homogeneous pattern of connectivity.

FIGURE 3-17 shows that the six standard cortico-cortical connections can subdivide the upper cortical columns (on the transversal axis): they relate the column with increasingly close areas as one goes along the transversal axis, from the deeper layer to the surface of the cortex.

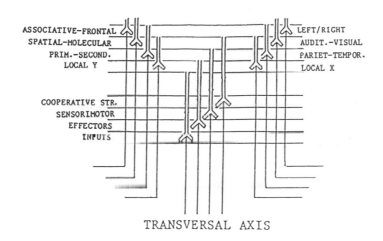

TRANSVERSAL AXIS

Figure 3-17 . Specialization of sublayers for standard connections of columns.

As illustrated in Figure 3-16 and 3-17, these standard connections can be named in the same way for all the cortical columns, whatever the cortical regions implicated. Standard connections are named by the symmetrical links that they form between two dichotomized parts of the cortical surface: the local columnar network (analyzed in chapter II) and the network between areas (analyzed in chapter III) are thus in complete correspondence:

1. left-right: contralateral connections link two symmetrical columns in the two cortical hemispheres;

2. associative-frontal: long range connections within each hemisphere link two columns symmetrical with respect to the central sulcus, one in associative and the other in the frontal pole;

3. spatial-molecular: intrahemispheric connections within each pole, link two columns symmetrical with respect to the upper convexity , one in the external face of

the cortex that processes "spatial" information and the other in the medial face with "molecular" representations;

4. visual-auditory: connections within the external face link two columns symmetrical with respect to cortical sulci, or on the privileged sensorimotor circuits that relate vision and manipulation, the other in the circuit that relate audition and phonation.

5. parietal-temporal: within each privileged sensorimotor circuits, connections link two columns symmetrical with respect to the temporal circuit, one in the parietal lobe (specialized in positioning) and the other one in the temporal lobe (specialized in recognition);

6. primary-secondary: More local connections within each lobe connect two columns, one in a sensory-motor pole (receptive or motor) and the other in a more associative areas.

The two more local sets of connections together form the privileged sensory-motor circuits, with two possible directions for the information flows: one from the somatic pole (motor or molecular) toward the "environmental" pole (receptive, visual or auditory) and the other in the reverse direction, from the environmental pole toward the somatic pole.

B) The process of construction by division-connection generates a 6-D hypercube network that optimizes communication between cortical areas.

a) The network between areas as an hypercube.

The six sets of symmetrical connections between areas are defined independently of the area connected. In the cortical network model proposed here, all the cortical areas have the same connective capacity. The six long-range cortical connections are the six basic symmetries of the cortical surface and are common to all cortical areas: they are directly linked with the dichotomies of the cortical surface. The same connectivity pattern is repeated throughout the cortical surface.

This geometry is very close to an hypercube (Burnod and Daegelen, 1988). This is due to the very simple mode of construction of the cortical network, that is successive "divisions-connections" where each division of a set in two subsets is automatically compensated by a direct connection between the two new subsets. Six successive steps form an hypercube with six dimensions: six successive dichotomies form 2 to the power 6 functional cortical areas and each area is connected with six other areas . The hypercube geometry is a very efficient structure used in parallel computers because it optimizes the communication between processors: if there are 2 to the power N nodes in the network, each one is only linked to N processors and the pathway between two nodes has a maximal length of N intermediary nodes. For the cortical hypercube with sixty-four areas, each area (and each columnar zone in the area) is only connected with six areas, and the maximal pathway to link another area is formed by six intermediate columns.

b) Standard connections of a cortical zone.

As illustrated in Figure 3-16, the repetitive pattern of columns projected on the cortical surface form a repetitive pattern of cortico-cortical connections sites; for example in Figure 3-16, four minicolumns have eight connection sites and six of them could be occupied by the six standard cortical connections; but we have also to take into account the two possible types of connections with distant columns of the same area, along the two lateral axes of the surface. This pattern with eight connections is a minimal one; the basic combination should be larger than the four minicolumns shown in Figure 3-16, and its spatial period should be closer to the size of a maxicolumn.

As illustrated in Figure 3-16 and 3-17, cortical outputs toward the other neural structures can also be viewed as standard connections (Figure 3-16) and are also organized with respect to cortical layers (Figure 3-17). Four standard output connections could represent four types of adaptive actions: command of "cooperative" structures (striatum, cerebellum, or hippocampus), command of the major sensori-motor functions (colliculus, reticular formation), direct command of muscular activity (motoneurons in the spinal cord) and command of cortical inputs (thalamus).

Thus the same standard connections, cortical and extracortical, can be repeated throughout the cortex for each cortical column, as shown in Figure 3-16, with four extracortical outputs in the lower layers, six possible long-range connections through the cortical network in the upper layers, four direct connections with the four adjacent modules, and two types of connections with distant columns in the same cortical area.

3. The cortical matrix for sensori-motor combinations

References

1. *Thalamo-cortical connections are organized in a system of "stripes" or "bands" - elongated rectangular zones oriented in the same direction. Within each band, neurons share the same functional property, the same peripheral significance:*

- In somatomotor areas, bands represent parts of the body (Woolsey 1958, Kaas 1981); representation of somesthetic units like vibrissae in the rat, have a "barrel" shape in layer IV (Woolsey 1970).

- In visual areas, cortical zones tuned for different orientations of receptor fields alternate in parallel stripes (Hubel, 1974), which are not necessarily continuous, as shown by simultaneous optical recordings of neuronal populations (Blasdel, 1986). A second system of alternating bands represents the activation of each eye (Hubel 1972,1974); these bands are about 300-500 microns wide and several millimeters long.

- In auditory areas, a similar pattern of stripes represent frequencies of sound (Imig 1978).

2. *Cortico-cortical connections, for instance between somatosensory and motor areas, are also organized in the form of bands or stripes (Jones, 1975). Inputs from ipsi- and contralateral cortical areas alternate in a regular pattern (Jones 1975). In frontal areas, inputs from intra-hemispheric connections (with limbic areas) and inter-hemispheric ones also form alternate stripes (Goldman 1977, 1981).*

3. *When two groups of inputs project to the same cortical zone, they form alternate bands; this pattern is produced by a process of active segregation (Hubel, 1974; Rakic 1981, Goldman 1981): bundles of afferent compete for post-synaptic zones*

within limited cortical layers; groupings are favoured by functional homogeneity while alternation is stabilized by balanced activation of competing axons, especially during "critical" developmental periods (Hubel 1974).

4. The bands that represent different sensory-motor features within each cortical map are often organized perpendicularly to a sulcus, for example the central sulcus for the different parts of the body (Woolsey 1958); the cortico-cortical connections are also oriented with respect to cortical sulci: they link columns which are symmetrical with respect to a sulcus and they form redundant connections on the axis parallel to this sulcus (Jones 1975).

A) Relations between cortical maps: bands of afferents alternate within a layer and cross in different layers.

1. Dimension and boundaries of cortical modules are defined by functional homogeneity of component neurons. This homogeneity is due both to the anatomical pattern of afferent axons and to the sensori-motor significance of these inputs.

Extrinsic inputs enter the cortex with the same form of thalamic projection in layer IV. During growth of the cortical network, two axonal bundles which have the same cortical target (lateral axes) and the same layer (transversal axis) are in

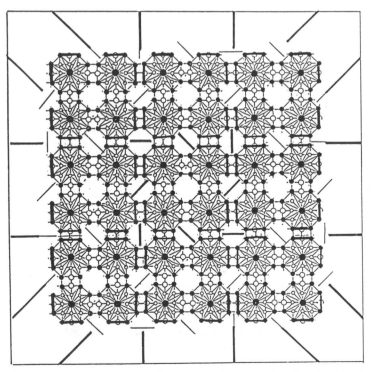

Figure 3-18 . Relative orientations and crossing of afferent bands which form standard cortical connections of columns.

competition and their connections are stabilized as a function of their functional homogeneity (coactivation): stable connections tend to follow the main axes of afferent bundles and to form alternating bands, stretching in a lateral direction. For example , in the visual area, the thalamic afferent system represents, in an alternating pattern, the two eyes within layer IV.

The cortico-cortical axons also form alternating parallel bands. However, afferences are not competitive when they arrive in different layers and they may cross with different orientation.

Thalamic and cortical afferences are organized in a double system of alternating and crossing bands : parallel and alternating bands for the afferences that arrive in the same layer, and crossed bands for afferences that arrive in different layers.

2. FIGURE 3-18 illustrates the geometry of alternating and crossed bands in relation with the standard connective pattern that was presented in Figure 3-17.

Each cortical afferent band form repetitive inputs to a set of columns aligned on a axis of the cortical surface (as shown by lines with different orientations). The six standard cortico-cortical connections with other areas form a system of crossed and alternate bands: two sets of connections can alternate in the same functional sublayer with a common orientation (as shown in Figure 3-17) and connections which arrive in different layers may have different orientations and cross within the same module in different sublayers.

This general pattern can be repeated throughout the cortical surface.

3. An afferent band formed by a thalamic or a corticocortical input has an homogeneous activity; for example this band corresponds to a part of the body in the somatomotor region, to the stimulus orientation in the visual areas, or to the frequency of a sound in the auditory areas. The functional modules will tend to group and to differentiate along these afferent lines. Crossing of afferent lines will form modular zones which are groups of columns sharing the same combinations of afferent functional properties.

B) Crossed and alternate bands of inputs form a cortical matrix with systematic combinations of sensori-motor representations.

a) Systematic combinations.

The facility to learn new sensorimotor patterns is related to the presence of already-existing anatomical connections that proposes the appropriate combinations. On the contrary, learning facility decreases markedly when several intermediate columns are necessary to form a new functional pathway. Thus, the multiplicity of connections already wired into the cortical network considerably facilitates the learning of a new behavioral sequence.

From this point of view, the cortical network has a remarkable geometry which organizes systematic combinations between two sensorimotor subsets, like a correlation matrix. This cortical "matrix" is shown in FIGURE 3-19 at the level of columns and in FIGURE 3-20 at a larger level (modular bands).

Each sensory-motor action (for example contraction of a muscle) is redundantly represented in the cortex by several columns which form a modular band; different actions of the same type (for example, muscular activation of neighboring parts of the body), are represented in parallel bands and are differentiated by reciprocal inhibitions. For example, two modular horizontal bands that command two different actions are shown in the lower part of FIGURE 3-19, separated by a continuous line that illustrates the inhibitory border.

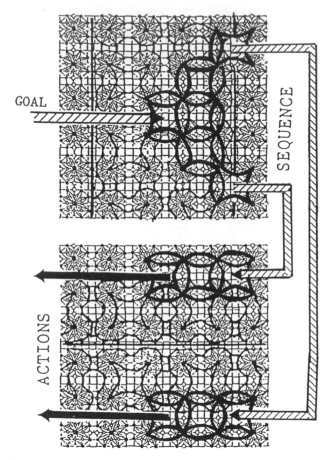

Figure 3-19 . New functional circuits which relate modular bands of columns in different cortical areas.

These bands are often oriented perpendicular to a sulcus (for instance, the somatic representations are redundant on a axis perpendicular to the central sulcus). The intrinsic axes of the cortical maps follow the orientations of the main cortical sulci. But the different cortical sulci have different orientations (as illustrated in figure 3-7) and consequently the modular bands of two specialized maps are oriented in a different way on the cortical surface. Cortico-cortical connections link cortical regions that are located symmetrically across sulci (as illustrated in Figures 3-19 and 3-20). Orientations of modular bands is conserved in the symmetrical connections across the sulci and two systems of bands from two different maps project to a common area with different orientations : consequently they form multiple crossings which represent multiple sensorimotor combinations.

For example, in Figure 3-19, the modular bands of two maps have perpendicular orientations (vertical and horizontal); cortical connections from the upper (arrows with stripes) reproduce modular bands in the target area, with similar orientations. Consequently, each afferent band from the first map crosses all the modular bands of the second map: this pattern form a "matrix" where each possible combination is represented by a modular zone formed by several minicolumns in a redundant way.

This pattern is again shown with a lower resolution a higher level in Figure 3-20 where two areas project to a common target, with symmetrical connections oriented by two perpendicular sulci; thanks to their diverging orientations, each modular band of the first map is thus linked with all the modular bands of the target map.

b) Redundancy of combinations.

Intermediate associative areas organize such matrix combinations between parts of the peripheral maps, with a large cortical surface, thus increasing the combinatorial capacities and the redundancy of each combination.

For example, within the two privileged sensorimotor circuits (vision-manipulation and audition - phonation) the parietal region organizes a systematic combination:

- each part of the the visual map can be related to each part of the muscular map that controls position of the hand in space;

- each part of the auditory map can be related with the different motor commands of the vocal apparatus.

In the same way, the temporal lobe organizes systematic combinations between the various parts of the visual map and the various parts of the internal, hypothalamic map (significance of visual forms).

In the frontal region, the two main axes, "time" and "sensorimotor" (described with Figure 3-7) form a whole set of combinations: each sensorimotor pattern can be organized at different temporal levels. Nevertheless, these two frontal axes are not perpendicular and their correlation induces a privileged relation between each sensori-motor modalities and a temporal level; for example the somatosensory system organizes briefer movements than does vision, which is in turn briefer than audition, then olfaction.

The cortical network produces a "matrix" with many available combinations and each combination is redundant ; many sequences can be constructed from the same component actions, in a parallel and non-competitive way. We saw in Chapter I that the hippocampus and the cerebellar cortex both have a matrix organization at the neuronal level; in the cerebral cortex, each combination involve a whole modular zone in a redundant way.

C) The cortical matrix favours progressive construction of call trees.

a) Call tree: continuous chaining of sensory-motor actions.

Cortico-cortical connections cross thalamic bands which are linked with closely related parts of the sensorimotor systems. Consequently, a cortical call tree can easily combine several modules that have slightly different sensori-motor significance. For example, in Figure 3-19, a call network in the upper map is depicted with accented lines for reinforced connections between cells; it combines two actions of two adjacent bands in the lower map and consequently two close sensory-motor features.

This anatomical organization favors "chaining" of successive calls to closely related sensorimotor activities. These call trees can perform continuous motor actions or continuous explorations on the parallel information flow that a rives in a cortical area. We will see in chapter IV that such explorations are efficient way for extracting stable forms during changes of visual information in the retina.

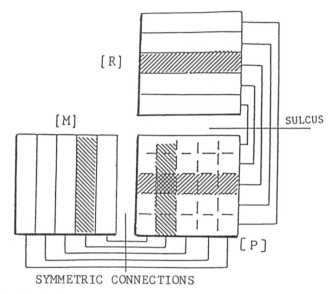

Figure 3-20 . Cortical matrix with systematic combinations formed by connections symmetrical across sulci.

b) Interrelation between successive call trees.

New call trees are first formed upon the connections between two areas, on the anatomical pattern of the cortical matrix. But each module of the call tree also forms connections with several other cortical regions (up to six, as shown in Figure 3-18). Thanks to the local repetitive pattern of cortical connections, all the functional relations that are learned between two cortical areas can be integrated within another call tree originating from any of the six other connected regions . FIGURE 3-19 (in the upper map) illustrates a functional network that call two actions in the lower map; this whole combination is then called by a connection from another cortical area..

In the last chapter, we will see that successive integration of cortical call trees by the six standard cortico-cortical connections is of major importance for development of cognitive capacities in the early childhood.

III. Functional reorganization of the cortical space.

1. Differentiation and sequences.

In the preceding chapter, we saw that the functional unit, the "cortical module", has a variable lateral extension that can change with learning. "Lateral uncouplings" reorganize the modular dimensions; they progressively subdivide the cortical space into distinct functional zones. In alternation, "transversal couplings" sequence the actions of these modules to form call trees. The new functional circuits that develop in the cortex (call trees) are constructed with maximal possible redundancy, on a maximum number of cells.

Functional rules of the cortical automaton are relatively independent of the spatial dimensions of the modular zones. But the anatomical extensions of cortical subsets are important because they determine the subsequent learning capacities.

A) Uncoupling mechanisms of columnar automata subdivide cortical zones into independent modules.

Lateral uncoupling (inhibitory reinforcement) delimit new modules, from the maxicolumn to the minicolumn level; they progressively separate the cortical space. A modular zone can be split into two half-sized modular zones, when activities in these two sub-groups have a different effect with respect to attaining a specific goal.

This process is recursive, as shown in Figure 3-21. New lateral uncouplings can again subdivide the newly-formed modules and so increasing numbers of modules can appear on the same cortical surface. At each step, the new modules multiply, but share the same total surface area.

This process can continue to the level of a small group of pyramidal cells that can be "isolated" by an inhibitory circuit: the minimal cortical output module is the "minicolumn" with a diameter of about 30 microns.

The maximum number of functional dichotomies within a cortical zone depends upon the ratio between its surface and the minicolumn dimensions (30 microns). In this perspective, the number of minicolumns in a modular zone that forms a behavioral unit represent the maximal number of call trees in which the behavioral unit can participate. These zones are more or less extended : they have the dimensions of a maxicolumn in a primary map but are extended by the redundant cortical connections in the associative areas.

The maximum number of new cortical networks is determined by the relative extensions of anatomical subsets. This capacity is discussed in Annex VI.

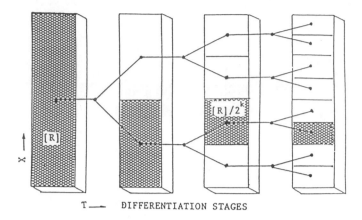

$$[R]/2^k$$

$[R]$

X

T ——— DIFFERENTIATION STAGES

Figure 3-21 . Successive functional subdivisions of a cortical zone.

The total learning capacity of each area is directly linked to its RELATIVE extension compared to the sensory and motor maps. Frontal areas in the human species has great capacities, since they occupy half of the cortical surface, as illustrated in our model (Figure 3-11). These relative dimensions condition the cognitive capacities of the child.

B) Successive subdivisions of cortical modules conserve sequences previously learned.

Sequence construction entails a three-dimensional reorganization - transversal and lateral- of the upper layers of cortical modules:
- lateral uncoupling differentiates neighboring modules in call trees.
- transversal uncoupling between layers in a column differentiates its relations with different regions of the cortical network.

This functional reorganization of the cortical space is discussed in Annex VII.

A behavioral sequence is redundantly constructed by reinforced connections within the largest possible lateral zone: this process facilitates ulterior differentiation. All the functional links which form a sequence are conserved for all the new modules which may be created by a subsequent lateral differentiation.

This property is illustrated in FIGURE 3-22. Recursive lateral uncouplings occur in parallel in two cortical areas (R and M). Constructions of new sequences between these modules are made redundantly, with the largest possible lateral extension: if one of the modules is again differentiated, each of the two newly formed modules will conserve the functional relations previously learned by the parent module.

We will see in Chapters V the importance of this process for language learning. For example, phoneme differentiation alternates in a cooperative way with construction of phonemic sequences in order to match the adult model : new phonemes (lateral uncoupling) are immediately integrated in previously acquired sequences (transversal coupling). In the same way the differentiation of grammatical categories (lateral uncoupling) conserves syntactic rules already learned (transversal coupling).

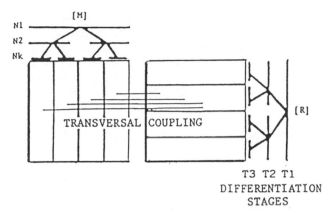

Figure 3-22 . New modules formed by functional subdivisions conserve previously-acquired transversal couplings (sequences).

C) Successive subdivisions of cortical modules produce new sub-goals which call actions that favour contrasted activities in these zones.

a) Differential activity in a modular zone.

New modules are not differentiated in an a priori and permanent way, but rather as a function of the type of behavior: several modules coexist at different spatial levels and the call determines the modular extension.

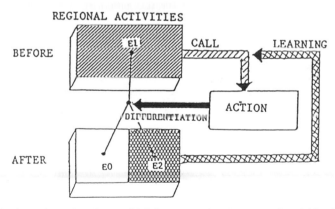

Figure 3-23 . Learning of actions which increase the contrast of activities in a cortical zone.

The cortical matrix (alternation and crossing of afferent bands) produces functional opposition within a group of cells that share a common property: for example, in the visual system, preferential perpendicular orientations oppose cells that

share a   common receptor field. This functional opposition depends upon the
environmental situation, and inside the cortex, it depends upon the goal to be attained:
for one external situation, two neighboring modules will have an opposed functioning
(contrasted activity E2-E0), while in another situation, they will have the same
functioning (similar levels E2-E2). Reinforcement of their functional opposition (E2-
E0) will be specific to each cortical "call". Thus different calls can produce different
activity patterns within a given cortical zone.

b) Differentiation actions

Each lateral subdivision reinforces a functional opposition between two
neighboring modules: one of them can be intensely active (level E2) while the adjacent
module is inhibited (level E0). Consequently each newly-differentiated module can
become the root of a call tree : its action becomes a possible goal for other modular
actions.

FIGURE 3-23 illustrates a cortical zone with two successive activities: a
moderate activity of all the cells (upper diagram:E1) or a strong activation for half of
the cells (lower diagram E2).

In the first case, when the module is activated only to the lower level (E1), it will
call those cortical actions that will favour its own reactivation at the higher level, that is
a contrasted activity with other modules until the maximal difference (E2-E0) is
reached (equilibrium position). Such cortical actions have a "differentiating" effect on
cortical activities.

FIGURE 3-24 depicts the new functional links at the columnar level (equivalent
circuit): for instance a module in a receptive area (at left) call the action of a motor
module (at right) that orients the body and amplifies the signal reception: this action
increases the lateral difference between activities of two neighboring columns in the
receptive areas.

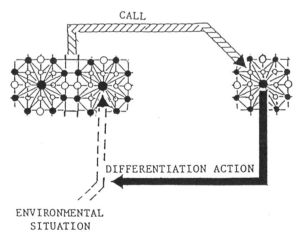

*Figure 3-24 . Call of an action which results in a contrast of activity in two adjacent
columns, by an external feedback loop.*

Thus, when a cortical zone has already been differentiated into more limited
modules, its moderate activity is an unstable state: all the active module will call a

series of actions until the goal is attained, that is a contrasted activity, with a group of modules at the higher level (E2) and all the others inhibited (E0). This stable state is reached faster thanks to the oriented calls toward effective actions that favour this contrasted activity. These "differentiation algorithms" are described with further details in Annex 7, Figure A-20 . They will be used in the process of recognition analyzed in chapter IV.

2. New bases of integrated cortical actions

A) Construction of new call trees in intermediate cortical areas produces generalization of learning.

Call trees are functional circuits between modules that can belong to different cortical areas. In general, several anatomical pathways can be used in their construction. As illustrated by the model in Figure 3-11, the cortical network forms several possible transversal pathways for identical inputs and outputs; the call tree organizes the relations between sensory and motor activities by using these various pathways, from the most direct to the most "circuitous".

The intermediate cortical areas are more than simple "relays" for transmission or processing of information. They effect new combinations : for each cortical area used in a call tree, there can be a supplementary adaptation.

a) Generalization.
In FIGURE 3-25, two areas (L and R) are directly connected; but they also have indirect connections via an intermediate associative area (M) : call trees are constructed on the direct pathway, but they will also be constructed on the parallel pathway in the intermediate area (M).

New circuits constructed by learning do not concern isolated cells, but rather involve the largest possible cell populations. In the direct pathway, the redundancy of learning is limited because of the reciprocal inhibitions between modules. But in the intermediate area new couplings can be very extensive: redundancy is amplified.

The newly-formed "coupling module" in the intermediate area not only links the sensorimotor modules whose activity is responsible for learning, but also links many others that are simply "close to" these modules. In this way, the new coupling module is activated by a variety of environmental situations similar to the learning situation. This overlap produces "generalization" of learning.

For successive associations, the dimensions of the coupling modules are greater for early stages, and then decreases with lateral inhibitions.

b) Differentiation.
The "generalized" coupling modules enhance the characteristics of a whole set of environmental situations in relation with a specific behavior. Consequently, they also enhance their differences. New differentiation will again subdivide the coupling modules; each new daughter-zone conserves the previously-acquired functional connections of the parent-zone: two circuits are formed that effect two variations of the

same adaptive process. Thanks to the large redundancy, many different variations can be successively formed on the same large functional pathway.

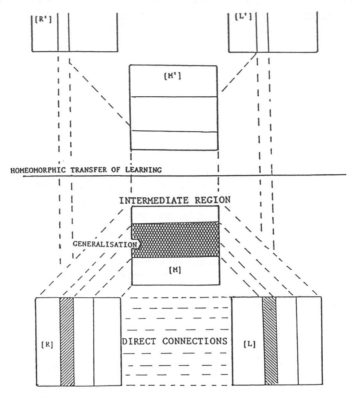

Figure 3-25 . Generalization of learning in intermediate areas and transfer of learning by symmetrical connections.

The capacity to learn multiple sequences is greatly enhanced in intermediate cortical areas: this capacity is no longer limited by the dimensions of the upper layer of sensory or motor modules, but depends upon the lateral dimensions of the intermediate "associative" area.

B) Successive associations form new sets of integrated cortical actions which are reciprocally organized in "cortical bases".

New functional relations are "amplified" in associative and frontal areas (generalization), and new call trees have reciprocal mutual inhibition within these areas (differentiation) .

The set of call trees formed in an intermediate area by the double process of generalization and differentiation has two properties:

- The call trees effect the same type of adaptation (initial, "generalized" coupling in the intermediate areas): they produce sequences of cortical actions that share a common behavioral property. They generate "integrated actions".

- These call trees are linked by reciprocal inhibitions in the intermediate associative area. Because of these reciprocal inhibitions, the new cortical "integrated actions" can themselves be combined by the columnar automaton, exactly like the elementary modular actions.

The group of new integrated cortical actions, constructed in the intermediate area, sharing a common behavioral property and linked by reciprocal inhibitions, constitute a new "base of cortical actions".

Each base of cortical actions is defined by three components:

- by its behavioral result, which is a set of similar integrated actions, for example the "words" of a language.

- by the call trees that generate these actions; they are functional networks with their reciprocal relations.

- by an anatomical substratum, which is a part of the cortico-cortical network and which includes intermediate associative and frontal cortical areas.

Bases of cortical actions integrate many new learned associations in a structured way thanks to the redundancy and the geometry of the cortical network. In the last chapter we will study the construction of several bases that form main stages of cognitive development of the child: exploratory movements, mental images, words, syntactic relations, logical operations, etc. Many bases are cultural (for instance base of "words") and are learned after exposure to relatively few examples, thanks to the rapid processes of generalization and differentiation.

C) Construction of new sets of integrated actions is a recursive process ordered by the properties of the cortical network.

Formation of new bases of cortical actions is a recursive process. The cortical mechanism can generate new combinations in two ways:

- new integrated actions can be used by any call tree to participate in new sequences;

- new integrated actions are new potential goals and can thus organize new call trees in other cortical areas.

Integrated actions of different levels are interconnected by call trees: each action is called by upper-level actions, and in turn calls lower-level actions, as a partial goal. The human capacity to assimilate several bases is intimately related to the existence of several intermediate cortical areas and alternative pathways in the cortical network: the successive associations are not competitive. Furthermore, all these integrated actions can be combined by the columnar automata, since they are subsets of elementary modular actions.

a) Symmetry and transfer of learning.
Connections between cortical areas are systematic and symmetrical. Thus, in FIGURE 3-25, areas are linked by a set of symmetrical connections. Every connection in one area has a symmetrical representation in the other area, and each new memorization in one area will reinforce a parallel memorization in the symmetrical

area. A cortical base of integrated actions established in one area guides the construction of an isomorphic base in the symmetrical region.

b) Frontal areas and assimilation of rules

Associative areas form intermediate pathways on more direct sensorimotor circuits, and frontal regions form higher-level intermediate pathways between associative regions.

Consequently, new networks in a frontal area couple "sets of integrated actions" in associative areas; the call trees between two frontal regions do not link specific sensory-motor actions, but rather link sets of actions: they form "rules" between categories. We will see, in the last chapter, the example of the assimilation of "syntactic rules" of language by call trees in the frontal regions.

c) Maturation of the cortical network and stabilization of integrated actions.

In the human species, learning is ordered by a slow maturation process of the cortical network. "Generalization" in associative and frontal areas occurs when the anatomical network continues to grow.

We have seen that the anatomical substratum gives limits to the transmission coefficients which memorize new relations: if learning occurs during neural growth, these limits will be surpassed , both in extension (new connections) and in intensity (more contacts). The cortical integrated actions learned during this period will be the roots of many new call trees.

IV. Cooperative processing
by other neural structures.

Several nervous structures cooperate with the cerebral cortex to perform a behavioral function. We will now focus on three structures that receive information from the cortex, process it and send it back to specific cortical areas: cerebellum, nigro-striatal system and hippocampus.

1. Cerebellum

References

Comparison of tissue structure and function can clarify the relative roles of cerebral and cerebellar systems in motor learning.

1. The cerebellum is connected in parallel with three systems which command movements (Eccles 1969, Oscarsson 1976):

- the vestibular system that commands equilibrium reflexes;

- the reticular system that commands basic motor programs (breathing, walking, etc..);

- the cortical system that commands voluntary goal-directed movements, and in particular precise movements of the hand.

2. The Purkinje cells in the cerebellar cortex receives two very different types of inputs (Eccles 1969):

- the climbing fibers represent a proprioceptive information from the olivary nucleus; each climbing fiber strongly and specifically influences one Purkinje cell;

- the mossy fibers represent a general information from the sensory parts of the motor command systems (for example from associative cortical areas), and project to the granule cells of the cerebellar cortex; the axons of granule cells, the parallel fibers, are perpendicular to dendritic trees of Purkinje cells and make only one synapse per target neuron; each Purkinje cell integrates the activity of a great number of granule cells.

3. From this architecture, a model of learning by the cerebellar system has been proposed (Marr 1969, Albus, 1979) and experimentally analyzed (Ito 1982): transmission coefficients between each parallel fiber and Purkinje cell can change in an associative way when the weak input from parallel fibers and the strong input from climbing fiber are coactivated. After learning, sensory information via mossy fibers can selectively modulate Purkinje cells and anticipate climbing fiber activity.

4. The Purkinje cells are inhibitory on cerebellar nuclei that project back toward the motor command systems: for instance the dentate nucleus projects (via the the thalamus VL) to the motor area of the cerebral cortex. The connections from the cerebellum to cerebral motor cortex correspond to a complete muscle map.

The cerebellar nuclei integrate activities of many Purkinje cells and their outputs quantitatively modulate motor cortex neurons that command movement (Thach 1978, Lamarre 1978, Brooks 1972).

5. The cerebellar mechanism amounts essentially to a fine adjustment of gain between sensory inputs and motor outputs, as shown in the vestibulo-ocular reflex (Ito 1978). It thus plays an important role in the quantitative determination of rapid movements in order to make anticipatory corrections before proprioceptive feedback (Thach 1978, Gilbert 1977).

The cerebellar cortex adjusts commands of muscle to maintain a global body equilibrium during goal-directed movements learned by the cerebral cortex.

FIGURE 3-26 illustrates the parallel role of cerebellar and cerebral cortex (upper part) in the learning of two correlated movements (lower part): a voluntary movement (M.A) and a compensatory movement (M.B) that corrects the disequilibrium provoked by this voluntary movement.

Neural structures which command these movements are arranged on the vertical axis, and two parts of the muscular map which are concerned are arranged on the horizontal axis ("A" and "B").

New functional links produced by learning are accented by black arrows within the two cortical structures (cerebral and cerebellar); the causal modification of behavior is also shown by a black arrow: after learning, the compensatory movement is anticipated at the onset of the voluntary movement.

Two main sensory inputs are represented by dashed lines: an information about the environmental context of the voluntary movement (O.A) and a proprioceptive information about disequilibria produced this movement (O.B).

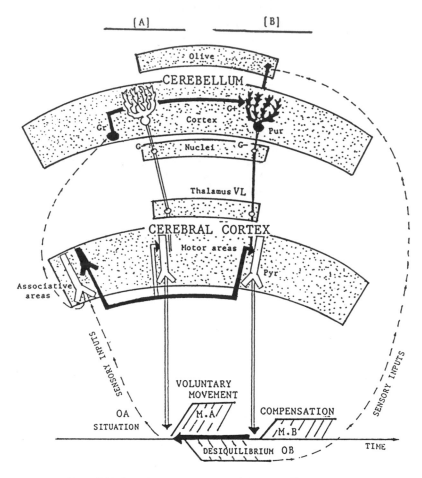

NEW FUNCTIONAL CONNECTIONS (IN BLACK)
PRODUCE DIRECT LINKING BETWEEN MOVEMENTS

Figure 3-26 . Cooperative learning of a movement by new functional links (in black) in cerebral and cerebellar cortex.

"Qualitative" learning of the voluntary movement "M.A.", is first effected by the cerebral cortex; this movement is triggered in the environmental situation "OA"; this sensory information activates the associative areas of the cerebral cortex, which in turn call the modules in motor area that command the voluntary movement "M.A".

When this "principal" movement is executed, it provokes disequilibria (measured by a proprioceptive effect O.B) that in turn trigger reflex movements for re-equilibration (compensation M.B).

In both cerebral and cerebellar cortical structures, a tissue zone "A" commands the principal movement and a zone "B" commands the compensatory contractions. Since the two muscular maps are in register, the zones "A" of the two cortical structures are interconnected, as are the two zones "B" :

- the environmental situation "OA" activates the cerebral cortex (associative area) that in turn activates the cerebellar granular ("Gr") neurons (circuit "A", at left);

- the proprioceptive disequilibrium "OB", via the olivary nucleus and the Purkinje ("Pur") neurons disinhibits the cerebellar nuclei, which in turn excites the thalamic input of the module in motor area that commands the compensatory movement (B): the "thalamic" activation of the cerebral cortex by the cerebellar system represents the appropriate muscular command for re-equilibration (circuit "B" at right).

The two sensorimotor circuits [A] (voluntary movement) and [B] (compensatory movement) are linked within each cortex by their intrinsic recombination networks; disequilibrium produces critical learning conditions in the coupling circuits between the two zones "A" and "B" within each cortex.

But the architecture of the two cortical structures are different and induce two types of learning:

1. In the cerebellum, the parallel fibers (Gr[A]) are activated by the triggering conditions of the voluntary movement, and project to the Purkinje cells (Pur[B]) which receive also climbing fibers activated by the disequilibrium "OB"; this coactivation modifies the transmission coefficient between the granular and Purkinje cells. Consequently, after learning, as soon as the conditions "OA" for a voluntary movement occurs, the granular cells will modify the firing frequency of the Purkinje cells, and the cerebellar cortex will immediately command the compensatory movement "M.B.", before the disequilibrium produced by this voluntary movement. The new functional network (granular layer [A] -Purkinje cells [B]) recognizes the sensorimotor conditions of voluntary movements before its onset (mossy fiber inputs) and anticipates the compensatory movement.

Cerebellar memorization is more continuous than in the cerebral cortex and is directly dependent upon the temporal coupling between two aspects of a movement : its triggering context (parallel fibers) and the proprioceptive consequences of the resulting disequilibrium (climbing fiber).

2. By contrast, the construction of motor sequences in the cortex is essentially goal-directed and the goal may have no natural relation with the movement since the recombination network of the cerebral cortex form recursive combinations between many motor and sensory activities which are all possible subgoals.

The modular actions which command the voluntary movement (goal A!) are such sub-goals: they selectively call the modules that command the corrective movement (actions B!) because muscular reequilibrations prior to and during the principal movement increase the efficiency of goal attainment. Furthermore, the call will be directed preferentially toward the compensatory modules ([B]) whose thalamic inputs are already activated by the cerebellar nuclei. In this way, the cerebellum "guides" cortical learning. This new functional network in the cortex anticipates compensatory movement ("M.B") before execution of the voluntary movement ("M.A").

The cerebral cortex contains several sensory and motor maps. In contrast, the Purkinje cells redundantly form a precise motor map, that converges onto the cerebellar nuclei, and then projects to the muscle map of the cerebral cortex. A large cerebellar zone can be devoted to the quantitative modulation of a single module in the motor area of the cerebral cortex. Thus, the cerebellar cortex considerably amplifies the cerebral capacities for storage of motor information.

In summary, new motor learning involves both the cerebral and the cerebellar cortical structures which both can produce anticipatory correcting movements. One might say that the two cortical structures "cooperate" in that for each type of movement triggered by the cerebral cortex, the cerebellum "proposes" precise muscular readjustments that prevent disequilibrium. The two cortical structures learn in parallel, each according to its own logic; the modifications produced by one are automatically integrated by the other, since in both cases selection occurs on the basis of the overall effect of the activity: proprioceptive reafferences for the cerebellum and goal attainment for the cerebral cortex.

2. Striatum.

References

The striatum has two parts: the putamen which receives information from the frontal cortical areas and the caudate nucleus from the limbic areas. These two structures send inhibitory projections to the pallidum and the substantia nigra : the output of this entire system is to the thalamus (VL) and to the premotor cortex (Kemp 1971).

The substantia nigra forms an internal loop with the striatum and releases the neuromodulator dopamine, that can control the transmission between cortex and striatum with a prolonged effect even after a transient activation (Llinas 1984). The nigrostriatal system plays an important role in the organization of large movements with a long time constant (Kornhuber 1974, DeLong 1974) and when they are effected in a general context even without direct sensory stimulation (Schultz, 1982, Evarts 1984).

The nigro-striatal system transforms a cortical disequilibrium into a context that drives specific motor programs.

Relations of the cerebral cortex with the nigro-striatal system are organized in the same way as those with the cerebellum; we have illustrated them in FIGURE 3-27 with a similar schema as cerebellar relations in FIGURE 3-26. The nigro-striatal system is composed of three parts, from top down in figure 3-27:

1. The substantia nigra plays an "instructive role" with respect to the striatum that is quite similar to that of the olivary nucleus with respect to the cerebellum. The substantia nigra (pars compacta) projects toward the striatum (caudate nucleus and

putamen), with a strong dopaminergic influence that can modify the cortico striatal transmission for long periods.

2. The striatum has an "informative" role similar to the cerebellar cortex. It has two inputs, one from the cerebral cortex (Glutamate G+) and the other one from the substantia nigra (dopamine). The cortical input represents a precise sensori-motor information, ([A] or [B] in Figure 3-27) and the nigral input represents a global condition.

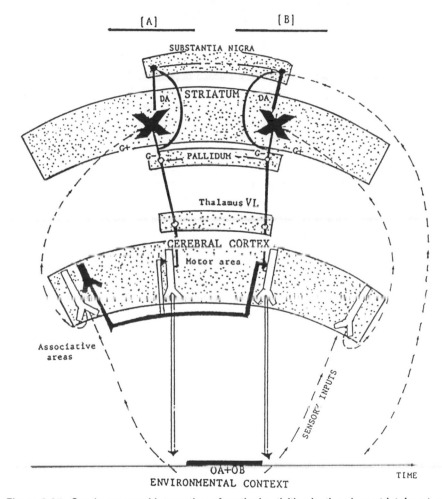

Figure 3-27 . Spatio-temporal integration of cortical activities by the nigro-striatal system.

Like Purkinje cells, the main striatal neurons have an inhibitory projection on the output structure (pallidum).

3. The pallidum is the output structure that integrates large information from the striatum and activates the thalamic input (VL) of the motor cortex ; the striatum can

ultimately modulate the output activity of the motor cortex in a way quite similar to that of the cerebellum, by a precise thalamic input. The striato-pallidal system effects a spatial integration of information that come from large cortical regions and send the result to the thalamic input (VL) of the motor cortex.

The nigrostriatal system can function in two ways, depending upon the spatio-temporal characteristics of cortical activity:

1. Phasic cortical activity: When motor cortical modules are locally active in a phasic way (for instance, during a reflex), this local excitation inhibits the pallidum and the substantia nigra ; resulting activity in the thalamus decreases and thus prevents direct reactivation of the modules in motor area.

2. Extensive cortical activation ("context"): during extensive, prolonged cortical activation (for instance, when a goal is not quickly attained), neurons of the substantia nigra are not inhibited, and consequently release dopamine. The effect is to globally decrease the cortico-striatal transmission and thus to activate the pallidum: the result is a global, sustained activation of the cortical motor area. When the cortical activity is sufficiently widespread and of sufficient duration (exploration , fundamental programs, etc), the thalamus has a prolonged activity that reactivates the cortex, and more precisely those cortical regions (frontal and motor) that command motor programs and can suppress the disequilibrium. The nigrostriatal system is important for the organization of cortical intrinsic programs which have a long time constant and integrate the activities of large cortical regions (context).

The nigrostriatal system effects spatial and temporal enhancement of widespread cortical activities; this operation is a "slow filtering" of cortical activities in both the spatial and temporal dimensions. Its result in the thalamic nucleus (VL) can be viewed as a context to perform a movement which can compensate for a general "cortical" disequilibrium.

3. Hippocampus.

References

The hippocampus receives information from the temporal regions of the cerebral cortex. This information integrates data from several sensory maps-- visual, olfactory, auditory. The hippocampus also has a privileged relation with the septum, whose activity is in turn linked to that of the hypothalamus. Hippocampal outputs return to limbic cortex via the mammillary bodies of the hypothalamus, and then via the thalamus (Papez 1937, Isaacson 1975); several complementary roles have been attributed to the hippocampus: sensory correlations (Marr, 1970), short-term memory storage and spatial orientation (O'Keefe 1978).

The hippocampus can recognize regular patterns of cortical activation.

Connections between the hippocampal system and the cerebral cortex are depicted in FIGURE 3-28, with the same arrangement as in Figures 3-26 for cerebellum and 3-27 for striatum:

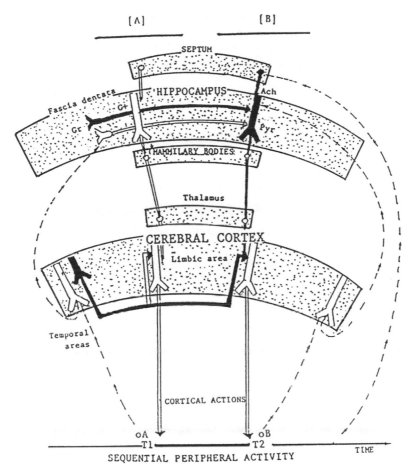

Figure 3-28 . Correlations of cortical activities by the hippocampus.

1. The septum is the "instructive structure" (similar position as olivary nuclei or substantia nigra); the septo-hippocampal pathway release acetylcholine which has a strong facilitatory effect on hippocampal neurons.

2. The hippocampus is the "informative structure" (similar position as striatum and cerebellar cortex); it has a spatial selectivity for sensory-motor information and its granular division forms a specific recombination network (as in the cerebellar cortex).

3. The mammillary bodies form the "convergent output structure" that projects back to a limited part of the cortex (limbic areas) via the thalamus (similar position as cerebellar nuclei or pallidum in the two other systems).

Thanks to the geometry of the recombination network (see figure 1-12), hippocampal pyramidal cells can integrate two successive afferent messages from the cerebral cortex: a hippocampal pyramidal neuron receives simultaneously a message "OA" produced first at an instant "T1" in temporal areas and relayed by the granular layer, and a message "OB" produced at an instant "T2" and relayed by the direct inputs from the temporal lobe. Each hippocampal cell is strongly activated for an optimal time interval (T2-T1) which is a continuous function of the cell's position on the hippocampal "spiral". Each pyramidal neuron integrates two delayed messages and its position measures the temporal interval between the two messages: this operation is very close to an autocorrelation function. Instead of producing a goal-directed recognition algorithm as does the cerebral cortex, the hippocampal system effects a correlation that detects regularities of sensory information.

For longer time intervals, oscillations of the hippocampal neurons (theta rhythm) can memorize transient information and produce overlap among successive messages. This short term memory is potentiated by cholinergic inputs from the septum; intrinsic features of sensory information ("OA.T1 - OB.T2") are memorized by hippocampal neurons when they occur during a fundamental program that activates the septal cholinergic inputs.

When the same sensory characteristics reappear in the temporal lobe, the hippocampus recognize them and activates the limbic cortex (via the mammillary bodies) in the same way that the fundamental program would.

In summary, the hippocampus recognizes sensorimotor information pertinent to fundamental programs, and reactivates the limbic cortex when similar situations occur. This recognition system is relatively independent of the nature of the stimuli, depending instead on their spatial and temporal features.

4. Thalamus.

References

1. Thalamic relay neurons have two afferences: a "peripheral" input (for instance, visual information in the optic tract) projects on the proximal dendrites, with a large number of synapses per axon, and a cortical input projects on more distal dendrites, with a small number of synapses per axon (Libermann 1983). Inhibitory interneurons form a synaptic "triad" between the peripheral input and the relay cell, frequently at the border between the two receptive dendritic regions (Szenthagothai 1970, Hadju 1974, O'Hara 1983).

2. For the pulvinar nucleus of the thalamus, linked to temporal and parietal regions, the synaptic pattern previously described (glomerular triads) is unchanged, but the "proximal" and "distal" afferences are both of cortical origin (Robson 1977, Graybiel 1981).

Cortical actions upon the thalamus adjust thalamic transmission of peripheral information toward the cortex.

FIGURE 3-29 depicts the thalamic cells in order to illustrate their integrative function on their two main inputs: strong input from the periphery (sensory stimulus "oA1", dotted), that arrive on the proximal dendrites, close to the soma, and weak cortical inputs ("cA1") that arrive on the distal dendritic tree.

The local feedforward inhibitory network (glomerular synaptic triads) is activated by sensory inputs and affects primarily the distal cortical input (due to its intermediate position in the dendritic tree): it inhibits the cortical feedback ("cA1") that immediately follows a peripheral sensory stimulation.

But the glomerular triads do not inhibit cortical inputs (cA1) that precede a sensory input (oA1); consequently, anticipatory cortical actions reinforce the transmission of sensory inputs towards the cortex. Thus the sequential order of cortical and sensory activation is important: cortical actions preceding a sensory information can amplify this information; if not, the information is simply transmitted towards the cortex without reactivation of a cortico-thalamic "loop".

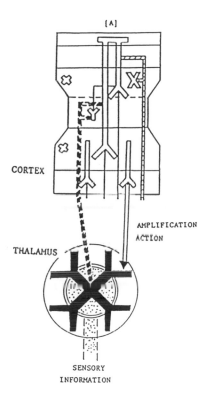

INPUTS TO THALAMUS			THALAMIC ACTIVITY
PERIPHERY oA1	followed by	CORTEX cA1	TRANSMISSION tA1=oA1
CORTEX cA1	followed by	PERIPHERY oA1	AMPLIFICATION tA1=oA1+cA1

Figure 3-29 : Selective anticipatory amplification of thalamic inputs by cortical columns.

Cortical modules can thus effect selective filtering actions upon sensory information at the thalamic level: we will see in Chapter IV that these actions participate in recognition algorithms.

In the thalamic nucleus connected to the parietal and temporal associative regions (pulvinar nucleus), strong inputs that project on proximal dendrites of relay neurons and form glomeruli, do not come from the periphery, but they come also from the cortex ; they represent a cortical activity which is processed by the pulvinar just as retinal activity by the geniculate nucleus . Consequently the cortical actions upon the pulvinar can control cortico-cortical transmission in the same way as other cortical areas can control inputs from sensory organs.

Regional specialization
of cortical function.

In Chapter IV, we will examine in detail how behavioral functions are constructed by columnar automata in each cortical region.

We focus on the three main cortical regions and the behavioral adaptations that they produce:

- What are the specific properties of parietal, temporal and frontal regions?

- How can parietal areas place the hand and the body in a predetermined final position, whatever their initial position?

- How can temporal areas recognize stable forms, although their images are changing all the time on the retina?

- How can frontal areas produce structured programs with a variable number of nested levels, like sequences of words that form sentences?

I. Specialized cortical actions

We first examine the regional variations of the cortical operation:

1. At the more global level (S4), the specific input-output connectivity of each cortical area gives the significance of the basic components of the columnar automata: "actions", "environmental situations", "goals" and "calls". We shall use the model of network analyzed in Chapter III, and we shall be guided by anatomical works and neuro-psychological studies on the behavioral consequences of damages restricted to each cortical region.

2. At the tissue level ("S3"), the internal organization of each cortical map determines the sensori-motor combinations that are most easily learned. A certain image of the world is wired into the cortical interconnections, and this primitive image serves as a nucleus for all subsequent learning. We shall use the models of the cortical maps and cortical "matrix" examined in Chapter III and we shall be guided by the experimental mapping studies in sensory and motor areas.

3. At the modular level (S2), the cortical texture (layer thickness, thalamic relations, etc) changes from one area to the next; these anatomical variations modulate the basic in-out operation of the cortical column studied in chapter II. At this level we shall use the model of "call trees" developed in chapter II and we shall be guided by experimental analysis of cell activities during stereotyped behavior. These cellular activities are due to privileged relations with peripheral maps, but also to the different cortico-cortical connections of the modules. Cell activity has a temporal pattern in relation with sensory inputs or motor outputs; but quantitative modulation during the behavioral sequence is also related to the distance from the goal; cell activity may

gradually increase (anticipation) up to the moment of the goal-action (strong activation and terminal inhibition).

II. Parietal and motor areas: positioning

In motor areas, cortical automata command movements of the hand: in our model the spatial organization of motor and somatosensory maps have an important role in a "natural" sequencing of muscle contractions of the upper limb.

In associative parietal regions, experiments have shown that columns perform a "matching test" upon two sensory activities. These associative modules will call motor actions that can match the two sensory activities and consequently they will become partial goals for muscular sequences that bring two parts of the body into contact.

We examine the construction of a parietal function which guides hand movements with respect to an object, in spite of variations in the initial position of the hand. In parietal areas, call trees combine motor commands with respect to a final goal which is a specific digital-foveal matching, and partial goals which are somesthetic/visual correlations.

In our model, the cortical function that positions the vocal apparatus for producing sounds is constructed in the same way as that which positions the hand in the visual field; partial goals are somesthetic/auditory correlations. The phonemic sequence that produces a word is constructed like any other new movement: what is particularly significant is the great combinatorial richness of the vocal apparatus which is redundantly mapped in the cortical network and the memorization capacities of the temporal lobe.

III. Visual areas: pattern recognition

Researchers have described several visual maps which are each specialized in a particular mode of processing the retinal image. In our perspective, it is important to note that primary maps can effect selective amplifications of different visual features; secondary maps related with parietal regions can effect "matching tests" between retinal images and corporal positions. In temporal areas, visual maps can correlate two distinct retinal activities. We show how call trees in secondary maps can effect an "internal translation" between two parts of the image, like eye movements that effect an external translation between two parts of the visual field; but contrary to eye movements, different internal translations can be simultaneously effected in parallel on different parts of the visual image. In the same way, internal rotations of the retinal image are also possible, thanks to the mapping of orientations in the primary map. Call trees that combine translations or rotations interrelate different features of the image, and can memorize a description of environmental patterns; in these call trees transmission coefficients register the proportions which are stable characteristics of external forms. These algorithms can recognize stable external patterns from perpetually changing retinal information. We show how construction of such algorithms generates new "recognition categories": as an example, we shall consider the progressive facial recognition by the newborn human.

IV. Frontal areas: structured sequences

Frontal cortex is important for the temporal organization of behavior and the planning of complex behavioral programs; frontal lobe has been subdivided into areas specialized by their in/out connections, for example for visuo-motor or language processing. In our perspective, specific adaptive capacities of the frontal lobe are due to two properties of the frontal network: thanks to their relations with associative areas, these frontal regions can effect several recombinations of sensory and motor information. Furthermore, frontal areas can memorize activities from associative regions at several temporal levels thanks to two complementary properties: (1) specific ionic channels in frontal neurons that can change transient inputs into continuous output (flip-flop property) , and (2) connections with other neural structures (reticular formation, striatum, amygdala) which function with a long "time constant": consequently, . Modular actions in frontal regions can be viewed as "dynamic memorizations". We show how call trees in frontal areas become specific mechanisms that can transform an branching structure into a structured sequence, in a way very similar to the "stacking" mechanisms used in computers: "call memorization" corresponds to "stacking", and "execution of a partial goal" corresponds to "unstacking". These frontal stacks can produce and recognize structured sequences of sensori-motor information with a variable number of nested levels, like sequences of words that form sentences. The number of possible levels in each stack and the number of parallel stacks are directly linked to the extension of the frontal lobe: this relation can explain the powerful capacities of the human frontal cortex.

I. Specialized cortical actions.

A) Sensory correlations in parietal areas are partial goals for muscular sequences in motor areas

a) Sensory correlations in associative regions.

In parietal regions, the columnar automaton that combines thalamic and cortical inputs becomes a "matching test" that correlates somatic and visual information.

FIGURE 4-1, at right, depicts the thalamic and cortical connectivity in the associative parietal cortex (SV). The thalamic input comes from the pulvinar nucleus, whose main afferences do not come from periphery but represent activity of these cortical associative areas: the thalamic operation described in Chapter III becomes a selective amplification of cortico-cortical relations, controlled by cortical actions.

Thus, in FIGURE 4-1 (upper part, at right), the associative module (in parietal area [SV]) receives cortical inputs from two other cortical areas (somatic [S2] and visual [V2]). It effects a temporal "matching test" which functions like a correlation between two cortical inputs (from S2 and V2): the parietal module is strongly activated only when the two cortical inputs are simultaneously active. This combination is not a simple sum, but a correlation which is amplified by the non-linear nature of the columnar operation.

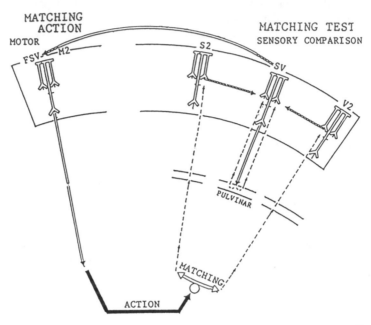

Figure 4-1 . Columns which test sensory correlations in parietal areas call matching actions which produce these correlations by an external feedback loop.

b) Matching action in motor areas.

As described in chapter II, modular action in associative areas, that is the result of a "matching test", can become a goal for other cortical actions. The network is depicted in FIGURE 4-1. The cortical associative module (in parietal area SV at right) tests the temporal correspondence between two sensory activities, somatic (from area S2) and visual (from area V2). When only one of these inputs is active, the associative module (SV) is excited only to the low level of activity (E1) ; the associative module will call, preferentially, those modules in the motor area (M2, at left) whose actions can synchronize the two sensory inputs (in S2 and V2), thus producing its strong reactivation (at the higher level E2). The called module in motor area (in M2, at left) effects a "matching action" between the two sensory information, for example by moving the hand (somatic information) toward the foveal region (visual information).

In this way, the parietal call trees organize motor actions on the basis of their sensory results. This priority is important for commanding movements: movements will have a cortical representation that relates the sequences of muscle activations to their global effect, as measured by the temporal correspondence between two sensory stimulations.

Reciprocal connections between parietal associative areas (SV that effect the tests of sensory matching) and the premotor areas (FSV and M2 that perform the matching action by means of muscular contractions) give these mechanisms a great importance in adaptations of positioning: sensory combinations are "partial goals" that organize muscular combinations. For example in the somatic associative area, modules are strongly activated by the contact between two parts of the body, for example between the fingers and the lips (matching test); this contact can become a goal. When the parietal module is persistently activated by only one of its two sensory afferences (for example the lip), it will call the cortical actions likely to effect the sensory correlation (simultaneous stimulation of fingers and lip): it will thus call selectively the modules in motor areas that command the matching movement (flexion of the arm that brings the finger toward the lip).

This model is predictive for neuronal activity which can be recorded in parietal regions during stereotyped behavior. The parietal module has a first activity just before and during the movement (call of the matching action), and next, a strong activation at the end of the movement (sensory matching test). Such activities are frequently observed in cortical associative areas (see ref. in section II).

B) Cortical actions in secondary areas can effect internal translations of sensory information

a) Simultaneous activations of a primary sensory area [V1] and actions of the secondary area [V2].

FIGURE 4-2 depicts the functional relations between the modules of the primary and secondary visual maps during simultaneous activation by a group of visual stimulations:

- Each of the primary modules corresponds to both a retinal position ("pi") and an elementary feature (for example, a preferential orientation "fi").

- Modules of the secondary area [V2] receive convergent inputs from the primary map. They are more strongly excited during coactivation of two distinct modules of the primary area: for example, in Figure 4-2, a module in the secondary map tests for coactivation of two modules in the primary map with two different positions "p0" and "p1". Its strong activation thus represents the simultaneous presence of two visual characteristics ("f0" and "f1"), on two different positions of the retinal map (p0-p1). We call "p0p1" the secondary module that tests the co-activations of two positions "p0" and "p1" in the retinal map.

b) "External" and "internal" matching: translations.

As we have seen before, modules that effect a "matching test" between two sensory stimuli learns to call specific "matching actions" that can produce their co-activation by some external feedback loop: as shown in Figure 4-2, eye movements are "matching actions" that can correlate two characteristic elements of the visual field, by placing them successively on the fovea.

The primary visual map controls eye movements by its output to the colliculus: in the colliculus a stimulus position "p1" commands an eye movement that positions the fovea on the stimulus. When a module in secondary area ("p0p1") is activated by a stimulus in position "p1" , it can call (via the primary area) an eye movement that translates the stimulus from position "p1" in the retinal map toward a new position "p0" in the foveal region. This oculomotor "matching" action is "external" to the cortical system.

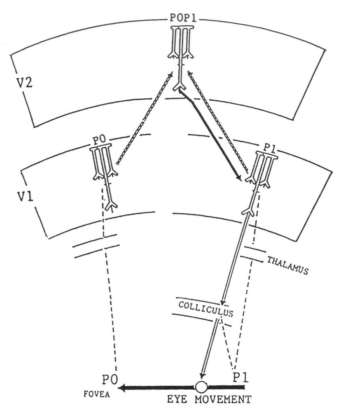

Figure 4-2 . External matching: columns in secondary areas [V2] can call eye movements which translate visual information into the fovea.

But modules of the secondary area [V2] can effect the same type of "matching" action between two activities of the sensory map, in a way "internal" to the cortex, in that there are no eye movements; in this case their actions are differential enhancements of activity in the successive visual maps on the feedforward connections.

FIGURE 4-3 illustrates these "internal matching actions" and can be compared with Figure 4-2 that illustrated the "external matching actions". The modules of the secondary map (for example "p1p2") are strongly activated when two different primary modules ("p1" and "p2") are simultaneously active. But this strong activity will also occur when there is only one primary module which is active ("p1" or "p2"), and when there is a call by another cortical module (for example a call from the secondary module "p0p1"). In this case, one of the inputs of "p1p2" is an actual information in the primary map (p2) and the other one is an expected information relative to a possible recognition.

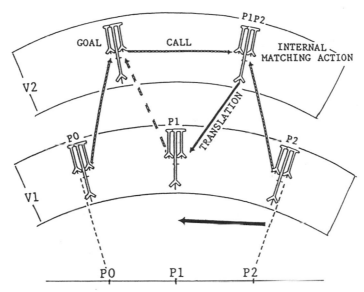

Figure 4-3 . Internal matching: columns in secondary areas can virtually translate a part of the image in order to match an expected pattern.

The strong activity in the secondary module (p1p2) evoked first by the information "p2", represents a virtual activation of the other position "p1" of the primary map. In this way, action of the secondary module "transfers" activity of an initial position "p2" toward a final position "p1" of the receptive map, as in the case of an eye movement. The action of the secondary module is similar to a virtual translation "p2 --) p1" of visual information on the retinal map. The important property is the fact that this translation is not permanent (as in any convergent system) but depends upon cortical goals and subgoals.

The spatial characteristics of these elementary translations depend upon the connectivity pattern between primary and secondary areas; there is not a point to point selectivity but rather shifts which are more or less extended, with a rough specificity in orientation and amplitude.

c) Translation sequences.

The call trees constructed in the secondary map [V2] sequence elementary translation actions, as depicted in FIGURE 4-3.

Suppose that a call tree in secondary area expects an information in the central position "p0": if this information is not present, it will call selectively another secondary module such as "p0p1" that can transfer internally an activity from position "p1" to position "p0"; if "p1" is not present, the secondary module "p0p1" directly calls another module "p1p2" which searches an information in "p2. If there is an information in "p2", the action "p2p1" is triggered and virtually translates the activity from "p2" to "p1", and then the action "p0p1" can effect a translation to the final position "p0" (goal). Any initial activity (p2) can thus be actively transferred to a final point (p0), by several intermediate links.

The learning logic of the columnar automaton construct call trees that sequence translations which have similar orientations but different amplitudes, in order to translate an information to a final central position, whatever its initial position. The function of such call trees is similar to that which commands eye movement to bring a visual stimulus in the foveal region, whatever its initial position in the retinal map.

Actions of the secondary map [V2] locally imitate eye movements. According to the connectivity pattern between primary and secondary areas, internal translations have a coarse selectivity in orientation and amplitude. There is thus a set of internal exploratory actions that correspond to a set of "fictitious" eye movements: these internal exploratory actions can, like actual eye movements, follow a moving point, the contours, or the axes of an object projected on the primary map.

But, contrary to the eye movements that change the whole retinal activity, internal translations affect only limited parts of the visual map. Many different internal translations can be effected in parallel in various parts of the retinal map: thus the secondary area can simultaneously perform a whole set of exploratory actions on the visual information flow. The functional result is much more rapid than sequential eye movements. Furthermore, the equilibrium position is not necessarily the fovea, and can be functionally redefined.

C) Long lasting activities in temporal and frontal areas represent two types of short term memory

a) "Melodic memorization" in temporal areas.

In temporal areas, successive sensory correlations are made possible by short term memory processes at the level of each cortical column. But for longer periods, activity of temporal areas can be memorized by the hippocampus in the form of repetitive reactivations.

This "oscillatory" mode of memorization is very effective to learn sequences occurring at a regular rhythm within a single time level, such as sequences of phonemes: thanks to the repetitive, regular reactivation, each phoneme of the sequence can be recombined with a phoneme previously heard.

b) Memorization with several temporal levels in frontal cortex.

In frontal regions of the cortex, the thalamic inputs come from neural structures that function with a long time constant, and form a "time axis" on the frontal pole (see chapter III): the pallidum and the substantia nigra effect a slow spatio-temporal filter of cortical activities , the reticular nuclei produces long-lasting oscillations, and the hypothalamic nuclei represent fundamental programs of the organism.

Outputs of the frontal cortex project to the input structures: striatum, reticular formation, hypothalamus. Modular actions in frontal areas reactivate input-output "loops" formed between the frontal cortex and other neural structures: these "loops" correspond to various behaviors having long time constants: integrated movements (striatum), intrinsic rhythms (reticular formation) and fundamental programs (hypothalamus).

Furthermore, direct inputs from reticular nuclei which release neuromodulators with long-lasting effects on cellular activities (dopamine, peptides) have a higher density in the frontal regions. Thalamic and reticular inputs can induce long-lasting activities in the frontal pyramidal cells.

Activities in the associative areas are transitory, since they are linked to visual, auditory, or somesthetic stimulations. But a frontal module excited by a transient input from associative areas, produces a steady continuous activity which stops when the module receives an inhibitory signal; this mechanism is similar to a flip-flop mechanism which memorizes one of two states - active or inactive. This flip-flop property may be due to two complementary properties: (1) intrinsic membrane properties such as channels which remain open in depolarized conditions; (2) network properties, such as loops with other neural structures which have long time constants. Consequently, activity of the pyramidal cells in the frontal cortex increases duration of associative information. Activities of frontal modules are "dynamic memorization" of transient information. The storage duration depends upon excitation-inhibition patterns (flip-flop) and upon extrinsic connectivity of frontal modules (with striatum , reticular formation, etc): several "temporal levels" are possible on the "time axis" of the frontal cortex and correspond to duration of a movement, a motor program, a fundamental program. These temporal levels are not fixed durations; they are rather order of magnitudes.

The input-output connections of these "loops" are not coincident within the frontal areas. If the reactivated zone lags behind the activating zone, frontal actions can re-activate different "loops", of increasing time constants. The frontal cortex can thus produce successive memorizing actions and memorize an activity "on demand" for a given duration.

Temporal and frontal areas perform two different types of dynamic memorization:
- The temporal areas favour the construction of sequences, organized upon regular basal rhythms, like phonemic sequences that form words.
- By comparison, dynamic memorization in the frontal lobes involves sequences with different "temporal levels": it is more important to produce and recognize sequences such as sentences which are sequences of words with an internal multi-level structure.

II. Parietal and motor areas : positioning.

References

A. Motor areas

a) Motor cortex commands muscular contractions via the pyramidal tract.
The motor cortex projects in an ordered way through the pyramidal tract onto various groups of motoneurons responsible for the activity of each muscle.

Phylogenetically, one can see an increase of direct projections on motoneurons that is parallel to an increase in the adaptive capacities of the hand: lesions of motor areas have increasingly dramatic effects as one mounts the phylogenetic scale, particularly on the fine movements of the hand (Phillips 1970).

b) Motor cortex output is directly controlled by somatosensory inputs.

There are various somatosensory maps, specialized according to different types of somatic reception , sequentially interconnected (Jones 1975, Darian-Smith 1984): area 3B (slow-adapting mechanoreceptors), then area 1 (fast-adapting mechanoreceptors), then area 2 (joints), then motor area 4.

c) Motor and somatosensory maps are symmetrically organized on a proximo-distal axis.

The somatosensory and motor maps extend symmetrically on each side of the central sulcus (Rolando), with a parallel somatotopic organization (Woolsey, 1950). They are interrelated by symmetrical and redundant connections (Jones 1977). The cortical dimensions for each part of the body are proportional to their functional importance (Woolsey 1950, 1958); in fact, it is possible to recognize a concentric organization in which the proximal parts are arranged around the distal parts. This organization is found in the motor area (Strick 1982, Kwan 1978) as well as the somatosensory area (Kaas 1979, McKenna 1982).

d) Neuronal activities in motor areas represent parameters of intended movements.

Activity in motor area neurons anticipates the parameters of movement, particularly regarding the intensity of muscular contraction (Evarts 1965, Fetz 1977), and the direction of movement (Georgopoulos 1984); the vectorial sum of the neuronal activities is a faithful representation of the characteristics of the movement executed. Furthermore, a large part of the neurons specifically control fine movements (Evarts, 1974).

e) Neuronal activities in motor areas depend upon the distance from the goal.

Privileged input-output relations of each module in the motor area favor cortical reflexes (Asanuma 1972, Strick 1982). But it is primarily the goal that organizes voluntary movement (Bernstein 1967): whatever the type of movement, cortical activity is dependent mostly on the difference with respect to the goal (Phillips 1977); activity of command neurons is a direct function of the distance from the equilibrium position: for example, modular activities in motor cortex compensates for perturbations of an intended movement (Evarts 1974, Fetz 1980). Cortical neurons have an anticipatory activity that precedes triggering of movement; this anticipation depends upon the instructions that indicate the type of movement to be executed (Evarts 1974, Kubota 1978).

B. Parietal areas

a) In parietal regions, neuronal activity is dependant upon correlation of somatosensory and visual inputs.

In parietal cortex, the cortical columns are strongly activated by coordinated stimulations, visual and somatosensory: for example, contact of two parts of the body, or by visual and somesthetic stimulations with parallel orientation (Hyvarinen 1973, Sakata 1975). Cells in posterior parietal area integrate information about eye position and retinal position (Andersen, 1985).

b) Parietal neurons are also active during movements that produce sensory correlations.

Neurons are active not only by coordinated stimulations, but also before the movements that provide this kind of stimulation, for instance a movement bringing two parts of the body into contact (Robinson 1975), or a projection arm movement in the surrounding space (Mountcastle, 1975). Such movements are favored by the direct connections between parietal and premotor areas (Pandya 1969, Jones, 1975).

c) Parietal lobe effect visuo-somatic coordinate transformations.

Parietal lesions produce a large deficit in the capacity to effect transformations between the corporal coordinate and the visual coordinate systems: these lesions produce a deficit in the visual guidance of the hand in space (Mountcastle 1975, Le Doux 1977).

Positioning the hand toward an object occurs after the visual fixation of this object; this movement has first a ballistic component due to a visuo-somatic calibration, and then precise regulations with sensory feedbacks; such movements adapt very quickly to changes of sensori-motor quantitative ratios, and this adaptation is generalized between articulations with a proximo-distal hierarchy (Paillard, 1975; Jeannerod, 1975) .

d) Visuo-somatic coordinate transformations are learned from visuo-somatic correlations.

In posterior parietal areas, neural responses are tuned for locations of targets on retinal axes, but this tuning is eye-position dependant: this information is sufficient to construct by learning functional circuits that would read out the position of targets in head-centered space independent of eye position (Andersen, 1987).

e) Parietal areas are important for the production and recognition of phonemes.

Verbal production and recognition are done by cortical circuits constructed between the auditory areas, the parietal areas, and the motor areas of speech (Broca 1861, Wernicke 1874, Hecaen 1983): phonemic structure is recognized by parietal areas intermediate to audition and somesthesis, and recognition of phonemic sequences is done in temporal areas connected with the hippocampus (Luria 1978; Milner 1974); semantic structure of words is recognized in associative areas intermediate between audition and vision (Wernicke area), and the syntactic structure of sentences is produced by frontal areas directly connected with speech motor areas (Broca area).

f) Cortical organization is similar for auditory and visual recognition

Processing of auditory information by the auditory cortex is very similar to that effected by the visual cortex (Miller 1974, Godstein 1982), with a spatial organization of the auditory map that is also in terms of modular bands (Imig 1978)

1. Learning of movements by motor areas

A) Modules of motor areas act on several levels of motor commands

FIGURE 4-4 depicts sensori-motor information flows in the model of cortical network developed in chapter III ("closed" form of figure 3-10): through the primary [M1] and secondary [M2] motor areas, and somatosensory areas [S1] and [S2].

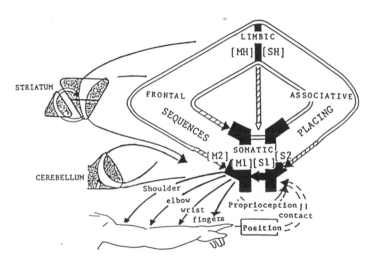

Figure 4-4 . Information flow in the cortical network: somesthetic activations are potential subgoals for muscular commands.

A modular action in the motor area produces direct activation of a group of motoneurons, with two possible effects: the cortical module can directly command a muscular contraction if it activates alpha motoneurons; it can act upon postural adjustment if it activates gamma motoneurons. These cortical modules can participate in various motor adaptations, depending upon their projections on the corporal anterior-posterior axis: they can command orientation of the body axis (if they project more anteriorly); manipulation of external objects (if they project more medially); walking toward distant targets (if they project to lower limb muscles).

Modules nearer the central sulcus act upon localized and independent muscular contractions (for instance, of the fingers), while modules of more frontal areas act rather upon motor programs of the reticular formation (for instance, walking).

Since each modular action can become a goal, all these motor commands can be partial goals; they can call preliminary movements that favour their own execution; for instance, such as postural adjustments before a large movement.

B) Thalamic inputs of motor areas represent three types of disequilibria.

Thalamic inputs to the motor cortex originate primarily in the VPL and VL thalamic nuclei; activities of these nuclei represent, for the motor cortex, three types of disequilibria in which movement becomes necessary.

1. Somatosensory inputs (thalamus VPL) represent a disequilibrium measured by the tactile or muscular receptors, for instance a perturbation in the position or the direction of a limb movement. Each somatosensory stimulus can thus activate appropriate corrective movements. This is a reflex-type situation, but one that is highly dependent upon cortical goals.

2. Inputs from the cerebellum (thalamus VL) reflect the "corporal" disequilibrium produced by a voluntary movement; cerebellar inputs represent the compensatory muscular contractions that can maintain overall corporal equilibrium (see chapter III). This compensation is learned by the cerebellum, after each new voluntary movement learned by the cerebral cortex.

3. Inputs originating in the pallidum and the substantia nigra (thalamus VL) represent a general disequilibrium that is due to an extensive cortical activation (limbic, frontal or associative) when a cortical goal cannot be immediately attained: for instance, in repetitive movements, large slow movements, or unreinforced movements (Chapter III-4). This thalamic input globally activates cortical regions that command motor programs ("walk","take") rather than a precise muscular contraction.

Representations of these three types of disequilibria are relatively separated in the motor area: cerebellar inputs (postural disequilibrium) produce thalamic activation of the primary area (precise muscular contractions); in contrast, nigrostriatal afferences (general "cortical" disequilibrium) produce thalamic activation of more frontal areas (global motor programs).

C) Direct cortical inputs to motor areas represent cortical subgoals for simple movements.

Goals organize voluntary movements. Cortical inputs to motor areas represent natural goals of motor sequences.

Motor cortex belongs to four fundamental loops of the cortical network (see models of cortical network in chapter III): these four loops correspond to four behavioral types of learning that all implicate the same fundamental mechanism at the modular level.

a) Connection with somatosensory areas: learning of the "body image".

Motor areas are directly connected to somatosensory areas. Consequently, the goal of a sequence of muscular contractions can be a tactile or proprioceptive stimulation. Modular actions of somatosensory areas are partial goals for many movements; for example, if a perturbation deviates a movement from its trajectory, somatosensory partial goals can call the compensatory motor command, which will correct the deviation and bring the movement back to the intended trajectory.

Each type of somatosensory sensation (tactile, mechanoreceptive, joint) successively orients the call toward the most effective compensatry movement, with increasingly precise muscular activations. Construction of call trees on these connections represents learning of a body image.

b) Connections with the associative regions: learning "by imitation".

The secondary motor area (M2) and the adjacent frontal areas (FSV) are directly connected to the parietal areas (SV) . Modular actions of the parietal areas, and therefore the goals of movements, are temporal correlations between somatosensory and visual stimulations. These partial goals that direct positioning movements toward visually defined stimuli and movements guided by a visual model. Consequently they favor learning by imitation.

c) Connections with limbic regions: "pavlovian conditioning".

The motor area (M2) is also connected to the limbic areas (importance of the "supplementary" motor area). This cortical connection represent long-term goals, such as execution of fundamental programs (activation of limbic areas by hypothalamic receptors). These connections favor pavlovian and operant conditioning, where goals are food rewards.

d) Connections with frontal regions: "conditional learning".

The motor area is also connected to the frontal areas that organize, over prolonged periods, structured sequences at several temporal levels (studied in detail in Chapter IV.4). Activation of frontal modules has three possible effects upon motor areas:

- Frontal modules can be long term goals that produce sustained call of successive muscular actions with a selective anticipatory activity; frontal connections favour "conditional learning".

- Frontal modules can produce "suspension" of movement execution, when a triggering condition is required; frontal connections favour "delayed learning" (Chapter II).

- Frontal modules can suppress activity in the motor areas, such as the patterns previously acquired that become irrelevant. Frontal connections permit "reversal learning" .

D) Columnar automata learn movements with an alternate process of repetition and differentiation.

FIGURE 4-5 depicts, in three stages (1-3) learning of a new movement, first by combinations of muscular contraction (1,2), and then integrating triggering conditions (3).

The diagrams illustrate the "call trees" as described in chapter II (same conventions as figures 2-24 and 2-25) with their three dimensions: the possible actions

(A,B,C,D, etc.), the distance from the goal (vertical axis) and the temporal sequence (from left to right on the horizontal axis).

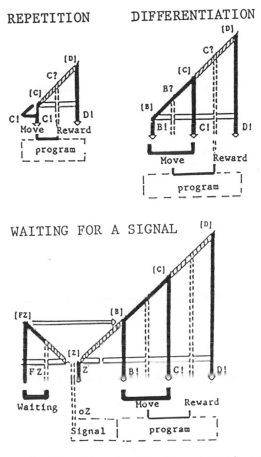

Figure 4-5 . 3 successive steps of learning of motor programs by columnar automata.

In operant conditioning (related to fundamental programs by food reward), the learning process is guided by an external program that introduces longer and longer sequences of muscular actions: D!, then C!D!, then B!C!D!, and finally A!B!C!D!: success at each stage is reinforced until a stereotyped pattern is produced; the conditioning program is then changed in order to lengthen the sequence.

In imitative learning (depending upon connections with temporo-parietal regions), the learning process is guided by the sight of a model performing the effective movement "A!B!C!D!". Disequilibrium is produced by the ineffectiveness of the movement and perception of differences with the model.

a) Repetition of movement already acquired (upper diagram 1)

New movements are obtained from natural movements of the behavioral repertoire. For example, in operant conditioning, learning occurs from a natural "food intake" movement; in the upper diagram of FIGURE 4-5 , we start from a cortical module ([D]) that commands such a natural movement. When this goal cannot be attained, the calls from this module ([D]) will first activate movements of the repertoire (for example [C]).

If the closest natural movements are ineffective, the call spreads through the motor cortex, and produces larger and larger exploratory movements. The columnar automaton learns to direct the call toward motor command modules that are effective with the global result; a module will be selectively called because its action favors a sequence that can attain the goal, whatever the output pathway of the motor cortex (motoneurons, reticular formation, or cerebellum).

A simple consequence of columnar mechanisms is the repetition of movements when cumulative effects permits goal attainment: the new movement learned ([C]) will be repetitively "auto-initiated" when a general call is issued with respect to the global goal related to reward (for instance "hunger").

b) Progressive differentiation (middle diagram).

Cortical learning is a perpetually active process; as long as a movement is not totally effective, the cortical mechanism produces, in alternation:

- repetition of the movement, since it is not immediately inhibited by attainment of the goal;

- progressive modification of the movement, because neuronal activity spreads through the cortico-cortical network (call from the goal); this extension first changes amplitude of movement (call of neighbouring modules having the same muscle target), and then the type of movement (call of more distant modules with a different muscle target).

These two phenomena create new movements:

- a call (D?) produces learning of the motor action that is closest to the goal (C!..D!)

- if the goal is not attained, persistence of the call (D?-C?), produces a repetition" of this first component (C!- C!..D!)

- cortical spread of the call (D?-C?-C?) modifies the first part of the sequence (B! - C!..D!)

- this process continues until complete adjustment of the sequence defined by the conditioning program (A!-B!-C!..D!).

At first, this learning is qualitative, determining the joints and muscles to be activated. Afterwards, learning can be more quantitative, determining the kinetic parameters of the movement. This progressive adjustment is favoured by the connections of pyramidal cells on motoneurons: one subset of pyramidal neurons has qualitative effects (spatial limits of a motoneuron group) while another subset determines quantitative parameters (force of muscular contraction or kinetic parameters for constant force).

Call trees integrate more and more cortical actions that decrease the variability of the kinetic parameters, and thus increase the precision of movement. Columnar automata in the motor cortex can learn successive muscular contractions with their relative intensities; transmission coefficients between command modules register the optimal ratio between two contractions (chapter II). Consequently it is the form of a movement (ratios of muscle contraction) and not its absolute amplitude that can be more easily memorized by cortical call trees.

c) Integration of triggering signals into a muscular sequence.

Call trees can integrate active receptions of external triggering conditions (see chapter II, figure 2-23). The lower diagram of FIGURE 4-5 illustrates such a call tree, where a signal is introduced by the conditioning program when the form of the movement (B!-C!-D!) is already learned.

Reception of the signal by a receptor module ([Z]) becomes a partial goal that favors the effectiveness of the motor sequence: since the movement is not effective without a time adjustment to the signal, the receptive module ([Z]) will in turn call modules of the frontal cortex ([FZ]) whose actions suspend the movement and favor signal reception.

Modules of motor cortex ([B]-[C]) are both called by the final goal ([A]) and inhibited by the frontal "waiting" actions ([FZ]); they arc in an attentive state (see Chapter II). When the signal occurs, the receptive module is strongly activated, it suppresses the frontal "waiting" activity (at a lower call level) and thus it reactivates (at a superior call level) the motor command modules : the that trigger the movement. Behavior thus oscillates between these two types of cortical actions: waiting (FZ) and movement (B).

When several movements are successively learned, differential instructions can selectively reinforce the call toward one of the possible movements. Increasingly complex triggering conditions necessitate the use of more and more modules in the frontal lobe.

E) Cortical somato-motor maps favour the natural and progressive sequencing of muscles of the upper limb.

a) Functional property of the whole cortical motor map.

The cortex is not the only neural structure that commands movements: the spinal cord and the reticular formation also effect motor programs integrating muscle groups on the anterior-posterior corporal axis; for example, the reticular formation can generate fundamental programs with progressive motor sequences depending upon the distance from the goal (for example, food): "eat" (jaw activation), "seize the food" (upper limb), "move toward the food" (lower limb), etc.

In the same way, the geometry of somato-motor maps in the cortex correspond to the progressive sequencing of various motor organs from the most "internal" part (mouth) toward the more "external" parts (activation of the upper limb, then the lower limbs if the goal is distant..). Cortical motor sequences are primarily learned with respect to the fundamental programs of the organism.

Motor commands occur in parallel in several neural structures: spinal cord, reticular formation, cerebellum, motor cortex. But, because of its adaptive columnar mechanism of progressive sequencing, the cortex is uniquely suited for the execution of complex sequences and the coordination of multiple, temporally dispersed sensory conditions. The cerebral cortex can learn motor sequences for goals that have very little to do with fundamental programs. The redundancy of its somatomotor map determines the number of sequences which can be learned, with larger zones devoted to the hand.

b) Functional property of the cortical map for the upper limb.

The phylogenetic evolution of pyramidal tract targets shows a growth of direct connections to "distal" motoneurons that coincides with evolution of the hand. Optimal use of the hand is under direct cortical command because positioning of the hand and fingers is accomplished by a complex set of muscular contractions; it cannot be commanded by a simple "coding" of a sensory position into a muscular intensity (often sufficient for postural orientation of the eyes or the body axis).

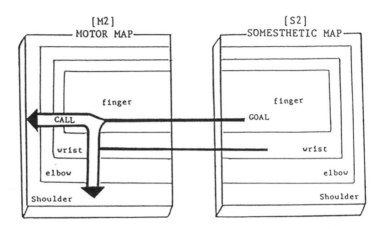

Figure 4-6 . Proximo-distal hierarchy in somato-motor maps: calls from fingers (goal) to shoulder, and muscular commands in the reverse direction.

FIGURE 4-6 depicts the motor and somatosensory maps in relation to the upper limb: the organization in modular bands is almost concentric, with the representation of the more proximal parts surrounding that of the more distal parts. Thanks to these maps, modular actions that command the finger muscles (in motor map [M]) and those that represent their sensory activation (in somesthetic map [S]) thus become "natural" goals for actions sequences of more proximal muscles. For example, if the fingers are not in contact with a target object (goal not attained), "finger" modules progressively call adjacent cortical zones: because of the geometry of the cortical map, they thus call increasingly proximal muscle contractions, producing larger and larger movements, as illustrated by the thick arrows in FIGURE 4-6. The concentric geometry of somato-motor maps favors a "natural" proximo-distal hierarchy: proximal muscles are implicated only if the goal is not attained by a more precise, limited movement with more distal muscles. progressively call adjacent cortical zones: because of the geometry of the cortical map, they thus call increasingly proximal muscle contractions, producing larger and larger movements, as illustrated by the thick arrows in FIGURE 4-

6. Because of the map's concentric geometry the proximal muscles are implicated only if the goal is not attained by a more precise, limited movement.

2. Parietal areas: visually-guided movements

A) Parietal modules which test visuo-somatic correlations call movements which can produce these correlations.

Positioning the hand relative to objects is capital for their recognition and use. This positioning is very rapid when it can be visually guided. The guiding function cannot be effected by a simple coordinate transformation between retinal positions of objects and intensities of muscular contractions.

The cortical mechanism is responsible for the progressive construction of the function that visually guides the hand toward an object. The cortical call trees are quite efficient to position a part of the body with respect to a final equilibrium point that is defined, not in an absolute way, but rather by an activity in the visual map, and with a starting position that may be quite variable.

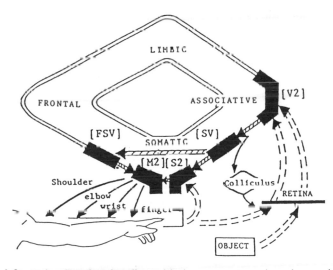

Figure 4-7 . Information flow for visually- guided movements: subgoals are visuo-somatic correlations in parietal areas.

The part of the cortico-cortical network that is used for guiding hand movements is depicted in FIGURE 4-7. This behavioral adaptation is effected in two steps:

1. Positioning visual receptors with respect to the object: the fixation point (ocular axis + convergence point) is thus placed upon the object .

2. Positioning the hand with respect to the visual fixation point: this goal is attained when the image of the hand is in the center of the fovea, at the distance of convergence, that is to say, for zero disparity between the two retinal activations.

Execution of these two positioning steps in succession brings the hand onto the object. Modules of the parietal area ([SV]) are partial goals that "test" the temporal correlations between visual and somatosensory stimuli (matching test):

- some parietal modules test correlations between the position of the stimulus in the visual field and the direction of movement toward the center of the field; they will be strongly activated by the sight of hand movement toward the visual fixation point;

- other modules test the correlations between the direction of movement in the visual field and that of proprioceptive stimulations on the corporal map; they will be strongly activated when the hand moves in a particular direction.

Furthermore, the cortical network forms direct connections between the parietal area ([SV]) where module test the sensory correlations, and motor command areas ([FSV] and [M2]) where modules can command hand movements which produce these correlations. Parietal actions (visuomotor correlations) are goals for muscle sequences that move the hand in a particular direction of the visual field.

B) Parietal maps relate visual and somatic maps from their centers to their periphery.

The various visuomotor correlations are not independent, and the parietal map can include implicit relations between retinotopy and somatotopy, as depicted in FIGURE 4-8. The curved lines illustrate the trajectory of the hand within three cortical maps (somesthetic S2, visual V2 and parietal SV) when the hand moves toward the visual fixation point.

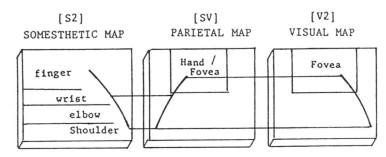

Figure 4-8 . Combinations of visual and somatic information in parietal maps organized around central positions, fingers and fovea.

During positioning of the hand toward the visual fixation point, increasing peripheral positions of the image of the hand on the retinal axes (in [V2]) implicate more and more proximal muscles of the upper limb (in [S2]); approach toward the fovea implicates increasingly distal muscles.

These natural relations can be included in the connections between the visual and somatosensory maps: connections interrelate the "central" modules of the two maps, that represent fovea and fingers. Thus, increasingly proximal muscles will be called by large peripheral positions of the image. The "central" cortical modules (fingers and fovea), are redundantly represented and consequently the sensory correlation can be more precise as the hand approaches the fixation point.

Proper hand positioning necessitates use of more and more proximal muscles for increasing distances, measured by increasing left-right disparities. This implicit relation can also be included in the connections of parietal maps with motor command modules.

C) Columnar automata construct a function that guides the hand toward a visual target, whatever its initial position

The function that brings the hand toward a target is depicted in FIGURE 4-9, by a call tree, as it was represented in Chapter II, with its three dimensions: possible actions (A,B,C,D), the sequence executed (on the horizontal axis), and the distance from the goal (on the vertical axis).

The parietal modules ([A], [B], [C], [D]) are strongly activated when the hand crosses a region of the visual field, with an orientation toward the foveal region. Each

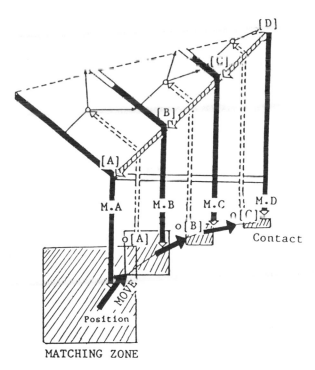

Figure 4-9 . Cortical call tree for placing movements: subgoals are visuo-somatic correlations in different matching zones.

parietal module ([A]) corresponds to a "matching zone (o[A]) within the visual field. Furthermore, parietal modules can call motor modules that command hand movement: thus, by learning, a parietal module ([A]) will precisely call that movement (M.A) that brings the hand into its "matching zone" (o[A]).

Columnar automatA construct a call tree that guides hand movements toward the visual fixation point and do so from any initial position of the hand.

1. The goal (D) is the strong activity of the modules that represent the position of the hand at the visual fixation point (foveal region with no left right disparity).

2. These modules, when they are not strongly active, call other parietal modules specialized for "matching zones" that are further and further from this central position: "C", then "B", then "A".

3. These parietal modules (SV) in turn call matching actions of the motor areas. The call spreads toward larger and larger motor actions- "M.C.", then "M.B.", then "M.A.".

4. When a "matching zone" meets the initial position of the hand (for example "o[B]"), a partial goal is attained: it inhibits lower-level partial goals (for instance, the more distant matching "o[A]"); only modules that control correlations in intermediate zones ("o[C]") closer to the fovea will continue to call motor actions.

5. The image of the hand approaches the fovea on the retinal map (and the position of zero disparity). In space, the hand approaches the object which is already at the visual fixation point.

6. The final goal, that is touching the target ("D") then inhibits further calls for hand movements.

The call tree activates larger and larger motor actions when the positions of the hand image are further and further from the fixation point: it thus effects a function in space, that brings the hand to the visual fixation point, whatever its initial position.

Learning of this function is cumulative since each correlation (hand in a visual zone) is a partial goal for the matching between hand position and visual zones closer to the fovea; the parietal map ([SV]) favors this construction.

3. Recognition and production of phonemes

FIGURE 4-10 illustrates the cortical network: the model that we proposed in chapter III stresses the privileged sensorimotor circuit between audition (area [A2]) and speech (motor area [M2]), with intermediate temporal ([AT]) and parietal areas ([SA]).

FIGURE 4-11 depicts the sensory-motor maps in these areas, in order to illustrate the combinatorial properties of the cortical network.

"Words" are sequences of "phonemes" that are themselves muscular combinations of the vocal apparatus. Words and phonemes correspond to two circuits in the cortical network:

- The structure of each phoneme is dependent upon the relation between audition and somesthesia of the vocal apparatus: each phoneme is a specific configuration of muscle contractions in the vocal tract (somatosensory activation in [S2]), guided by an auditory result (in the auditory area [A2]); phonemes are produced and recognized within the "parietal" network ([A2] - [SA] - [S2] - [M2]).

- Sequences of several phonemes that form words, are associated with a meaning, which is for instance the end result of an algorithm of visual recognition. In addition, combination of phonemes necessitates short-term memorization: consequently recognition and production of a phonemic sequence occurs especially within the temporal region ([AT]), directly related to the meanings ([VT]), and in association with hippocampal short-term memory.

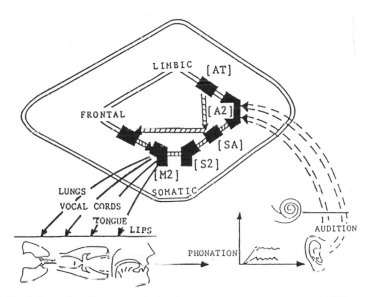

Figure 4 10 . Information flow for verbal imitation: subgoals in temporal [AT] and parietal [SA] regions.

A) The cortical function that positions the vocal tract for sound production is similar to the function that positions the hand in the visual field.

a) Auditory forms
The cochlea transforms an auditory frequency into a "position" on a neural map. The peripheral auditory system produce contrast enhancements. The primary cortical area ([A1]) amplifies the specific orientations of the stimulus, as does the primary visual area, and thus accents specific changes in sound frequency. Both characteristics of auditory information (frequency and frequency changes) are represented in the primary cortical area by parallel modular bands.

Vowels are defined by a relation between two sound frequencies, independently of the particular frequencies used; consonants are defined by a relation between two transient changes of frequency. Consequently, auditory recognition of vowels and consonants is quite similar to visual recognition of forms as discussed further in Chapter IV-3. Columnar automata construct recognition algorithms that are descriptors of auditory patterns independent of frequencies: transmission coefficients between modules of these call trees represent the ratios of two simultaneous frequencies (vowels) or two changes in frequency (consonants) independently of absolute values.

b) Consonant and vowel productions

Phonemic production is accomplished by a set of coordinated muscle commands that shape the vocal apparatus.

- Contraction of the vocal cords produces a vibration in the air flow from the lungs.

- Contraction of the mouth muscles controls the horizontal and vertical dimensions of its opening, thus giving a "form" to vowels.

- Brief contacts of two parts of the vocal tract stops the air flow and its opening produces the different types of consonants: "gutturals" by the contact of the tongue and the palate, "dentals" by the contact of the tongue and the teeth, and "labials" by the contact of the two lips.

Before learning of phonemes, spontaneous activity of the vocal tract (babbling) produces a temporal link between the contact of two parts of the vocal tract (somatic correlations in [S2]) and the muscle sequence that produces this contact (matching actions in the motor area [M2]).

Somatosensory modules which test correlations due to the contact of two parts of the speech apparatus, are partial goals for consonant production. These modules (in somato-sensory area [S2]) call muscle sequences (in motor area [M2]) that in turn produce contact between two parts of the vocal tract that results in the specific consonant.

These call trees position the tongue with respect to the vocal tract independently of its initial position. The general principle is the same as for positioning of the fingers on a part of the body. Furthermore, the cortical map of the tongue muscles can be concentrically constructed (like that of the limb muscles), with the proximal parts "surrounding" the distal parts, as illustrated in Figure 4-11 (map [S2]): the position of the distal parts is thus a subgoal for the contractions of proximal muscles of the tongue.

c) Learning of phonemic forms.

Spontaneous activity of the vocal apparatus (babbling) also introduces a relation between the sound that is heard (goal in auditory area [A2]) and the contact of two parts of the vocal tract (somatosensory area [S2]) which are partial goals for sound production (in motor area [M2]).

The parietal map ([SA]) organizes redundantly privileged relations between the somatosensory region for the vocal apparatus and the auditory sensory area, as depicted in FIGURE 4-11:

- the modules that test for changes in sound frequency (auditory area [A2]) can call somatosensory modules that test the contact of two parts of the vocal tract (in somatosensory area [S2]); the redundancy of parietal combinations is important to produce various consonants (labial, guttural, dental).

- the modules that test combinations of frequencies ([A2]) can call the mouth-muscle command modules ([S2]-[M2]); the redundancy of parietal combinations is important to produce a variety of vowels.

Thanks to partial goals in parietal and somato-sensory areas, columnar automata can construct call trees that command phonemic production upon simply hearing the sounds .

Memorization of phonemic patterns is similar to the memorization of motor patterns (described in chap IV.2) : the cortex learns a position, that is a contact between two parts of the vocal tract (consonants) and it learns the ratios of the intensities of the muscular commands (vowels).

Vowels and consonants are not produced in the same part of the muscular map; systematic connections between these two regions permit all the possible combinations of vowels and consonants.

In the same way that the cortical mechanism constructs visual guidance of hand movements with respect to the body, it constructs auditory guidance of tongue movements with respect to the vocal tract.

B) Fixed phonemic sequences (words) are learned in the temporal lobe which has a specific property of melodic memorization.

a) Cortical matrix in temporal areas and melodic memorization.

FIGURE 4-11 depicts the temporal map ([AT]) and the parietal map ([SA]). The cortical connections between these two maps form a "combination matrix", as described in chapter III (figure 3-20): each modular band of the temporal map is directly related to

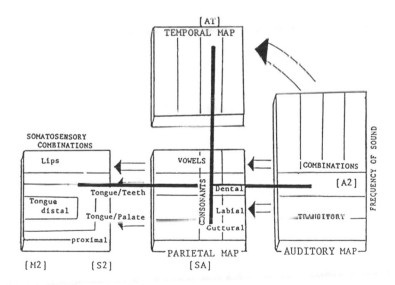

Figure 4-11 . Verbal imitation: systematic combinations of auditory and somatic information in parietal maps.

all the modules of the parietal map, each of which can produce a consonant or a vowel; this matrix facilitates the construction of various phonemic sequences in the temporal region.

Furthermore, in the temporal regions, call trees can register long sequences of phonemes, organized upon basal rhythms (see chapter IV.1). This "melodic" memorization in temporal regions is efficient in the first stages of language learning: it will later be complemented by memorization in frontal lobes, which can learn the internal structure of words.

b) Recognition and production algorithms.

FIGURE 4-12 depicts in three steps the construction of an algorithm for the recognition and production of a phonemic sequences, during initial language learning in the child. The diagrams represent "call trees", as described in Chapter II, with their three dimensions: possible actions (phonemes), the phonemic sequence executed (horizontal axis), and the distance from the goal (vertical axis).

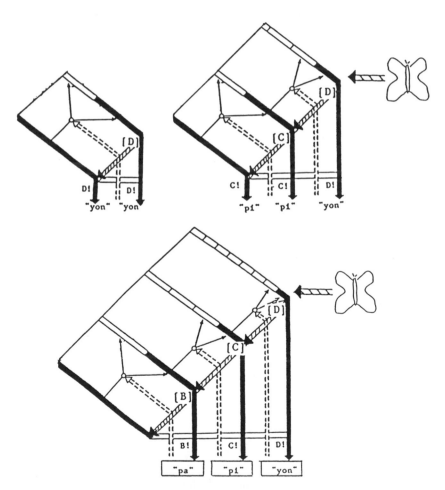

Figure 4-12 . 3 steps in the construction of call trees which produce and recognize phonemic sequences (words).

The final goal is a contrasted activity in an another cortical circuit, that gives the meaning of the phonemic sequence heard or produced: for example, this meaning is itself the result of a visual recognition algorithm (for example a butterfly in figure 4-12).

Recognition and production share common call trees : recognition uses the cortical circuit between areas [A2]-[SA]-[AT], and production uses the cortical circuit [AT]-[SA]-[M2]: somato-auditory correlations in the intermediate parietal map [SA] are partial goals both for recognition and production of phonemic sequences. But these partial goals can be attained by two different sequences of actions that will recognize or produce words:

- Actions of the recognition algorithm are internal explorations or selective amplifications that differentiates between the various possible meanings. The auditory recognition algorithm of a word, in a way, complement the visual recognition algorithm of an object and thus contributes to a fuller familiarity with the object.

- But the same partial goals are attained by muscular commands of the vocal apparatus, and this process result in production of phonemes.

c) Construction of phonemic sequences.

Learning of word production occurs in the same way as the learning of any sequence of movements, beginning with a goal (activation of a meaning) and progressively approximating the model constituted by the word that is heard; the expression of this progressive approximation will vary over languages and over words within a language, its precise form for a given word depending upon such factors as stresses, accents, familiarity of the syllable.

As illustrated in the first step of Figure 4-12, one phoneme is learned (for example D!) in relation with the meaning (goal). The difference between the word pronounced and the model heard (non-attained goal), provokes a disequilibrium . The persistence of the call lengthen the sequence, first by repetition (D!D!); the extension of the call through the cortical network produces progressive diffrentiation of the "new" phoneme pronounced, until its adjustment to the corresponding phoneme of the model (C!D!). If the disequilibrium persist the process continue (C!D! becomes C!C!D!and then B!C!D!), until complete overlap with the adult model. The word produced is thus a progressive approximation of the model heard.

This construction of phonemic sequences is especially important in the very first stages of language acquisition, to associate a symbolic sequence to an external meaning. But after this stage, learning of new sequences can include "position rules" between phonemes (prefixes, suffixes, etc.), and these hierarchical sequences implicate the frontal regions.

d) Verbal call trees.

The goal of recognition is the complete assimilation of a phonemic sequence that activates in an intense and unequivocal way a single meaning (sequence A!-B!-C!-D! in the lower diagram of figure 4-1) . As for visual recognition, this progressive differentiation is accomplished in two ways:

- Bottom-up in the direction of the auditory information flow (A!B!C!D!): each phoneme limits the set of possible meaning circuits (selection by call reinforcement).

- Top-down in the direction of the call (D?C?B?A?): the set of possible meanings at each step (limited by context and antecedent activations) selectively calls the possible continuation of the sequence: the call trees anticipate at each instant the most probable meanings of partial sequences of phonemes.

Similar call trees can produce words by commanding fixed sequences of phonemes beginning with the call by a meaning; the call occurs in the direction D?C?B?A? and the word is then pronounced in the reverse direction A!B!C!D!. Production of the complete sequence (ABCD) attains the goal, which is the maximal reactivation of the meaning.

The cortical representation of a word is much more than a simple chain of phonemes arranged in order of pronunciation; it is also a call tree constructed from a meaning. This tree represents a set of latent possibilities (at level E1), that are not competitive with ongoing actions (level E2), and that produce anticipations during recognition and increased control during production.

III. Visual areas : pattern recognition.

References

a) Recognition is both a parallel and a hierarchical multi-step process.

Vision has been described by a set of processes that transform the retinal image into successive representational stages: representation of local properties of the two dimensional image, representation of properties of visible surfaces in a viewer centered coordinate, and object-centered representation of the three dimensional structure of the viewed shape (Marr, 1982).

b) Modules in primary areas effect specific filtering actions on the visual image.

The successive stages of the visual system amplify specific characteristics of visual information: for example the retina first enhances contrasts and transmits information via three types of ganglion neurons ("X", "Y", "W"), each having specific dynamic properties (Stone 1973, Ennoth-Cuggel 1983).

The thalamus (lateral geniculate body), relays the retinal activity toward the cortex. The primary visual area selectively enhances orientations (Hubel 1972, 1977) and processes differential activation of the two eyes (Hubel 1972, Poggio 1977), that is the basis for stereoscopic recognition in three-dimensional space (Poggio 1984).

The primary visual area has direct outputs that control the reception of the visual image:

- pyramidal neurons of layer VI control the transmission of retinal information at the thalamic level (Creutzfeld 1971);

- pyramidal neurons of layer V project to the superior colliculus that commands ocular positioning; collicular neurons are activated by the position of the stimulus in the visual field (sensory aspect), and command the ocular movement oriented toward this position (motor aspect) (Robinson 1975).

c) Recognition uses multiple representations in different cortical maps which form three main pathways: temporal areas for pattern recognition, parietal areas for visually-guided positioning and frontal areas for exploration programs.

Several "visual maps" with specific functional characteristics are organized in a connective sequence as defined by "feedforward" and "feedback" connections (Zeki 1978, Van Essen 1979, Cowey 1981). Maps and cortico-cortical connections form two main functional pathways : a parietal pathway which analyzes positions (where? or where to go?) and a temporal pathway which recognizes forms (what?) (Ungerleider, 1986). For example the parietal pathway is formed by maps like "V3" where the neurons are specialized in the recognition of movements in three-dimensional space, and "VIP" related to eye movements, and is linked with somato-motor maps (area 5 and 6). The temporal pathway is formed by maps like "V4" specialized with colour discrimination and "STS" or "IT" where neurons have invariant properties for face recognition (Gross 1972, Rolls 1982) and this pathway is linked with the hippocampus and limbic regions (significance of forms which are important for the organism). Several maps, such as "MT", where the neurons are selective for directions, have intermediate positions toward the two main pathways, parietal and temporal ; parieto-temporal links favour recognition of structure from motion (Perret, 1987).

d) Recognition is both parallel and sequential with successive internal transformations of the image.

Recognition is both a parallel and a sequential processing: parallel for local forms and sequential for more global forms, for example via successive eye movements (Julesz 1984). In sequential processing, the time required to recognize a form is directly related to the extent of transformations involved in order to match a standard pattern previously learned; for example the time before recognition is proportional to an angle of rotation (Kosslyn, 1980; Shepard, 1984).

Mental representation of an external object may be local (Barlow 1972) but more generally, this representation can be distributed over a group of neurons by "synaptic weights" that change with learning and store patterns which are repeatedly presented to the network (Kohonen, 1977; Hinton 1981). Distributed representations have very interesting properties similar to biological recognition processes such as completion of novel patterns, content addressability, resistance to noise and degradation, and spontaneous generalization (Rumelhart 1986).

e) Invariant recognition is an adaptive process using a variety of methods.

Algorithms that have been developed for invariant recognition of forms use highly-varied methods: parametric, correlative, structural, and syntactic (Simon 1981)

The problem of invariant recognition of forms was tackled by parallel processes like combination of perceptrons (Fukushima 1980), but adaptive process are more efficient such as correlations of unit activities based on a rapidly-changing synaptic plasticity (Von der Malsburg 1981, Bienenstock 1985).

Invariant recognition of faces was analyzed in temporal areas (Rolls, 82; Perret, 87): cells respond to a face despite changes in position within very large receptive fields , changes in viewing distance and changes in face orientation. While cell responses generalize to unusual views, they are often slightly decreased in magnitude and increased in latency.

This recognition is based on several encoding processes that proceed in parallel.
For example many cells are responsive to part of the face, and particularly to the eyes.
For other cells, maximal response requires a normal arrangement of features in the
face. Some cells are strongly responsive for different perspective views of the head (full
face, profile etc). Other cells are more sensitive to identity and respond more to one
individual than to others, whatever the perspective view.

1. Specialized visual maps

FIGURE 4-13 depicts the visual information flow in the cortical network. The
primary visual area receive information processed by the retina and the thalamus. The
retina amplifies spatiotemporal characteristics of visual signals like contrasts. The "X"
and "Y" ganglion neurons independently transmit two spatio-temporal levels of retinal
activity to lateral geniculate body of the thalamus and the corresponding thalamic
neurons project to different sublayers within the fourth layer of the primary visual area
[V1] (area 17). The cortical network inter-relates this receptive pole with the secondary
visual area [V2] (areas 18 and 19).

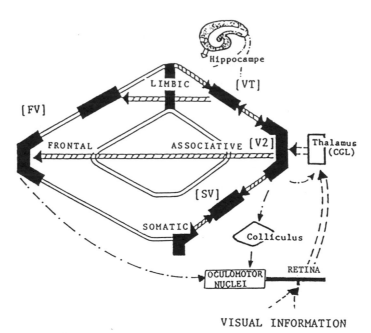

Figure 4-13 . Vision: information flow in the cortical network towards parietal, temporal and
frontal regions.

The "visual" cortical region is distributed over several specialized maps.
Secondary visual maps form three pathways towards three cortical regions: parietal

(SV), temporal (VT) and frontal (FV). This organization is illustrated in FIGURE 4-14, that is an "enlargement" of FIGURE 4-13.

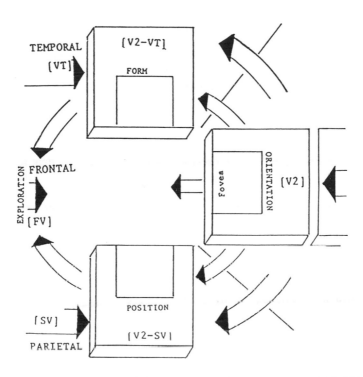

Figure 4-14 . Specialization of visual maps in the main directions of the visual information flow.

We have grouped visual maps in two functional subsets corresponding to the two main pathways, parietal and temporal:

1. The "occipito-temporal" maps [V2-VT] organize the relations with the temporal area [VT]; this functional region corresponds to experimentally- defined areas like "VP","V4","MST" and is specialized in the recognition of forms and colors.

2. The "occipito-parietal" maps [V2-SV] organize the relations with the parietal area [SV] (area 7) ; this functional region corresponds to experimentally- defined areas like "V3", "PIP", "PO", "MST", and is more specialized in the analysis of movement in three-dimensional space. This region is particularly important for visual guidance of hand movements.

Learning of new visual functions in these different subsets depends upon their input-output relations which give significance to the components of the columnar automaton (see chapter II): "thalamic inputs" which represent external situations, "elementary output actions" of columns, and "partial goals" on cortico-cortical connections.

A) Actions of modules in the primary visual map [V1] selectively enhance reception

Each cortical module in the primary area [V1] represents a combination of several visual parameters (due to the combination of afferent axonal bands):

1. Positions: they correspond to retinal coordinates ("pi", two-dimensional vector with foveal origin); input intensity represents contrasts previously enhanced by the retinal function.

2. Ocular dominance: inputs activated by each eye alternate, for each position in the visual field; cortical activity depends upon disparities between left and right retina ("dg");

3. Orientation tuning: Cortical transfer functions extract local features of visual information, like orientations of contrasted stimuli ("f").

4. Wave lengths ("c") : they optimally activate subsets of retinal receptors and are transmitted by parallel channels toward the cortex.

Modules of the primary area [V1] effect two types of actions that selectively enhance visual information:

1. Activity of pyramidal neurons in layer VI selectively amplifies the activity in the thalamic map; this amplification occurs only if cortical activity precedes retinal activity (Chapter III, figure 3-29): transmission of retinal activity to the cortex can thus be controlled by cortical goals.

2. Activity of pyramidal neurons in layer V commands ocular positioning via the superior colliculus: the in-out function of the colliculus transforms a stimulus position into command of ocular muscles . This function positions the stimulus on the fovea. If the eye movements are not sufficient, the collicular function progressively orients the head, then the body.

Because of the direct connections between the primary visual area [V1] and the colliculus, a cortical module activated by a visual stimulus (retinal position "p") can command an eye movement (direction and amplitude "-p") that will bring the stimulus onto the fovea (stimulus enhancement).

B) The "occipito-parietal" maps [V2-SV] and the parietal areas [SV] correlate visual and somatosensory information.

The "occipito-parietal" map [V2-SV] is specialized for the detection of disparity between the two retinal inputs produced by a common stimulus: the distance ("d") of an object is represented in addition to its retinal position ("p") and this combination produces a system of three-dimensional visual coordinates.

Parietal modules effect visuo-somatic correlations between positions on the corporal axis and positions in the visual field: they call two types of movements that can produce these sensory correlations:

a) Command of body movements in a system of visual coordinates.

Each position of the hand in a system of visual coordinates is a possible subgoal for hand movements. This process was fully discussed in the preceding section (II-2).

Columnar automata construct call trees that can guide the hand toward an object which is already situated on the fovea.

More generally, various body movements can be progressively called to effect a visual exploration of the surrounding space.

b) Command of eye movements in a system of corporal coordinates.

In the somatosensory areas, body movements are defined with respect to body coordinates (left-right, internal-external, and front-back). An environmental element thus occupies a position ("P") on these corporal axes.

Eye movements position the visual fixation point in various parts of surrounding space, including parts of the body (already defined by their own "P" coordinates). They activate the parietal modules that test these visuo - somesthetic correlations . Cortical calls from these partial goals can in turn command ocular movements that will match the fovea with a corporal position.

C) The "occipito-temporal" maps [V2-VT] and the temporal areas [VT] integrate visual components of an image.

Cortico-cortical connections of the primary map [V1] toward the temporal area [VT] are characterized by an increase in the size of the receptor field.

We saw in section I (Figures 4-2 and 4-3) that modules in temporal areas can correlate different cortical inputs, such as different positions or orientations in the visual field. From these partial goals, call trees can command active "matching actions" between different features of an image: either by eye movements which produce an external translations of visual information (Figure 4-2) or by virtual translations internal to the cortex (as explained in section IV-1 with Figure 4-3). These call trees correlate characteristic elements of the visual image and match them with expected patterns previously stored.

Furthermore , temporal visual areas have privileged connections with the hippocampus that recognizes spatio-temporal correlations in the afferent information flow (chapter III). In interaction with the hippocampus, the temporal area can memorize activity, and compare this activity to another activity pattern occurring at another point in time. This process is very important for comparing similar but temporally separated information.

D) The oculomotor frontal areas [FV] produce structured ocular scanning of an image.

Visual maps which have intermediate positions in the parietal and temporal pathways not only recognize orientations and relative positions with respect to the retinal axes, but also detect directions. These maps have reciprocal connections with the frontal area [FV] (corresponding to the frontal eye field), that commands eye movements by a direct action upon the oculomotor nuclei.

On these connections, the cortical call trees can command eye movements that are more independent of the visual characteristics of the image, but more linked to the behavioral programs or to the intrinsic properties of external objects .

The frontal oculomotor area [FV], like the other frontal areas, can memorize temporally successive information in a structured way. In this area, call trees can produce structured eye movements that explore an image at successive levels. Each detail of the image can call an exploration sequence whose result will be an element of exploration at a superior level. These ocular sequences can have goals unrelated to the image, such as verbal communication.

2. Recognition of elementary forms

A) Cortical call trees can recognize forms independently of their retinal position and size by internal transformations of the image.

In our perspective, invariant recognition of elementary forms independently of their size and their retinal positions is an active process due to external and internal "matching actions" that transform the retinal image. These cortical actions have been described in the first section of this chapter, in Figures 4-2 and 4-3.

Modules in the primary area represent both retinal positions ("pi") and elementary features ("fi") which already have invariant properties, such as orientations and colours. Modules of the secondary map [V2-VT] test the coactivation of two distinct modules of the primary map; their high activities represent the simultaneous presence of two characteristics ("f1" and "f2"), on two distinct positions of the retinal map ("p1 and p2").

But a similar activity (a cortical action) is produced in secondary maps by only one visual feature when it occurs during a cortical call; these actions represent a shift between an actual information and an "expected" one in another position of the primary map. Modules in secondary areas can effect virtual "translations" of visual information in order to match an expected pattern.

The call trees constructed in the secondary area [V2-VT] combine and sequence such elementary actions to produce any type of translations (see section 1 of chapter IV). Furthermore, the intensity of activity in the call network represents the amplitude of the translation since it increases with the goal distance that is the distance between the starting and final positions.

Function of these call trees constructed by learning is similar to that which commands eye movements according to activations of retinal positions. Call trees in the secondary map [V2-VT] form a set of exploratory actions that corresponds to a set of "fictitious" eye movements activated in parallel. These internal exploratory actions can, like actual eye movements, follow a moving point, the contours, or the axes of an object; they are much more rapid and can occur in parallel in several retinal regions. Furthermore, the equilibrium position is not necessarily the fovea, and can be functionally redefined.

In the same way that they effect translations, the modules of the secondary map [V2-VT] can also effect rotations of the visual image (or part of it). Since the orientations of stimuli on the retinal map (f1,f2) are represented by different positions in the primary map, translations between these cortical positions represent rotations of the visual image ("f1 - f2") in the retinal map. Call trees in the temporal map can effect either translations (large distances) or rotations (small distances) on the retinal inputs.

B) Transmission coefficients between translations (or rotations) are the parameters that memorize proportions of elementary visual forms.

a) Construction of a descriptor.

Call trees formed in the secondary map [V2-VT] effect translations (or rotations) and the intensity of their activity is proportional to the amplitude of the translation.

These translation actions are guided by specific features of the visual image; the elementary forms of external objects guide a series of internal translation actions, just as they guide successive exploratory eye movements. The ratio of the amplitudes of two successive translations is relatively independent of the size (or the position) of the image on the retina, and depends instead on the proportions of the object. The ratio between the activity levels in the two call trees that effect the two successive translations thus directly represents the proportions of an object, independently of its retinal position.

Moving the object nearer or further produces a variation in the intensity of the two actions that effect translations, but the ratio of these two intensities remains constant. Since it is precisely this ratio that is registered by the transmission coefficient between the two call trees, it is in fact the transmission coefficients that "memorize" the proportions of an object.

Representation of elementary visual forms at the cortical level can thus occur via the construction of a "descriptor" which is a call tree in the occipito-temporal map [V2 VT] :

- component call trees that produce elementary translations and rotations represent the principal axes of the external form;
- transmission coefficients represent the proportions of the form;
- intensity of activity represents the size of the form in the retina: it calibrates all the other related cortical actions.

These call trees constitute primitive descriptors of external forms. Movement of a form across the retina activates the same descriptors, with an intensity varying inversely with distance.

Form learning occurs first by a succession of eye movements guided by the contours of the object ("external" matching), then by a succession of translations and rotations effected by call trees in the secondary map [V2-VT] ("internal" matching). The second process, initially guided by the first but later autonomous, is much faster and can occur in parallel in several parts of the visual image.

Color recognition can be produced by a process comparable to that of form recognition: a comparison is made between light received from a colored area ("c1") and neighboring regions ("c2"). Since wave lengths are also represented by different positions on the visual sensory map, color recognition can occur by the same type of successive internal translations as those that produce elementary form recognition.

b) Recognition in three dimensions.

The call trees which describe the forms by translations and rotations recognize the coarse form of an object in two dimensions (internal relations between salient details of a given object). This global form can serve as a partial goal for further cortical actions. In this way, recognition of objects in three dimensions corresponds to a supplementary stage in a recognition algorithm. Two types of actions can explore an object in three dimensions:

  - commands of body movements with respect to the object in order to change the perspective;

  - internal matching actions between the images that come from the two retina; in a way these two retinal images are equivalent to a permanent, fixed visual displacement (at the distance between the two eyes).

During visual fixation of an object, these cortical actions provide changes in perspective and form. Two perspectives of the object can be linked by successive exploratory actions (translations, rotations, amplitude changes). The three-dimensional form of an object can thus be memorized by coefficients between the exploratory actions that allow one to pass from one perspective to another.

3. Recognition algorithms of objects and people.

A) Recognition algorithms of objects and people are cortical call trees.

Recognition of complex forms is an active process that proceeds via learning; recognition algorithms have the general properties of call trees (Chapter II):

a) Goal.

The algorithm is built up from a cortical "goal", as any other call tree: this goal is a complete recognition which corresponds to a contrasted cortical activation with the higher intensity level in a defined subset of modules (a "multi-module" as described in chapter III). This final subset interrelates the visual percept with other cortical algorithms, and defines the "meaning" of the recognition algorithm. At first, such goals are linked with fundamental programs, but as soon as the cortical circuits can be differentially activated, each contrasted pattern becomes a partial goal. Figure 4-15 depicts three steps in the construction of a recognition algorithm, by three successive aspects of a call tree . Darker lines on the upper part represent the differential activation of an increasingly precise cortical network.

b) Cortical actions and visual information flow.

Construction of recognition algorithms results from a disequilibrium, when cortical activity does not match subsets of modules previously differentiated. Columnar automata select, by learning, exploratory actions that favour contrasted activities, by transforming the image projected on the primary map. In Figure 4-15, such cortical actions are depicted by downward dark arrows, and successive projected images by upward dotted lines.

c) Call trees.

Structures in the environment are recognized by successive approximation. Cortical activities interact with the visual information in two ways (as illustrated by call trees of figure 4-15):

   - In the direction of calls (D?C?B?A?): on the basis of previous learning, each external form partially recognized produce differential activity that call new actions; each call tree anticipates a possible form and effects specific explorations on the image.
   - In the direction of actions (A!B!C!D!): these exploratory actions selectively transform the image building on the   results of the preceding step. Cortical re-activations after each exploration progressively restrain the set of possible meanings. The algorithm continues to function until complete recognition: full activation of a meaning extinguishes the call network.

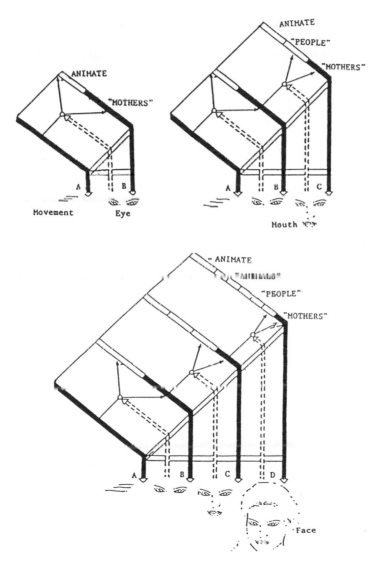

Figure 4-15 . 3 steps in the construction of a recognition algorithm for faces with parallel differentiation of categories.

d) Progressive sequence.

The recognition process is both parallel and sequential: each step in the call trees transforms in parallel the various parts of an image by a combination of internal explorations (rotations, translations); several steps produce recursive transformations which permit rapid recognition by successive dichotomies (exponential efficiency).

Only those cortical actions necessary for goal attainment are triggered: at each instant they depend upon the information arriving on the visual cortical map. The sequence is not fixed, but depends upon the information already present in the retina; sequence is always of the minimal length that will permit attainment of the goal (i.e activation of a meaning).

In an unfamiliar situation, a whole group of possible "meanings" call, in parallel, exploration actions that could ultimately lead to a contrasted activity. This general disequilibrium not only produces a group of exploratory actions, it is also a driving force for new learning (effect of "novelty").

e) Transmission coefficients.

Transmission coefficients between successive exploratory actions memorize specific forms, as described in preceding sections:

- each exploratory action, guided by the main visual features of an object, serves as a reference for ulterior exploratory actions;

- transmission coefficients memorize the relative amplitudes of successive exploratory actions: they anticipate the other parts of a form. Call trees

are descriptors which define the forms independently of the position, the orientation, and movement of the object on the retina. The form that is recognized will have a stable cortical representation, regardless of ensuing changes in retinal position.

B) Call trees combine parallel and sequential transformations of the retinal image.

All of the possible cortical actions are used in the recognition process.

a) Comparisons and internal explorations.

Spatial filtering and extraction of local characteristics are effected in parallel by the visual areas upon the afferent retinal information relayed by the thalamus. The cortical tissue compares this afferent activity with an intrinsic function that enhances features such as orientations. This first step is more efficient for recognition of continuous patterns.

Sensory correlations (areas [V2] and [VT]) are then effected between non-adjacent parts of the visual image. The temporal correlation between two stimuli permits recognition of discontinuous forms on the retina. These comparisons of retinal information are also executed in parallel.

The internal exploratory actions (translation and rotation) are effected by call trees in the temporal maps; several translations can be effected in parallel when they involve different parts of the image.

b) "External" explorations: eye movements and positioning of the body.

Eye movements produce a global translation of the image . Call trees can describe forms by a sequence of eye movements. This processing is sequential, but very rapid compared to other motor programs and this recognition seems "instantaneous". When the visual angle is very large, eye movements are supplemented by rotation of the head and then the axis of the body. Furthermore, algorithms in the frontal cortex can command multi-level ocular scanning of a visual scene, with goals which are quite varied, ranging from a detail of the image to grasping a global meaning.

Generally speaking, all the cortical actions (like movements) can participate in recognition algorithms. Positioning actions of different parts of the body become partial goals for recognition, and local recognitions become partial goals for these positioning movements.

c) "External" explorations are progressively replaced by "internal" explorations.

Eye movements are the first exploratory actions effected from the primary visual area, guided by the characteristics of the object; these eye movements in turn guide the formation of internal exploratory sequences such as virtual translations and rotations in the temporal areas; these algorithms constitute adjustable descriptors of objects.

In this way, visual properties of an external form are progressively assimilated by the recognition algorithms; they perform larger and larger anticipations with more and more limited exploratory actions. They recognize increasingly complex forms with increasing rapidity (parallelism of "internal" exploratory actions).

C) Algorithmic developments generate new recognition categories.

The temporal area is connected to the limbic areas; various recognition actions will first be combined in order to favor the execution of fundamental program. Forms and colors, extracted by temporal call trees, are characteristics of objects, and the fundamental programs give significance to these objects. The most significant "objects" are of course other people: face recognition is the first to be developed in the infant, during maternal interactions.

FIGURE 4-15 illustrates as an example the development of the "face recognition" algorithm in the newborn baby. In this case, the "meaning" (the goal) that orients construction of the algorithm, is at first linked to execution of a fundamental program (food, heat).

Three steps are illustrated (N1-N3); at each step, a schema shows the call tree with its three dimensions: the possible exploratory actions, the sequence actually executed (horizontal axis) and goal distance (vertical axis) . The darker lines on the upper part of the prism depicts the differential activation of an increasingly precise cortical network.

The first exploratory actions "A!", "B!" etc. are eye movements guided by the external form; these eye movements are progressively replaced by internal exploratory actions of the foveal image.

Each step in the construction of call trees increases sharpness of recognition and produces new categories:

a) Recognition of "eyes" (step N1).

Activation of visual cortical areas is at first evoked by movements of external objects; the face of the mother is a mobile element of the external world that anticipates activation of fundamental programs. But since this recognition is insufficient, it produces a disequilibrium. The call tree extends toward exploratory actions centered upon the moving face.

The eyes of the face have a very particular structure. "Eyes" form a stimulus pair that engender an oscillation of ocular positioning (two equilibrium points). This oscillation can be integrated in the recognition algorithm.

At this stage, the sequence of exploratory actions is the following: positioning upon the moving face (A!), then oscillation upon the two "eyes" (B!). Such call tree effects a primary visual recognition of the face of the "mother", and can distinguish two sub-sets in the visual environment, that of "animate forms" and that of "mothers", who are "animate" but also have "eyes".

b) Recognition of the principal axes of the face (step N2).

The following step is a differentiation between several "faces"-- that of the mother and that of other people. This differentiation is favored by a supplementary action of ocular positioning upon another facial element, for example the "mouth", that is visually distinct (color) and mobile (smile). This new step produces a new call tree that can differentiate "people" from "mother" and "animals" from "people".

c) Recognition of particular features (step N3).

The process continue with more precise exploratory actions that can recognize familiar people among others.

The meaning circuit "mother" thus successively calls recognition actions in the order D? ("facial feature"?), C? ("mouth"?), B? ("eyes"?) and A? ("moving"?). If the visual information in the retina so permits, actions closest to the goal (for instance, "eyes" B!) can be directly triggered; they then inhibit recognition actions that are more general and thus further from the goal (for example "animate forms" A!). It is not always necessary to effect the entire sequence from general to particular; only the terminal steps necessary for total recognition are effected.

The very mode of construction of the call tree creates "recognition categories" . Such categories correspond to combinations which define increasingly general characteristics in the direction of the call and more and more precise properties in the reverse direction (effective actions).

The first general characteristic recognized is that of "movement": this step in the algorithm is insufficient for distinguishing a person or an object, but does create a category that includes "people"+"animals"+ "other animate objects". A new step that enhances specific characteristics such as "eyes" defines a new subset constituted of "moving things" possessing "eyes", that is living subjects "people + animals". Another step in the algorithm, for instance a sequence of eye movements that detect a "mouth" ("C"), will demarcate a more restricted category "persons" and reject the "animals".

The algorithm continues to grow and create more and more categories: the more precocious step will form the more general categories.

C) Several subsets of coefficients can store an image.

This model of visual recognition produced by call trees is intermediate between algorithmic and connexionist models, as illustrated in FIGURE 4-16.

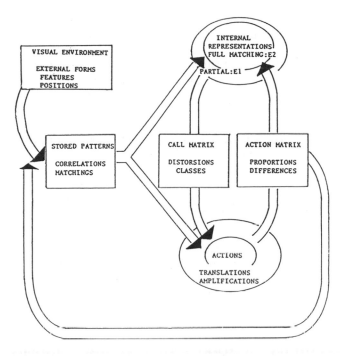

Figure 4-16 . Subsets of transmission coefficients which can store knowledge on visual information.

Visual environment (at left) generates an internal representation that is a set of cortical activities, distributed over a wide set of modules; these activities are illustrated by circles, with two possible levels:

- high level activities (E2: inner circle) represent fully recognized objects, due to complete matching;

- Low intensity activities (E1: outer circle) represent possible objects, anticipations and expectancies.

Figure 4-18 illustrates by squares the different subsets of coefficients that participate in the storage of images. These transmission coefficients -inter and intra modular- can be grouped in three types of "connectivity matrices":

1. Some subsets of coefficients act as pattern associators; a first cortical representation of an object is obtained by correlation of the visual information flow by these distributed weights. The weights (continuous coefficients) change with activity in order to match distributed input patterns. The set of coefficients can learn several distinct "correlative" patterns and recognize external forms when they are correctly centered, with standard positions and dimensions. The product of the visual information by this correlation matrix produces an internal representation with two levels of activity, the fully recognized objects (E2) and the possible ones (E1).

2. The low-level activities correspond to partially recognized objects: they produce a disequilibrium and generate "calls" toward actions that can explore the expected patterns. The set of "call coefficients" (the "call matrix") store the possible changes in the different images (retinal projections) of the same object (distortions); furthermore, this matrix store classes (or categories) of objects that correspond to the same sets of cortical exploratory actions. These subsets of coefficients represent a qualitative description of objects.

3. The exploratory actions (translation, amplification) that fit the visual image are triggered . The ratio of intensities between two successive actions represents a proportion . These "action coefficients" can change with learning and they can fit the expected proportions of the external objects. This subset of coefficients stores proportions of objects, independently of their real sizes and positions, and represent a quantitative description of proportions of an object.

The exploratory actions which are triggered change the cortical image of the visual environment and increase the probability to match the expected patterns in the internal representation (reactivation at the E2 level). Resulting set of cortical actions correspond to the real aspect of objects.

4. Systems of representation and stability of the visual world.

A) Cortical maps and pathways form three parallel systems of representation of the visual world.

Visual information is represented within the cortex in three ways, corresponding to three coordinate systems: retinal, somatic, and object-centered coordinates.

These three systems are illustrated in the three parts of FIGURE 4-17. In this figure, the left part represents the relations within the cortex and the right part represents the relations in the external world.

The three representations of the visual world coexist in the three main regions of the visual system in relation with the three input poles:
- the occipital region [V2] receives the visual information flow with retinal coordinates;
- the parietal region [SV] receives both visual and somatic information and can represent an image on a system of corporal coordinates.
- the temporal region [VT] receives both visual information and information about the internal state of the organism (relation with fundamental programs); it can give significance to visual patterns and define visual information in object-centered coordinates.

Figure 4-18 focuses on the cortical network and the regional processing of visual information, with relations derived from the model of network developed in chapter III. The three main regions are related by intermediate visual maps: occipito-temporal maps [V2-VT] for recognition and occipito-parietal maps [V2-SV] for positioning.

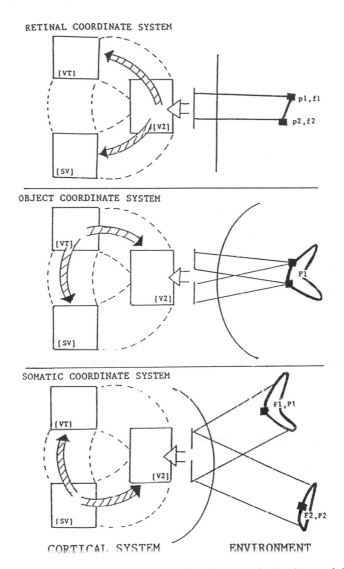

Figure 4-17 . 3 coordinate systems of the visual environment in 3 subsets of the cortical network.

The symmetrical connections of the cortical network interrelate the three areas (V1,VT,SV) and the two intermediate sets of maps (V2-VT,V2-SV) by 6 parallel and systematic connections: these six relations form a "fundamental loop" of visual recognition.

There are two opposite information flows through these cortical regions: one is the visual flow from the retina in the feed-forward cortical connections (from right to left in figure 4-17 and 4-18) and the other is the set of calls in the "feed-back" connections. These calls in the feed-back direction originate from the cortical goals in the somatic and internal "hypothalamic" pole (from left to right). Visual information is progressively "assimilated" by anticipatory calls intrinsic to the subject (internal world), either from the molecular pole ([MH]) that represents fundamental programs or from the somatic pole that represent corporal space ([M]). These intrinsic calls shape the continuous information flow from the retina.

a) Retinal flow from the primary area [V1] and retinal coordinates.
In the occipital pole (V1), the flow of visual information is organized with respect to the retinal axes. Modules represent retinal positions "pi" and local features "fi" of visual information .

The two secondary maps [V2-VT] and [V2-SV] represent, respectively, elementary forms and their relative positions on the retinal axes.

b) Call by the molecular pole and object-centered coordinates.
The molecular pole [MH] calls cortical actions that increase recognition of forms and colors as a function of their meaning for the organism: these call trees break down the visual information flow in basic forms ("Fi") in the temporal region [VT], thanks to adjustments in the intermediate map [V2-VT] which effects internal translations (or rotations) and eye movements.

In the temporal area [VT], call trees represent descriptors of forms "Fi" related to objects in the external world , relatively independent of retinal positions. Transmission coefficients represent the proportions of the object's form ("Fi"), its color ("Ci"), and the relations among its various perspectives.

For a given object, the same final subset in the call tree ("Fi,Ci") is activated, whatever the size and position of the object on the retinal axes. The internal and external explorations are centered upon the "object" axes: visual information is defined by a system of intrinsic axes of the object.

c) Call by the somatic pole and somatic coordinate system for visual information.
The "somatic" pole [M] calls positioning actions in surrounding space: these call trees define positions ("P") on the intrinsic corporal axes ([SV]).

Thanks to the matching properties of parietal areas, corporal positions can in turn call ocular fixations. Eye movements (and convergence changes) move the visual fixation point along a series of positions that are defined with respect to corporal axes ("P"), that is to say, with respect to a subject-centered coordinate system.

As shown in the right part of Figure 4-17 (lower diagram), two successive focussing positions defined on the corporal axes (P1 on "f1" and P2 on "f2") represent the relative positions of visual information (f1-f2) projected upon the intrinsic corporal axes.

In this way, the parietal area [SV] can represent the positions and relative orientations of visual stimuli with respect to the corporal axes, and transmission coefficients can represent the relative positions of visual elements that are stable on these axes.

Representation of external information in subject or object centered coordinates is not made by strong cortical activities (E2) on contiguous cortical maps, but by a set of expectancies (E1) which relate pieces of information by possible cortical actions (call trees).

B) Cortical call trees interrelate the three systems of representation of the visual world in order to maintain a stable image of the environment.

a) Parallel representation of visual information

Call trees originating from somatic and molecular goals organize visual information: they "fill" temporal areas with forms ("Fi") and parietal areas with positions ("Pj") on the corporal axes. A minimum of familiar forms and positions serves

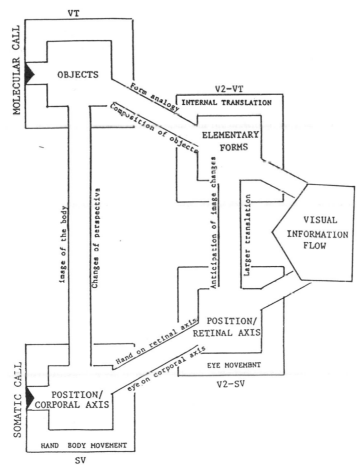

Figure 4-18 . Recognition loop between specialized cortical areas: internal cortico - cortical adaptations produce a stable visual environment.

as a general framework for the construction of an inner representation of surrounding visual space.

The parallel flow of retinal information through the two main pathways, parietal and temporal, continually produces a set of forms (temporal) and a set of positions on both the retinal and corporal axes (parietal).

Connections between the two cortical regions form "matrix" combinations (as illustrated in figure 4-18B) where forms and positions can change independently. Call trees constructed between these two regions can follow forms whose positions change in a continuous way. These call networks anticipate the transformations of the retinal image produced by movements.

The retinal flow produces synchronous activation of the different visual maps (five in figure 4-18) and thus synchronizes the parallel representations of the different objects of the surrounding world (VT) with their relative position on the corporal axes (SV) and their component elementary forms (V2-VT) with their relative positions on the retinal axes (V2-SV).

b) Adjustments between the different representations of visual information.

The cortical call trees continually produce exploratory actions that integrate the different aspects of successive retinal images; these call trees represent "natural" relations between the three projections, centered on retinal, somatic or objects axes. Call trees around subgoals produce bidirectional adjustments in the 6 symmetric connections between the five cortical regions of the "recognition loop":

- call trees search positions on the retinal axes (in V2-SV) that are related to positions on the corporal axes (from SV), and reciprocally; call trees search the various simple forms (in V2-VT) that constitute an object (from VT), and search analogy between forms on the reverse connections;

- call trees search possible movements (in SV) that explore different perspectives of an object (from VT) and reciprocally search for fixed relations among elements of the external environment (in VT) on order to move with respect to those objects (from SV);

- call trees search ocular movements (in V2-SV) that supplement the internal translations (from V2-VT) on a larger scale (recognition of three-dimensional forms), and reciprocally search for internal translations (in V2-VT) that can anticipate movement of a form on the retina provoked by an eye movement (from V2-SV).

The spatial relations between two forms (in VT) are established by an eye movement defined on the corporal (SV) and retinal (V2-SV) axes; this operation is accompanied by internal translation and rotation (in V2-VT) that maintains the coherence of the global form in the temporal region during the eye movement.

This set of adjustments between the five cortical areas thus furnishes a "global" image with objects, forms, and their relative positions with respect to corporal and retinal axes.

This global image changes relatively continuously over time. In a given environment, the set of objects and positions is relatively stable in the subjective "corporal" reference, whatever the projection of the surrounding world on the retina.

D) Calls between cortical maps implicitly represent body and object in an external frame.

As shown in Figure 4-14, the different maps of the recognition loop form two parallel pathways, (1) an inner circle more related to "central" positions and recognition of objects and (2) an outer circle more related to peripheral positions and recognition of the external frame:

- in the inner circle, including experimentally defined maps such as "MT" or "FST" in the temporal sulcus, or "VIP" in the intra-parietal sulcus, cortical operations are more specialized for recognition of objects in foveal or perifoveal regions in relation with hand representation and manipulation; connections between parietal and temporal zones of this inner loop are important to recognize structures from local motions and then to recognize articulated objects such as hands with fingers; calls in these cortico-cortical connections define positions of objects with respect to the body frame.

- in the outer circle (including maps such as "V3" or "PO") cortical operations are more specialized to recognize the external frame ("world frame") and the places in which the body moves, in relation with feet representation in somatic regions (parietal side), and in relation with the "cognitive maps" of the environment in the hippocampus (temporal side); calls in this network (expectancies) define the positions of the body with respect to the external frame and this global relation is controlled by vestibular inputs (in S2) which indicate the vertical axis.

These two pathways, for central and peripheral processing, are reciprocally linked by parallel and systematic connections:

- in parietal links, cortical automata relate the different motor coordinates (feet, hand, head, etc);

- in temporal links, they relate global forms that represent the external frame of the environment (distant and peripheral vision) and the local forms of manipulable objects (more foveal); analyses of surfaces with colours (in the map "V4") in connection with relative movements (in "MT") are important to discriminate objects from external frames.

IV. Frontal areas : structured sequences.

References

The frontal cortex, particularly developed in the human species, has an important role in the temporal organization of behavior into structured sequences (Jacobsen 1931; Luria 1978; Fuster 1980).

The specific role of frontal cortex has been investigated by studying the effects of lesions of its various parts. These lesions always have a double effect, a general "frontal" effect and a specific effect related to the part of the frontal lobe which is damaged.

a) Temporal organization of behaviour.

Whatever the frontal region, the lesions have a general disruptive effect on the temporal organization of behavior (Jacobsen 1931; Fuster 1980). Frontal areas are thus important for delayed-response learning (Jacobsen 1931). Frontal lesions produce a repetition of stereotypical movements and make it impossible for the subject to organize a sequence using external cues (Luria 1966); to spontaneously generate varied combinations (Milner 1984), and to modify behavior in response to a new element of information (Denny-Brown 1951).

This temporal organization role of frontal cortex receives support from the analysis of neuronal activity during delayed-response performance. Frontal pyramidal cells have sustained activity during the delays between the stimulus and the response established by the learning program; frontal neuronal activity can even predict the behavioural response that will occur after a delay (Fuster 1972; Sakai 1981; Kubota 1980); prolonged activity of frontal cells, specific to a given behavior, represents a memorization of transitory activity. Long-lasting frontal information processing could be favored by a dopaminergic modulatory afference that is especially dense compared with that of other cortical regions (Thierry 1975).

b) Specific sensori-motor integration.

More specific effects of frontal lesions can be explained by differences in the input-output organization of the various frontal areas (Nauta 1962). Differences in the specific functional roles of various frontal areas is also suggested by metabolic measures of cortical tissue activity during various tasks (Roland 1984).

1. The frontal region related to parietal areas (Pandya 1969, 1971), that we have called [FSV], is more specialized in the kinesthetic organization of movement; its destruction provokes an apraxia for precise movements (Walter 1973; Hecaen 1983). This region is particularly active during abstract problems of a spatial nature (Roland 1984).

2. The frontal region connected with visual areas (Chavis 1976; Astruc 1971) that we have called [FV], organizes structured ocular scanning: its destruction provokes an inertia in eye movements and reading problems (Hecaen 1983; Luria 1967); neurons in this zone are active before structured eye movements (Bizzi 1968). This region is very active during visual discrimination tasks (Roland 1984).

3. The polar region of the frontal lobe, that we have called [FVT], connected with the temporal lobe, is very active during tasks with categorization of objects (Roland 1984).

4. The frontal region directly connected to the somato-motor language production areas (Krieg 1949; Crosby 1962), that we have called [FSA], organizes the syntactic structure of language, and its destruction produces a production aphasia (Broca 1861; Hecaen 1983).

5. The directly adjacent frontal region, connected to the auditory areas and that we have called [FA], also plays an important role in the syntactic organization of language: its destruction provokes an "agrammatical" aphasia (Hecaen 1983; Lhermitte 1972; Perret 1974). This region is active during both verbal expression and listening to a story (Roland 1984).

6. The frontal region just more anterior, which is also connected to the temporal area (Crosby 1962) that we have called [FAT] plays a more global role in the organization of language: its destruction results in loss of spontaneous speech and verbal initiative (Benton 1895; Ramier 1970; Hecaen 1981), as well as the impossibility for the subject to organize behavior in response to instructions (Luria 1966). This region is active when one listens to a story in order to repeat it afterwards (Roland 1984).

7. The supplementary motor area, that we have called [M-H], shows sustained activity during voluntary movement (Roland 1984).

8. The polar region situated on the medial face of the frontal cortex that we have called [FT-H] is active during periods of sustained attention during abstract tasks, such as mental arithmetic, that have both auditory and visual components.

9. Frontal regions connected with the olfactory areas, the hypothalamus (Papez 1937, Yakovlev 1948) and the amygdala (Akert 1964) that we have called [FO], play a role in the global organization of behavior in relation to fundamental programs: their destruction produces akinesia and general apathy (Hecaen 1981; Livingston 1973); this lesion also has an important effect on food-motivated learning.

1. Sensori-motor integration and dynamic memorization

A) The frontal cortex is subdivided into several functional areas specialized by their sensori-motor relations.

In Chapter III, we subdivided the frontal regions in 9 functional areas and we proposed a model for the network that connects them (Figures 3-10 and 3-11); this model focus on two properties of the frontal region:

1. The frontal areas are organized along a "time axis" with longer and longer time constants from the somatomotor pole (central sulcus) to the molecular pole (see figure 3-7).

2. The frontal areas are symmetrical with respect to associative areas, and their internal relations are symmetrical with respect to the connections between the associative areas.

In this chapter we will define a mechanism shared by all the frontal areas ; this "frontal mechanism" is a specialization of the general columnar automaton (described in Chapter II): frontal automata can construct sequences (general cortical property) with an internal structure and a variable number of nested levels (frontal characteristics). Such call trees will effect specific functions in each frontal area, depending upon its connections with associative areas; these specific functions constructed by learning can explain the experimental results concerning the different parts of the frontal lobe; automata in frontal areas give an internal structure to sensori-motor combinations performed in symmetrical associative areas:

1. [FSV] linked to [SV] (hand positioning) organizes movements of manual exploration (fine, structured movements).

2. [FV] linked to [V2] (visual translation) organizes structured visual exploration (for instance, ocular scanning during reading).

3. [FVT] linked to [VT] (recognition algorithm) organizes exploration of a complex visual scene as a function of the meaning of the various elements.

4. [FSA] linked to [SA] (positioning of the vocal apparatus) organizes the syntactic structure of language on the basis of the relative positions of words.

5. [FA] linked to [A2] (auditory forms) organizes the syntactic structure of language with respect to function words (prepositions, conjunctions, etc.).

6. [FAT] linked to [AT] (auditory sequences) controls the long term organization of language; it permits spontaneity, verbal initiative, and the general organization of behavior by language.

7. [FT-H] linked to the temporal areas [FVT] and [FAT] (visual and auditory recognition) and to the limbic areas [MH] (fundamental programs) is important for structuring the auditory and visual patterns in the environment so as to relate them to the execution of fundamental programs.

8. [M-H] ("supplementary" motor area) along with the motor area [M2] (motor sequences) and the limbic area [MH] (fundamental programs) is important for general motor initiative and to structure the various movements implicated in the satisfaction of a fundamental need.

9.[FO] linked with the limbic areas [MH] and the olfactory area [O] globally control behavior in relation with the fundamental programs.

B) Frontal modules can temporarily memorize transient activities from associative areas.

We saw in the first section of this chapter that modules in the frontal areas produce "memorizing" actions. They can dynamically increase the duration of a transient information which comes from associative areas. This memorization is effected at several temporal levels, depending upon the position of the module on the frontal "time" axis.

a) Afferences and time axis.
The thalamic afferences of frontal cortex come from systems that function with a long time constant (Figure 4-19 similar to Figure 3-10):

- For the lateral surface of the frontal lobe ([FV], [FA], [FSV]. [FSA] convexity), the thalamic afferences come from the pallidum and the substantia nigra. The "thalamic" input of this part of frontal cortex represents a global cortical activity as seen through the slow spatio-temporal filter of the nigro-striatal system (Chapter III.4). This activity represents a general context of disequilibrium, originating in the prolonged activity of large cortical regions when a goal is not rapidly attained: fundamental programs, exploratory movements, motor programs, slow and large movements. This thalamic input reactivates the frontal areas as long as the "cortical" disequilibrium persists.

- For the orbitofrontal surface of the frontal lobe ([FO]), the afferences come from the olfactory lobe; activity in the olfactory system has often a long lasting time course which is related to that of the fundamental programs.

- For the medial surface of the frontal lobes ([FT-H], [M-H]) the thalamic inputs come from the amygdala, the hypothalamus, and the reticular formation. Activity of the reticular nuclei is in the form of oscillations with a long period (circadian rhythms, for instance); activities of the hypothalamic nuclei represent molecular activations linked to fundamental programs of the organism; activities of the amygdala are also long-lasting, since they depend upon the significance of environmental patterns for the fundamental programs.

"Reticular" type inputs can also modulate frontal cortical activity during long periods (for example, by dopaminergic inputs).

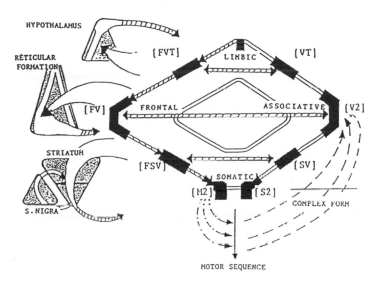

Figure 4-19 . Information flow in frontal areas: sensorimotor combinations (from associative regions) long-term programs (from subcortical loops).

b) Outputs and memorizing actions.

Outputs of the frontal cortex project to the input structures: striatum, reticular formation, hypothalamus. The actions of the frontal modules can command long-term programs of the reticular formation, motor programs of the pontine nuclei, and molecular programs of the hypothalamus (hormonal secretion); frontal actions can trigger or reactivate input-output "loops" that maintain a temporal continuity in various behaviors having long time constants: inertia of movements (striatum), long-term behavioral coherence as a function of the significance of environmental patterns (amygdala), intrinsic rhythms (reticular formation) and activation of fundamental programs (hypothalamus).

These input-output "loops" have two characteristics:
- thalamic inputs to frontal cortex are separated: this separation gives a "temporal selectivity" to each frontal area;
- outputs from the frontal cortex to another structure (for example striatum) are larger than inputs from that same structure. Consequently a frontal area can reactivate (via extracortical loops) other frontal areas that correspond to different temporal levels.

There is a global shift on the time axis of the frontal cortex; frontal actions can re-activate "loops" with increasing time constants.

By comparison input output loops in other cortical region are less extended and this can explain the fact that destruction of frontal cortex tends to produce repetitive, stereotyped movement (narrow loops in associative areas) in contrast with structured behaviour (large loops in frontal areas with a global shift).

c) Memorization with several temporal levels.

Frontal neurons memorize transients inputs from associative areas by a continuous activity, thanks to 2 basic properties (see section I): (·1) membrane properties (channels) which transform a transient pulse in a continuous step (like a flip-flop mechanism), and (2) activation of the input-output loops which increases the duration of activity in frontal modules.

Duration of memorization by the intrinsic flip-flop mechanism depends upon the activation patterns: it starts with transient excitation and stops with transient inhibition. Duration of activities in the input-output loops depend upon the place of the frontal area on the "time axis", with quite variable "temporal levels": duration of a movement, a motor program, a fundamental program. This property generates new learning capacities. For example this process favors delayed response learning: if there is a delay between a stimulus and a movement, the frontal modules can conserve the "instructive" aspects of stimuli (inputs from associative areas), anticipate the characteristics of movements to be effected (output to motor areas), and wait for a triggering signal .

Furthermore, this memorization is an active process controlled by frontal automata; storage duration depends upon the position of the frontal modules on the time axis, and this system favours learning of fixed temporal intervals (with no ending inhibition).

We have already seen how temporal areas memorize regular activity sequences of the same time level. By comparison, dynamic memorization in the frontal lobes can occur over quite different temporal levels, depending upon the input-output of each frontal region .

C) The frontal network interrelates longer durations with larger combinations of sensori-motor information.

a) Subgoals.

Frontal regions form an alternative pathway, parallel to connections formed by associative areas between sensory and motor maps (chapter III):

1. The goal of frontal actions can be a correlation between two sensory stimuli (connections with associative areas) when these two stimuli are not simultaneous; frontal actions (dynamic memorization) participate in recognition algorithms. Frontal areas can modulate the meaning of a sensory message depending on a set of quite different sensory inputs.

2. The goal can be the execution of a motor sequence, when the elementary components are not immediately contiguous (connections with the motor area). Frontal areas can integrate several successive conditions occurring at different moments with different time constants, before triggering of the motor action.

Frontal regions receive thalamic inputs which represent sets of sensorimotor information rather than precise stimuli. For example thalamic inputs are the result of the nigrostriatal processing which transforms a set of transitory cortical activities into a "context" (Chapter III.4, Figure 3-28). In the frontal areas, sensory information can thus be integrated into a much larger context that can change the meaning of the message.

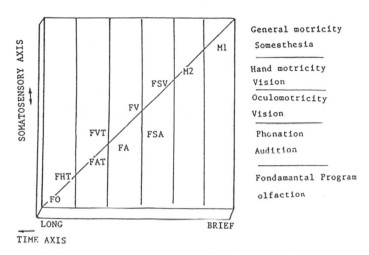

Figure 4-20 . Frontal maps form coherent combinations of sensorimotor and temporal information.

b) Temporal levels and sensori-motor combinations.

The frontal areas form several alternative pathways between sensory and motor activities (Chapter III, Figure 3-11 and 3-12). These pathways correspond to several levels of recombination in sensorimotor information, and larger combinations are linked with longer temporal levels.

As illustrated in Figure 4-20, the frontal areas are nodes between temporal levels (due to thalamic inputs, on the horizontal axis of the table) and sensorimotor combinations (due to inputs from other cortical areas, on the vertical axis).

The architecture of this "frontal map" generates implicit relations between temporal and recombination levels of sensori-motor information, which both increase from the back toward the front of the frontal cortex:

1. Different sensorimotor modalities have different behavioral time constants and the frontal map conforms to this relation: somesthetic positioning (in [M2]) have short durations, then manipulation is a more complex program ([FSV]); then vision-exploration ([FV]) and audition-speech ([FA]) correspond to longer durations; then molecular reception ([FO]) and fundamental programs ([FHT]) have very long time constants.

2. Within each sensorimotor modality, increasing temporal levels (thalamic inputs) are related to increasingly long sensorimotor activities (cortical inputs). For

example, in the visuo-motor system combinations increase from the back to the front of the frontal cortex:

    - The motor areas organize fast muscle contractions (duration in the range of 100 milliseconds).

    - The next frontal area on the time axis (FSV) receives inputs from the parietal region, where visual and proprioceptive information are combined. These visuo-somesthetic combinations are important for local and fast positioning (duration in the range of seconds) .

    - In contrast, the frontal area farther on the time axis ([FVT]) receives inputs from the temporal region where algorithms recognize pure visual information ([VT]): complex recognition is often responsible for long-term motor actions (in the range of minutes).

    In the cortical circuit that relates audition and phonation, the frontal levels (temporal and recombination) correspond to organizational levels of language (see Chapter V): muscular contractions of the vocal apparatus ([M1]), words ([M2]; position rules within sequences of words (FSA]), complex sentences ([FA]) and coherent discourse ([FAT]).

    3. Each frontal area that is related to a sensory or motor modality (positioned along the sensorimotor axis) is redundantly organized along the temporal axis ; several temporal memorization levels and several recombinations levels coexist for the same sensory or motor information.

    In associative and motor areas, activation has an intrinsic sensori-motor significance. But in frontal areas, modular activation also corresponds to a time level. Any sensory or motor message can be independently prolonged: a shift on the frontal axis produces a change in temporal levels. The maximal number of intrinsic levels that structure a sensorimotor pattern is directly related to the redundancy of connections and to the size of frontal areas.

2. Frontal stacks: organization of structured sequences.

A) Temporal and combination levels shape the internal structure of sensori-motor patterns in frontal areas.

a) Structured sequences.

FIGURE 4-21 and 4-22 depicts frontal call trees. As developed in chapter II (Figure 2-24), they can be depicted by three-dimensional prisms. Furthermore, they occupy a "mirror" position with respect to the call trees in associative areas.

    The two specific properties of the frontal region are memorizations (shown on the horizontal axis) and sensori-motor recombinations (on the vertical axis). These two properties give the capacity to produce and to recognize structured sequences with several nested levels:

    - The frontal mechanism can produce structured motor programs. Thus, from a set of motor actions A,B,C,D,E,F, although general columnar automata can organize only sequences at one level A-B-C-D (for example, the phonemes of a word), frontal automata can organize hierarchical sequences of the type A-((B-C)-(D-E)-F) where internal levels of the structured sequence are symbolized by parentheses.

- The frontal mechanism can recognize structured sensory patterns in the outside world; for example, from a set of sensory messages A,B,C,D,E,F frontal automata generate a structured information of the type $A*((B*((C*D)*E)F))$, where parentheses are internal levels and

operations (*) are sensory correlations in the associative areas.

Figure 4-21 illustrates a structure with two levels $A*(B*F)$, and Figure 4-22 a structure with four levels $A*((B*((C*D)*E))*F)$.

b) Context-dependent significance.

In associative areas, a call originating from a module "A" toward a module "B" facilitates the action of the calling module "A". But often the efficiency of "B" depends on another condition "F" which has a quite different nature or time constant. In terms of combinations, it is not "B" that directly favors "A", but rather the preliminary combination of "B" and "F" that can be represented by "(F*B)".

In the frontal areas, the compound condition (F*B) is an autonomous cortical action that can participate in a call tree: for example the stimulus "B" from associative regions is integrated into the context "F" (for example, input from the nigro-striatal loop) and the combination becomes a frontal action (F*B). The compound stimulus (F*B) may have a different, even opposite meaning from that acquired by the first stimulus (B) in previous learning ("reversal" learning). For example, after learning of a compound sequence "(F*B)-A", the frontal automata can easily learn two different contexts (F1 and F2) that favor two variants of the same sequence: "(F1*B)-A1" and "(F2*B)-A2", even with opposite effects.

Several levels of preliminary combinations (for instance "G1*F1*B") can be established in frontal areas as preconditions for triggering a motor sequence ("B-A").

B) Frontal automata transform a branching structure into a structured sequence with several nested levels, as do the stacks used in computers.

Structured sensori-motor information with a variable number of nested levels can be represented in an branching form, with binary branching. These structures are depicted in FIGURE 4-21 and 4-22, in lower parts:

The terminal branches represent basic information like peripheral sensory or motor activity.

Forks in the tree represent a combination; the two branches leaving the fork are the combined elements. This combination is effected by columnar automata: either a sensory correlation in the associative areas, or an elementary motor sequence in the motor areas.

Execution of any of these combinations is a partial goal, and depends on the preliminary accomplishment of the branches forming the fork of this partial goal. The base of the tree represents the total combination and thus the global structure.

The relative position of the branches with respect to the base defines the combination "levels". These levels correspond to larger and larger sets of elementary sensori-motor actions.

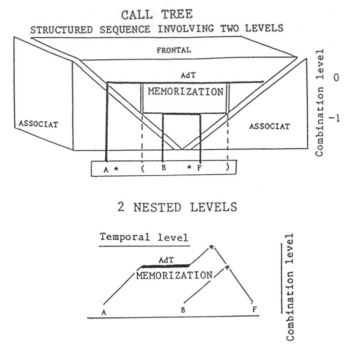

Figure 4-21 . Call tree in frontal cortex (upper diagram) : structured sequence with 2 nested levels (lower).

Structured information are represented in neural networks by a spatial hierarchy (recombination level) but also by a temporal hierarchy (temporal levels). We saw how the frontal network links both spatial and temporal levels. Frontal automata execute a double transformation:

- they can recognize a sequence of sensory information as an branching structure.

- they can transform an branching structure into a motor sequence;

In computers, transformation of an branching structure into an equivalent sequence is effected by a "stacking" mechanism. "Stacks" are sets of ordered registers, manipulated by two operations:

- stacking: an element is placed on top of the stack, in a "stand-by" status, as long as it cannot be combined with the following elements.

- unstacking: the element on top of the stack is removed as soon as it can be combined.

These two operations correspond to level changes.

The frontal call trees are analogous to these "stacks": they transform in the same way structured sequences into branching structure and reciprocally.

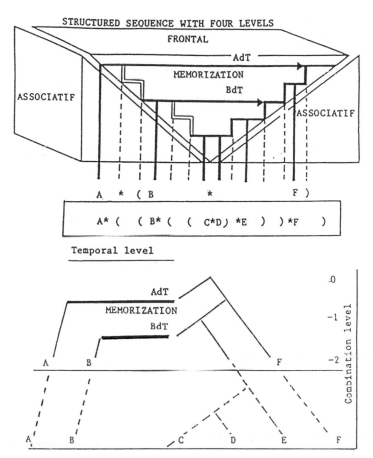

Figure 4-22 . Development of a frontal call tree (upper diagram): structured sequence with 4 nested levels (lower).

a) Frontal memorization of calls is comparable to "stacking".

Sequence-structure transformations require transitory memorization, in order to combine operations at a lower level.

If two messages of the same level are to be combined but are not simultaneously present (for instance A and X=B*F), the associative module that tests this correlation (A*X) produces a call. This call is transient in the associative area, but it can be dynamically memorized by a frontal module: the new prolonged activity in the frontal region is depicted as "AdT". Even if the call from the associative module "A" diminishes, the call from the frontal module "AdT" will persist. The expected combination becomes a goal in frontal regions; the associative modules can be re-used with shorter time constants.

Several "partial" sensory messages can be successively memorized in a non-competitive way by the activity of other frontal modules. For example, a new call from associative areas (B) can also be stored in a frontal module (BdT) ; the expected intermediate combination "BdT" becomes a partial goal in frontal areas, at a lower level (FIGURE 4-22).

In any oriented call tree, the number of effected actions is variable and depends upon environmental conditions. In the same way, the number of nested levels in frontal call trees are variable and can be adjusted to multiple sensory and motor conditions. These levels are not absolute but defined relative to the goal of the sequence, which has the maximal level of recombination "r0" and the longest level of memorization "t0". In our example, the frontal module "AdT" has the maximal level (r0,t0) and the second call (BdT) generates another level (r0-1,t0-1).

b) Attainment of a partial goal is comparable to "unstacking".

A partial goal is attained when a combination occurs between a call previously stored in a frontal region (for instance "BdT") and a new sensory information in associative regions (for example, "F" in Figure 4-21). The combination (B*F) reactivates the frontal module that was calling. This frontal modular action has two consequences:

- It prolongs the dynamic memorization of the upper-level calls (AdT) : the same call (AdT) can have longer and longer time durations (flip-flop properties and reactivation of loops with a longer time constant). Selective reinforcement of the call at superior levels produce an intense "behavioral" attention.

- On the other hand, the frontal modular action extinguishes the lower-level calls; dynamic memorization of inferior-level calls stops.

Inhibition of lower levels and reactivation of superior levels produces a "level lag".

The "stacking" and "unstacking" processes continue until attainment of the final goal, that is execution of the maximal-level combination (extinction of all the calls by combination with "A").

New levels in the sequence are produced by the general process that extend call trees: for example the two-layered structure A*(B*F) of FIGURE 4-21 can be differentiated into a three-level structure A*(B*(E*F)) and then a four-level structure A*(B*(C*(D*F))) as depicted in FIGURE 4-22.

c) Rules and relations.

Construction of the frontal algorithm involves specifically the direct symmetrical connections between the associative areas and the frontal cortex.

But the frontal areas are also interconnected symmetrically with respect to the connections between corresponding associative areas. Call trees in associative areas have images in frontal areas (see chapter III), but call trees in frontal areas couple modules which correspond to large sets of sensori-motor information: they constitute "rules" that will in turn guide combinations effected in the associative areas. Call trees between frontal areas do not have the same role as the symmetrical associative call trees : in the associative area, a call tree represents information linked by a relation but in the symmetrical frontal areas a call tree can represent the "relation" itself. In the following chapter we will analyze, in detail, learning of syntactic rules by such a frontal mechanism.

d) The human frontal cortex.

The frontal cortex properties that we have been discussing (temporal levels, recombination levels) are not supplementary properties that have appeared in the course of phylogenesis, but rather a regional specialization involving the separation of temporal from spatial processing.

We saw that the frontal mechanism is similar to "stacks" in computers. But the frontal areas form as many "stacks" as there are frontal modules: the capacities of the frontal lobe are directly related to its dimensions compared with the associative cortex.

The unique qualities of the human frontal cortex are not so much due to a new functional mode, as to its relatively large size: half of the cortical surface, in humans, is specialized in this "stacking" function.

The growth of frontal areas has favored the development of language, which is a structured symbolic communication system.

Language exploits two different coding possibilities offered by the cortical network:

- Symbolic coding is first effected by auditory forms and muscular actions of the speech apparatus (implicit coding).

- But symbolic coding is also effected by structured sequences of cortical actions: combinations of symbols can code relations between symbolized information. The frontal mechanism is well suited to code structured sets of relations (branching structures) by symbolic sequences with intrinsic levels (syntactic coding). Redundancy of frontal areas multiplies the coding levels; furthermore the geometry of the network between frontal areas (symmetry with the associative network) favours the learning of rules from examples.

Cortical adaptive mechanism and language learning.

In chapter V we study the brain processes involved in the cognitive development of the child and language learning, addressing five related problems:

1. What are the properties of the cortical system that permit language assimilation by the child ?

2. How are "mental images" that will be coded by "words" formed in the child's brain?

3. Why can children learn general language rules from only few examples ?

4. What are the neuronal processes that produce the semantic and syntactic components of language?

5. How can successively learned associations coexist in the child's brain in a cooperative rather than competitive way?

I. Cognitive development: properties of the cortical system

In our analysis, the processes of language acquisition are considered to be refinements or more general processes of sensori-motor adaptations; in other words, language is not produced by a new, specialized mechanism. For example, the columnar automata that construct call trees can form phonemic sequences to make "words", and then sequence them to form sentences; the two types of sequences- words and sentences- correspond to the two memorizing states in the cortical column: words are "fixed" combinations of phonemes and sentences are formed by "oriented" calls of words since many combinations can express the same ideas. The adaptive qualities of columnar automata are responsible for the large variety of possible combinations in language.

But language is also a parallel process at the semantic level: the basic geometric features of the cortical network such as symmetries are important for systematic coding of mental images by words and sentences. We interpret in this way the hemispheric specialization of the brain. Hemispheric symmetry favours the autonomous development of symbolic relations (words and sentences), isomorphic but independent of natural relations (mental images).

Cognitive development is an ordered process with features common to all children: we explain each stage of cognitive development by the acquisition of a new set of integrated cortical actions with three organizing factors: (1) COLUMNAR AUTOMATA produce an active and permanent learning since each new acquisition produces new disequilibria that call for new learning. (2) The geometry of the

CORTICAL NETWORK guides whole sets of new associations in a structured and coherent way. (3) Differential MATURATION of cortical regions orders the first stages of cognitive development and favours the development of integrated cortical actions related to communication, like words and sentences.

II. Adaptive construction of mental images

We consider that "mental images" are produced by cortical call trees in exactly the same way as sensori-motor adaptations. The only difference is that they realize adaptations between the activities of cortical areas: they are cortical goals attained by cortico-cortical interactions.

These cortical images are not a-priori structures but are constructed in a very progressive way since the child's birth.

For example, innate reflexes induce cortical call trees that will be the roots of cortical images of simple movements. In the same way, images of "people" are constructed from recognition algorithms of faces and voices. The cortical images of "objects" develop in parallel with new motor algorithms, in a very progressive way: first grasping isolate objects, manual exploration project them on different sensory maps, visual imitation gives them a useful aspect , and frontal exploration an intrinsic structure. We analyze how development of the frontal cortex is important to construct "images of relations", that are "concepts"; although they implicitly exist in associative regions, in frontal lobes images of relations become autonomous cortical actions and then partial goals. In the frontal network of human species, these representations can be recombined by columnar automata and form the roots of sentence production.

III. Language acquisition

Communication and language learning by the child is an adaptive process. Learning of "words" correspond to the construction of call trees by columnar automata in direct continuity with the construction of "mental images". Cortical images call cortical actions such as phonemic sequences that form "words". This process is much more than a simple "associative" phenomenon. It is a constant active learning due to successive disequilibria produced by the development of cortical call trees; this process is only stabilized by a complete overlap of "cultural bases" of cortical integrated actions: images, phonemes, words, and syntactic relators. Furthermore, "words" become powerful means to assimilate new "images" from adult language: in our perspective, words are new sub-goals that produce re-organizations of previous call trees; the assimilation of "categories" by the child is not a complex process but is merely due to isolation of basic cortical actions which pre-exist in other simple cortical images.

Words relate images with sensory-motor symbols. Diversity of symbolic coding is due to the extension of the cortical network and to the dual learning property of columnar automata: lateral subdivision form new phonems and sequencing of phonemic forms produces new words. Learning of syntactic structures develop with the same dual process in the frontal regions: lateral subdivision form grammatical categories, and their sequencing produce syntactic rules. The two processes cooperate in a recursive way:

new grammatical rules do not change those which were previously learned but instead shape more local relations.

IV. Cortical process of language production

The geometrical properties of the cortical network are very important for organizing the various semantic and syntactic levels of language.The model of network between areas that we proposed forms two possible sets of functional circuits interrelated like concentric circles and their radii.

The first set of cortical circuits (the concentric circles) correspond to the major semantic categories of images and words; they are constructed in different poles of the cortical network since there roots are the different types of sensorimotor adaptations: for example, in the temporal pole, the columnar automata construct "names" from "images of people", and in the symmetrical frontal pole, they construct pronouns from "concepts of relations centered around people"; in the parietal pole, they construct "adverbs" from "images of spatial relations", and in the symmetrical frontal pole, "syntactic rules of positions" from "concepts of oriented relations".

The second set (the radii) correspond to the different aspects of symbolic coding: the cortex produces "images" in the visuomotor circuit, codes them by "words" in the auditory-phonation circuit and expresses their "relations" by "sentences" in the two frontal symmetric circuits. Thanks to the parallel connections in the cortical network, this symbolic coding is systematic: every cortical image can be coded by at least a word and every word can construct a cortical image. Symmetries induce isomorphic functioning between cortical images and words.

The cortical circuits which produce "images" and "words" cross all the circuits which correspond to the main semantic categories; their parallel activation leads to an equilibrium position that results in a minimal semantic combination with actors, actions, circumstances of space and time; in the same way, parallel call of "relations" in the symmetrical frontal circuit produces the representation of a story and the resulting call toward "syntactic rules" shapes the narrative. When one listens to a narrative, minimal semantic combinations are also equilibrium positions; if they are not reached, the call spreads in the cortical network and produces inferences and questions.

The columnar automata organizes speech in a sequential way, with several nested levels generated along the "time axis" of the frontal cortex, with a global pulsation: the general frame of the narrative is often centered around actors (frontal region symmetric to the temporal pole), then the global syntactic structure of sentences is shaped by structured explorations of the environment (frontal part symmetric to the receptor poles), and at shorter time levels the polarity of each simple phrase depends upon polarity of actions (frontal region symmetric to parietal lobe), and the phonemic sequence in verbs is varied in order to represent elementary temporal relations (somato-motor).

V. Coherence of the cortical system for structured learning

The cortical substrata of learning is a limited physical structure. But the geometry of the cortical network gives a powerful coherence to varied learning experiences in early childhood; we shall examine the relations produced by this network between successively learned associations.

As an example we will discuss the problem solving capacities of the human brain. The basic process of problem solving is a direct consequence of the general properties of columnar automata: search, progressive sequencing, and registration of successful combinations. But the efficiency of this process is dependent upon previous acquisitions: we examine how, thanks to the cortical geometry, the newly formed integrated cortical actions cooperate to solve a problem: they can be behavioral adaptations, cortical images or symbolic combinations. Several representational levels can coexist in the frontal network and their relations by frontal automata correspond to the inductive properties of the human brain. But many contradictions appear, since results of combinations are not always in register. Such contradictions are resolved by new cortical actions; for example logical relators are cortical actions which maintain word combinations in register with combinations of cortical images of the outside world.

I. Cognitive development :
properties of the cortical system.

In FIGURE 5-1, we have illustrated the principal properties of the cortical system that are responsible for cognitive development and language learning: THE COLUMNAR AUTOMATA, THE GEOMETRY OF THE CORTICAL NETWORK, AND THE PROCESS OF CORTICAL MATURATION.

1. Columnar automata

A) Columnar automata learn two types of combinations: fixed sequences for words and oriented sequences for sentences.

The columnar automata constructs new integrated actions by combining existing cortical actions in the form of call trees (as described in chapter II).

In a novel situation, the modular mechanism produces a search of an efficient combination of cortical actions likely to attain a specific goal; the resulting adaptations can be memorized at two levels: by the construction of "oriented" sequences that gate external inputs or "fixed" sequences that directly trigger cortical actions.

Words and sentences are sound sequences generated by the cortical mechanism; but "words" are fixed phonemic sequences, while "sentences" are varied combinations of words. The two generative processes correspond to the two memorizing states in the cortical column (see chapter II):

1. In WORDS, combinations of phonemes is stabilized by a strong coupling between upper and lower layers of cortical columns; as a result, call trees generate

	CORTICAL SYSTEM	CAPACITY	HUMAN SPECIFICITY
MECHANISM	SEARCHING ADJUSTMENT	SENSORIMOTOR ADAPTATION	
	FIXED SEQUENCES ORIENTED SEQUENCES	WORDS LEARNING SENTENCE LEARNING	PHONEMIC CAPACITIES
	INTEGRATED ACTION BASES	GENERALIZATION DIFFERENTIATION	COMMUNICATION ACTIONS
NETWORK	FRONTAL SPECIALIZATION	SYNTACTIC CODING/DECODING	LARGE FRONTAL AREAS
	RELATIVE SIZE OF AREAS	STORAGE CAPACITIES	REDUNDANCY: MULTIPLE COMBINATIONS
	PRIVILEGED CIRCUITS	PHONEMIC IMITATION	LARGE COUPLING AUDITION-PHONATION
	SYMMETRIES	SYSTEMATIC CODING LEARNING TRANSFER	HEMISPHERIC SPECIALIZATION
	PARALLEL PATHWAYS	SEMANTIC POLES	
MATURATION	POST-NATAL MATURATION	RELATIVE STRUCTURATION	SLOW MATURATION
	DIFFERENTIAL MATURATION	IMPORTANCE OF COMMUNICATION	MOTOR RETARDATION
	SUCCESSIVE DESEQUILIBRIA	FULL OVERLAP OF ADULT BASES	CULTURAL BASES

Figure 5-1 . Properties of the cortical system for cognitive development and language learning.

phonemic combinations which are fixed. The sequence depends only upon the call by a goal which is the activation of a CORTICAL IMAGE.

2. But in SENTENCES, the appropriate combination of words is a transitory relation. Many combinations of words may be used to express the same idea. Possible relations between words correspond to the weaker coupling between the upper layers of columns; the sequence is not fixed but there are many semantic and syntactic links that orient sentence construction . For example, syntactic rules can be interpreted as weak couplings between upper layers of frontal modules that represent grammatical categories.

B) Stages of cognitive development correspond to learning of coherent sets of new integrated cortical actions

References

Cognitive development occurs in successive steps, or "stages" (Piaget 1950,1975). Each stage is constituted by a learning sequence that gives new capacities to the growing child. Each new learned set produces new disequilibrium, which becomes the incentive for further learning. The age at which a given stage appears can vary from one child to another, but the temporal order is relatively fixed, and this fixed order strongly suggests that each stage's existence depends directly upon development of prior stages.

There is, at least to some extent, an innate capacity for the various types of behavioral adaptation that we have considered in chapter IV: recognition, positioning, intrinsic programs (Bower 1970, 1978; Vurpillot 1972). These innate "diagrams" are the roots of increasingly structured sets of actions, by a learning process of relative assimilation (Piaget 1948,1968).

Each stage of cognitive development, in our analysis, can be explained by the acquisition of a new set of integrated cortical actions.

As described in chapter III-3, these new integrated actions are constructed by columnar automata in intermediate cortical areas: alternate stages of "generalization" and "differentiation" gives an internal coherence to these new cortical "bases". The process is recursive since new integrated actions can be combined by columnar automata to attain specific cortical goals and they become new possible sub-goals for other combinations of cortical actions.

The first integrated actions assimilated by the child effect the principal sensori-motor adaptations: positioning movements, recognition algorithms and imitative functions. Then columnar automata generate new call trees that effect internal adaptations between cortical areas; these call trees produce CORTICAL IMAGES that are internal representations of the external world: image of a "person", of an "object", or of a "movement".

Call trees that produce WORDS are then constructed by elaborating upon those that generate cortical images. Furthermore, columnar automata can combine cortical images and then sequence the corresponding words to form SENTENCES.

Learning is cumulative. Cooperation between different types of integrated actions is possible since the cortical operation is recursive (action=goal) and independent of sensori-motor meaning. Several bases of integrated actions can function in parallel in different part of the cortical network.

C) Cortical learning generates subgoals that induce new learning.

Each new acquisition provokes a disequilibrium, because each new cortical action becomes a possible goal which calls new combinations that favor its execution. Consequently the child is always learning.

At birth, initial disequilibria are due to a general lack of motor development . The slow maturation of motor capacities in fact stimulates learning of cortical actions that are more distant from direct execution of fundamental programs. Language learning is facilitated because it is not competitive with direct motor learning, and because it compensates, to some extent, for the motor deficiency. In the very young infant, communicative actions are the only ones possible for effecting most positioning and a certain number of recognitions. In a sense, by communicating with an adult, a child uses that adult as an intermediate means for interacting with people and objects. As an example, crying is an action that may put the child into contact with a desired object, via a cooperative adult.

Communicative actions other than language are at first more expressive for the child: postures, gestures, etc. But verbal communication permits a greater expressive diversity. As soon as the child begins to understand or produce words, these words become goals in themselves. The permanent disequilibrium between the child's production and the adult model stimulates learning of the various components of language: words are combinations of phonemes that activate cortical images . But learning of words induces learning of new phonemic forms; moreover, words are symbolic actions which become partial goals to assimilate cultural images, like categories of the adult language. The learning process is stabilized ultimately when there is complete overlap with adult bases of integrated actions-- phonemes, words, cortical images, but also syntactic rules that order combinations of words, and logical rules that resolve the disequilibrium due to the fact that combination of words create many new images that do not exist in the external world.

2. Geometry of the cortical network: hemispheric specialization

References

Each cortical hemisphere is specialized for particular behavioral functions: a certain number of associations are acquired in only one hemisphere (Sperry 1967, Gazzaniga 1970, 1975).

There is an hemispheric "geography" of cortical functions related to language; they are produced for the most part in the dominant hemisphere, usually the left (Hecaen 1983). Language specialization on the left, particularly the capacities for processing vowels and consonants, is precocious (2 years) (Kimura 1963). This functional specialization becomes accentuated during development.

Words and sentences are memorized on the left temporal lobe, while melodies and spatial tasks are treated on the right (Milner 1979). Subsequently, a more general functional specialization of the two hemispheres develops (Levy 1979): the right hemisphere shows more global, spatial processing, while the left hemisphere has a more analytic, sequential functional mode, related to the symbolic function.

Hemispheric symmetry favours the development of symbolic relations, isomorphic with but independent of natural relations

The second major property of the cortical system is due to its geometry, in particular the symmetries between cortical areas (as described in chapter III). The first one is the left-right symmetry between the two cortical hemispheres.

FIGURE 5-2 depicts the relations between the two cortical hemispheres: the cortical network is represented by the model developed in Chapter III ("closed" form of the network, like Figure 3-10).

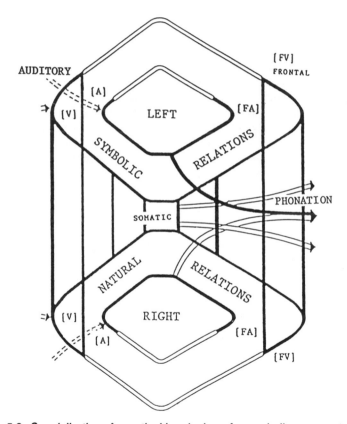

Figure 5-2 . Specialization of a cortical hemisphere for symbolic representations.

Parallel, systematic connections link symmetrical parts of the two cortical hemispheres, right and left. This architecture has two properties:
- newly-learned relations can be constructed independently in the two hemispheres;
- in favorable circumstances, newly-constructed relations in one hemisphere can induce isomorphic functional relations in the symmetrical parts of the other hemisphere. A new learned association can be transferred in a complete, "isomorphic" way to the

symmetrical regions. Even if the sensorimotor meaning of two groups of "symmetrical" cortical actions is not the same, their internal relations can present remarkable similarities.

a) Motor lateralization.

At birth, each cortical hemisphere has a sensory and motor specialization for the contralateral half of the body.

Connections systematically effected by the corpus callosum between the two hemispheres favor functional coupling between cortical zones related to symmetrical body parts. Furthermore the density of interhemispheric connections can control this functional dependency. For instance, a lower density between zones which command hand movements may favour independent actions of the two hands.

In the developing child, sensori-motor learning tends at first to be constructed in both hemispheres, in a parallel fashion. Interhemispheric symmetry favors isomorphic transfer of sensorimotor learning involving symmetrical parts of the body: a new call tree that produces a motor skill in the left or right hemisphere favors the construction of a symmetrical call tree in the other hemisphere.

But central muscular systems, like the speech apparatus, do not need a double cortical command. Development of call trees within a single hemisphere is sufficient for speech. In addition, this lateralization avoids the competitive aspect of double commands.

Cortical call trees coding words will thus be constructed in the hemisphere that commands speech movements; these initial associations favor the subsequent development and accumulation of new learning in the same hemisphere, and thus the command of language will be more and more lateralized.

b) Symbolic and natural relations.

The first bases of integrated actions acquired by the child's brain pertain to the logic of sensori-motor relations; symbolic bases, acquired later, are essentially cultural. Children learn language by imitating an adult model: this model implicitly contains a great number of structured relations, phonetic, semantic and syntactic. This internal structure is the result of a long social process and is specific to each language. Its formation is not the result of an individual effort of trial-and-error learning, but rather reflects a gradual historical and social accumulation process.

With language learning, two types of relations become possible between a sound and the perception of an object:

- NATURAL relations link visual perceptions of objects and sounds that they produce: these natural relations are due to the acoustic structure of the environment;

- SYMBOLIC relations link visual perceptions of objects with sounds produced by the vocal apparatus: these symbolic relations are due to social conventions.

These two types of relations would be competitive if they were constructed in the same cortical region; hemispheric specialization permits their coexistence, and therefore the systematic aspect of symbolic coding, as illustrated in FIGURE 5-2:

- SYMBOLIC relations are preferentially learned in the left hemisphere, implicating the command circuits of the vocal apparatus; cortical bases of integrated actions linked to language development, are lateralized on the left side.

- NATURAL relations are preferentially developed in the other hemisphere.

Non-linguistic cortical bases can develop in both hemispheres, but in the right hemisphere, they are less competitive with linguistic symbolic relations.

This twofold relational system (natural and symbolic) is elaborated in two different places, thanks to hemispheric specialization, and is therefore non-competitive. An excessive interdependence between these two systems would complicate acquisition of symbolic relations; for instance, if the two systems co-existed in the same cortical space, each external stimulus would be analyzed to determine if it was a signal or a symbol. Use of a separate space provides a convenient means of defining the symbolic domain.

Language profoundly reorganizes our representations of external reality. Words permit cleavage of reality into distinct elements, thus generating new cortical images. In sentences, these cortical images can be recombined independently of structures in the external world: these analytical treatments are thus essentially accomplished in the left "symbolic" hemisphere.

By contrast, links that are not symbolic and arbitrary, but that correspond to natural relations in the external world, favors direct spatial and synthetic processing, in the right hemisphere.

Systematic connections between symmetrical zones of the two hemispheres have a double importance:

- they permit isomorphic transfer of learning between relations of the "real world" and those of the "symbolic world", while at the same time respecting their functional independence;

- inter-hemispheric relations imply a series of adjustments. Combinations within one hemisphere are compared with combinations within the other; a disequilibrium in this comparison constitutes an important factor for the assimilation of logical operators.

3. Cortical maturation

References

Cortical maturation of cortical tissue continues after birth. Growth of cortical circuits (dendrites, spines, synapses) continues during the whole period of cognitive structuring. But there is a differential development of cortical areas; furthermore, the development of each area is roughly correlated with acquisition of new behavioral functions specific of this area (Rabinowiz 1979; Sauer 1983):

- Maturation of visual areas occurs during the first year, when development of visual recognition is faster.

- Maturation of motor areas, particularly the hand region, occurs between the first and the sixth year, when manipulation becomes well-organized.

- Maturation of the speech area also occurs between the first and the sixth year, lagging slightly behind that of the hand area: this correspond to the period of language structuring.

- Development of the frontal areas continues slowly until adulthood: during this period, the complex processes of logical symbolic manipulation are elaborated.

Differential maturation of the cortical network orders the first stages of cognitive development in a systematic way

Thanks to the slow process of maturation after birth, stabilization of the anatomic network (dendrites, synapses) becomes an integral part of learning: the transmission coefficients which are the substrata of memory can then be modified in a more extensive way, since their limits of variation are determined by anatomical parameters (as developed in chapter I).

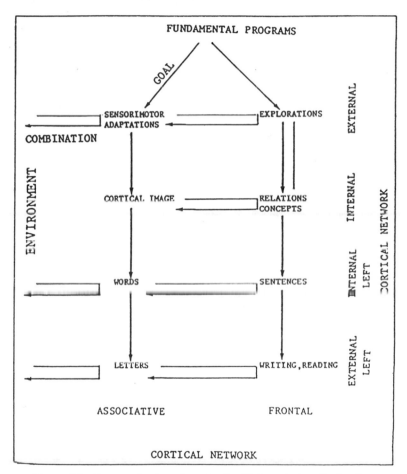

Figure 5-3 . Progressive learning of sets of integrated cortical actions.

Thus at each step, differential cortical maturation demarcates those regions where construction of new functional networks will be more intense: the integrated actions learned during this critical period will be very stable. Thanks to sequential maturation, each set of integrated actions can be formed in an independent and complete way.

The maturation sequence induces a natural "logic" in the order of learning. The different cortical pathways are successively structured from the most direct to the most "recombined". For instance, the frontal areas mature and learn structured sequences after learning of simple combinations by associative areas. We have seen that frontal lobes can learn rules from examples, and differentiate them from subsequent particular cases (chapter IV-4). The slow maturation of large frontal areas explains the particularly human capacity to memorize the multiple rules of language and the multiple levels of symbolic sequences .

Language acquisition is due to three properties of cortical tissue (TABLE 5-1): the columnar automaton, the geometry of the cortical network and its maturation process (slow and differential). The columnar automaton is not exclusive to the human brain. But the slow maturation process of the frontal network is an essentially human phenomenon that may be critical for development of a structured language.

We interpret each stage of learning in the young child as the construction of a

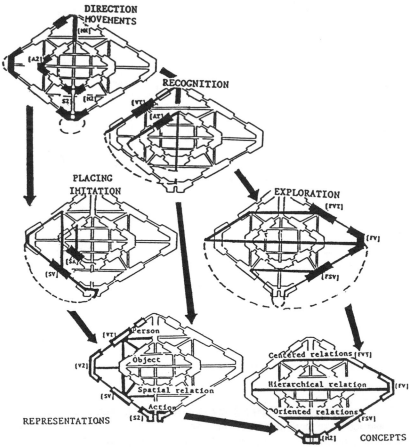

Figure 5-4 a . Cortical network as a substratum for learning mental representations from sensorimotor adaptations.

new basis of integrated actions. The main stages are listed on FIGURE 5-3:

- Each new "integrated action" is a combination (sequence) of existing cortical actions, generated by a call tree (depicted by a double arrow).

- Call trees are organized with respect to a "goal" that is itself a cortical action (depicted by a single arrow). Each sequence favors the accomplishment of a particular goal, but it acquires its own autonomy and become a goal for new call trees.

FIGURE 5-4 shows how the anatomical substrata orders the construction of these new cortical bases: this figure summarizes the progressive use of the cortical network during cognitive development of the child.

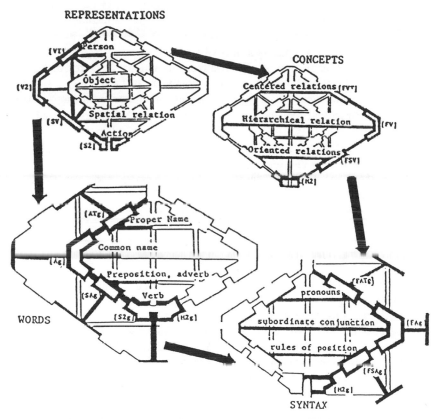

Figure 5-4 b . Cortical network as a substratum for learning words and syntax from mental images.

Each of the eight diagrams is a reproduction of the model of the network between cortical areas that we proposed in Chapter III ("closed" form, as Figure 3-10). Each schema represents a stage of cognitive development: it highlights the priviliged cortical circuits that favor the acquisition of new behavioral functions; this substrata is depicted with accented dark lines.

The vertical axis of Figure 5-4 represents the time during which cognitive development occurs: later bases of integrated actions (lower diagrams) are constructed upon earlier ones (upper diagrams).

The lateral extension of new functional networks in cortical areas is larger for early learning, but at each new step, it decreases and it is mostly the number of transversal connections between areas that increases in the call tree:

- Each new learning experience implicates neurons which are not grouped in a restrained zone, nor are they randomly scattered. But they are denser in privileged poles given by the logic of network connections: relations with sensory or motor organs and combinations formed by the cortical network.

- The new call trees are constructed upon one of the six standard connections of every cortical zone that correspond to the six basic symmetries of the cortical network (see chapter III). Each of the six symmetries favors new types of learning.

a) Sensory motor adaptations (A1-A4).

Primitive construction of sensori-motor adaptations structures first the main cortical regions: directional movements in primary areas (stage A1) , recognition algorithms in temporal areas (stage A2), positioning and imitative functions in parietal (stage A3), and structured sequences of exploration in the symmetrical frontal areas (stage A4).

b) Cortical images and internal adaptations (R1-R2).

From these sensori-motor bases, columnar automata construct CORTICAL IMAGES of movements, of people, of objects (stage R1). Cortical representations of "relations" between these images (stage R2) are autonomous in the frontal regions; their roots are the structured explorations previously formed in these frontal areas.

Cortical images are constructed on the same anatomical areas as the "parent" sensorimotor adaptations; their substrata share common parts but have a specific organization:

- call trees that generate sensori-motor adaptations are functionally related with the external world and they use the input-output connections of the cortex: they form an EXTERNAL functional network;

- by contrast, other call trees can generate cortical images on the internal cortico-cortical connections: they form an INTERNAL functional network. In Figure 5-4, we have depicted these two functional network , External (A1-A4) and Internal (R1-R2), in a different way, but with a common anatomical substrata.

c) Linguistic bases and symbolic adaptations (L1-L2).

Language acquisition has two aspects: symbolic and phonetic.

1.   Language is first a symbolic process : word code images by symbols. The symbolic linguistic bases will develop in the left hemisphere while the right hemisphere will be the main substrata for images independent of symbolic coding.

2. But language is also a verbal process that uses the phonation capacities to communicate. Figure 5-4 (stage L1) enlarges the cortical network to more clearly show the specialized circuit of verbal imitation upon which words are learned. As illustrated in this schema, the call trees that code the various types of images (persons, objects, movements) will be constructed in relation with different poles of the cortical network.

Afterwards, syntactic bases are formed in the symmetrical frontal regions (stage L2). Different types of verbal control will be constructed in different poles of the frontal network.

d) Reorganization of cortical bases.

All these new functional networks change in two ways:

1. First, new integrated actions are produced by call trees constructed from goals which are pre-existing cortical actions (downward movement in Figure 5-4).

2. Second, each new integrated action becomes a partial goal which reorganizes the pre-existing actions into larger combinations (upward movement in Figure 5-4). For example, words that define categories are cultural and predefined for the child; they restructure existing cortical images and construct new ones. Similarly, the new syntactic rules that the child learns reorganize the base of words previously acquired: each word becomes a multi-level phonemic sequence expressing a group of hierarchical relations (agreement of number, conjugations, etc.)

The geometry of the human cerebral cortex permits a remarkable coherence among successive learning experiences. The new bases of integrated cortical actions will represent external reality in two very different ways, natural and symbolic, from three sensory modalities (vision, audition, somesthesia) and with three sets of motor commands (ocular, manual, and vocal); furthermore, they will organize at least five different temporal levels in language production: phonemes, words, word pairs, sentences, and coherent discourse.

II. Adaptive construction of mental images.

In our perspective, mental images are produced by cortical call trees. The call trees that generate "mental images" are constructed and function in exactly the same way as sensori-motor adaptations. The only difference is that they effect adaptations between the activities of different cortical areas, independently of external stimuli or motor outputs; they produce an oriented call toward cortical actions that are triggered when they are in register with other cortical inputs (same process as developed in chapter II).

In chapter IV, we have already analyzed the construction of the different types of sensori-motor adaptations (positioning, recognition, structured programs); these behavioral adaptations are the roots of the different "cortical images" that represent the external world in the cortex: cortical images of movements, of people, of objects, and then of various spatial and temporal relations of the external world.

Construction of these "cortical images" is, in fact, very progressive. For example, the "image of a movement" is at first the representation of the direction of the movement; then it includes a final "somesthetic" position, and then it takes into account the effect of the movement upon another sensory modality, visual or auditory, etc...

The same holds true for the cortical image of an object: the object is at first simply an element of the environment that can be isolated by a visual or manual exploration; then this object is distinguished by manipulation sequences and then on the basis of its utility ; the next step is the progressive assimilation of the intrinsic structure of the object.

The stage of construction of "cortical images" that we are discussing here corresponds to a state preceding language learning; these images will be goals to learn phonemic sequences that form words.

A) Columnar automata construct images of simple movements from reflexes

The newborn baby is equipped with a certain number of positioning reflexes (for example orienting the head as a function of an odor) and repetitive motor responses (sucking after lip contact). There are also a number of spontaneous repetitive movements that occur without external stimulation: eye movements, crying, etc....

These various activities are not produced by the cortex; but their simple repetition will structure the primary cortical areas, because they provoke in the cortex regular activity patterns and recurrent coactivations linked with the geometrical features of the sensory and motor systems. Few coactivations can create new functional networks related with the geometry of movement (orientation, direction) because of the critical periods of cortical growth. Since actions of these new cortical circuits become partial goals, cortical automata will be able to sequence these simple directional movements to attain other cortical goals.

During maturation of primary visual area ([V1]), an eye movement coactivates cortical modules that preferentially respond to a stimulus oriented in the same way. Rapid registration during these critical periods stabilize new circuits selective for orientations, for each position of the visual field; new call trees in the visual cortex can control the orientation and the final position of eye movements. We saw that these cortical commands are very important for the construction of recognition algorithms (chapter IV-3).

The primary somatosensory ([S1]) and motor ([M1]) areas are similarly structured by various reflexes and spontaneous movements, and resulting call trees will command beginning, stopping, orientation and direction of simple movements of various parts of the muscular map. In the same way , crying favours a primitive structuring of the motor region which command the different parts of the vocal apparatus.

B) Columnar automata construct mental images of people from recognition algorithms

Whenever a reflex or spontaneous movement is produced, external forms in the environment induce temporal correlations between sensory inputs. We have already seen that these correlations are not stable in receptive areas, although they can be in temporal areas that form an information pathway between sensory activity and fundamental programs. First call trees in temporal areas are primitive recognition algorithms which combine sensory "matching actions" with respect to fundamental programs (goal).

In the visual temporal regions, "faces"-- and particularly the mother's face-- are the first forms recognized, since they are directly associated with most of the fundamental programs (heat, food, etc.). The cortical process has a double effect (as analyzed in chapter IV.3):

1. It constructs a recognition algorithm for "mother's face" by a descriptor which combines exploratory actions directed toward the "eyes", the "mouth", etc..

2. It produces increasingly accurate distinction between different faces , familiar or novel, since each exploratory action amplifies a difference.

Auditory recognition follows the same process: a recognition algorithm for "mother's voice" is constructed by a combination of actions that differentiate either sound frequencies or voice modulations; in parallel, each exploratory action enhances the differences perceived between various voices.

Call trees become polysensory; for example, auditory and tactile information can be included in recognition algorithms of people. Since these algorithms function internally between cortical areas independently of external stimuli, they will constitute primitive cortical "images" of people. These representations become more and more precise as recognition algorithms continue to develop.

C) Columnar automata construct images of object from positioning and recognition algorithms

Call trees progressively include more and more features in the cortical images of "objects", in this paragraph we will analyze the first four stages.

a) Grasping: the object as an independent element in the environment.

Simultaneous eye and hand movements produce sensory correlations that induce two call trees : the first produces visual fixation of the hand, and the second positions the hand at the point of visual fixation. The cortex can thus control movement of the hand toward a visually-fixated object (Chapter IV.2) and a grasping action can isolate the object from the environment. The "fixation-grasping" algorithm generates the first cortical image of an object, as something independent from other parts of the environment.

b) Manual exploration: the object as a manipulable element

The "fixation-grasping" algorithm is then extended by manipulative or moving actions. Repeated contact with objects induces the construction of exploratory actions independent of the object's nature, consisting of movements such as " take", "grab", "shake", "drop".

These movements facilitate interaction of the object with the main cortical sensory inputs ("put in the mouth", "make a noise with") and they are included into recognition algorithms. The cortical system will produce new exploratory movements by the general process of repetition ("align", "stack") and differentiation ("turn", "strike"). Then new cortical sequences will depend upon the intrinsic properties of each object. Images of objects will progressively include images of manipulative movements.

c) Visual imitation: the object as a useful element.

Imitation of other people accelerates object recognition. Visual imitation is possible because of a double property of the cortical system (Chapter IV.2):

- temporal regions can match the perception of the movements of another person and the perception of one's own movements;

- parietal regions can match the perception of one's own movements and the muscle commands that produce those movements.

The cortical mechanism integrates this double relation to construct "imitation" call trees that can command movements on the basis of perception of a model (call by one of two elements of a sensory correlation). This visuo-motor imitation is very powerful for internalizing new combinations of effective motor actions: a child can economically learn appropriate responses by observing adult models.

d) Frontal exploration: the object as a structured element.

In the previous stage, cortical goals are no longer just fundamental programs; they can also be "recognitions" or "motor actions", as soon as these call trees are constructed. The curiosity for people and objects seen in the child at this stage is due to the generalization of cortical goals. Frontal activity prolongs interest for an object that has disappeared from the visual field and reinforces the autonomy of its cortical image.

But the frontal call trees can also organize hierarchical sequences of exploratory actions with several nested levels (Chapter IV.4). This ordered exploration will assimilate the internal structure of an object.

D) Columnar automata construct images of relations from combinations of cortical images.

a) Combination of cortical images.

Before the symbolic function of language, "images" of motor actions, people, and objects are produced by cortical call trees which function autonomously between cortical areas.

These "cortical images" have combinatorial possibilities independent of language: they are cortical actions and can be combined by columnar automata. These "spontaneous" combinations of cortical images are well expressed in the child's play, independently of language.

b) Cortical images of relations: concepts.

In the frontal regions, the call trees represent "relations" between the cortical images produced in the symmetrical associative areas. Relations between cortical images, independent of sensory or motor activity, will be defined here as "concepts": for instance, the concept of "giving something to someone" represents a directional relation between two people. (The distinction between image and concept can be illustrated by another example: one can have an image of "movement"; the concept of "haste" involves, in addition to the image of movement, reference to an external time limit or an internal state of stress. Roughly speaking, a concept, in our analysis, is a relation between two or more images.)

Cortical images of relations exist implicitly in the call trees between images in the associative areas, but they become autonomous actions in the symmetrical frontal areas, and consequently they become partial goals for image combination.

Thank to these partial goals, image sequences become increasingly complex according to the same general plan that directs combination of sensori-motor actions: repetition, differentiation, level changes. For example, in the child's play, sequencing of motor actions occurs first from an actual object (for example a toy-car), but after it can occur from a cortical image evoked by the object (for instance "to drive"); then the sequence will be triggered without an external support but directly from partial goals that are "representation of relations". The next step is the imagination of a story by combination of images based on the "representation of a set of relations" centered about actors.

c) Concepts and structured language.

Combinations of cortical images will lead to combinations of the words that code them. Developments of concepts in the form of autonomous cortical actions in the frontal areas favor the development of structured language since these concepts can serve as partial goals for large combinations of images (of people, actions, and objects).

Before this concept stage, the cortical tissue can combine "images" only in response to an external situation: the environmental conditions shape the sequence. This stage of cognitive development is reached by the great apes. The next stage, specifically human, is the capacity to combine cortical images with partial goals that are themselves cortical images of relations: for instance, the concept of "absence" or "presence", linked to a strong call activity in the frontal areas, is frequently expressed by the first sentences pronounced by a child.

III. Language acquisition.

References

Language is basically a specific expression of a more general adaptation of communication. Communication exists in several animal species, but human language is characterized by an extremely powerful intrinsic organization showing both a systematic, symbolic code of mental images (words) and an hierarchical, sequential code (sentences) that together permit the expression of multiple, varied relations between the mental images.

Language learning is a structured process, organized in successive stages; the order in which these stages appear is relatively fixed from one child to the next, and is relatively universal across cultures (Richelle 1971, Liberman 1973, Oleron 1976).

a) Words.

1. Language builds upon associations between mental images (an object, person, or action) and symbols; such associations can be acquired by the great apes (Premack 1976).

2. Symbols developed by humans are mostly phonetic. Children learn phonemes by relative differentiation from the most clearly opposed forms (Jacobson 1956; Pierce 1974) ; they learn in parallel sequences of phonemes whose length progressively increases with the development of memory capacities (Oleron 1973).

3. The relation between a "symbol" and its "meaning" is not fixed in the child's brain, but rather evolves by successive approximations of adult usage (Reich 1976, Halliday 1975), including stages of overgeneralization and overdiscrimination (Clark 1973). The child's acquisition of vocabulary occurs rapidly, even exponentially (Smith 1926).

b) Syntax.

1. Language is also a combination of words in an ordered way, in the form of sentences: the spoken sentence expresses various relations between people, objects, and actions symbolized by words. The internal structure of the verbal sequence becomes progressively more complex, representing various relational levels. First sentences originate from isolated words ("word-sentences") that express both an image (for instance, a person) and a relation (for instance, an absence) (De Laguna 1967, Greenfield, 1968). Next the child assimilates, from adult models, combinations involving two words (Bloom 1973, Brown 1973), especially from words that imply a relation (Braine 1976).

2. Children learn syntactic rules by context-guided generalization, then restrictions corresponding to successive adjustments to models from the adult culture (Rondal 1978).

3. Assimilation of new syntactic rules by the child produces the construction of increasingly complex tree-structures: subordinate clauses, conjugations, etc. (Menyuk 1971). In the "syntagmatic" model (Chomsky 1971), sentences are represented by an branching structure beginning with an initial "axiom" (the root), then developing according to a certain number of "rewriting rules" (the nodes) that extend each grammatical category (the branches) and that are repeatedly applied to each category. The terminal branches are the elementary components of the sentence (words, terminations). This "deep structure" of the sentence is then modified by a certain number of "transformation rules", which are operational diagrams applied to the trees which generate the sentence: these rules produce the "surface structure" of the sentence which is then pronounced.

c) Semantic representation.

But production and comprehension of sentences depends also upon a semantic representation, in which the meaning of the words is specified in relation to the context. The meaning of each word is also a multi-level structure: for instance, verbs, representing "actions" (for example "give") have "primitives" that contain a sensori-motor representation (for instance, "transfer of something to someone") (Schank, 1975). When a word is pronounced, its component representations generate a certain number of possible "expectations"; consequently, in a sentence, many elements are not directly expressed, being instead guessed by inference . The meaning of a sentence can be represented by a schema of "conceptual dependency" between the different representations and expectancies included in each word (Schank 1975).

1. Learning of words and semantic categories

FIGURE 5-5 illustrates the natural pathways of the cortical network which are the substrata of language acquisition.

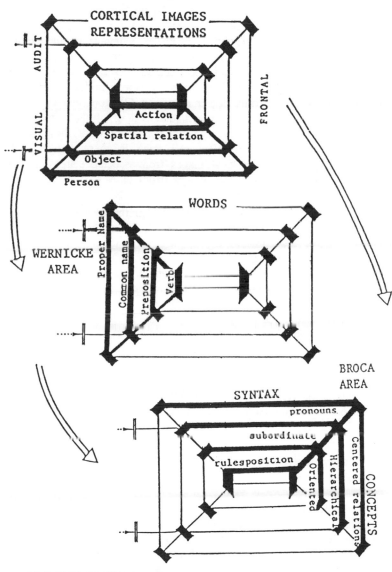

OPEN FORM OF THE NETWORK

Figure 5-5 . 3 steps in the learning of linguistic bases until a global equilibrium due to the circular geometry of the cortical network.

Three diagrams show the three main learning stages on the model of cortical network (that we developed in chapter III ,Figure 3-11: open form). Columnar automata construct new integrated actions on the different symmetrical connections of this network: (1) CORTICAL IMAGES on connections between associative and frontal areas (upper diagram); (2) then WORDS between the auditory and visual circuits (associative areas including Wernicke area, middle diagram); (3) then SYNTACTIC RULES on connections with symmetrical frontal regions (Broca area), which are also linked with representations of relations (concepts) by the frontal network.

The lower diagram shows that the circular aspect of cortical geometry results in an equilibrium point in the acquisition of language: language production will be a circular and recursive process. During the whole period of language learning by children, new functional networks (call trees) spread over the cortical network from mental images in two directions: (1) from images to words (middle diagram) and then to ordered combinations of words (lower diagram); (2) from images to images of relations (upper diagram) and then to symbolic coding of these relations (lower diagram). Thanks to the circular geometry of the cortical network, these two sets meet in frontal regions (Broca's area). New call trees in these regions will adapt combinations of words that code cortical images (from associative areas), and symbolic coding of concepts which relate these images (from other frontal areas): they form syntactic rules which structure sentences.

We begin with the learning of words. The disequilibrium underlying the learning of each word is the lack of correspondence between the child's word and the adult model; construction of new cortical integrated actions is stabilized only when there is complete overlap of three cultural bases: phonemes, words" and cortical images. These three bases are constructed in a cooperative way by columnar automata in large associative and frontal regions with alternate processes of sequencing (transversal coupling) and differentiation (lateral uncoupling):

1. A word is at first a sound called by a cortical image ; each cortical image can be coded by a sound symbol that is easily transmitted.

2. Various cortical images differentiate new phonemes and induce new phonemic sequences; these two processes generate an extensive diversification of words.

3. Words of the cultural base are not directly adjusted to the cortical images of the child; words will become goals for the cortical construction of new mental images.

A) Cortical images call actions of communication such as phonemic sequences

a) Word comprehension: symbolic coding of cortical images.

Auditory recognition of words extend the visual and somatosensory recognition algorithms that are the roots of cortical images. A word pronounced by an adult in the presence of an object becomes an integral part of the recognition algorithm of the object. In fact, parents behave in such a way as to accelerate this learning-- by repetition of more significant words, accentuating separations and modulations, use of visual ("showing") and tactile ("giving") aids. Adaptation of adult language to the capacities of the child guides the construction of the original set of words.

b) Word production from cortical images.

Word comprehension is, like visual recognition, an all-or-nothing phenomenon that triggers a cortical image. The "word", considered as a combination of sounds, is a partial goal of the recognition algorithm: it is called by an image and gains an autonomy inside the cortex. Word production is a consequence of this autonomy: cortical images are goals and "auditory words" subgoals for the call trees that produce words. Thanks to the circuits for vocal imitation which are already learned, each "word" , as a partial auditory goal, can call cortical actions that favour its reactivation (as developed in chapter II); consequently it calls appropriate commands of the vocal apparatus since pronunciation of words attain this subgoal.

c) Diversity of symbolic coding.

Because of the systematic connections between cortical areas (symmetries left/right and auditory/visual), "cortical images" can be systematically coded by sounds: each cortical representation is a call tree that can be extended by a specific branch toward a phonemic sequence.

The cortical region that can couple the "images" and the phonemes is very large and includes whole areas like the area of Wernicke. In this region, "words" are constructed as partial goals, and acquire autonomy with respect to both images and phonemes.

The variety of symbols needed to code the diversity of "images" is obtained by two parallel processes: the cortical mechanism can combine positions of the vocal apparatus to produce different sounds (phonemes) and it can combine these phonemes by sequencing them with increasing length (chapter IV.2):

1. Phonetic differentiation conforms to the successive dichotomies of a cortical zone (chapter III.3): the most obvious phonetic oppositions will be first learned, and differentiation continues with the learning of less marked transitions, up to mastery of phonemes involving fine transitions between consonants and vowels (such as fricatives).

2. Well before complete differentiation of the phonemic base, columnar automata construct fixed sequences of phonemes, in the same way as any goal-directed motor sequence (Chapter IV.2): one of the syllables is first associated with the recognition algorithm of the word (for instance "dy" for the cortical image of a candy); the disequilibrium provoked by the mismatch with the model leads to persistence of the cortical call which results in repetition of the syllable ("dy-dy"); extension of the call through the cortical network results in a progressive differentiation ("can-dy"). Whatever the number of phonemes, this repetition-differentiation process can assimilate any adult model until complete matching.

The two aspects of word learning (diversification of phonemes and prolongation of sequences) are not competitive and can occur in parallel thanks to the redundancy of cortical circuits (Chapter III.3). Every cortical action that participates in the algorithm of word production amplifies the perception of discrepancies from the model, and hence favors new differentiations. Each word that is learned serves as a reference in the comprehension of adult language: consequently learning speed is, initially, proportional to the number of words learned; thus this number will grow exponentially.

The internal structure of a word (prefix, ending) can come to express a particular relation and will be learned by the frontal mechanism (chapter IV.4), as soon as the phonemes have acquired a certain functional autonomy.

B) Semantic categories: words are new subgoals which can isolate parts of recognition algorithms that represent categories.

a) Words become new goals.

In the same way that cortical images of the child organize the learning of words, these words in turn can reorganize cortical images, or even construct new ones.

As the phonemic base becomes more and more solidly consolidated, word learning becomes more rapid; the child can learn a new word by recombining phonemes, even if the resulting word is not necessarily linked to one of his cortical images.The numerous words proposed by adults (cultural base) exceed the simple representations of the child: these words then become goals to construct new images. Consequently, the representations of the child become progressively adjusted to the adult model, via verbal communication.

b) Recombination of cortical algorithms from words: proliferation of cortical images with different representational levels.

Many words represent CATEGORIES that are natural characteristics of objects and people: shape, size, movement. The cortical images fitted to these categories exist implicitly in single steps of many recognition algorithms. They are directly related to simple cortical processes. For example "adjectives" (colour, size) are directly related to activation of a limited part of the sensory map.

Since recognition algorithm proceeds from the general to the particular, each isolated stage in the algorithm implicitly represents the category of all elements which possess the common characteristics of this stage. In the example of the visual recognition algorithm of a person (Chapter IV.3), the first action explores the "eyes": its isolation generates the representation of a new category--"people". Partial combinations across algorithmic stages also lead to elaboration of new categories: for example, the exploratory sequence "eyes+mouth" differentiates two new categories, "people" and "animals".

Words of the cultural base are goals from which columnar automata can extract individual steps of recognition algorithms and thus produce new images that are new "categories". Thanks to words, columnar automata can isolate and recombine the pre-existing cortical actions in many ways to adjust mental images to the categories of the adult model.

2. Syntactic rules

A) Cortical automata in frontal regions construct syntactic rules in order to express hierarchical sets of relations between cortical images.

Combinations of cortical images exist at a pre-linguistic level (Chapter V.2). The capacity to combine words is initially linked to the capacity to combine cortical images.

The global goal that calls a verbal sequence is the communication of a story, formed by an ordered group of relations between cortical images: columnar automata in frontal areas can attain this goal by combining words in a structured way, with several nested levels (see chapter IV).

Subgoals are specific relations between cortical images, such as:
- temporal relations between two successive actions (for example "eat" and then "sleep");
- oriented relations between two people ("give"); the nature of the relation expressed (for instance, "position" or "possession"), and especially its orientation will be important for coding sequential order of words.
- relations centered around a person ("actors" of the story) or around a "theme".

The cultural coding of these relations has two aspects: "Syntactic rules" code a relation by the relative position of words; "syntactic relators" (for example, the pronoun "who") code both the relation and the level changes of the word sequence.

Children learn this cultural coding in a very progressive way. The various temporal levels of a sentence are assimilated in parallel with growth of the verbal sequence.

1. Initially, the image of a relation ("absence of a parent", for instance) is a subgoal that calls a single word, a "word-sentence" that expresses either the relation (absence) or its elements (the absent parent).

2. The ambiguity of such an expression produces a disequilibrium that leads to associate two words. At first, this association has no particular temporal order.

3. But in adult speech, word order is guided by syntactic rules that specify the relation (for instance, its orientation : "give to"): new call trees orient sequences of words in a similar way in order to express a relation. The verbal sequence is directly copied from the underlying story (representations of successive relations), but word pairs are occasionally arranged by a syntactic rule.

4. This first organizational level (word pair) filters the adult sentence and highlights "syntactic words" (prepositions, conjunctions) that specify the type of relation existing between two elements: for example, the relative position of two objects, or the temporal relation between two actions. New functional networks from images of relations not only orient word sequences, but also call a phonemic sequence which is a syntactic relators; these new words serve as level markers for the frontal mechanism in order to decode several nested levels of relations (subgoals) in a verbal sequence.

B) Grammatical categories are formed in frontal regions by progressive lateral uncoupling and syntactic rules by transversal coupling.

Figure 5-6 illustrates the learning of syntactic rules by columnar automata in the frontal areas with the dual process of generalization and differentiation:

1. The progressive dichotomy in the frontal areas is depicted in the left part of FIGURE 5-6, learning time is shown on the horizontal axis, and frontal areas are arranged on the vertical axis ("frontal" time axis described in chapter IV.4). Differentiation of frontal modules produce increasingly precise grammatical categories which are called by sets of words in the symmetrical associative areas (call from the left part of the figure).

2. Syntactic rules are shown by an branching structure, in the right part of Figure 5-6; they are produced by large couplings between frontal zones that represent

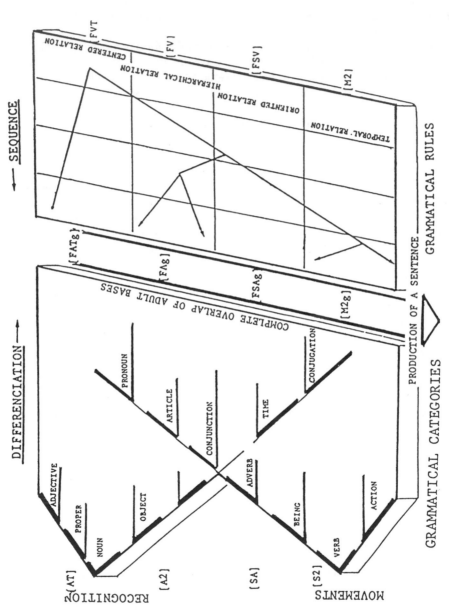

Figure 5-6 . Grammatical rules (right part) are call trees which relate more and more precise categories of words (left part) in frontal areas.

grammatical categories. Each rule expresses a meaningful relation and is called by a "concept" (image of a relation) already constructed in the other frontal areas (call from the right part of the figure).

a) Differentiation of grammatical categories.

Grammatical categories are thus differentiated by successive opposites and correspond to successive dichotomies of frontal regions.

First, the category "nouns" specifies a whole frontal region linked with recognition algorithms of people (in temporal areas) and is differentiated in opposition to the category "verbs", which specify the whole frontal region linked with movements (motor areas).

In a second stage, adverbs and prepositions are differentiated from verbs, since they represent results of actions (frontal region linked with sensory correlation in parietal areas) rather than the actions themselves (primary motor area).

Then several types of syntactic relators can specify different relations: first the relation between two words (preposition), between a word and a context (article), then between two sentences (conjunction), between a sentence and a context (pronoun), etc.

This process continues until complete adjustment to the adult cultural base of grammatical categories and syntactic relators.

b) Multi-level syntactic rules.

Syntactic rules are learned in several stages. At each stage, the rule is established by a global, large transversal coupling between two frontal zones that involves grammatical categories, not just isolated words.

Within each grammatical category, words can become more and more numerous (differentiation in the associative areas), but they call globally the same frontal region. Subsequent differentiations in associative areas conserve the transversal relations in frontal areas and, consequently, the syntactic rules previously acquired.

The new rules are not competitive with the older ones since they correspond to more local transversal couplings : for example, position rules pertaining to "verb-noun" are constructed before differentiations "article-noun", and remain unmodified by acquisition of the latter.

Thus, syntactic rules are hierarchical couplings between frontal zones corresponding to more and more precise grammatical categories. Sentences produced by children, become longer and more structured as these "syntactic bases" become more differentiated.

As illustrated in Figure 5-6 (in the right part) a sentence is produced by columnar automata from a set of sub-goals (syntactic rules) which can be depicted by an branching structure (from left to right):
- each node is a syntactic rule (coupling between two frontal zones);
- each branch provides supplementary specification of a grammatical category.
- forks couple increasingly restricted frontal zones which correspond to increasingly precise categories.

A global call is produced by a set of images of relations (from right in figure 5-6). As described in chapter III, global activity of a cortical zone spontaneously moves towards contrasted configurations (equilibrium states); these configurations in frontal areas correspond to the expression of the more precise grammatical categories (maximal differentiation). But there are intermediate configurations that correspond to more general categories coupled by more general syntactic rules; a rule is activated at each level of precision.

This "cortical activation" tree shown in Figure 5-6 is similar to the generative process of sentences described in linguistics (by syntagmatic models) : the tree defines the "re-writing rules" (intermediate nodes) that permit passage from a "initial axiom" (initial global call) to the "deep structure" of the sentence (final configurations with actions of the most differentiated cortical zones).

IV. Cortical process of language production.

1. Cortical circuits and symmetries

A) The cortical network form two orthogonal sets of circuits which correspond to the semantic and temporal aspects of language.

Language is generated by cortical tissue: production and comprehension of language depends upon both the columnar automaton and the geometry of the cortical network.

FIGURE 5-7 illustrates the whole process of language production and comprehension on the cortical network; this network is represented again by the model that we proposed in chapter III.2 in order to more clearly illustrate its geometrical properties (see Figures 3-11 to 3-14, "open" form). Functional relations within this network are the results of the learning processes developed in part III of this chapter (see Figure 5-5 and 5-6).

Figure 5-7 shows that language is globally organized by its anatomical substratum formed by two sets of cortical circuits inter-related like radii and concentric circles:

a) "Convergent circuits": syntagmatic organization.

The first set formed by the four CONVERGENT radii (or diagonals) includes the two privileged sensorimotor circuits (vision-manipulation and audition-phonation) and their two frontal symmetric counterparts: the cortex produces "IMAGES" in the visuo-motor circuit, codes them by "WORDS" in the auditory-phonation circuit and expresses their "RELATIONS" by "SENTENCES" in the two frontal symmetrical circuits.

The cortical network link these circuits with parallel connections: every image can be coded by at least a word and every word can construct a cortical image. Furthermore, the cortical symmetries produce a functional isomorphism: a relation between two images induces a relation between two words.

b) "Concentric circuits": semantic organization

The second set of cortical circuits are formed by the four CONCENTRIC circles (or rectangles) which relate associative and frontal areas; they correspond to the four

INFORMATION FLOWS IN THE CORTICAL NETWORK

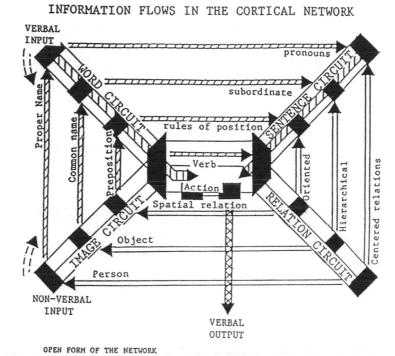

OPEN FORM OF THE NETWORK

Figure 5-7 . Concentric and convergent circuits of the cortical network interrelate semantic and syntactic components of language in a coherent structure.

main "poles" of the cortical network which are the substrata of the four major semantic categories of images and relations: "movements" in the somatomotor circuit, spatial and temporal "relations" in the fronto-parietal circuit, "objects and explorations" in the fronto-receptor circuit, "people and their relations" in the fronto-temporal circuit.

The various lexical and grammatical categories induced by these images will be constructed with a similar regional specialization in these four "semantic poles".

c) Cortical areas as nodes between two orthogonal circuits.

In parallel, FIGURE 5-8 represents these two sets of functional circuits on a table. Each circuit is formed by four cortical areas linked by four sets of symmetrical and systematic connections. Each area is a node between two cortical circuits and consequently columnar automata within this area produce internal adaptations between two major information flows:

- Through the four "CONCENTRIC CIRCUITS" (columns in table 5-7), call trees effect symbolic coding and decoding of words within each semantic category. These four circuits can function in parallel, and their reciprocal relations induce a primitive semantic organization of language.

- Through the four "CONVERGENT CIRCUITS" (lines in table 5-7) , call trees interrelate the different semantic categories of images and the corresponding words in a coherent structure: actor, action, circumstances, etc.. In the frontal circuits, cortical

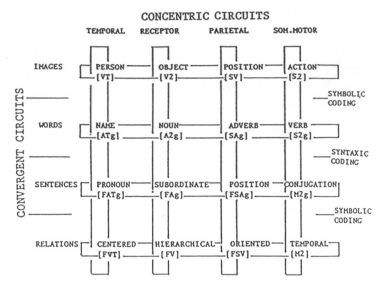

Figure 5-8 . Linguistic relations are learned in cortical regions which are nodes between two sets of cortical circuits.

automata organize speech in a sequential way, and the four parts of these circuits correspond to four basic temporal levels of language (time axis of the frontal cortex): the general frame of the narrative (centered relations), the global syntactic structure of sentences (hierarchical relations), the polarity of each simple phrase (oriented relations) and then the phonemic sequence of words (temporal relations).

The cortical network coordinates all these various local adjustments in a coherent global movement, and the whole set of internal adaptations is responsible for language production.

The regional specializations described here should be loosely interpreted as organizational tendencies rather than strict functional separations.

B) Cortical symmetries favour systematic symbolic coding and isomorphic functioning between cortical images and words.

a) From images to words

Cortical images are constructed in a subset of associative areas that we call the "IMAGE-CIRCUIT" (one of the four concentric circuits).

Language leads to a hemispheric specialization because of the symbolic nature of coding, and within this hemisphere, there is another specialization because of the phonemic nature of the symbols. We called this set of areas the "WORD-CIRCUIT" . The image-circuit and the word-circuit are related by systematic symmetrical connections. Using this symmetry, the call trees interrelate cortical images and vocal sequences: in one direction they effect a symbolic coding of each cortical images, and in the other direction they effect decoding of each word.

b) From images to concepts

In the frontal regions symmetrical with the image-circuit, the call trees define relations between cortical images. We call this set of frontal areas the "RELATION-CIRCUIT". Via the symmetrical connections, the call trees interrelate images (associative regions) with the representation of their relations (frontal region) in the form of autonomous concepts: these new partial goals can be coded in a symbolic form.

c) From words to sentences.

Syntactic relations organize word sequences at several levels in the frontal areas symmetrical with the word-circuit. We call this set of frontal areas the "SENTENCE-CIRCUIT". Via symmetrical connections, call trees organize word pairs (in associative areas) with syntactic relations (in frontal regions). This adaptation generates the syntactic structure of the sequence of words.

d) From relations to syntactic relators.

Via the symmetry between the two frontal circuits, the relation-circuit and the sentence-circuit, the call trees adapt relational concepts and syntactic rules. This adaptation produces the temporal descriptive structure of a story: sequence of events, exploratory description of a complex scene, centered relations around actors, etc..

2. Semantic categories in the cortical "concentric" circuits

Regional specialization of behavioral adaptations (EXTERNAL network) induces regional specialization of cortical images (INTERNAL network) that in turn induces regional specialization of words; the four concentric circuits (concentric rectangles of Figure 5-7) form four major semantic "poles": images of motor actions and verbs involve mainly the somatomotor regions, images of people and names implicate temporal regions, and images of objects and nouns are produced in the parieto-temporal regions.

Within each circuit, symmetrical and systematic connections between areas establish parallel, isomorphic, non-competitive relations between : a semantic category of cortical image (node with the image-circuit), its symbolic coding by a lexical category (node with the word-circuit), the principal concepts related to the image (node with the relation-circuit) and the syntactic coding of these concepts (node with the sentence-circuit). Consequently, the coding and decoding of the main semantic components of a sentence (person - object - relation - action) are effected IN PARALLEL.

A) Cortical automata construct names from images of people in the temporal pole, and pronouns from concepts of centered relations in the symmetrical frontal pole.

a) Temporal pole: cortical images of people and names

Images of people are generated by call trees in temporal areas (area [VT], Internal network); these call trees are progressive extensions of recognition algorithms for faces ([VT], external) and voices ([AT]).

Names of people are then learned from images of persons mainly in the symmetrical temporal region of the word-circuit ([ATg]).

b) Symmetrical frontal pole: the concept of centered relations and pronouns

In the frontal areas symmetrical to the temporal pole ([FVT]), the call trees represent relations that are "centered" around a person and that pertain to that person's history. It is important to note that the concept of a "central theme" that structures a story is often based upon the relations among the characters.

Syntactic relators that refer to people (particularly pronouns) will be mostly constructed in the frontal part of the sentence-circuit ([FATg]), symmetrical to the temporal area ([ATg]) that organizes "personal names" and linked (by the auditory-visual symmetry) to the frontal area ([FVT]) that represents relations "centered" around a person.

In this "fronto-temporal circuit", recognition of voices and faces (External network) generates images of people (Internal network) that are themselves coded by proper names (left hemisphere) and in the frontal part, the call trees produces concepts of relations "centered" around these people (Internal network) and code them by pronouns (left hemisphere).

B) Columnar automata construct nouns from images of object in the parieto-temporal pole and syntactic words from concepts of hierarchical relations in the symmetrical frontal pole.

a) Parieto-temporal pole: cortical images of object and nouns.

Cortical images of objects are generated by recognition algorithms which include both purely visual recognition (temporal area [VT]) and manipulative (parietal area [SV]): the call trees are constructed in the intermediate parieto-temporal pole, that includes also the secondary receptive areas (recognition of elementary visual forms).

Names of objects are then learned from the recognition algorithms in the parieto-temporal (or "receptor) pole of the word-circuit (region [A2g]).

b) Symmetrical frontal pole: concepts of hierarchical relations and syntactic words.

In general, concepts involving hierarchical relations are constructed in frontal regions. Representations of "inclusion" or "category membership" can develop in the frontal areas from call trees which produce visual explorations of complex scenes with several organizational levels ([FV]). Syntactic relators will be learned from these concepts in the symmetrical frontal area within the sentence-circuit ([FAg]), which is also linked (by the frontal-associative symmetry) to the recognition of an auditory pattern; a word is thus associated with a syntactic organization (denomination of relators).

In this "fronto-receptor circuit" recognition (External network) generates images of objects (Internal network) that are themselves coded by nouns (left hemisphere); in the frontal part, structured visual exploration (External network) generates concepts of hierarchical relations among these objects (Internal network); these relations are then coded by syntactic relators (left hemisphere).

C) Columnar automata construct prepositions from images of spatial relations in the parietal pole, and syntactic rules of positions from concepts of oriented relations in the symmetrical frontal pole.

a) Parietal pole: cortical images of relations and adverbs.

Images of spatial relations are generated by call trees that command positioning movements. These cortical images are mostly constructed in parietal areas ([SV]).

Images of spatial relations (for instance, the relation of "contact") are later differentiated according to whether the relation concerns a "person" or an "object", or according to the type of movement that can modify the relation (movement of the hand, of the body, etc.).

Names of spatial relations (prepositions, adverbs), are learned from placing functions in the symmetrical region in the word-circuit ([SAg]).

b) Symmetrical frontal pole: concepts of oriented relations and syntactic rules of position

Cortical automata can sequence the spatial relations constructed on the parietal pole: for instance "give" includes a double spatial relation (involving an object and two persons), and a hand movement. In this way, columnar automata produce concepts of "oriented relations" that combine two spatial relations linked by motor actions. These concepts, that include at least two levels (the spatial relation and the movement) will be organized in the frontal area ([FSV]) symmetrical with the parietal area ([SV]: image of spatial relations), and also connected to the motor area ([M2]: representation of movement).

The syntactic coding of order, will be mostly learned in the symmetrical frontal area within the sentence circuit ([FSAg]), which is also linked to the parietal area that codes spatial relations ([SAg]) with adverbs and prepositions.

In this fronto-parietal circuit, positioning (External network) generates "images of spatial relations" (Internal network). These images are coded by adverbs or prepositions (left hemisphere). In the frontal part, "structured" positioning (External network) generates "concepts of oriented relations (Internal network). These representations are coded by rules governing positions of words in word pairs (left hemisphere).

D) Columnar automata construct verbal representation of motor actions in the somato-motor pole.

Cortical representations of motor actions are generated by call trees that effect somatosensory matching ([S2]) and muscle sequences ([M2]).

Representation of the dynamic aspect of movements will be mostly organized in motor areas ([M2]) while representations of their somesthetic results will be formed in somatosensory areas ([S2]).

The cortical image of an action thus has an "associative" part, linked to a spatial relation (result of the action), and a frontal part, more linked to a temporal relation and hence more conceptual (dynamic aspect of the movement).

Verbs are then learned from images of motor actions in the symmetrical somato-motor region ([S2g] and [M2g]) in the word circuit .

In the somato-motor circuit, motor adaptations (External network) generate images of motor actions (Internal network) that are then coded by verbs (left hemisphere). In its frontal part, movement sequences (External network) generate "concepts of temporal relations" between these actions (Internal network); these relations are then grammatically coded by a reorganization of the verbal structure (left hemisphere).

E) Cortical call trees integrate semantic relations from each cortical pole over the six standard cortico-cortical connections.

We saw that semantic differentiation is first regional on four poles of the cortical network ; then call trees are differentiated on the lateral axes by the sensori-motor maps, and on the transversal axis by the six possible standard connections of every cortical zone with other areas (as described in chapter III, Figure 3-17).

For instance, images of various movements are constructed from the somato-motor pole:

- first, motion verbs can be distinguished as a function of the motor system implicated (for example "say" is related to the mouth, while "do" concerns the hand, and "go" involves the legs).

- then verbs are distinguished by the six possible cortical connections: verbs linked to fundamental programs ("eat") or verbs indicating state of being ("to be") involves the connection with limbic areas; position verbs ("catch") involve connections with the parietal region; and verbs with a temporal component ("wait") or verbs organizing actions ("say","do","go") involve connections with the frontal areas .

The anatomical substratum of a cortical image could be described by a more and more complex combination: from the four main poles call trees extend to other areas by the six basic cortico-cortical connections .

We saw that the regional differentiation of words (call trees) is induced by that of cortical images (goals) in different cortical poles. But regional specialization of words can also be considered in relation to their phonemic structure. The cortical network induces a relation between the four main semantic poles and the four main regions specialized in phonemic production (as described in chapter IV-2):

1. In the temporal pole, proper names are related to fixed sequences of phonemes.

2. In the parietal pole, spatial relation are linked to phonemes; spatial relations are often expressed by prefixes, suffixes in "adjustable" phonemic sequences.

3. In the intermediate parieto-temporal region, common names have intermediate phonemic properties ; they are more modifiable than proper names (gender and number coding).

4. In the somato-motor region, verbs are more linked to the basic phonemic components; they can be easily modified (verbal endings) to code time and person (dynamic aspect of the sentence).

3. Minimal combinations and inferences in the cortical "convergent" circuits.

As shown in Figures 5-7 and 5-8, the cortical network contains four privileged circuits that recognize and produce "images", code them by "words" and express their "relations" by "sentences".

The columnar automata within each circuit adjust two different cortical inputs, via two symmetries of the cortical network (visual-auditory and associative-frontal). These inputs are widespread calls which concern in parallel the different semantic categories (actions, position, objects and people in the "semantic poles"). These calls to pre-differentiated cortical regions are unstable states (Chapter III) and cortical activities tend towards an equilibrium position which is a contrasted activity with production of "cortical actions"; this differential activation concern increasingly precise functional networks which correspond to previous stages of learning. All these intermediate links produce multiple inferences. Consequently global calls result in the final activation of a minimal combination: a set of differentiated actions and a set of inferences.

A) Parallel activation of "images" in associative regions results in the representation of an "elementary situation".

The cortical areas on the visual information flow form a general recognition loop which represents in parallel the various features of the visual world in their relative positions (see chapter IV-3). The associated Internal network between cortical areas is the "Image-circuit". The symmetrical loop in the frontal lobe forms the "Relation-circuit". These two loops are illustrated in FIGURE 5-9 on the closed form of the model of cortical network.

Images of different types, such as images of people and images of actions, are not competitive because they implicate different poles of the image-circuit (temporal and somatic) and corresponding call trees can function in parallel. However images may be locally competitive within each semantic category (for example two actors or two actions).

As shown in the Figure, connections within the image-circuit relate the different semantic categories: on these connections, call trees can relate action and actor, action and object; they can also represent spatial relations between objects, relations between actors, relations between an actor and objects (possession), relation between an action and its results.

a) Parallel activation: elementary situation.

Global activation of the image-circuit produces simultaneous representations of a person, an action, an object, and a position . This complementary set represents an elementary "situation" that forms the semantic nucleus of a simple sentence: that is a relation between an actor, an action, and a target, with circumstances of place and means and specifications concerning relative positions and possession.

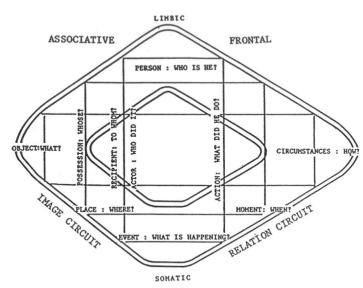

Figure 5-9 . Inferences and questions generated by calls in the different poles of the cortical network.

The richness of an elementary sentence is due to pre-existing differentiations in the image circuit: as long as these various elements are not expressed (partial goals), there is a disequilibrium that provokes expression of supplementary information. As in the case of recognition, the image circuit "fills up" beginning with the central calls (people and actions) and then continuing with more sensory areas (circumstances of action).

This "elementary situation" becomes increasingly precise, in proportion with the previous differentiations; children's sentences gradually become richer as soon as they learn new lexical categories.

b) Listening: Inferences in the "image" circuit.

When one hears a phrase, verbal decoding generates calls toward the image circuit. In this circuit, an equilibrium state is reached with the parallel activation of the most differentiated parts, and this set corresponds to an elementary sentence, with actor, actions, circumstances, etc....

In order to reach this equilibrium position, the call extends to component categories that have not yet been expressed. The pre-existing call trees produce multiple inferences in order to complete an elementary situation in the image circuit.

B) Parallel activation of a subset of "relations" in frontal regions results in the representation of a "story".

a) Cortical representation of a story.

In the frontal relation-circuit, symmetrical with the image-circuit, columnar automata construct autonomous "concepts" (Images of relations, Internal network) and different categories of relations can coexist in the semantic poles of the frontal cortex: relations between people, hierarchical relations in structured scenes, oriented relations, temporal relations.

Several images of relations can be activated in parallel in the frontal circuit: they structure a set of elementary situations in the form of a "story" (events with a coherent sequence in time) . Each of the relations in the story corresponds to an elementary situation in the image-circuit (by the associative-frontal symmetry).

b) Inferences in a story.

When one listens to a story, the call extends to all the possible relations (personal, scenic, temporal, etc) previously stored in the frontal regions. It generates a series of inferences that tends to immediately complete the story. These inferences will be used implicitly in the succeeding sentences; for example, they will induce the use of pronouns instead of repetition of the proper names.

C) Parallel activation of words results in an elementary sentence.

a) Production: various forms of sentences

A simple sentence is produced in the word-circuit by columnar automata that adjust two parallel calls:

1. The parallel call from the images toward the words form a coherent set (elementary situation): for example, this call will include a noun, a verb, and complementary circumstances.

2. The parallel call from the frontal sentence-circuit defines a syntactic template between words, depending upon activity in the relation-circuit that structures the story.

Outputs of automata in the word-circuit form an elementary sentence, (subject-verb object circumstances). As in the process of visual recognition, each new cortical action (a word) explores a "situation" that becomes more and more precise in the image-circuit. The word sequence produces a "trajectory" within the image circuit that has all the properties of a cortical sequence: it is a progressive adjustment until a goal is reached (expression of an elementary situation). This trajectory can vary: many distinct verbal forms allow achievement of the equilibrium position in the image circuit.

A stereotypical trajectory can follow the general call in the "recognition loop" , originating from the internal somatic regions and going toward the external sensory poles (see chapter IV-3) : this call activates first the relation "actor-action", followed by the relation "actor-object" with intermediate trajectories such as "object-owner" or "action-consequence" and spatial circumstances.

Each word pair is oriented by syntactic rules that restrain the variety of possible trajectories within stereotyped patterns.

b) Calls in the "word" circuit: inferences and questions.

As one listens to sentences, parallel calls produce first a maximum of inferences in the image circuit and then they can generate questions in the word circuit. Questions are the verbal extensions of internal calls that "fill" the different poles of the image circuit, as illustrated in Figure 5-9: "Who?" in the temporal pole, "What?" in the parieto-temporal pole, "Where?" in the parietal pole, and "What's happening?" in the somato-motor pole, etc..

D) Parallel activation of syntactic rules and words in frontal regions results in a narrative.

Structured sequencing of words is done by call trees in the frontal sentence-circuit. The frontal mechanism produces and recognizes several nested levels of the speech sequence, by associating the syntactic aspect (symmetrical connections with the word-circuit) with the semantic aspect (symmetrical connections with the relation-circuit). Call trees in the sentence-circuit generate the narrative by adjusting both relations to be expressed and word categories:

a) Calls from a story.

Each frontal zone of the sentence-circuit is symmetrically linked to another frontal zone already specialized in the image of a relation. Through this connection, the cortical mechanism effects the symbolic coding of concepts, both by syntactic rules and syntactic relators.

Parallel activity in different parts of the relation-circuit represents a coherent story which produces a widespread call to the sentence-circuit. The result is a set of cortical actions which generates the corresponding narrative: description of the sequence of events, their orientation, exploratory description of a complex scene, etc.

Reciprocally, when one listens to a narrative, calls towards the story-circuit produces a maximum of inferences (equilibrium state) . The calls that do not have an internal response (inference) will generate general questions in the sentence-circuit, as illustrated in Figure 5-9: for example "Why?" comes from regions that orient motor action (FSV), and "How" is produced in the region that organizes the description of structured scenes (FV).

b) Calls from words.

Each frontal zone of the sentence-circuit is also linked to associative zones of the word-circuit: a grammatical category in the frontal cortex is associated with an entire group of words in the associative regions; call trees between frontal zones produce sequencing rules between grammatical categories. These syntactic rules are learned and activated as hierarchical sets with each level corresponding to an increased precision in grammatical categories (Figure 5-6).

4. Temporal organization of a narrative on the frontal "time" axis.

Frontal call trees organize narrative in the sentence-circuit as a function of content in the story-circuit. They decode several levels of relations in a verbal sequence and, inversely, encode several levels of relations in the form of a word sequence. As we have seen, these levels are both temporal and sensori-motor recombination levels (as described in Chapter III-5).

Four main levels are determined by the four poles of the frontal axis, as illustrated in Figure 5-7. These levels decrease on the frontal time axis as one moves from the fronto-temporal pole, involving fundamental programs (global goal of communication), toward the somato-motor pole (elementary verbal actions). In passing from the fundamental pole to the motor pole, not only do the time constants become more and more precise, but also the representations become less and less integrated. We go from characters of the story all the way to actions that they perform, passing "en route" the circumstances of these actions.

a) The theme of the narrative: the general frame.

By its position on the frontal "time" axis, the fronto-temporal pole ([FATg]) effects long term organization of narration:

- This region is linked with the fundamental programs that provoke the general call of communication, the global goal of speech.

- This region can express a whole series of relations centered on specific persons.

From the global goal of communication, the goal of each narrative segment ([FATg]) is the expression of a set of relations centered around specific actors ([FVT]) or more generally around a specific "theme".

b) Syntactic levels of the sentence.

The next position on the frontal time axis, is the frontal region symmetrical to receptor areas ([FAg]). this region is linked to spatial and temporal descriptions of situations (chronology) based upon structured explorations of the surrounding world (pole [FV]).

This region can organize nested phrases thanks to the syntactic relators that mark the various levels of a sentence ([FAg]). Whenever a sentence is produced, a partial goal is attained; the more global level ([FAT]: general theme) then calls a new set of relations to be expressed.

c) Polarity of actions and relations.

The next position on the frontal axis is the frontal region symmetrical to the parietal pole ([FSAg]); this region can organize sequences of two simple actions within each level of the sentence ([FAg]). This frontal region is structured by position rules that define the order within word pairs, according to the image of an "oriented" relation (for example actor-action or subject-object in [FSV]).

d) Elementary actions.

The last position on the frontal time axis, is the motor pole ([M2g]) that represents the shortest temporal level: verbs impose the basic rhythm of the word sequence.

Each "elementary action" (a verb) is expressed with a specific phonetic structure that depends upon representations of temporal relations (M2). Expression of an "elementary action" leads to a basic pulsation in the cortical network:

- in the image-circuit, the equilibrium position generates an elementary situation: actor- action- object- circumstances;

- in the word-circuit, the corresponding trajectory subject- verb- object is strongly oriented by the frontal calls that represent the permanent elements of the story (for example, the same individuals in successive actions); they activate personal or relative pronouns in the place of personal names;

- in the relation-circuit, the elementary sentence expresses a specific concept; longer-term trajectories progressively dispose of the various relations that constitute the whole story.

V. Coherence of the cortical system for structured learning.

A) Cognitive development acquires the geometrical coherence of the cortical network.

The geometry of the cortical network gives a global coherence to the different integrated actions that are learned in the early childhood,as illustrated in FIGURE 5-10 ("open" form of the model, as in Figure 3-11).

a) External and Internal specialization: behavioral adaptations and cortical images.

Call trees function in relations with sensory and motor organs in the "External" network and they perform behavioral adaptations, or they produce cortical images in the "Internal" network. As shown in Figure 5-10 these two networks are coextensive over the cortico-cortical connections (internal network is shown with dots): the same adjustment that occurs with external world occur also with its images.

b) Right and left hemispheres: natural and symbolic relations.

The two hemispheres are symmetrically represented on the upper and lower halves of FIGURE 5-10 . The left and right hemisphere are systematically interconnected; symmetric connections induce homeomorphic relations: for example relations between symbols (sentences) can code relations between images (story); reciprocally, symbol combinations (for example letters of a word) can induce new sensori-motor adjustment (for example, reading and writing).

c) Two complementary sets of cortical circuits: syntactic and semantic components of language.

Sixteen functional areas in each hemisphere form sixteen nodes in the cortical network and areas can be grouped in two complementary sets of circuits (concentric and convergent as described in Figure 5-7 and 5-8):

- the cortical areas can be grouped in four convergent circuits (radii or diagonals) which form four coherent internal combinations: images are grouped in a coherent

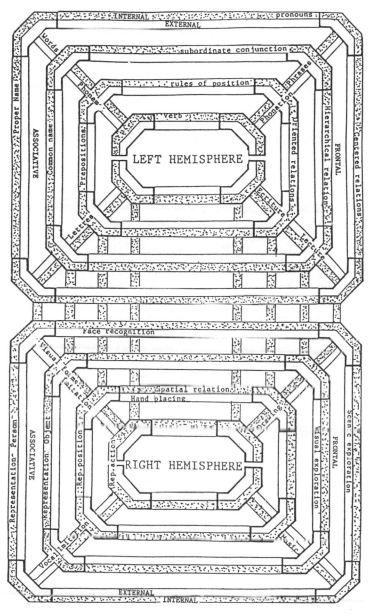

Figure 5-10 . Inter-hemispheric and inter-regional concordance of adaptive and linguistic integrated cortical actions.

situation, words in a coherent sentence, relations in a coherent story and sentences in a coherent narrative;

- the same cortical areas can also be grouped in four concentric circuits (circles or rectangles), each of which correspond to a semantic pole (for peoples, objects, positions and actions). Within each pole , the network coordinates the symbolic coding of two images by two words with the symbolic coding of their relations by a syntactic rule between their lexical categories.

B) The columnar processing is a general problem-solving mechanism but its efficiency depends upon previously learned integrated actions.

a) The modular searching mechanism.

The overall problem-solving capacity of the human brain is directly related to the properties of cortical tissue: "searching" mechanism of columnar automata and

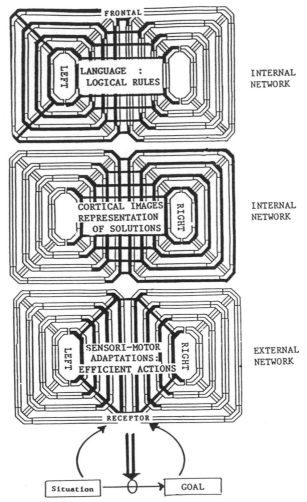

Figure 5-11 . Network configuration of 3 sets of cortical actions which can be used to solve a problem.

combination of information flows by the network between areas.

Columnar automata common to all cortical areas effect adaptations in a very general way, and can in fact be considered as a general "problem solving" mechanism, since they seek out optimal combinations of actions in order to achieve a goal:

- they sequence possible actions in a progressive way from any "initial situation" until a goal is attained.

- they produce "explorations" in new situations.

- they memorize effective combinations and partial goals; such memorizations increase resolution speed for analogous problems.

This mechanism remains the same throughout the cortex, whatever the external actions used.

But for any given problem, its efficiency is dependent upon the pre-existence of appropriate integrated cortical actions: for example movements, representations, symbols, categories, or logical operations.

b) Selective use of a cortical base of integrated actions.

FIGURE 5-11 illustrates the anatomical substrata of the three types of cortical integrated actions that correspond to the three principal stages of cognitive development: sensorimotor adaptations, cortical images and language components.

These three types of integrated cortical actions can function in parallel, since they use three subsets of the cortical network, as shown in the three diagrams of Figure 5-11 which are designed on the model of cortical interactions detailed in Figure 5-10:

- lower diagram: sensori-motor adaptations function in the external network, in both left and right hemisphere (E,dg);

- middle diagram: images which are independent from language function in the right internal network (I,d);

- upper diagram: symbolic words function in the "internal" network of the left hemisphere (I,g).

FIGURE 5-12 illustrates the process of problem solving by the cortical mechanism (horizontal axis) acting within each of these three bases of integrated actions (vertical axis):

1. On the first bases of sensori-motor adaptations , columnar automata effect recognitions, positioning, and motor programs to realize the goal.

If no combination proves sufficient, a disequilibrium is produced, and the cortical mechanism generates an exploration. In motor areas, the mechanism produces new movements (muscular combinations); in the parietal areas, it produces an exploration of the surrounding world; in the frontal areas, it produces structured visual and manual exploration (like the "stack" search by a computer--see Chapter IV.4).

Whatever the ultimate cognitive stage (symbolic, for instance), these sensori-motor bases are indispensable to effect actions upon the outside world.

2. On the bases of cortical images, columnar automata can simulate sensori-motor adaptations and can thus make choices that do not necessarily involve actual motor actions.

The bases of cortical images allow the problem-solving system to overcome the energy and time limitations inherent in motor action. Furthermore, construction of

INTEGRATED ACTION BASES	CALL	ACTION	SEARCHING	MEMORIZATION	SUCCESSIVE ASSOCIATIONS
SENS.MOTOR ADAPTATIONS	NEW SITUATION	MOTOR	EXPLORATION	ENVIRONMENT REGULARITIES	GENERALISATION DIFFERENTIATION
CORTICAL IMAGES	PROBLEM	INTRA CORTICAL	POSSIBLE SET	PREVIOUS RESULTS	INDUCTION INFERENCE
LANGUAGE	QUESTIONS	RULES	HYPOTHESE	KNOWN SOLUTIONS	LOGICAL INFERENCES

Figure 5-12 . Expression of cortical operations for problem solving with 3 sets of integrated actions.

hierarchical relations among exploratory actions in the frontal cortex insure a systematic exploration to find a solution.

   3. On linguistic bases, columnar automata can organize different levels of relations between images.
   Symbolic coding permits social communication of cortical images, and learning of many relations by concepts. Consequently, children can assimilate adult representations independently of their direct personal experience; for example "categories" defined by words of the cultural base increase the number of representational levels, and integrate knowledge acquired by the human species.

   The most efficient base for problem resolution depends upon the type of problem. For example, the actions to be used may be predefined, such as in school problems. The cortical combination that permits achievement of the goal occurs on a fixed, limited base.
   When search within one given base does not permit goal attainment, the call extends progressively to other bases. Several bases can be used in parallel, since they can function in different circuits of the cortical system, as depicted in Figure 5-11. Columnar automata can combine all types of integrated actions since all these actions have the same homogeneous physical reality in the cortex .

C) Disequilibria between combinations of words and combinations of images are removed by logical rules.

   Problem solving is enormously facilitated by the frontal network where columnar automata generate categories and rules between categories.
   In frontal areas, cortical automata learn relations from examples which activate associative areas. The new frontal link has the largest - possible extension (generalization) and thus involves many more cortical images than those provoking it. The new relation creates a "rule" between groups of representations that form new

categories. We have described in this way the construction of grammatical categories and syntactic rules (see Chapter V.3).

Induction, the process that creates new rules between categories on the basis of individual examples, is thus a general property of the cortex; in frontal regions these rules are autonomous call trees and their activation corresponds to the mental representation of a relation (a concept). Inference, the process that applies the rule to relations between elements of the category, represents the symmetrical complement of induction capacity: several rules are applied when the activity becomes more and more contrasted (as detailed in section V-3) since cortical images belong simultaneously to several categories.

Construction of several levels of relations in the form of "rules", on the basis of individual examples, and the parallel construction of several levels of representations in the form of "categories" are cortical properties that are critically important for the complex, profound adaptations of which only human beings are capable.

Syntactic rules allow multiple combinations of words and a certain narrative autonomy. These symbolic combinations create new relations between the corresponding cortical images. In certain cases, these combinations correspond to real ("natural") relations, while others simply represent abstract permutations that have no relation to reality. The distinction between the imaginary and the real comes about through learning based on "experience".

Symbol combination according to syntactic rules, on the one hand, and image combination according to relational concepts, on the other, do not necessarily give concordant results. Each time that the combination of cortical images doesn't match a "natural external relation", or even a concept of relation, a disequilibrium is produced. This disequilibrium favours learning of a new cultural base, that of "logical relators" and logical rules.

Logical relators are differentiated from syntactic words; they restrain use of syntactic relators so that symbolic combinations are made consistent with combinations of cortical images; in this way, language comes to anticipate the result of cortical image combinations.

Logical rules, like the syntactic rules, are large, transversal relations between frontal zones; they produce an isomorphic between "natural" and "symbolic" combinations, which is to say between mental images and language.

Cortical automata oriented by these logical relations result in the process of "deduction", that we define as the anticipatory use of language, controlled by increasingly precise rules. When a problem produces a disequilibrium, the cortical exploration generates the formulation of an hypothesis ("symbolic" exploration). It is just what we tried to do in this work.

Formal description
of an adaptive system.

A) An analytical table guides the analysis of the cortical system.

An analytical table represents the four levels of the cortical system: cell, module, tissue, and organ. At each level, the analysis considers three complementary processes: the structuration of an interactive network, its functioning, and its memorization properties.

Diagrams of these interactive networks and their activities at the four levels are presented in Figure A-1 and are explained in more details in the different chapters. The four levels of the cortical system are represented on the vertical axis of Table A-2 and are symbolized by the letter "S", from "S1"(cellular level) to "S4" (organism).

Functional rules of the cortical system are specializations of general rules for cellular groups, with a generality which decreases as the organizational level increases: the system involved at the cellular level S1 is the nervous cell; at the modular level S2, we consider a "general" cerebral cortex; at the tissular level S3 we focus on the cortex of primates, and at the general level S4 we develop the properties of the human cortex.

To ensure the internal coherence of our model, we define the descriptive categories ("structure", "activity", etc..) in the most general way, independently of the level considered. Symbolic abbreviations are assigned to each of these categories in order to give logical rigor. This formalism is presented in detail in this Annex, in Figures A-2 to A-20. The number of symbolic abbreviations may appear elevated, but it is quite small compared with the number of independent parameters of the real cortical system: any further simplification would have meant a drastic loss of the system's richness.

a) Structuration of interactive networks.

At each LEVEL, any system is formed by GROUPS OF ELEMENTS that mutually interact. This definition is recursive, since the elements are themselves systems at a lower level: cell is the basic element of a module that itself is the basic element of a tissue. Figure A-2 shows the main subgroups of the cortical system with their symbolic abbreviations.

The subgroups of elements are defined by their TYPES (AXES OF DIFFERENTIATION), and their position along the SPATIAL AXES. Biological systems are produced from a single cell by a double process of division and differentiation:

1. The "differentiation axes" represent the type of cells (and the types of nervous structures). These "types" are defined in a relative way: the type "K" defines first the

organ and the nervous structure (level S4), then the modular type (S3), the specific cell type within the module (S2). At the cellular level (S1), differentiations of the membrane (axons, dendrites, synapses) can be represented on a local axis of differentiation "k" (channel or receptor types).

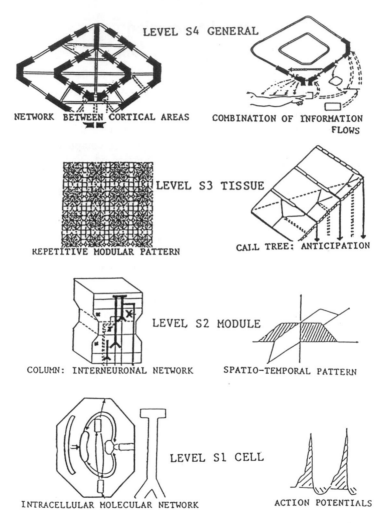

Figure A-1 . Interactive networks (left) and activities (right) at the four organizational levels of the cortical system.

2. Each organizational level has its own spatial INTRINSIC AXES (or proper axes). At the global level "S4", these are the corporal axes (internal/external, left/right, back/front). At the tissue level (S3), these are the proper axes of the tissue layer: two surface axes ("lateral" axes X,Y), and the axis perpendicular to the tissue layer

```
LEVEL S4 GENERAL
  Axes: Int-external/Left-right/Back-front        IE,DG,AA
Motor and sensory organs
Coordinate systems Retinal/cochlear/somato-motor
Neural structures:
  Thalamus                                         Th
  Cortex                                           Co
  Reticular formation                              Ret
  Cerebellum:cortex/nuclei/olive
  Striatum/Pallidum/S.Nigra
  Hippocampus
  Retina/Spinal cord/Olfactory bulb
  Hypothalamus
Cortical hemispheres:
  Axes: ant-posterior/med-lateral
Cortical regions  Central/Parietal/Occipital/Temporal/Frontal
Cortical areas                         VT  V2  SV S2  AT  A2  SA
                                      FVT FV  FSV M2 FAT FA  FSA
```

```
LEVEL S3 TISSUE
  Axes: 2 Lateral (Surface) / 1 Transversal        X,Y,Z
Spatial zones: subdivisions
  Cortical maps                                    R,M,P
  Modular bands
  Maxicolumns
  Modules                                          A,B,C,D
  Minicolumns
```

```
LEVEL S2 MODULE
Cortical layers:
  Upper layers : Supragranular                     CoH
  Lower layers : Infragranular                     CoB
  Middle layer : layer IV
Cortical neuronal types
  Pyramidal neurons: upper layers                  PyrH
  Pyramidal neurons: lower layers                  PyrB
  Stellate cells                                   Ste
  Basket cells                                     Pan
  Chandelier cells                                 Pac
  Bipolar cells                                    Cbp
  Double bouquet                                   Cdb
```

```
LEVEL S1 CELL
  Axis: Int-exterior/proper axes                   x,y;z
Specialized membrane zones:
  Presynaptic zone (transmitter release)           m
  Receptor zone                                    e
  Homogeneous dendritic zone                       a,b
  Global cell                                      K
Molecular types:
  Channels
    Ca++;K+;Cl-;Na+
  Transmiters/Receptors
    Glutamate                                      G+
    GABA                                           G-
  Modulators
    NA,DA,5-HT
```

Figure A-2 . Symbols used for axes, spatial zones and cellular groups at the four levels of
the cortical system.

("transversal" axis Z). At the cellular level, the configuration of the neurons, with their dendritic branching patterns, imposes the axes (x,y,z) of the cell.

The subsets of elements at a given level (for example cells at the modular level) are defined both by their TYPE "K" and by the spatial ZONE [A] that they occupy. We are essentially interested in sub-groups having homogeneous behavior, formed of type "K" elements in a spatial zone [A]. We denote such a subgroup by K.[A], or more simply K.A, giving first the type "K" and then the spatial zone [A] (for example, see figure A-12).

Thus, each cellular subgroup is defined both by a spatial zone [A] and a "K" level of differentiation: all K.[A] cells share the properties of their specific molecular network "K" and of their common spatial position [A] in the anatomical network. Similarly, at the subcellular level, k.[a] represents a membrane zone of homogeneous behavior.

Generally, two subgroups of a system, K.A and I.B, have reciprocal interactions that form an interactive network "K.A-I.B" (for example see Figure A-13). Neurons construct interactive networks that are always doubly determined:

1. Local junctions, the synapses, link neuron according to their molecular types: the synaptic network "K.A-I.A" links two cell groups of type "K" and "I" within the same spatial zone [A].

2. Membrane extensions (axons, dendrites) of a given neuron link two spatial zones of the tissue: this "membranary" network "K.[A]-K.[B]" links two zones [A] and [B] of the tissue with a K neuronal type.

The ontogenic STRUCTURATION of the neuronal interactive network is based on a cellular "logic"; this construction mode is critically important because the whole network is implicit in the genome of a single cell and can adapt across phylogeny.

b) Functioning and activity of interactive networks.

"Structure, "functioning", and "memorization" of an interactive network are very relative notions, that depend upon the time scale used. One can define them on the basis of temporal modifications of the distances between subsets:

1. Fixed distances define the STRUCTURE of a system; IRREVERSIBLE modifications result in STRUCTURATION of the system.

2. Variable, REVERSIBLE distances between elements defines the FUNCTIONING of the system.

3. Modifications that depends upon activity define the MEMORY of the system.

ACTIVITY is a function of space and time that represents change in the reversible positions of elements: each homogeneous subgroup K[A] has an activity that we note as K.A.E(t). For example, this formalism is used at the modular level in Figure A-12. Several descriptions of the temporal pattern "E(t)" are possible; for example, we use "intensity levels" from "E0" to "E2" as critical parameters in the cerebral cortex. We could use the term INFORMATION to designate the spatio-temporal form of the activity.

An "ACTION" is the result of an activity that is able to modify another interaction. For instance, a motor action is the result of muscle activities upon the distance between an organism and its environment. Actions grouped in stable sequences constitute PROGRAMS. Programs entirely produced by the system are INTRINSIC PROGRAMS.

FUNCTIONAL RULES relate the activity of a system to its structure. For example, a molecule has an atomic "structure" and an electronic "activity" ; this activity can be deduced from analysis of the atomic geometry by a group of rules such as Schrodinger's law. In electric circuits, rules determine the input-output relations from the values of resistance, capacity, inductance, etc. On another scale, a computer has a "structure" of memories and logic circuits; the "activity" is defined by the successive states of different registers; the "programs" determine the sequences of activation.

For the nervous system, the FUNCTIONAL RULES determine the operations that the nervous network can effect upon sensory or motor activity: for example, a neural tissue can generate a spatio-temporal pattern of activity.

These rules are not necessarily completely deterministic: part of the activity can be random. For instance, the rules can simply give upper and lower limits of the activities .

c) Transmission coefficients and memorization.

The parameters of the interactive network that influence activity are called TRANSMISSION COEFFICIENTS.

The transmission coefficient between two subgroups K.A and J.B is a parameter of the network "K.A-J.B". For example, this formalism is presented in Table A-13 at the modular level.

These transmission coefficients can be functions of time . MEMORIZATION RULES specify the possible changes of the transmission coefficients resulting from activity. The memorization rules account for learning capacities. In these terms, learning is the behavioral adaptation based on the memorization process.

ADAPTIVE CAPACITIES are generated by the three basic components of a system: its structure (the potential of the system), its functioning (the actions that are performed), and its memorization processes (its learning capacities).

B) The result of an adaptation, its "goal", is an equilibrium position which optimizes an interaction between an organism and its environment.

In FIGURE A-3 we have illustrated the interactions between a system (a cell, a neural tissue, or a whole organism) and its environment.

Figure A-3 shows a very general interactive network: two subgroups K.A and K.B might represent two molecules of the same cell, two parts of a genome, two cells linked by a hormone, or two organs linked by a neural network.

The two subgroups of elements "K.A" and "K.B" perform specific , appropriate actions (M.A,M.B) when they receive specific information (in R.A and R.B) from the external environment (O.A, O.B). These actions can modify the interactions between the system and its environment.

A set of actions is adaptive when it OPTIMIZES one of the interactive parameters: the interaction becomes maximal or minimal. For example, since most interactions increase when the distance decreases, a movement directed toward an object maximizes the interactions with that object.

Table A-3 shows different types of behavioral adaptations (on the vertical axis), with the interactive parameter that is optimized (a distance for example) and the actions that modify this parameter (a movement for example):

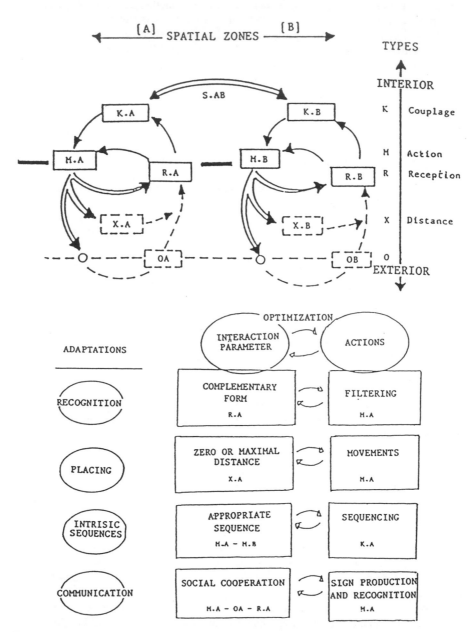

Figure A-3 . *Behavioural adaptations (lower diagram) are optimizations of interactive parameters with the environment (upper).*

a) Recognition.

The mechanism of recognition optimizes the receptiveness of a system to a given external situation. For example, the adaptive mechanism generates a series of actions (M.A) which remodel the receptive structure of the system (R.A) in order to increase its complementarity with an external model (O.A). The mechanism produces a "complementary form".

b) Positioning.

The mechanism of placing or positioning optimizes a distance. This mechanism can first optimize the orientation of the system with respect to an external object: since most interactions vary inversely with distance (X.A), oriented movement (M.A) toward a target (O.A) continuously increases its interactions with the target; the end result is a new relationship (contact or connection) with the target.

c) Intrinsic programs.

Temporal optimization of an intrinsic sequence of different elementary actions in a program is another kind of adaptation; for example, from a pool of elementary transformations of an external object (M.A,M.B), the mechanism can simply choose the sequence of actions (A then B) to optimize interactions with this object.

d) Communication.

Optimization of social interactions by communication leads to cooperations: an the organism "emits" an action (M.A) that "calls" another organism (OA), which in turn modifies the interactions of the first organism with the environment. The adaptive mechanism requires not only the production but also the recognition of "communicative actions" such as "signs" or "words".

C) A behavioral adaptation is due to structural, functional and learning properties of the interactive network.

In FIGURE A-4, we have illustrated some properties of structure, function and memorization that produce adaptative mechanisms.

The interactive networks are illustrated on the left as in FIGURE A-3, with two coupled circuits, "A" and "B":

- the circuit R..A-M.A is postulated to be functionally important for the organism: we call it a "principal circuit";

- the circuit R.B-M.B is less critically important; we call it an "alternative circuit".

- the couplings K.A and K.B determine the cooperative or competitive aspects of the two circuits.

The adaptive mechanisms are illustrated on the right part of Figure A-4.

a) Progressive linking: STRUCTURAL properties of the network.

"Principal circuits" determine the appropriate actions for each type of external situation (R-A/M-A); but "alternative circuits" (K-B/K.A) which are connected "in parallel" with the principal circuits, supplement it when variations in the external environment make the principal circuit less appropriate.

CONSTRUCTION
PROGRESSIVE LINKING

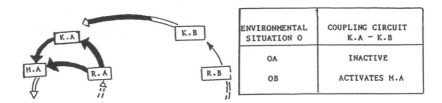

ENVIRONMENTAL SITUATION O	COUPLING CIRCUIT K.A - K.B
OA	INACTIVE
OB	ACTIVATES M.A

ACTIVITY
PROGRESSIVE SEQUENCE

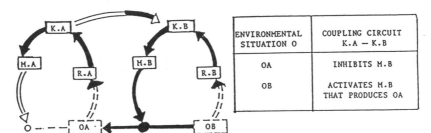

ENVIRONMENTAL SITUATION O	COUPLING CIRCUIT K.A — K.B
OA	INHIBITS M.B
OB	ACTIVATES M.B THAT PRODUCES OA

MEMORIZATION
ASSOCIATIVE COUPLAGE

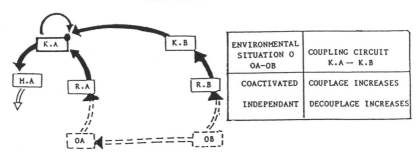

ENVIRONMENTAL SITUATION O OA-OB	COUPLING CIRCUIT K.A — K.B
COACTIVATED	COUPLAGE INCREASES
INDEPENDANT	DECOUPLAGE INCREASES

Figure A-4 . Adaptive mechanisms are due to structure (upper diagram), function (middle), and memorizing properties (lower).

We will see that neural circuits are constructed with the general pattern of "progressive linking" with alternative circuits which supplement principal fundamental circuits.

b) Progressive sequencing: FUNCTIONAL properties of the network
The interactive network can organize the successive triggering of various alternative actions, thus preparing the triggering of the principal action.
- in the environmental situation "OA", the principal action M.A is executed; a coupling circuit (K.A-K.B) inhibits the other possible actions (such as M.B);

- in the environmental situation OB, the coupling circuit (K.A-K.B) "activates" the alternative actions (M.B) that first bring the organism to the situation OA until finally the principal M.A action can be executed

Many alternative actions can be hierarchically sequenced in this way. For example, when the goal is a contact with an object, several actions are possible and can be sequenced: move toward the object (M.C), grasp it (M.B), or manipulate it (M.A); these different actions are triggered as a function of the distance of the object, and each action brings the system into the triggering zone of the next, more "proximal" action.

We will see that the basic function of the cortex generalizes this "progressive sequencing" mechanism.

c) Associative coupling: MEMORIZATION properties of the network.

The interactive network can change the COUPLING between circuits in an "associative" way: the relation between two circuits (R.A-M.A and R.B-M.B) is modified in a permanent way as a function of the temporal correlation of their activities:

- coupling increases if the two circuits are coactivated;
- uncoupling increases if the activities of the two circuits are temporally independent.

The mechanism of "associative coupling" provokes anticipation of an appropriate action on the basis of the regular appearance of antecedent conditions; furthermore , in association with "progressive sequencing" , this mechanism can construct new efficient actions, by linking those actions that,together, permit goal attainment.

On the other hand, "associative uncoupling" can differentiate two external situations and even eliminate irrelevant actions, whose execution is not regularly followed by positive results.

Each cortical module has several levels of associative coupling-uncoupling mechanisms (chapter II).

ANNEX 2

Construction of neural networks.

A) Cell groups, their activities and transmission coefficients (memory) are described by symbolic combinations: "K.Z.EZ.[A].[a].Ci.Tj+.Et"

"K": cell type.

"K" represents the cell type: in a neural tissue, several cell types coexist   K= Kh,Kb for two main layers, K= K',K" for interneurons. Each cell type functions and memorizes activity with its own logic.

For the cerebral cortex, we consider two principal types of pyramidal neurons, "PyrH" and "PyrB" and we have arranged the cortical interneurons into five categories

(Ste,Pan,Pac,Cbp,Cdb), each symbolized by three letters; thus the cell type "K" has seven possible values for a cortical cell "K"= Co = (PyrB, PyrH, Ste, Pan, Pac, Cbp, Cdp).

Three types of inputs to the cortex give three possible values K = "Ret" (reticular), "Th" (thalamic), "Co" (cortical).

"Z": Laminar transversal position.

Each neuron's position in the tissue is defined by its X,Y,and Z coordinates on the tissue's intrinsic axis. For a given cell type "K", the position of its soma on the transversal axis will be called "K.Z".

Pyramidal cells (Pyr) are differentiated along the transversal axis of the cerebral cortex: this supplementary differentiation is called "Pyr.Z" and its two principal branches are the infragranular "PyrB" and supragranular "PyrH" cells.

"EZ": Transversal extension.

Each neuron has dendritic and axonal branching patterns with three extensions "EX","EY", and "EZ" on the three intrinsic axes of the tissue. The axonal and dendritic extensions of a cell "K" occur along both of the lateral axes (K.EX, K.EY) and the transversal axis (K.EZ).

The two spatial parameters of position Z, due to migration, and of extension EZ, due to maturation, are important, since they determine the relative strength of the different afferences on each neuron.

Since afferences are organized by layers, it is important to compare cellular extensions, Pyr.EZ or EZ(Pyr), to the extensions of the layers : for example, extension of layer IV is named Co.IV.EZ or EZ(IV) and we can compare EZ(Pyr) / EZ(IV) .

"[A]": Lateral zone on surface.

The "surface" or laminar X,Y position on the lateral axes is due to cellular division along the intrinsic axis of the body.

"[A]" represents the spatial zone around the position X,Y with an extension EX,EY; K.[A] thus defines a cell group. Functioning and memorization generally don't concern isolated neurons, but rather regions of tissue depending upon relations with sensory or motor organs.

A cortical column or a module which is a group of contiguous columns is a subset "Co.[A]" : "Co" is the set of the different neuronal types in the cortex and [A] is a lateral zone of the cortical tissue.

"[a]" : homogeneous subcellular zone.

The principal parameters of the neuronal transmission are directly related to the properties of specific molecules (channels, receptors) and their membrane distribution on a neuron.

A neuron has four specialized membrane zones: synapse pre "m" and post "e", homogeneous receptive zone "a" , and global cell "K". They corresponds to four spatial level: "m" is a presynaptic bouton, "e" is the post -synaptic receptor zone of a single afferent cell, "a" is a dendritic zone that receive an homogeneous group of afferents and "K" is the global neuron which integrates all inputs from groups of afferent cells.

"Ci" : Molecular parameters.

Molecular parameters are then specified within these homogeneous subcellular zones [a]. A molecular type which influences transmission is symbolized by "Ci", with

"+" or "-" for its main excitatory or inhibitory effect: for example transmitter Glutamate is symbolized by "G+" and GABA by "G-". Molecular matching between transmitters and receptors in pre and post synaptic cells generate connections: In the cortex the main connections are due to a double mediator/receptor matching, first "G+" (glutamate) then "G-" (GABA).

"Tj": Time range.

A time range Tj (with an index j from 1 to 4) defines the temporal variation level (from T1 to T4, on the vertical axis);"T1" represents parameters with short term changes (for instance channel opening), "T2" the parameters that are stable during behavioral time constant but can change with short term memory (for instance channel modulation), "T3" the parameters that are stable during long durations and can only change with long term memory (for example a channel density), and "T4" represent the morphological parameters that change during the construction of te network.

At each temporal level, a neuron has two possible states: a "change" state "Ti+", which favors transmission and longer term memorizations of afferent activity , and a state "Ti-" that decreases the transmission.

"Ti+" represents the temporal level of memorization that moves progressively from "T1" to "T4" as a function of the characteristics of the input activity.

B) Molecular affinities between cell groups guide neuronal programs to construct a transmission network at four spatial levels (from "S1" to "S4").

The connectivity and the parameters of neuronal transmission are not genetically determined in an exact way for each individual cell; this determination is progressive and occurs at different spatial levels. The construction of the neural network can be seen as a series of adaptations, of successive adjustments that are increasingly precise. Regulations at successive stages place increasingly strict limits upon the possible values of functional parameters.

FIGURE A-5 shows the construction stages on the basis of known cellular mechanisms and molecular affinities between cell types: the figure depicts an "transmitter" cellular group ("I" on the right) that projects toward a "receptor" cellular group ("K" on the left).

a) Target zone and support zone.

The cellular actions responsible for network construction are guided by successive "molecular affinities" that give specificity to the network.

The growth cones of the neurons can move independently of the cell body and thus form the polarized extensions of the membrane (axon, dendrites). They can divide and bifurcate. Each growth cone is guided by two molecular affinities (illustrated by the horizontal and vertical arrows of FIGURE A-5):

1. They move toward a "molecular source", or a growth factor produced by the potentially receptor cells; this "target affinity" guides the growth cone towards a "target zone" (horizontal arrows); several inputs can compete for the same target zone.

2. They are guided, by "adhesion molecules", to elongated cells that constitute a "support zone" (vertical arrows).

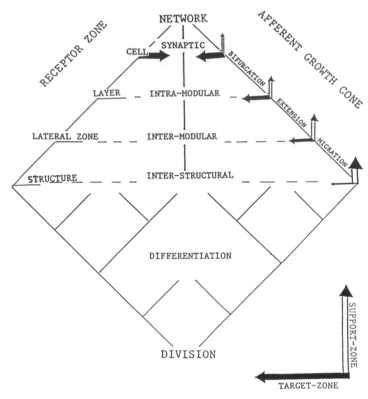

Figure A-5 . Progressive construction of neural networks by cells is guided by successive support-zones and target-zones.

Synaptogenesis proceeds by "automatic" adjustment on the basis of molecular target affinities. Growth cones are "attracted" by membrane zones of the target cell. The post-synaptic receptors then adapt their position relative to the growth cones: their "support zone" is the cell membrane and their "target zone" is the afferent growth cone; in moving together within the post-synaptic membrane, they stabilize the position of the growth cone. The directed extension of the axons is thus completed by synaptic formation which can be resumed as a set of positional adaptations between (a) the zones of transmitter released by the growth cone moving in three dimensions and (b) the receptors of the target cell moving in two dimensions under the post-synaptic membrane.

b) Levels of construction and precision of connectivity.

The neural network is determined by a double molecular affinity (support zone/ target zone), that changes during construction: the "support zone" become less and less constraining (increasing freedom of movement) and the "target" zones become more and more precise (approach).

This pattern of construction does not produce precisely determined connections for each individual neuron, but rather four relational levels of increasing precision (vertical axis of FIGURE A-5), from the overall structural level (S4) to the subcellular level (S1):

- S4:   The neural structures are first differentiated with respect to the intrinsic axis of the embryo; the "general" network "I-K" between neural structures can be defined on these global axes. It organizes the main information flow between sensory or motor organs. We describe the main features of this network in chapter III.

- S3: Each nervous structure acquires a specific form (tissue level), with intrinsic axes:"lateral X,Y" (surface of the cell layer) and "transversal Z" (perpendicular to the cell layers); molecular affinities form an inter-modular network [A]-[B] or "recombination network" between different "lateral" zones of the same structure. The geometry of this network is important for learning. We describe a "geometrical model" of the network between cortical areas in chapter III.

- S2 : Several neuronal types become differentiated on the transversal axis of the tissue and form a repetitive modular network I.Z1-K.Z2 between the layers Z1 and Z2 of the structure ; this network determines the local processing performed by each nervous structure. We describe the modular cortical network in chapter III, in order to explain the basic operation performed by the cortex.

- S1 : The receptor molecules are specified on subcellular "zones" [a],[b] on the intrinsic axis (x,y,z) of each cell: soma, axon or dendrite, proximal or distal ; a "synaptic network I[m]-K[a]" links different cells and the cell membrane of each cell form a "membranary network K[A][a]-K[B][m]" between synapses. We describe the "transmission" and "combination" properties of this double network in chapter II.

c) Differentiation of in-out connections of a column by the transversal positions (layers).

The intra and inter-columnar networks are produced by cellular processes.

FIGURE 2-2 in chapter II depicts the transversal differentiation of the columnar outputs:

- a column is a lateral zone symbolized by [A], with a central position X,Y; position on the lateral axes is due to cellular division along the intrinsic axis of the body;

- the "laminar" Z position on the transversal axis is due to the progressive migration of cells from the same ventricular division zone; laminar position is directly linked to the time of migration.

Pyramidal cells (type "Pyr") are differentiated along the transversal axis: this supplementary differentiation is called "Pyr.Z" and its two principal branches are the infragranular "PyrB" and supragranular "PyrH" cells. The Z position of the soma on the transversal axis has semiquantitative values corresponding to the layers and sublayers.

We have linked neural network formation to the double guiding of successive "support zones" and "target zones" . In the cortex, pyramidal cell axons begin growth downward on the transversal axis (support zone); the destination of this axon will depend upon its target affinities "Pyr-K" with other neuronal populations (target zone "K"). Differential maturation along the Z axis "Pyr.Z" permits several different targets "Pyr.Z-K(Z): during cortical maturation, these connections are established progressively.

Lower ("PyrB") cells of infragranular layers V and VI, the first to migrate in the Cortex, connect with other neural structures: the type "K" of the target changes with the position "Z" of the soma, but the motor or sensory significance of the target cells (related to the position [A]) does not change. For the very first neurons that migrate, the target is the principal input structure, the thalamus. The most precocious cortical axons travel the greatest distances and there is thus a relationship between the transversal, "Z" position of the cell body and the distance of the target (d[K]): spinal cord, medulla, red nucleus, then striatum.

This extrinsic affinity "Pyr-K" is complemented by the "G+" glutamate affinity that produce a coupling between pyramidal cells (Pyr-Pyr). Unlike the lower cells, "upper" pyramidal axons, following an initial downward growth (transversal support zone), are strongly determined by this molecular affinity (cortical target zone), and form connections essentially with other cortical regions, thus forming the cortical recombination network. The distance of the target zone "d[A]" will decrease with the maturation of pyramidal cells on the transversal axis (Pyr.Z). The closer the cell to the cortical surface, the closer the cortical target: adjacent regions, then distant ipsilateral zones, then contralateral cortical zone. Lower cells will have the most distant targets ("d[A]" on the lateral axes).

Cortical convexities and concavities (gyri and sulci) , may also have an organizational role: cells closest to the folds form the first contacts with zones on the other side. In this way, cortico-cortical connections are organized in symmetrical, "mirrorlike" fashion around the gyri and sulci. We stress the importance of these symmetries in the learning processes.

Because of the G+ affinity, higher pyramidal cells that form the long-range intracortical network project simultaneously to upper and lower pyramidal cells, thus forming a recursive network. This G+ affinity induces direct excitatory influences between pyramidal cells of the same column, mostly from the upper to the lower layer; these two layers are connected, but the main direction of influence is downward (main downward directions of axons). Lateral axonal branches of the pyramidal cells extend toward pyramidal cells of the same layer.

d) Coupling levels of the interneuronal network determined by successive molecular affinities.

An important factor in construction of the network is the molecular affinity between the transmitters and the receptors of the different neuronal types. The construction of the connection matrix between the cortical types is depicted in Figure 2-1 in chapter II; the network is shaped by two successive affinities: the Glutamate affinity (G+) and the GABA affinity (G-). The matching between transmitters and receptors in different cells at each time controls the nature of the interconnections.

Successive molecular matches , G+ then G-, involves connecting new types of interneurons parallel to already-existing circuits:

1. A first affinity, G+, organizes reciprocal connections between pyramidal cells "Pyr-Pyr" and induces an interneuronal pathway "Th-Ste-Pyr" parallel to the direct pathway "Th-Pyr";

2. A second affinity G- produces inhibitory synapses; interneurons "Pan" receive their afferences from pyramidal neurons "(by their G+ receptors), and project to pyramidal neurons (having G- receptors): they thus form uncoupling connections "Pyr-Pan-Pyr" between pyramidal cells that are parallel to. the reciprocal pyramidal excitatory connections "Pyr-Pyr".

3. But inhibitory interneurons also develop GABA receptors (G-); consequently they receive inhibitory connections from "Cdb" neurons; "Cdb" interneurons will have

a disinhibitory effect on pyramidal neurons "Pyr-(CdB-Pan)-Pyr" thanks to this double inhibitory pathway.

ANNEX 3

Neuronal operations.

A) Four specialized regions of neurons control transmission of information.

a) The transmission steps.

Neuronal transmission can be schematically illustrated by an "equivalent circuit" (Figure A-6) that stresses its principal functional characteristics.

A neuron has four specialized transmission zones that correspond to four spatial levels: "[m]" is one presynaptic bouton, "[e]" is the post -synaptic receptor zone of a

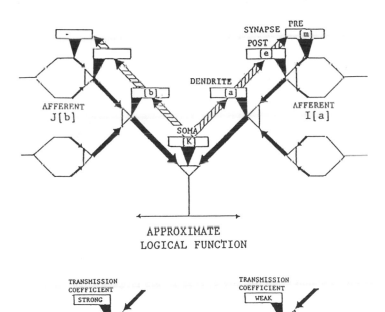

Figure A-6 . Functional circuit for a neuron with several transmission coefficients (upper diagram) and related approximate logical functions (lower).

single afferent cell, "[a]" is a dendritic zone that receive an homogeneous group of afferents and "[K]" is the global neuron.

The neuron "K" has two dendritic zones, [a] and [b] that are post-synaptic receptive zones of the two neuronal afferent groups "I" and "J". Thus,I[a] represents the afferents of cell group "I" on the dendritic zone [a]. It is composed of "na" cells each of which occupies an average zone [a]/na.

Each of the two inputs I[a],J[b] has a somatic effect that depends upon a prior combination with transmission coefficient specific to each receptive zone [a] or [b], with four successive steps (m,e,a,K) .

Transmission coefficients can vary over several time spans and they can change with learning (upward arrows). Spatial level of changes are important: modification of the transmission coefficient occurs either at a local level, for each afferent zone ([a]), or at a global level, for the entire cell (K).

Transmission coefficients thus correspond perfectly to the registers, or elementary memories of a computer. They have several possible "strength levels": for example, they can be strong, weak or zero. Activity changes the "strength" of the transmission coefficients and consequently inputs increase or decrease their access to the output.

In order to integrate such cellular equivalent circuit within larger networks, we use the simplified representation illustrated in Figure A-7, which depicts only the main transmission coefficients (local [a] and global K) and the combination effected by the neuron.

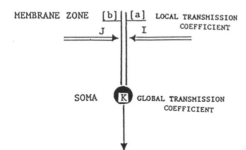

Figure A-7 . Simplified functional circuit for a neuron with 3 specialized transmission coefficients, used as a building block for columnar circuits.

b) Parametric table of a neuron: cellular space-time matrix.

FIGURE A-8 specifies the principal parameters of the neuronal transmission:

- these parameters are directly related to the properties of the molecules "Ci" (channels , receptors, etc..);

- they depends upon the membrane distribution of these molecules, as shown on the horizontal axis of Figure A-8): presynaptic "m", post-synaptic "e", homogeneous membrane zone [a], or whole cell K.

- the time range of their variations has four possible levels (vertical axis): "T1" represents parameters with short term changes (for instance channel opening), "T2" the parameters that are stable during behavioral time constant but can change with short term memory (channel modulation), "T3" the parameters that are stable during long

durations but can change with long term memory (for example a channel density), and
"T4" represent the morphological parameters that change during the network
construction (for instance a surface).

Thus each transmission parameter is defined by the combination of a letter
(e,a,K,m) that represents a specialized membrane zone (horizontal axis), and an index
(T1 to T4, on the vertical axis) that defines the temporal variation level; molecular
parameters are then specified within this space-time matrix.

B) Functional parameters can vary within intervals limited by the structural parameters of the network.

Neural information is coded at temporal level T1 by four intermediate activities:
presynaptic transmitter release and receptor activation ("eT1") on the post-synaptic
zones , is followed by channel opening ("aT1") in the post synaptic dendritic zones, and
then changes of the somatic membrane potential ("KT1") produces a propagated spike
and again transmitter release ("mT1") by axon terminals.

The neuron's output information combines the characteristics of the afferent
information with the characteristics of the four specialized zones, by means of four

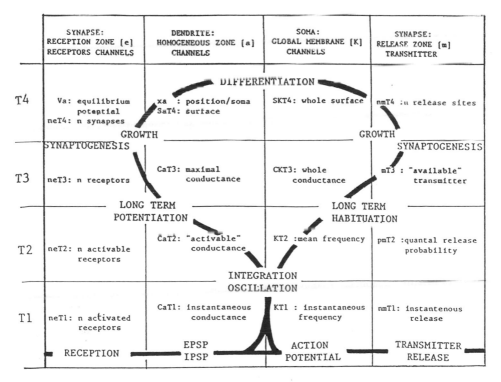

Figure A-8 . *Progressive memorization by a neuron: 4 types of subcellular locations
(horizontal) and 4 temporal levels (vertical).*

successive relations, specified on the lower line of TABLE A-6; the parameters of each zone (e,a,K,m) thus control the overall function of neuronal transmission.

a) Presynaptic release site.
Presynaptic parameters provide the successive limits to the random quantity of transmitter released per action potential: the release probability (mT1) and the transmitter content of each quantum (mT2).

b) Post-synaptic receptors.
At the post-synaptic level, the synaptic activity ("eT1") is the number of synaptic receptors "activated" by an afferent action potential . But this post-synaptic response is limited by the number of available receptors (eT2,eT3) and the extension of the receptive zone (eT4).

c) Homogeneous zones of the membrane.
The activity of homogeneous zones of the membrane (aT1) is defined by three complementary parameters: the number of open channels (conductance "CaT1" of the zone), the induced ionic flow and therefore the variations of membrane potential (V).

Afferent activity "I[a]" modifies the conductance "CaT1" of the zone [a]; its influence "dV" on the membrane potentia! "V" of the soma of neuron "K" is a function of three parameters:

1. Its influence increases with the difference "V-Va" between the membrane potential "V" and the equilibrium potential "Va" determined by the specific channels of the zone [a]; the maximum effect is to drive the equilibrium potential "Va".

2. Its influence increases with conductance (CaT1") activated by the inputs and decreases with the global conductance of the cell "CKT3" ; it depends upon the ratio "CaT1/CKT3". Conductance of each dendritic zone ("CaT1") has a maximal value ("CaT3"), related to the size of the zone ("SaT4=a"), for an homogeneous density of synapses;. The "maximal proportion of membrane activated by an afferent" ("CaT3/CKT3") depends upon the ratio "a/K" between the surface ("SaT4=a") of the afferences on the cell's membrane and the total surface ("SKT4=K") of the neuron.

3. Its influence decreases with the distance of the input zone ([a]) from the cell body; attenuation and especially slowing are more pronounced when the afference is farther from the soma. To define the relative positions of the afferents, we consider essentially the distances with respect to the soma, divided by the length of the cell ("scale principle"). Thus the zone I[a] occupies a position "xa" with respect to the soma, with "xa" varying from 0 to 1.

In a very general way, we can thus use the two geometric criteria (a/K and xa) to distinguish the "anatomical weight" of afferences: "strong" afferences (a/K) k0, xa (x0) and "weak" afferences (a/K (k0 , xa) x0). These weights are defined for neuronal groups: for each individual afferent cell, this weight is divided by the number of cells in the group ("na").

d) Global output.
At the level of the whole cell, for the neuron "K", the neural output activity KE(t) combines activities of several afferent groups: IE(t) on a receptor zone I[a] and JE(t) on another receptor zone J[b].

Each of the two afferences I[a],J[b] has a somatic effect that depends upon a prior combination with a transmission coefficient specific to each receptive zone [a] or [b] .

Neuronal integration of two inputs and can be schematically illustrated by an "equivalent logical circuit" (Figure A-6, lower part) that acts upon activity levels.

As summarized in Table 1-4, the integrative function depends:

- on the molecular parameters of the network that define equilibrium potentials "Va", "Vb" (vertical axis);

- on the geometric parameters of the network, such as the maximal proportion of membrane activable by an input "a/K", "b/K" and the relative positions of afferences "xa", "xb" (horizontal axis).

We first consider two afferences I[a] and J[b], both excitatory, with the same equilibrium potential (Va=Vb), above the threshold for the action potential (upper line in TABLE 1-4).

The influence of afferent activity on the soma ("dV") depends on the ratio between the synaptically activated conductance ("CaT1+CbT1") and the overall conductance ("CKT3") of the neuron: if this "proportion of excited membrane" ("(CaT1+CbT1)/CKT3") is high, there is an increased probability that the somatic potential ("V") reaches the triggering threshold for the action potential. Consequently, several integrative functions are possible and determined by the maximal proportion of excitable membrane (a/K and b/K).

If the two input coefficients are strong ("a/K" and "b/K" high), the global function of the neuron resembles that of the function "OR". But if the two afferences are weak, the global neuronal function resembles the "AND" function, stressing the importance of simultaneity.

Memorization changes the weights of the input and can change an "and" function into an "or" function.

When one of the two afferences is inhibitory, the integrative functions are illustrated on the second line of TABLE 1 4. The two afferences "I[a]" and "J[b]" have different equilibrium potentials "Va" and "Vb": the afference I[a] is excitatory and J[b] is inhibitory, with an equilibrium potential below the threshold potential. The inhibitory afferences that arrive directly on the soma have a powerful "shunting" effect on the excitatory activity, and can completely prevent triggering of an action potential. Consequently several integrative functions are possible and depend upon the relative position of inhibitory and excitatory afferences on the neuron (xa, xb).

C) The type of operation performed by a neuron on several inputs is shaped by the sequence of construction of the neural network.

a) Relative number of synapses between neurons.

We saw that the combination function of a neuron is a four step process from the lower (synapse) to the larger level (whole cell). The construction of the nervous network organizes these combinations in the reverse way from the larger (type of cell, groups of cells) to the lower level (individual cells).

Transmission coefficients and spatial integration functions of each cell depend upon "structural" parameters that are characteristic for each nervous tissue: an important

	1st AFFERENT "I"			2nd AFFERENT "J"		
	$\frac{a}{K}$	xa	$\frac{1}{na}$	$\frac{b}{K}$	xb	$\frac{1}{nb}$
CORTEX : UPPER LAYERS	M	M	M	M	M	M
CORTEX : LOWER LAYERS	W	M	M	W	W	M
CEREBELLAR CORTEX	S	S	S	W	W	W
THALAMUS	S	S	S	S	W	W

W: Weak
M: Moderate
S: Strong

Figure A-9 . Ontogenetic shaping of transmission coefficients by structural parameters (horizontal axis) for 4 neuronal types (vertical).

parameter is the relative number of synapses between cell groups, that will determine the two parameters "a/K" and "1/na".

- The total number of synapses on a neuron of type "K" depends upon its membrane extension and its size. Extension affects the global conductance and capacitance of the membrane.

- The maximum number of synapses between two neuronal groups "K" and "I" is a function of the "intersection surface" ("a") of the dendritic branching patterns of "K" and axonal branching pattern of "I". The relative influences of two inputs I[a] and J[b] depends both upon the maturation of the "K" neurons and the sequential arrival of the afferences "I[a]" and J[b] on the dendritic tree (see next paragraph).

- The maximum number of synapses between two individual neurons of type "K" and "I" depends not only upon the intersection surface ("a"), but in addition upon the number of afferent cells ("na") competing for the same dendritic surface ([a]). In several tissues, this number is a function of the deviation "dZ" on the transversal axis. The number of synapses between two cells of type "I" and "K" ("a/na") determines the maximal conductance of a type "K" neuron modified by the activity of a single type "I" neuron.

- The number of synapses between any two neurons depends not only upon the cells types, but also upon their position deviations on the lateral axes of the neural tissue (dX,dY); the number of synapses between two neurons diminishes as a function of the distances (dX,dY), because the density of the axonal and especially dendritic fields diminishes as a function of the distance from the cell body. This "connective" function 1/na(dX,dY), characteristic of a neural tissue, will be important to determine the response of the tissue to an input (I) which has a spatial pattern I(X,Y) on the axes of the tissue.

b) Different types of neuronal operations.

The construction patterns of neuronal integrative functions are illustrated in TABLE A-9 (as in FIGURE 1-5) for four cell types: the Purkinje cells of the cerebellum, the relay cells of the thalamus, and the pyramidal cells of the cerebral cortex, with two divisions: upper and lower pyramidal neurons. Table A-9 represents the functional parameters for two afferences (a/K,xa,na for input "I" and b/K,xb,nb for "J") with three possible values (W=Weak, M=Moderate,or S=Strong)

As in FIGURE 1-5, the construction sequence has two main stages "N1" (arrival of the afference "I") and "N2" (arrival of the afference "J".

At stage N1, the first afferent group "I" arrives in a "centered" way on the "K" neuron: its influence ("a/K") is maximal and the distance from the afferent group to the soma is minimal ("xa" small induces a strong influence).

At stage N2, the growth pattern of the second afferent group "J" can produce several spatial integrative functions (b/K and xb compared to a/K and xa).

For the Purkinje cells of the cerebellum, a single climbing fiber (I[a]) forms a large number of synapses ("a/K" maximum), while a great number of parallel fibers (J[b]) each makes only one synapse ("b/K" very weak); this pattern is regulated by the orientation of afferent axons (EX/EY(I)) with respect to the orientation of the dendritic branching pattern (EX/EY(K)): parallel fibers that are oriented perpendicularly to the dendrites of Purkinje cells make only one synapse, whereas climbing fibers, oriented along the principal axis, form a great number of synapses. The influence of the parallel fibers on the Purkinje cells is entirely conditioned by the activity of the climbing fiber : the integrative function may be approximated by a logical "if".

For the principal thalamic cells, the "spherical" growth mode of the dendritic tree gives great importance to the central "strong" peripheral afference ("a/K" large and "xa" is small), while the second afferent group, from the cortex, is "weaker" ("b/K" weak and "xb" large). The output activity represents primarily the central afferents (I[a]); the second afferent group (J[b]) reinforces this transmission if the component cells are simultaneously activated.

D) Transversal positions of soma and relative thickness of layers control the integrative operations performed by pyramidal neurons.

For the cortical pyramidal cells, the layered growth gives a more balance importance to the two types of afferences, inputs from the thalamus ("I=Th") and inputs from other cortical areas ("J=Co"). Within this organization, the anatomical position of the cells assumes a determining importance.

Separation of the transversal axis Z into limited horizontal layers controls the intersection surface (a,b). Cortical transmission parameters are thus determined by the position on the transversal axis.

STRUCTURATION OF CORTICAL FUNCTIONS BY LAYERS

	THALAMIC INPUT	CORTICAL INPUT	FUNCTION
GENERAL	$\dfrac{a}{K}$	$\dfrac{b}{K}$	
CORTEX	$\dfrac{EZ(IV)}{EZ(p)}$	$\dfrac{EZ(III)}{EZ(p)}$	
UPPER LAYERS	$\dfrac{EZ(IV)}{EZ(III+IV)}$	$\dfrac{EZ(III)}{EZ(III+IV)}$	"OR"
LOWER LAYERS	$\dfrac{EZ(IV)}{EZ(III+IV+V)}$	$\dfrac{EZ(III)}{EZ(III+IV+V)}$	"AND"

Figure A-10 . Transmission coefficients in cortical neurons: control by the relative thickness of cortical layers (EZ).

a) Relative strengths of inputs on dendrites.

The two spatial parameters, transversal position Z, due to migration, and extension EZ, due to maturation, are important, since they determine the relative strength of the two main inputs, thalamic "I=Th" and cortical "J=Co" on the pyramidal neurons.

During cortical growth, cellular migration occurs perpendicularly to the surface, along the transversal axis: new migrating cells cross cell layers already present, taking their place above them. Then maturation of each pyramidal cell (soma size, dendritic diameter) depend directly upon the transversal position of that cell's soma (Z).

Vertical dendritic growth is parallel to the thickening cortex: apical dendrites extend all the way to the cortical surface ; therefore their length (EZ(p)) will be equal to the cumulative extension of different layers: "EZ(III)" for the upper pyramidal cells and "EZ(III+IV+V)" for the lower pyramidal neurons.

b) Differences between upper and lower pyramidal neurons.

Thalamic inputs occupy the intermediate layer IV between the two main laminar divisions

Thalamic axons arrive in a period intermediary between the maturation of the upper and lower cortical cells and they form an intermediary layer (IV).

The thalamic afferents become thus connected in different ways to the two types of pyramidal neurons: with the apical dendrites of the lower ("PyrB") pyramidal cells, and then with the basal dendrites of the upper ("PyrH") pyramidal cells; so the upper and lower pyramidal cells have the same type of afference, but with quantitatively different parameters.

Supra and infragranular layers combine the two principal afferences , thalamic in layer IV (extension EZ(IV)) and cortical in layer III (extension EZ(III). But the intermediate position of the thalamic afferences differentiates the functions of the two layers.

For cells in the upper cortical layers, "a/K" and "b/K" are relatively equal ; "xa" and "xb" are also equal. These conditions result in a function like that of the logical "or". On the other hand, for the lower pyramidal cells, "K" increases, and then a/K and b/K decrease; "xa" and "xb" also decrease. These conditions produce a function like that of the logical "and".

c) Interneurons.

More generally, because of the laminar construction of the cortex, the operation performed by the pyramidal neurons, and their specific output (intra and extracortical) are both functions of the same transversal coordinate "Z".

For interneurons, integrative properties depend upon their axonal and dendritic extension with respect to the laminar organization (see table 2-2). These extensions can be defined coarsely:

- interneurons may have a preferential "transversal" extension that crosses several layers: they couple or uncouple the upper and lower divisions of a column;
- interneurons may have a preferential lateral extension that crosses several columns : they couple or uncouple neighboring columns.

ANNEX 4

From cellular memorization to learning rules.

The memorization process in a neural tissue has four complementary aspects:

1. Description of memorization: what are the transformed elements, and the spatial and temporal levels implicated?

2. Conditions for memorization at the cellular level: what are the parameters of activity that produce memorization at the cellular level?

3. Conditions for memorization at the modular level: what are the input patterns that change the modular coefficients?

4. Consequences of memorization: what are the resulting long term transformations of function?.

A) Description of the memorization process.

Memorization can occur independently for each cell type and each specialized region of the cell. For instance, increase in calcium concentration in the axon terminals produces an increase in mediator release without modifying the other neuronal functions. Each memorization is thus defined by: (a) the neuronal type ("K") and its position in the tissue ("A"); (b) the specialized part of the cell that changes ("[a]"); (c) the temporal level of change ("T1" to "T4") and (d) the direction of change which may be an increase or a decrease in transmission (Ti+ or Ti-).

Memorization is described by a combination "K.[A].[a].T3+"

- "K" represents the cell type: in a given neural tissue, several cell types can memorize activity with their own logic K= (Kh,Kb,K',K"); within the cerebral cortex, cell type that is transformed, (PyrH and PyrB, interneurons Ste, Pan, Pac, CdB, Cbp) imply a particular registration logic (depending upon the integrative function performed by each cell type)

- "[A]" represents the spatial zone and K.[A] the cell group which have long term transformations; memorizations generally do not concern isolated neurons, but rather regions of tissue depending upon relations with sensory or motor organs. The lateral "zone" ([A], [B], etc) of the transformed cell group is important because it specifies a relation with a sensory or a motor organ and the redundancy (lateral extension) of the new functional circuit created by learning;

- "[a]" represents the subcellular zone that changes; at least four are possible (synapse pre "m" and post "e", homogeneous receptive zone or spine "a", and global cell "K"); a more or less extensive subcellular region has different quantitative effects on the modular coefficients.

- "Ti+" represents the temporal level of memorization. This temporal level (from T1 to T4) explicits the passage from short term to long term and permanent memory.

B) Duration of memory traces depends upon several parameters of the spatio-temporal patterns of activity.

Memorization is progressive at four temporal levels (T1 to T4). Memorization at each temporal level "Ti" depends upon the state of the neuron and the parameters of the input activity, as illustrated in table A-10:

1. The "internal state" of the cell can facilitates (Ti+) or prevents (Ti-) further memorization at temporal level Ti.

2. The afferent activities have several critical features , both spatial and temporal, that can induce memorization processes at different temporal levels.

a) Temporal level T1: activity.
Input activity is defined by the instantaneous action potential frequency of the axons projecting on the afferent zone [a].

The nature (excitatory, inhibitory) of the input is determined by the equilibrium potential "Va" . The proportion of membrane activated "a/K" modulates the influence of each afference:

- a large depolarization and action potential (T1+) are produced if a large proportion of the membrane (a/K) is simultaneously activated by depolarizing afferences; memorization becomes possible;

- in contrast, the hyperpolarized state represents a stable state (T1-): there is no neuronal output and no memorization.

INTERNAL STATE	AFFERENT ACTIVITY	CRITICAL FACTOR	MEMORIZATION	
Depolarized	$I[a] \cdot E1$	a/K	$K \cdot T1+$	Action potential
Integrative	$I[a] \cdot E2$	$E2$	$K[a] \cdot T2+$	Post tetanic potentiation
Potentiated	$(I[a]+J[b]) \cdot E2$	$(a+b)/K$	$K[b] \cdot T3+$	Long term potentiation
Maturation	$Pe(K \cdot E2/J \cdot E2)$	$\frac{Pe}{Pu}$	$K[b] \cdot T4+$	Permanent memory Synaptogenesis, sprouting

Figure A-11. Critical conditions for cellular memorizations (horizontal axis) at four temporal levels (vertical axis).

b) Temporal level T2: short term memory.

For short-term memory (T2), intensity of activity (action potential frequency) is an important factor: elevated intensity levels ("E2") can produce short term memorizations. But we have to take into account as well the internal state of the neuron: its functional mode, either "integrative" or "oscillatory", regulates intracellular calcium concentration that is a critical factor in memorization:

- in the "integration" mode , successive activations have a cumulative effect (T2+) and can produce a post tetanic potentiation;

- in the "oscillation" mode, the neuronal parameters are stable (at T2 level) and independent of inputs.

c) Temporal level T3: long term memorization

For long term memorization (T3), important factors are intensity level of inputs (E2), and their spatial extension in the receptive membrane (a+b/K), due to the coactivation of afferent neurons. These inputs can induce prolonged modifications of receptors and channels:

- this long term memorization (T3+) can prolong post tetanic potentiation; it depends not only on the intensity (E2) of the afferent activity , but also on its spatial extension (a+b/K) ;

- in contrast, habituation can decrease the transmission and consequently the possible memorizing effects of afferent activities.

d) Temporal level T4: permanent memory

For permanent memory, the important factor is the recurrence of coactivations, measured by a "repetition factor . This "repetition factor" is a conditional probability "Pe": for instance Pe(K.E2/I.E2) is the conditional probability that the cell "K" will be activated at intensity level E2 after the activation of cell "I" at level E2.

Permanent memorization is dependant upon repetition of the afferent activity that produces long-term memorization (repetition factor) but there can be a competitive effect of long term depression.

Permanent transformations also depend upon a "maturation factor":

- during "critical" periods, strong input-output coactivations may result in the formation of new synapses (T4+) and for weak activities , synapses can disappear (T4-);

- after this critical period, the synapses remain stable.

B) Activation patterns and transmission coefficients at the modular level.

a) Modular pattern of activity.

Activities of the different layers of cortical modules [A] and [B] are represented by temporal trapezoidal functions with activity levels Ei. To symbolize activity sequences, we shall simplify the general activity term "K.[A].Ei" (activity level Ei of a K type cell in zone [A]) by the contracted form "KAi". This simplification is presented in TABLE A-12:

- the first letter (lower case) represents the cellular type : "o" is a sensory organ, "t" a thalamic afference, and "c" a cortical afference to the column;

	SYMBOLIC	SIMPLIFIED

CELL TYPE
  Thalamic
  Cortical
  -upper layers
  -lower layers
	K
	Th
	Co
	CoH
	CoB	

SPATIAL ZONE	[A]	A

CELL GROUP
Cortical module
  -upper layer
  -lower layer
	K.[A]
	
	CoH.[A]
	CoB.[A]
		KA

ACTIVITY	E(t)	Et

ACTIVITY LEVEL
      high
      low
      nul
	Ei
	E2
	E1
	E0	

ACTIVITY OF CELLULAR GROUPS activity level	K.[A].E(t) K.[A].Ei	KAt kAi
Cortical inputs Thalamus Cortex A-B	Th.[A].E1 Co.[AB].E1	tA1 cAB1
Cortical module		
-upper layers A B	CoH.[A].E1 CoH.[B].E1	A1 B1
-lower layers A B	CoB.[A].E2 CoB.[B].E2	A2 B2

ENVIRONMENTAL
SITUATION
  Signal
  Indifferent
	O
	
	O1
	O0	

Figure A-12 . Symbolic representation of activities of neuronal groups: definition of cell types and spatial location.

- the second letter represents the position of the modular zone, for instance "A" or "B";
- the last character is a figure that represents the activity level, E0, E1, or E2.

Upper layer activity of module [A] is defined by the output activity of its upper pyramidal neurons; this activity at the E1 level is symbolized by "A1". High activity of module [A], in both upper and lower layers, is symbolized by "A2" .

Similarly, we express the activities of module [B] by B1 and B2. The cortical afferences of the module [B] come from another module [A] and thus reflect the activities of the upper layer of module [A].

	SYMBOLIC		SIMPLIFIED
ZONES	[A]	[B]	A,B
TYPES	K	J	
Thalamic	Th		
Cortical	Co		
−upper layers	CoH		
−lower layers	CoB		
NETWORKS			
General	K.[A] −	J.[B]	KA−JB
Cortex			
−input/output	CoB.[A] −	J.[A]	
−inter-columns	CoH.[A] −CoH.[B]		A −B
SEQUENCE			
A before B	K.[A].Ei− J.[B].Ej		Ai−Bj
B after A	J.[B].Ej/ K.[A].Ei		Bj/Ai
LONG RANGE			
ACTIVATION	Pe(J.[B].Ej/ K.[A].Ej)		Pe(Bj/Ai)
PATTERN			
Coactivation	Pe(CoB.[B].E2/CoH.[A].E2)		P2
Inhibition	Pe(CoB.[B].E0/CoH.[A].E2)		P0
TRANSMISSION COEFFICIENT			
PROBABILIST	Pi(J.[B].Ej/ K.[A].Ei)		Pi(Bj/Ai)
Cortical:			
−upper−upper	Pi(CoH.[B].E1/CoH.[A].E1)		Ph
−upper−lower	Pi(CoB.[B].E2/CoH.[A].E1)		Pb
CONTINUOUS			
Cortical: Call			
−upper−upper	CoH.[B].Et/CoH.[A].Et		Ch1
−upper−lower	CoB.[B].Et/CoH.[A].Et		Cb1
Action			
−upper−upper	CoH.[A].Et/CoH.[B].Et		Ch2
−upper−lower	CoB.[A].Et/CoH.[B].Et		Cb2

Figure A-13 . Symbols for networks between groups of cells, sequences of activity in these networks, and transmission coefficients.

b) Long range activity patterns.

At the modular level, long range activity patterns (repetition factor) can be measured by conditional probabilities of close activation of a module and its inputs from other modules. These co-activations depend upon all the inputs and therefore upon activities outside the cortex. They are "external" conditional probabilities ("Pe").

We focus on two "external probabilities":

1. $P2 = Pe(B2/A2)$ is the conditional probability that a strong activity of module [B] precedes a strong activation of module [A]. The temporal order is important, and

this probability measures the high activities of [B] that occur BEFORE the high activities of [A].

2. P0 = Pe(B0/A2) is the conditional probability that module [B] is inhibited BEFORE a strong activation of [A]: the inhibitory cells, already activated to level E2, are reactivated in an important way by the cortical afferences.

The repetition coefficient "Pe" can have, as a first approximation, three possible values:

1. Pe=0 "never": coactivation never occurs; this condition can have an important effect upon inhibitory interneurons which are strongly activated in these circumstances;

2. Pe) 0 "sometimes": for certain cells in a critical position, a small number of coactivations can produce permanent memorization.

3. Pe =1 "always": for other cells, memorization occurs only when the activities are always correlated.

c) Modular transmission coefficients

At the modular level, we are particularly concerned with the relations between two modules, an transmitter [A] and a receptor [B] whose lateral extensions, we recall, are determined by considerations of functional homogeneity.

Upper pyramidal cells (CoH) of module [A], project to the upper (CoH) and lower (CoB) layers of module [B].

The transmission coefficient between two cell groups can be measured by an "internal" conditional probability "Pi" between the activities of the two cell groups: memorization is then due to modifications of this internal probability "Pi" that changes as a function of the values of the repetition factor "Pe". This memorization can be considered as the adjustment of an "internal" probability "Pi" of coupling between the cell groups, to a probability of external coupling "Pe" between two elements of the surrounding environment.

The modular transmission coefficients are determined by transmission parameters between two cellular groups [A] et [B]. We distinguish these coefficients for the upper and lower modular layers.

1. The coefficient of transmission between upper layers CoH[A] and CoH[B] is a set of conditional probabilities Pi(CoH[Bj]/CoHAk]), of triggering an output level Ej for an input level Ek, with "j" and "k" varying between 0 and 2. We focus on Ph=Pi(B1/A1) which is the conditional probability of activation of the upper layer of [B] at level E1, when the cortical afferences are at level E1.

2. The coefficient between [A] and the lower layers of [B] is the set of conditional probabilities Pi(CoB[Bj]/CoH[Ak]). We focus on Pb=Pi(B2/A1), conditional probability of activation of the lower layer of [B] at level E2, when the cortical afferences are at level E1.

D) Learning rules from cellular to modular levels.

TABLE A-14 shows, in four columns:
- the long-range patterns of modular activation Pe(Bi/Ai), as defined in paragraph (C) and Figure A-13;
- the corresponding activities in neurons of the cortical column;

- the consequences of these activity patterns upon cellular registrations, as defined in paragraph (A) and in figure A-11;

- and then the consequences of cellular registrations upon modular coefficients "Ph=Pi(B1/A1)" and "Pb=Pi(B2/A1)", as defined in paragraph (C) and Figure A-13.

MODULAR ACTIVITY	CELLULAR ACTIVITY	CELLULAR MEMORIZATION	MODULAR MEMORIZATION	
Pe(B0/A2) = 1	PanH.E2 + Co.E2 $\longrightarrow$	PanH.T3+	Ph $\longrightarrow$ 0	PROBABILISTIC COEFFICIENT
Pe(B2/A2)) 0	PyrH.E2 + Co.E2 $\longrightarrow$	Co[m].T3+ Cbp.T3+	Ph $\longrightarrow$ 1	
Pe(B0/A2)) 0	Pac.E2 + Co.E2 $\longrightarrow$	Pac.T3+ PanB.T3+	Pb $\longrightarrow$ 0	
Pe(B2/A2) = 1	PyrB.E2 + PyrH.E2 $\longrightarrow$	Cdb.T3+ Cbp.T3+	Pb $\longrightarrow$ 1	
Pe(B2/A1)) 0	Co.E1 + PyrH.E2 $\longrightarrow$ PyrH[a].T3+		Ch1 = B1/A1	CONTINUOUS COEFFICIENT
Pe(B2/A1) = 1	PyrH.E1 + PyrB.E2 $\longrightarrow$ PyrB[a].T3+		Cb1 = B2/A1	
Pe(B2/C2)) 0	Co.E1 + PyrH.E2 $\longrightarrow$ PyrH[c].T3+		Ch2 = B1/C2	
Pe(B2/C2) = 1	PyrH.E1 + PyrB.E2 $\longrightarrow$ PyrB[c].T3+		Cb2 = B2/C2	

Figure A-14 . Critical activity patterns that result in memorization: passage from the cellular level (center) to the modular level (left and right columns).

Each cellular memorization has both a temporal and a spatial consequence:

- Each cellular memorization facilitates longer-term memorizations , by changing the "internal state" and by increasing transmission. Memorization is thus progressive and several temporal levels are successively integrated in a sequential chaining.

- Each memorization has a specific spatial effect upon the cellular transmission coefficients; this effect may be local (a spine) with an associative coupling within each cell, or global (the whole membrane) with an associative coupling at a "modular" level (between cell groups).

The nature and the position of the transformed neuron within the network is particularly important (see Figure 2-2); an neuron (K) may have two opposite effects on the transmission between two cells groups, for example an associative coupling or an uncoupling if it is inhibitory.

On the vertical axis of TABLE A-14 (upper part), we represent the four possible reorganizations of the relations between two modules, derived from the activation conditions (P0 and P2):

a) If $Pe(Bo/A2) = 1$ then $Pi(B0/A1) = 1$

Receptor module [B] is "never" active before intense activity in the transmitter module [A]. This condition produces an uncoupling between the cortical afference and the rest of the module (Ph and Pb tend toward 0): we call "G0" this stable registration. In this state ("G0"), an activity "A1" inhibits [B].

If the two modules are adjacent, increased inhibition reinforces the subdivision of a cortical zone [A+B] into two new functionally independent modules [A] and [B].

b) If $Pe(B2/A2)) 0$ then $Pi(B1/A1) = 1$

Receptor module [B] is "sometimes" active at E2 before intense activation in the transmitter [A]. This condition reinforces the coupling between the cortical afference and the upper layers (Ph approaches 1): we call "G1" this registration level. In this new state, activity "A1" will produce "B1", but another input (for example thalamic) will be necessary to reach "B2". This registration state "orients" sequences of cortical activities but the actual sequence also depends upon activity of the thalamic inputs.

c) If $Pe(B0/A2)) 0$ then $Pi(B2/A1) = 0$

Receptor module [B] may also be "sometimes" inhibited before intense activities of its afferences. This condition produces an "active" uncoupling between the cortical afference and the lower layer (Ph remains equal to 1 and Pb approaches 0): this condition reinforces the stability of the new registration state "G1" (oriented sequences).

d) If $Pe(B2/A2) = 1$ then $Pi(B2/A1) = 1$

Receptor module [B] is always active at level E2 before the intense activity from transmitter [A]. This condition induces a coupling between the cortical inputs and the lower layer of the module (Ph=1 and Pb also approaches 1): this is a stronger registration state "G2". In this state, activity "A1" will produce "B2" , whatever the thalamic activation of the module.

If two modules are adjacent, increased coupling produces the merging of two adjacent cortical zones into a single module [A+B]. The global module will henceforth have a unitary and homogeneous activity.

E) Continuous coefficients refine the relations between modules which participate in the same call tree.

Functional links between modules are first the "probability" coefficients Ph and Pb, defined for each cortical input, but they are refined by "continuous coefficients" that also change with learning. These changes are shown in the lower part of Figure A-14.

These coefficients change when the module participates in a call network. Each module, for instance [B], has then two types of relations with other modules ([A] and [C]), first in the direction of the call (relation A-B) and in the direction of the actions (relation C-B).

a) In the direction of the call.

In the direction of the call (A-B-C), [B] is called by the pilot module [A] and the cortical connection coefficients between [A] and [B] represent in a way the force of the call:

1. The "upper-upper" continuous coefficient, symbolized by "Ch1", is the gain that determines the activities of the upper layers of a module in response to the call activity from the pilot module. It represents a "call coefficient". This coefficient will tend to decrease with the successive extensions of the call and will tend to be weaker when the distance from the final goal increases.

2. The "upper-lower" coefficient, that we have symbolized by "Cb1", is the gain that influences the lower layers during a call.It represents an "action coefficient". When the distance from the goal increases, fewer upper pyramidal cells are specialized to call other modules and more can be specialized to activate the lower layers of the module: the upper-lower coefficient can increase when the distance from the goal increases.

b) In the direction of actions.

In the direction of the sequence of actions (C!-B!-A!), the connection coefficients of [C] toward [B] represent in a way the "recall" force with which the action of [C] favours the action of [B] . These two coefficients are symbolized by Ch2 and Cb2: these are the "gains" that redefine the activity of the upper and lower layers of [B] following action of the module [C].

Specifically, the "upper-lower" continuous coefficient, that we have symbolized by "Cb2", can register the ratio of optimal intensity between two successive actions.It represents a "proportion coefficient". We shall see that this kind of registration has great behavioral significance: cortex does not learn the intensity of an action, but rather the proportion between two successive actions.

Global modifications of probabilistic coefficients shape the spatial extension of activated cell groups. Their behavioral significance is initially qualitative, for instance association of two types of movement.

Modifications of subcellular coefficients (for instance, a dendritic spine K.[a].C3+), produce increasingly fine adjustments of neuronal function: this supplementary memorization is more quantitative at the behavioral level. This fine memorization process can for instance control the quantitative relationship between two successive motor acts.

ANNEX 5

Columnar automata.

A) Columnar automata are searching mechanisms.

Columnar automata generate a spatio-temporal pattern of cortical activation. TABLES A-15 and A-16 illustrate the different possible chains of cortical events: to initial states (left column) functional and modular registration rules of Table 2-15 are applied (central column), generating event chains and thus an activity sequence (right column).

Spatial dimension is symbolized by letters that represent cortical zones. We use the simplification expressed in TABLE A-12: "Ei" activity of module [A] has a shortened form "Ai".

INITIAL STATE			EXTERNAL COUPLING	INPUT/OUTPUT RULES	SEQUENCES OF MODULAR ACTIVITIES	
cA	oA	oB				
cA1	oA1			cA1 + tA1 → A2 A2 → A! A2 → B0	A1 - A2	ACTION
cA1	oA0			cA1 + tA0 → A1 A1 → cB1	A1 - B1	CALL
cA1	oA0	oB0		cB1 + tB0 → B0	A1 - B1 - B0	CALL EXTENSION
cA1	oA0	oB1		cB1 + tB1 → B2	A1 - B1 - B2	ADAPTED ACTIONS
cA1	oA0	oB1	B! → oA1	B2 → cA1 cA1 + tA1 → A2	A1 - B2 - A2	EFFICIENT ACTION
cA1	oA0	oB1	C! → oA1	cA1→ cB1→ cC1 cC1 + tC1→ C2 C!→ A2 A2→ B0	A1 - B1 - C2	SEARCH

Figure A-15 . Different possibilities of cortical activation (right) determined by the rules of columnar automata (center) applied in different initial conditions (left).

a) Limited action or call extension.

In table A-15, we start from a prolonged activation "cA1". The ensuing activity sequence then depends upon the specific external situation "oA" that can activate the thalamic inputs of module [A] (tA1).

1. IF the specific environmental situation "oA1" is present, the coactivation of cortical "cA1" and thalamic "tA1" afferences produces a specific extracortical action A! and inhibits connected modules that have a weaker activity. The cortical activity sequence is then A1-A2 and is limited to the module [A].

2. IF the specific situation is absent (oAo), only the cortical afferences of [A] will be activated and the upper layer will call other modules, particularly [B. The cortical activation extends to other modules (A1-B1) .

b) Adaptation to the external situation.

Next we start from the call of [B] by [A]:

1. IF the specific situation "oB1" is present, the coactivation tB1+cB1 produces the action B!. The cortical activation is "A1-B1/B2-A2".

2. IF the specific situation "oB" is absent (oB0), the activation spreads through the cortical network.

c) Search for an effective action.

We start from the action B!:

1. IF the action B! modifies the situation "oA", by an external feedback loop, the action A! can be triggered, inhibiting the other, less active modules. The cortical activity sequence is "A1-B1/B2-A2" limited to the cortical network [A+B].

2. IF the action of [B] is inefficient on the external situation "oA", the activity spreads along the cortical network until finally actions of the called modules can modify in some way the situation oA, by an external feedback loop, and consequently trigger an action A!. Then the cortical excitation diminishes as previously described. If for instance it is a module [C] that modifies "oA", the cortical activity will be "A1-B1-C1/C2-A2".

B) New functional networks memorize efficient calls and sequences of actions.

We start from an efficient action B! that modify oA by an external causal link. The event sequence is "A1-B1-B2-A2": the sequence B2-A2 is the necessary precondition for changing the modular transmission coefficients between the upper layers of [A] and [B]. Two possibilities exist, as a function of the long term activity pattern P(B2/A2). The new functional links express then the values of the transmission coefficients "Ph" and "Pb": from inhibition when these values are equal to 0, to strong excitation when these values are close to 1.

a) Oriented sequences.

IF the repetition factor Pe(B2/A2) is different from 1 ("sometimes"), only the coefficient Ph will approach 1; relations between modules [A] and [B] will then be determined by the rules "G1" of Table 3-15. The pilot module [A] will selectively call [B], but the action B! will occur only in the environmental situation oB1.

Module [A] can call several modules in parallel: [B] and [B'] that represent two goal-directed actions. The two actions B! and B'! may be competitive and their functional relations in the cortical network which are antagonistic will become inhibitory. Module [B] can itself call another module, [C]. Thus module [B] will have three different functional specializations with three other modules: it is called by [A], it inhibits [B'], and it calls [C].

b) Fixed sequences.

IF the repetition factor Pe(B2/A2) is close to 1 ("always"), then the action sequence B!-A! will invariably permit goal attainment: the transmission coefficient Pb approaches 1. The functional rules "G2" of TABLE 3-15 can then be applied . The call from A! triggers the action B!, whatever the environmental situation oB. The sequence of cortical activity becomes "A1-B1-B2-A2" with a behavioral sequence "B2-A2" that is in an order inverse to that of the call sequence (A1-B1).

The sequence may become longer and longer. Module [B] is called by module [A] and calls module [C] . The action C! will be the first of the sequence. It will reactivate [B], and the action of [B] will be triggered. The order of actions "C2-B2-A2" is the inverse of the call order "A1-B1-C1".

C) Cortical sequences integrate attentive states for triggering signals.

TABLE A-16 represents sequence construction with a triggering signal. It is organized in the same way as Table A-15: the activity sequences (on the right) are determined from initial states (on the left) by the application of modular rules (center). The new functional network is shown in Figure 21C.

INITIAL STATE				INPUT/OUTPUT RULES	SEQUENCES OF MODULAR ACTIVITIES	
		SIGNAL				
cAB	oB	oZ				
cAB1	oB1	oZ0		cAB1 + oB1 -> B2 . oZ0 -> oA0	A1-B2	NO SIGNAL
cAB1	oB1	oZ1		A1 -> cB1 -> cZ1 cZ1 + oZ1 -> Z2	A1-Z2-B2-A2	SIGNAL
cAB1	oB1	oZ0	W1	cAB1 -> cBZ1 -> Z1 Z1 -> W1 cWB1 + cAB1 -> /B1/	A1-Z1-W1	WAITING
cAB1	oB1	oZ1	WO	oZ1 -> Z2 -> WO /B1/+ Z2 -> B1 B1` +oB1 -> B2 -> A2	W1-Z2-B2-A2	TRIGGER

Figure A-16 . Attentive state: integration of a triggering signal in a motor sequence.

a) Signal reception.
We start from a module [B] that is linked to a call network constructed around the pilot module [A]; the effectiveness of the action B! (to reach the goal A!) may

depend upon a signal "oZ1" in the sense that execution of B! coincides with maximum effectiveness when it is time locked with the signal.

When the signal is absent ("oZo"), the module [B] calls other modules that might potentiate its action, and thus it calls the sensory module [Z] that amplify the signal. The call is then A1-B1-Z1 and the signal "oZ1" produces the behavioral sequence Z2-B2-A2.

b) Readiness.

The signal ("oZ1") may be indispensable for the complete execution of the sequence: as long as this condition is not met, the actions B! are ineffective; they can even disrupt signal reception. In this case, the sensory module [Z] will in turn call another, "suspending" module [W] which will produce an inhibition upon [B].

Consequently, two opposed influences arrive on the same module [B] as shown in the equivalent circuit of FIGURE 21C : the afference "cWB" from the "suspending module" is inhibitory (Pi(B1/W1)=0) and competes with the cortical afference from the pilot module "cAB" that has an excitatory influence (Pi(B1/A1)=1).

Simultaneous activity of these two competitive afferences produces an "attentive state" of the upper layer of [B] that we call "/E1/": in this state, the activity of the upper layers of [B] is low, but the module has a heightened sensitivity. The functional relations are determined by rules "G1" expressed in Table 2-15 (activity "E1" is replaced by the attentive state /E1/). The inhibitory afference [W] has produced a supplementary temporal differentiation of the relation "G1" between the modules [A] and [B].

c) Signal.

When the external signal "oZ1" occurs, the receptor module [Z] performs an action Z! having two cooperative effects: it activates [B] and more importantly, suppresses the call of [Z] toward the "suspending" module [W] that inhibited the module [B]. Following this, the action of [B] is directly triggered. The global cortical sequence is the attentive state A1-Z1-W1-/B/ before the signal and the behavioral sequence Z2-B2-A2 when the signal occurs.

ANNEX 6

Redundancy of functional networks.

A) New functional networks are constructed with the maximal cellular redundancy.

The new functional circuits that develop in the cortex (call trees) are constructed with maximal possible redundancy, on a maximum number of cells, from a double process : "lateral uncouplings" reorganize the modular dimensions; they progressively

SUBDIVIDE the cortical space into distinct functional zones, and the "transversal couplings" SEQUENCE the actions of these module to form call trees.

Functional modules are "lateral zones" on the cortical surface. Each cortical module has an "address", that represents both its position and its lateral extension on the cortical surface: the position implies a specific input-output relation, and the extension gives an idea of the subsequent learning capacities.

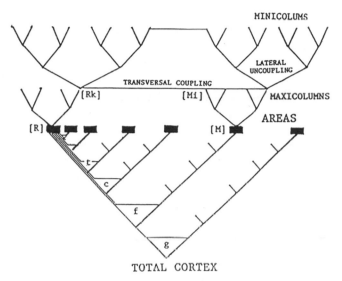

Figure A-17. *Progressive structuring of the cortical system by lateral uncoupling of cortical zones (forks) and successive transversal couplings (horizontal links).*

This address can be obtained by successive dichotomy of the total cortical surface, shown on FIGURE A-17 by a branching structure that starts from the total surface and goes to the minicolumn level. For example, a module first belongs to a cortical area, that implies both a cytoarchitectonic organization and a sensorimotor input-output relation. Call trees are formed by a set of new functional connections between cortical zones which can be defined with increasing precision: between two areas, between two bands within these areas, and then between two modular zones with a certain redundancy.

B) Systematic connections between cortical areas compensate dichotomies of the cortical surface.

a) Systematic "standard" connections

Cortical areas are produced by successive lateral dichotomies of the cortical surface: each division is compensated by formation of a new connection between the two new subsets; this connection is symmetrical about the border line and links the symmetrical modules in a parallel, systematic way.

The cortical surface can be subdivided by 6 successive dichotomies (FIGURE A-17): 6 systematic and symmetrical connections correspond to each of these subdivisions, and form 6 "standard" cortico-cortical connections at the level of each cortical zone. They can be named in the same way for all the modules, whatever the cortical region implicated:

1. "g" symmetry links the two hemispheres;
2. "f" symmetry links the associative and the frontal poles ;
3. "t" symmetry links the lateral and medial faces of the cortical hemispheres;
4. "c" symmetry links the two sensori-motor privileged circuits;
5. "h" symmetry links parietal and temporal areas;
6. "s" symmetry links secondary and primary areas.

Each basic module has other possible cortico-cortical connections with distant modules of the same area, along the two lateral axes ("x" and "y" connections).

b) Interrelation between successive call trees.

New call trees are first formed upon the connections between two areas. But each module of the call tree forms also connections with six other cortical regions. Thanks to these repetitive connections, all the functional relations that form the call tree between two areas can be integrated within another call tree that implies a third area: the whole sequence of cortical actions can be used by calls originating from any of the six connected regions.

For example a call tree constructed in an area [R] from a pilot module in another area [M] (connection "s"), can be used by a pilot module in a third area [L], (by the connection "c" for instance). The anatomical substratum of the call tree can be depicted by a "formula", that is a combination of cortical areas, each pair of areas being linked by one of the 6 basic symmetrical connections. For instance, the call tree has a substratum [L]-c-[M]-s-[R]-x-[R] . This formula will become increasingly long with several branches.

c) Combinations: modular bands and cortical matrix

More precisely, the module belongs to "bands" of "maxicolumns" (300 microns) with privileged relations with a specific part of a sensory or motor organ. New circuits are constructed on the "cortical matrix" formed by alternating bands within the same layer (for example "f-g"), and crossed bands in different layers (for example ("f/c"). The eight cortical relations correspond to four functional sublayers: g-f / t-c / s-h / x-y.

Modular bands ([R1] to [Rn] in an area [R], and [M1] to [Mk] in another area [M]) are oriented by the main axes of the sensory and motor maps ([R] and [M]); parallel and redundant corticocortical connections project these bands with the same orientation: for example the cortical afferent band t[Rn] that projects [Rn] by the symmetry "t" on an area [L] is parallel to [Rn], and c[Mk] on the same area [L] is parallel to [Mk]. Since the main axis of [Rn] and [Mk] are not parallel, c[Mk] is connected to all the modular bands t[R1],t[Rn].

C) The maximal number of new functional networks is determined by the relative dimensions of anatomical subsets.

Each module of a call tree is a group of cells with a lateral redundancy "EX" and a transversal redundancy "EZ", that represent both a spatial extension and a number of cells (homogeneous density of the cortical elements). To express the learning capacity of cortical regions, we use a binary quantitative approximation .

Lateral coupling and transversal uncoupling alternate in a dynamic way.

a) The process of lateral uncoupling (differentiation).

A modular zone [R] with a lateral redundancy EX0 may be subdivided by learning into two modular zones [R]/2 that are half as large EX0/2, when these two subzones have a different activity during attainment of a given goal.

"N" steps of lateral uncouplings can form 2 to the Nth new modules on the original surface [R] . If the lateral extension of the original module is "EX0", each of the new modules, at the stage 'n', occupies a surface "EX0/2pn".

The level of the minicolumn (30 microns) limits the maximum number of functional dichotomies. Due to their relative dimensions (300/30 microns), the number of minicolumns in a maxicolumn is about 2 to the 7th power: each maxicolumn has a capacity of at least 2 to the 7th differentiated circuits.

The total surface of an area determines the overall capacity for differentiation: at least 2 to the 10th maxicolumns having homogeneous peripheral significance can coexist within each area, that is 2 to the 17th elementary modules. The cortical surface is subdivided by 6 successive dichotomies into 2 to the sixth areas. The total capacity is then 2 to the 23rd.

b) The process of transversal coupling (sequences).

Upper layers are already differentiated into 8 sub-layers of transversal redundancy EZ0: a sequence of "K" actions subdivide a sublayer into "K" transversal zones whose redundancy is EZ0/K

The maximal subdivision "K" depends directly upon the ratio of upper to lower pyramidal cells. The number of neurons per minicolumn is about 100, with a large proportion of upper pyramidal cells: the maximal subdivision is 8, that limits the maximal length of the sequence.

The number of synapses per neuron affects the capacity for quantitative modulation of cellular transmission coefficients. The number of synapses for each pyramidal cell can be approximately 2 to the 16th power: therefore we shall consider that the transmission coefficients with each type of afference, specialized according to sublayer, include at least 2 to the 10th power synapses that will give a margin for quantitative variation.

ANNEX 7

Redundancy and transmission.

A) Relative dimensions quantify the limit values of transmission coefficients.

Each elementary module has six relations with other cortical areas; thus a great number of combinations are possible. Each of these cortical connections can memorize different functional relations (Chapter II): they can become inhibitory or execute oriented calls, or directly trigger a modular action.

The geometry of a call tree first depend upon the intermodular "probabilistic" coefficients; these coefficients determine call orientation and sequences of actions. The coefficients give two directions of functioning that do not have the same significance: one direction corresponds to the call and the other to the actions. In addition, the coefficients determine a hierarchy in the successive calls (call level "-k"), up to a minimum "-K" that represent the maximum length of the sequence.

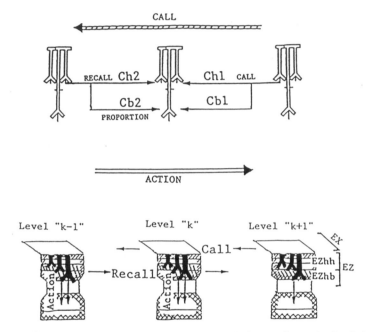

Figure A-18 . Continuous transmission coefficients within a call tree in the 2 directions, for calls and actions (upper) and dimensions (EX,EZ) of the component modules (lower).

But we have seen (annex 4) that a fine control also exists, expressed by four "continuous" coefficients (Ch1, Ch2, Cb1, Cb2). These coefficients are modified in a coordinated way, according to the logic of modular memorizations. Their values are dependant upon the number of cells that form the network, and thus they depend upon the transversal and lateral redundancy of the modular zones.

In order to represent the global behavior of a call tree, we quantify the limits of the four continuous coefficients as a function of their position on the call tree, that is as a function of the call level "-k". Relations between a module at level "-k" and another module at level "i" are defined by the continuous coefficients C(i,k). These coefficients successively orient the call and therefore the sequence of modular actions. At each instant, the intensity of the call upon a given module depends upon both the pilot module (by the call coefficient Ch1) and the execution of other modular actions (by the recall coefficient Ch2). The intensity of an action depends upon the thalamic afferences, the cortical call (Cb1), and recent actions (Cb2).

The values of the coefficients are dependent upon the number of cells that can form the network, and thus they depend upon the transversal and lateral redundancy of the module zones: lateral extension at the level of the call "k" will be called "EX(k)", and the vertical extension "EZ(k)".

That part of the upper layer specialized for the sequence will be called "EZhh", and the other part specialized for relations with the lower level will be called "EZhb".

B) Sequence construction and differentiation of modules alternate in a cooperative way.

FIGURES A-19 and A-20 depict the construction and function of call trees, by taking into account spatial constraints.
- The upper schema represents the function;
- The lower diagrams represent stages in the construction of the call tree: the first line represents the first stage with one action D!, the second the next stage with two actions C!D!, etc. At each stage, the number of modules called (lateral differentiation) and the length of the sequence (transversal differentiation) modify the lateral and transversal redundancy and thus the continuous coefficients: call (Ch1), recall (Ch2), action (Cb1), and proportion (Cb2).

Sequence construction entails a double spatial reorganization- lateral and transversal- of the upper layer of the modules

The functional connections within a call tree have both transversal and lateral redundancy. The transversal redundancy is limited by the sublayer that forms one of the six main cortico-cortical connections. The lateral redundancy is intermediate between an area and a minicolumn.

The construction of the call tree will progressively differentiate the upper sub-layer of the pilot-module. The pilot-module ([D]) has anatomical connections with the others modules ([A], [B], and [C]):

1. The first sequential relation (sequence C!-D!) is constructed with maximal redundancy within the upper sub layer of the pilot-module ([D]).

2. This sublayer can itself become subdivided into new sublayers when the size "K" of the sequence increases (for instance B!C!D! and then A!B!C!D!). The different stages specialize the anatomical layers into "K" functional sublayers.

3. For a sequence of a given length K subdivision can be lateral within each functional sublayer which correspond to a step of this sequence: for example several possible actions (B! or B'!) can be called by the same terminal sequence (C!D!). The various sequences of length K share the same zone that organized the original sequence of length K-1.

Diverse sequences are thus constructed by the repetition of lateral extension and transversal differentiations. At each new stage, the sequence is redundantly organized within the largest possible zone; this process facilitates ulterior differentiations.

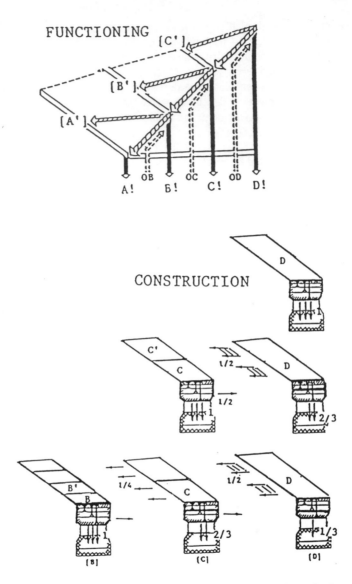

Figure A-19 . Redundancy of connections within a call tree (upper) determined by
subdivisions during construction (lower).

a) Call distribution.

The call coefficient Ch1(k,i) represents the influence of a module of level "-i"
upon a lower-level "-k" module during a call, that is to say, the ratio between the
activities "E1" of the upper layers of the modules for a decreasing call level. They
define the priority of activation in competitive situations when several modules of the
same call tree are simultaneously activated by their thalamic afferences.

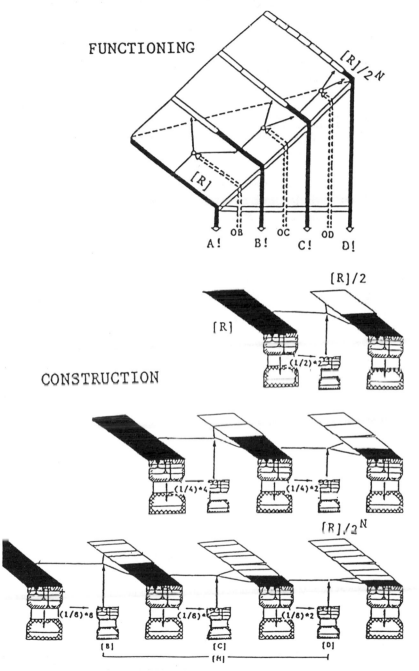

Figure A-20 . Recognition algorithms (upper diagram) integrate actions which increase contrast of activity within more and more precise cortical zones (lower).

The pilot module has a global "call capacity", related to its extension EX(0) and this call is distributed toward several modules having an extension EX(k). The call coefficient Ch1(k,0) depends upon the relative extension

EX(k)/EX(0) = 1/2 to the (k)th power.

The greater the number of modules called, the weaker the call coefficient. The call tends to diminish as the goal becomes distant. For an environmental situation that competitively activates several modules in parallel, upper-level actions have priority.

b) Action reinforcement.

The "action coefficient" Cb1(k) defines the influence of the upper layer of the module upon the lower layer: in other words, the ratio of upper to lower activity, in the direction of the call.

As sequence level "-k" diminishes, the vertical extension "EZhh" for the call decreases, and the direct influence of upper upon lower layer ("EZhb") increases but their sum remain constant; the sequence of K actions correspond to a differentiation into "K" sublevels as already mentioned; we can express these properties by two approximate equations:

EZhh(k) = EZ0(1-k/K)
EZhb(k) = EZ0(k/K)
The action coefficient "Cb1(k)" depends upon
EZhb(k)/EZ0 = k/K

The action coefficient can increase with the goal distance. When the goal is more distant, cells of the upper layer are less and less specialized for the call and can thus be more and more specialized for action. Action intensity (that depends upon the upper-lower coefficient Cb1) can increases as goal distance increases. Action intensity can be maximal for modules activated in situations far from the goal: the system will return faster to its equilibrium position.

c) Selective call reinforcement

Cortical connections are reciprocal. The recall coefficient Ch2(k,i) represents the reactivation of upper-level modules following execution of an action . By the recall "Ch2" coefficient, the modular actions reinforce calls toward upper-level modules that are situated in the activated branch of the call tree.

The recall coefficient "Ch2(k,k-1)" depends upon
(EZhb(k)-EZhb(k-1))/EZ0 = 1/K

Execution of modular actions reinforces activity in the calling modules. The call is enhanced, as the system approaches the goal, on all those branches "confirmed" by actions in fact executed. Reciprocally, if no action reinforces a call on a branch, this call is progressively extinguished. Execution of an action suppresses calls at a inferior or equivalent levels, and reinforces the call toward partial goals at superior levels.

d) Optimal ratio intensity.

The proportion coefficient Cb2(k,i) determines the quantitative relation between the intensities of two successive actions; by learning, it is adjusted to an optimal value for the attainment of a goal (optimal ratio intensity).

The "upper-lower" coefficient, in the direction of action execution ("Cb2") registers intensity ratios of two successive actions that bring the cortical system toward the goal in the most effective way. These coefficients do not register intensities per se, but rather ratios between two intensities, that is a "proportion": they will be important for the recognition of forms, where proportions are more stable than position and size.

e) Fixed sequence.

In the construction of a fixed sequence, each module calls only one "antecedent" module. The call coefficient remains constant. But the action coefficient increases with the goal distance; it is maximal for the last module called, and is thus sufficient to trigger an action, independently of "external" thalamic situations. The action of the last module called will be the first of the sequence executed.

Execution of this action strongly reinforces the call toward the module of the immediately superior level: this process determines a triggering order that is inverse to the call order, independently of external conditions: the proportion coefficient (Cb2) stabilizes the optimal ratio between the intensities of two successive actions.

f) Differentiation algorithms (Figure A-20).

When a cortical zone has already been differentiated into more limited zones, its activity at the low-level E1 is an unstable state; all the active modules will call a series of actions until the goal is attained: one of the more differentiated modules can pass to the higher level (E2) and all the others are inhibited (level E0). This stable state is reached faster thanks to a series of successive cortical differentiation actions.

Figure A-20 shows this mechanism. The upper part depicts the call of actions which favour differential activities in adjacent modular zone.

The lower diagram of Figure A-20 shows progressive functional subdivision of a modular region [R], by three successive "dichotomics":

- Each stage produces 2 new modules. Each newly-formed module becomes a potential pilot module.
- Each of these new goals is favoured by a cortical action (differentiation actions D!,C!,D!).

The equilibrium position of activity is the maximal activation (E2 level) of one of the modules that has already been differentiated. As soon as the external situation activates a modular region previously differentiated, this zone calls actions that lead to both more precise and more intense activity. As long as the goal is not attained, the process continues: a sequence of differentiation actions is triggered in order to obtain maximal activity in one of the newly differentiated modules of the modular zone; we will see the importance of this mechanism in the recognition process.

Bibliography

Abbs, J.H., Cole, K.J. (1982). Considerations of bulbar and suprabulbar afferent influences upon speech motor coordination and programming. In "Speech motor control" S. Grillner, B. Lindblom, J. Libke, A. Personn eds. Pergamon press Oxford.

Abeles, M. and Goldstein, M.H. (1970). Functional architecture in cat primary auditory cortex: Columnar organization and organization according to depth. J. Neurophysiol., 33:172-187.

Akert, K. (1964). Comparative anatomy of frontal cortex and thalamo-frontal connections. In J.M. Warren and K. Akert, eds., The Frontal Granular Cortex and Behavior, New York, Mc Graw-Hill, p.372.

Alberts, B., Bray, D., Lewis, J., Raff, M., Roberts, K., Watson, J.D.(1983). Molecular biology of the cell. Garland Publ. Inc. New York.

Albus, J.S. (1979). Mechanisms of planning and problem solving in the brain. Math. Biosci., 45:247-293.

Alger, B.E. (1984). Hippocampus: electrophysiological studies of epileptiform activity in vitro. In "Brain slices" R. Dingledine ed. Plenum Press NY.

Alkon, D.L., Lederhendler, I. and Shoukimas, J.J. (1982). Primary changes of membrane currents during retention of associative learning. Science, 215:693-695.

Allman, J.M. (1977). Evolution of the visual system in the early primates. In "Progress in psychobiology and physiological psychology" Vol 7 J.M. Sprague and A.N. Epstein eds. Academic Press NY.

Andersen, P., Sundberg, S.H., Sveen, O. and Wigstrom, H. (1977). Specific long-lasting potentiation of synaptic transmission in hippocampal slices. Nature, 266:736-737.

Andersen, P. (1983). Operational principles of hippocampal neurons; a summary of synaptic physiology. In Neurobiology of hippocampus, W. Seifert ed., Academic Press.

Andersen, P., (1975). Organization of hippocampal neurons and their connections. In "The Hippocampus" R.L Isaacson and K.H. eds. Plenum Press NY.

Andersen P. (1984). Brain slice work some prospects. In "Brain slices" R. Dingledine ed. Plenum Press NY.

Andersen, P (1983). Possible cellular prolonged changes of synaptic efficiency- a simple case of learning. In "Molecular and cellular interactions underlying higher brain functions" Changeux, J.P., Glowinski, J., Imbert, M., Bloom, F.E. eds. Elsevier Amsterdam.

Anderson, J.A., Silverstein, J.W., Ritz, R.S. (1977). Distinctive features, categorical perception and probability learning: some applications of a neural model. Psychological Review, 84, 413-451

Ariens-Kappers, C.U., Huber, G.C., Crosby E.C. (1936). The comparative anatomy of the nervous system of vertebrates, including man. New York, Mc Millan.

Arikuni, T., Sakai, M. and Kubota, K. (1983). Columnar Aggregation of Prefrontal and Anterior Cingulate Cortical Cells Projecting to the Thalamic Mediodorsal Nucleus in the Monkey. J. comp. Neurol., 220:116-125.

Asanuma, H. and Rosen, I. (1972 b). Topographical organization of cortical efferent zones projecting to distal forelimb muscles in the monkey. Exp. Brain Res., 14:243-256.

Asanuma, H. and Rosen, I. (1973). Spread of mono and polysynaptic connections within cat's motor cortex. Exp. Brain Res., 16:507-520.

Asanuma, H., Waters, R.S. and Yumiya, H. (1982). Physiological Properties of Neurons Projecting from Area 3a to Area 4 of Feline Cerebral Cortex. J, Neurophysiol., vol.48, no.4, Printed in USA.

Astruc, J. (1971). Corticofugal connections of area 8 (frontal eye field) in Macaca mulatta, Brain Res., 33:241.

Baddeley, A.D. (1975). Theories of amnesia. In A. Kennedy and A. Wilkes eds., Studies in Long-Term Memory, New York, Wiley.

Barlow, H.B. (1972). Single units and sensation: A neuron doctrine for perceptual psychology? Perception, Vol.1, 371-394.

Barret, J.N. and Crill, W.E. (1974). Specific membrane properties of cat motoneurons. J. Physiol., 239:301-324.

Barrionuevo, G. and Brown, T.H. (1983). Associative long-term potentiation in hippocampal slices. Proc. Natl. Acad. Sci. USA, Neurobiology, 80:7347-7351.

Baranyi, A., Feher, O. (1981). Intracellular studies on cortical synaptic plasticity. Exp. Brain Res., 41:124-134.

Barto, A.G., Sutton, R.S., Brouwer, P.S. (1981). Associative search network: a reinforcement learning associative memory. Biol.Cyber., 40:201-211.

Baughman, R.W. and Gilbert, C.D. (1981). Aspartate and glutamate as possible neurotransmitters in the visual cortex. J. Neurosci., 1:427-439.

Beaulieu, C. and Colonnier, M. (1983). The Number of Neurons in the Different Laminae of the Binocular and Monocular Regions of Area 17 in the Cat. J. comp. Neurol., 217:337-344.

Benton, A.L. (1895). Differential behavioral effects in frontal lobe disease. Neuropsychologia, 6:53-60.

Berger, B., Verney, C., Gay, M., Vigny, A. (1983). Immunocytochemical characterisation of the dopaminergic and noradrenergic innervation of the rat neocortex during early ontogeny. In " Molecular and cellular interactions underlying higher brain functions" Changeux, J.P., Glowinski, J., Imbert, M.,Bloom, F.E. eds. Elsevier Amsterdam.

Bernstein, M. (1967). Coordination and Regulation of Movements.Pergamon Press, New York.

Berson, D.M., Graybiel A.M. (1983). Subsystems within the visual association cortex as delineated by their thalamic and transcortical affiliations. In " Molecular and cellular interactions underlying higher brain functions" Changeux, J.P., Glowinski, J., Imbert, M., Bloom, F.E. eds. Elsevier Amsterdam.

Berthoz A. (1978). Rôle de la proprioception dans le contrôle de la posture et du geste. In "Du contrôle moteur à l'organisation du geste" H.Hecaen, M.Jeannerod eds. Masson, Paris.

Bienenstock, E. (1985). Une approche topologique de l'objet mental. In "Les théories de la complexité. Colloque de Cerisy. F. Fogelman M. Milgram eds. Le Seuil, Paris.

Bindmann, L.J., Lippold, O. and Milne, A.R. (1979). Prolonged changes in excitability of pyramidal tract neurons in the cat: a post-synaptic mechanism. J. Physiol., 286:457-477.

Bindmann, L. and Lippold, O. (1981). The neurophysiology of the cerebral cortex. Arnold, Lond.

Bizzi, E. (1968). Discharge of frontal eye field neurons during saccadic and following eye movements in unanesthetized monkeys.Exp. Brain Res., 9:69.

Blasdel G.G., Salama G. (1986). Voltage-sensitive dyes reveal a modular organization in monkey striate cortex. Nature Vol 321 : 579

Bliss, T.V.P. and Lomo, T. (1973). Long-lasting potentiation of synaptic transmission in the dentate area of the anaesthetized rabbit following stimulation of the perforant path. J. Physiol., 232:331-356.

Bloom, L. (1973). One word at a time. Mouton, La Haye.

Bloom, F.E. (1983). Chemical communication in the CNS: neurotransmitter and their functions. In " Molecular and cellular interactions underlying higher brain functions" Changeux, J.P., Glowinski, J., Imbert, M., Bloom, F.E. eds. Elsevier Amsterdam.

Boothe, R., Greenough, W., Lund, J. and Wrege, K. (1979). A quantitative investigation of spine and dendrite development of neurons in visual cortex (area 17) of Macaca nemestrina monkeys. J.comp. Neurol., 186:473-490.

Bonnet, A. (1984). L'intelligence artificielle: promesses et réalités Interéditions Paris

Bower, T., Broughton, J.M. and Moore, M. (1970). Demonstration of intention in the reaching behavior of neonate humans. Nature, 228:679-681.

Bower, T.G.R. (1974). Development in infancy. San Francisco, Freeman.

Bower, T. (1978). Le développement psychologique de la première enfance. Mardaga, Bruxelles.

Braak, H.T. (1984). Architectonics as seen by lipofuscin stains. In "Cerebral cortex Vol(1): cellular components of the cerebral cortex " A.Peters and E.G.Jones eds Plenum Press NY.

Braine, M. (1976). Children's first word combinations. Monographs of the Society for Research in Child Development, 41, no.164.

Braitenberg, V., (1978). Cortical architectonics: general and areal. In Architectonics of the cerebral cortex, M.A.B. Brazier and H. Petsche eds. Raven Press, New York.

Bresson, F., Vignaux, G. (1973). La psycholinguistique. In "Le langage" B. Pottier ed. CEPL, Paris.

Brinkman, C. and Porter, R. (1979). Supplementary motor area in the monkey: activity of neurons during performance of a learned motor task. J. Neurophysiol., 42:681-709.

Broca, P. (1861). Perte de la parole Ramollicooment chronique et destruction partielle du lobe antérieur gauche du cerveau. Bulletin de la Société d'Anthropologie, 2:235-237.

Brodal, A. (1969). Neurological Anatomy. New York, Oxford University Press.

Brodtrom, C.D., Huang, Y.C., Breckenbridge, R.M., Wolff, D.J. (1975). Identification of a calcium-binding protein as a calcium dependant regulator of brain adenylate cyclase. Proc.Natl.Acad.Sci.USA 72, 64-68.

Bronckart, J.P. (1977). Théories du langage. Une introduction critique. Mardaga, Bruxelles.

Brons, J.F., Woody, C.D. (1980). Long-term changes in excitability of weak intensity electrical stimulation of units of the pericruciate cortex in cats. J. Neurophysiol., 44:605-615.

Brooks, V.B., Adrien, J. and Dykes, R.W. (1972). Task-related discharge of neurons in motor cortex and effects of dentate cooling.Brain Res., 40:85-90.

Brooks, M.C., Koizumi, K. (1980). The hypothalamus control of integrative processes. In Medical Physiology, V.B.Mountcastle ed., C.V. Mosby Company.

Brown, R. (1973 b). A first language: the early stages. Cambridge, Harvard Univ. Press.

Bruce, C.J., Goldberg, M.E. (1984). Physiology of the frontal eye-field. TINS, 48:11.

Bruner, J.S. (1964). The course of cognitive growth. American psychologist, 19:1-15.

Buisseret, P. and Imbert, M. (1976). Visual cortical cells: their developmental properties in normal and dark-reared kittens. J.Physiol., Lond., 255:511-525.

Bullier, J., Henry, G.H. (1979). Neural path taken by afferent streams in striate cortex of the cat. J. Neurophysiol. 42:1264-70.

Bullier, J., Henry, G.H. (1979). Laminar distribution of first order neurons and afferent terminals in cat striate cortex, J. Neurophysiol. 42:1271.

Bushnell, M.C., Goldberg, M.E., Robinson, D.L. (1981). Behavioral enhancement of visual responses in monkey cerebral cortex. I. Modulation in posterior parietal cortex related to selective visual attention. J.Neurophysiol. 45:755-772.

Burnod, Y., Maton, B. and Calvet, J. (1982). Activity of neurons in area 4 and in area 5 of monkey during operant conditioning of a flexion movement. In Conditioning, C.D.Woody ed., Plenum Publishing Corporation, 265-280.

Burnod Y., Maton, B., and Calvet J. (1983). Neurons in Cerebral Cortex Area 4 and 5 increase their discharge frequency during operant conditioning. In Molecular and cellular interactions Underlying Higher brain functions. Progress in Brain Research, Vol 58, J.P. Changeux, J.Glowinski, M. Imbert and F.E. Bloom (Eds). Elsevier Science Publishers B.V.

Burnod Y. (1987). Possible mechanism of columnar processing in cerebral cortex. Neuroscience, 22, 2523P

Burnod, Y., Daegelen, P. (1988). Hypercube structure of the network between cortical areas (submitted).

Cajal, S. Ramon Y. (1911). Histologie du Système Nerveux de l'Homme et des Vertébrés. Maloine, Paris.

Calvin, M. (1969). Chemical evolution: molecular evolution towards the origin of living systems on the earth and elsewhere. Oxford University Press.

Carew, T.J., Hawkins, R.D., Kandel, E.R. (1983). Differential classical conditioning of a defensive withdrawal reflex in Aplysia californica. Science, 219:397-400.

Castellucci, V. and Kandel, E.R. (1976). Quantal analysis of hetero-synaptic facilitation underlying dishabituation. In Aplysia. Fed. Proc., 34:418.

Changeux, J.P. and Danchin, A. (1976). Selective stabilization of developing synapses as a mechanism for the specification of neuronal networks. Nature, 264:705-712.

Changeux, J.P. (1983). L'homme neuronal. Fayard, Paris.

Chauvet G. (1986). Habituation rules for a theory of the cerebellar cortex, Biol. Cybern., 55,1-9.

Chavis, D.A. and Pandya, D.N. (1976). Further observations on cortico-frontal connections in the rhesus monkey. Brain Res., 117:369-386.

Cheney, P.D. and Fetz, E.E. (1980). Functional classes of primate corticomotoneuronal cells and their relation to active force. J. Neurophysiol., 44:773-791.

Chomsky, N.A. (1964). Current issues in linguistic theory. In J.A.Fodor and J.J.Katz eds., The structure of language, Englewood cliffs.

Chomsky, N. (1970). Le langage de la pensée. Payot, Paris.

Chomsky, N. (1971). Aspects de la théorie syntaxique. Le Seuil, Paris.

Clark, E. (1973). What's in a word ? On the child acquisition of semantics in his first language. In T.Moore, Cognitive Development and the Acquisition of Language, Acad. Press, New York.

Colonnier, M. (1966). The structural design of the neocortex. In Brain and Conscious Experience, J.C.Eccles, ed. New York, Springer Verlag, pp. 1-23.

Colonnier, M. (1968). Synaptic patterns in different cell types and the different laminae of the cat visual cortex. An electron-microscope study. Brain Res., 9:268-287.

Colonnier, M. (1981). The electron microscopic analysis of the neuronal organization of the cerebral cortex. In The organization of the cerebral cortex, F.Schmitt et al., eds., Cambridge, Mass., MIT Press, pp. 125-152.

Connors, B.W., Gutnick, M.J. (1984). Neocortex: Cellular properties and intrinsic circuitry.In "Brain slices" R.Dingledine ed. Plenum Press NY.

Connors, B.W., Gutnick, M.J. and Prince, D.A. (1982). Electrophysiological Properties of Neocortical Neurons in vitro. J. Neurophysiol., vol.48, no.6, Printed in USA.

Cooper, L.N. (1981). Distributed memory in the central nervous system:possible test of assumptions in visual cortex. In "The organization of the cerebral cortex," F.Schmitt et al eds., Cambridge, Mass., MIT Press.

Cowan, W. (1979). Selection and control in neurogenesis. In The Neurosciences: fourth study program, F.Schmitt and F.Worden, eds., Cambridge, Mass., MIT Press, pp.59-81.

Cowey, A. (1981). Why are there so many visual areas? In "The organization of the cerebral cortex" F.Schmitt et al. eds MIT Press Cambridge.

Cragg, B. (1975). The development of synapses in the visual cortex of the cat. J. comp. Neurol., 160:147-166.

Creutzfeld, O., Lux, H.D., Watanabe, S. (1966). Electrophysiology of cortical nerve cells. In The Thalamus, D.P.Purpura, M.D.Yahr eds. Columbia University Press.

Creuzfeldt, O. (1978). The neocortical link: thoughts on the generality of structure and function of the neocortex. In Architectonics of the cerebral cortex, M.Brazier and H.Petsche eds., New York, Raven Press, pp. 357-383.

Crick, F.H.C. (1968). The origin of the genetic code. J. Mol. Biol., 28:367-379.

Crick, F.H.C., Marr, D.C. and Poggio, T. (1981). An information processing approach to understanding the visual cortex. In F.O. Schmitt, F.G. Worden, G. Aldelman and S.G. Dennis, eds., The Organization of the Cerebral Cortex, Cambridge, Mass., MIT Press, pp. 505-533.

Crick, F. (1982). Do dendritic spines twitch? Trends in Neurosci., 5, 44-46.

Crosby, E.C., Humphrey, T., Lauer, T. (1962). Correlative anatomy of the nervous system. Mc Millan, New York.

Curtis, D.R. and Felix, D. (1971). The effect of bicuculline upon synaptic inhibition in the cerebral and cerebellar cortices of the cat. Brain Res., 34:301-321.

Darian-Smith, I., Goodwin, A., Sugitani, M., Heywood, J. (1984). The tangible features of textured surfaces: their representation in the monkey's somatosensory cortex. In "Dynamic aspects of neocortical functions" G.M.Edelman, W.E.Gall, W.M.Cowan eds, John Wiley NY.

De Laguna, G. (1927). Speech: its function and development. Yale, University Press, New Haven.

De Long, M.R. and Strick, P.L. (1974). Relation of basal ganglia, cerebellum and motor cortex units to ramp and ballistic limb movements. Brain Res., 71:327-335.

De Long, M., Garete E., Alexander, E. (1986). Organization of basal ganglia. In "Diseases of the nervous System". Asbury, NcKahnn, Lc Donald. Ardmore medical books.

Denny-Brown, D. (1951). The frontal lobes and their functions. In A.Feiling eds., Modern Trends in Neurology, Lond. Butterworth 13-89.

Diamond, J., Gray, E.G., Yasargil, G.M. (1971). The function of the dendritic spine: An hypothesis. In "Excititatory synaptic mechanisms3 P.Andersen, K.Jansen eds. Universitetforlaget, Oslo.

Diamond, I.T., Hall, W.C. (1969). Evolution of neocortex. Science 164:251-262.

Dingledine, R. (1984). Hippocampus: synaptic pharmacology.In "Brain slices" R.Dingledine ed. Plenum Press NY.

Dowling, J.E. (1979). Information processing by local circuits: the vertebrate retina as a model sytem. In The Neurosciences Fourth Study Program, F.O. Schmitt, W.G. Worden eds., MIT Press, Cambridge.

Dunwiddie, T., Madison, D. and Lynch, G. (1978). Synaptic transmission is required for initiation of long term potentiation. Brain Res., 150:413-417.

Dow, B.M., Bauer, R., Snyder, A.Z., Vautin, R.G. (1984). Receptive fields and orientation shifts in the foveal striate cortex of the awake monkey. In "Dynamic aspects of neocortical functions" G.M.Edelman, W.E.Gall, W.M.Cowan eds, John Wiley NY.

Eccles, J.C. (1964). The Physiology of Synapses. Berlin, Springer Verlag.

Eccles, J.C., Ito, M. and Szentagothai, J. (1967). The Cerebellum as a Neuronal Machine. Berlin, Springer Verlag.

Eccles, J.C. (1981). The modular operation of the cerebral neocortex considered as the material basis of mental events. Neuroscience, 10:1839-1856.

Edelman, G.M. (1981). Group selection as the basis for higher brain function. In the organization of the cerebral cortex, F.Schmitt et al eds., Cambridge, Mass., MIT Press.

Edelman, G.M., Hinkel, L.H. (1984). Neuronal group selection in the cerebral cortex. In "Dynamic aspects of neocortical functions" G.M.Edelman, W.E.Gall, W.M.Cowan eds, John Wiley NY.

Emson, P.C. and Hunt, S.P. (1981). Anatomical chemistry of the cerebral cortex. In "The organization of the cerebral cortex", F.Schmitt et al eds., Cambridge, Mass., MIT Press.

Ennoth-Cuggel, C., Robson, J.G., Scweitzer-Tong, D.E., Watson, A.B. (1983). Spatiotemporal interactions in cat retinal ganglion cells showing linear spatial summation. J.Physiol. (Lond), 341:279-307.

Ernst, G., Newell, A. (1969). A case study in generality and problem solving. Academic press, NY.

Evarts.E.V. (1965). Relation of discharge frequency to conduction velocity in pyramidal tract neurons. J. Neurophysiol., 28:216-228.

Evarts, E.V. (1974). Precentral and postcentral cortical activity in association with visually triggered movements. J. Neurophysiol., 37:373-381.

Evarts, E.V. and Tanji, J. (1974). Gating of motor cortex reflexes by prior instruction. Brain Res., 71:479-494.

Evarts, E.V. (1984). Hierarchies and emergent features in motor control. In "Dynamic aspects of neocortical functions" G.M.Edelman, W.E.Gall, W.M.Cowan eds, John Wiley NY.

Evarts, E.V., Kimura, M., Wurtz, R.H., Hikosada, O. (1984). Behavioral correlates of activity in basal ganglia neurons. TINS, 48:11.

Fairen, A., DeFelipe, J., Regidor, J. (1984). Non-pyramidal neurons: General account. In "Cerebral cortex Vol(1): cellular components of the cerebral cortex " A.Peters and E.G.Jones eds. Plenum Press NY.

Fauconnier G. (1973). La grammaire générative. In "Le langage" B.Pottier ed. CEPL, Paris.

Feldman, M.F. (1984). Morphology of the neocortical pyramidal neuron. In "Cerebral cortex Vol(1): cellular components of the cerebral cortex " A.Peters and E.G.Jones eds. Plenum Press NY.

Fetz, E.E. (1984). Functional organisation of motor and sensory cortex: symmetries and parallells.In "Dynamic aspects of neocortical functions" G.M.Edelman, W.E.Gall, W.M.Cowan eds, John Wiley NY.

Fetz, E.E. and Baker, M.A. (1973). Operantly conditioned patterns of precentral unit activity and correlated responses in adjacent cells and contralateral muscles. J. Neurophysiol., 36:179-204.

Fetz, E.E. and Cheney, P.D. (1980). Post-spike facilitation of forelimb muscle activity by primate corticomotoneuronal cells. J. Neurophysiol., 44:751-772.

Fifkova, E. and Van Harreveld, A. (1977). Long-lasting morphological changes in dendritic spines of dentate granular cells following stimulation of the entorhinal area J. neurocytol., 6:211-230.

Filliolet, J. (1973). Phonologie et phonetique. In "Le langage" B.Pottier ed. CEPL, Paris.

Fischbach, G.D., Berg, D.K., Cohen, S.A. and Frank, E. (1976). Enrichment of nerve-muscle synapses in spinal cord-muscle cultures and identification of relative peaks of ACh sensitivity at sites of transmitter release. In The synapse, Cold Spring Harbor Symp. Quant. Biol., 40:347-357.

Fregnac, M., Imbert, M. (1984). Development of neuronal selectivity in primary visual cortex of cat. Physiological Reviews 64(1).

Freund, T.F., Martin, K.A.C., Smith, A.D. and Somogyi, P. (1983). Glutamate Decarboxylase-Immunoreactive Terminals of Golgi-Impregnated Axoaxonic Cells and of Presumed Basket Cells in Synaptic Contact with Pyramidal Neurons of the Cat's Visual Cortex. J. comp. Neurol., 221:263-278.

Fromm, C. and Evarts, E.V. (1977). Relation of motor cortex neurons to precisely controlled and ballistic movements. Neurosci. Letters, 5.259-265.

Fromm, C. and Evarts, E.V. (1981). Relation of size and activity of motor cortex pyramidal tact neurons during skilled movements in the monkey. J. neurophysiol., 1:453-460.

Fukushima, K. (1980). Neocognitron: A self-organizing neural network for a mechanism of pattern recognition unaffected by shift in position. Biol. Cybernetics, 36, 193-202.

Fuster, J. (1984). Behavioral electrophysiology of the prefrontaal cortex. TINS, 48:11.

Fuster, J.M. (1977). Unit activity in the prefrontal cortex during delayed response performance: neuronal correlates of short-term memory. J. Neurophysiol., 36:61-78.

Fuster, J. (1980). The prefrontal cortex. New York, Raven Press.

Fuster, J.M. (1982). Cortical neuron activity in the temporal organization of behavior. In Conditioning: representation of involved neural functions, C.D. Woody ed., Plenum Press.

Garey, L.J. (1976). Synaptic organization of afferent fibres and intrinsic circuits in the neocortex. In Handbook of EEG clin. Neurophysiol., Vol.2, Pt. A. Sect. IV. A.Remond, ed. Amsterdam, Elsevier, pp. 57-85.

Gazzaniga, M. (1970). The bisected brain. New York, Appleton Press.

Gazzaniga, M. and Blakemore, C. (1975). Handbook of psychobiology. New York, Acad. Press.

Georgopoulos, A.P., Kalaska, J.F., Crutcher, M.D., Caminitti, R., Massey, J.T. (1984). The representation of mouvement direction in the motor cortex : single celles and population studies. In "Dynamic aspects of neocortical functions" G.M.Edelman, W.E.Gall, W.M.Cowan eds, John Wiley NY.

Geschwind, N. (1965 a). Disconnexion syndromes in animals and man. Part.I, Brain, 88:237-294.

Gilbert, C.D. and Kelly, J.P. (1975). The projections of cells in different layers of the cat's visual cortex. J. comp. Neurol., 163:81-106.

Gilbert, C.D. (1977). Laminar differences in receptive field properties in cat primary visual cortex. J. Physiol., Lond., 268:391-421.

Gilbert, C.D. and Wiesel, T.N. (1979). Morphology and intracortical projections of functionally identified neurons in cat visual cortex. Nature, Lond., 280:120-125.

Gilbert, C.D. and Wiesel, T.N. (1980). Interleaving projection bands in cortico-cortical connections. Neurosci. Abstr., 6:315.

Gilbert, C.D. and Wiesel, T.N. (1981). Laminar specialization and intra- cortical connections in cat primary visual cortex. In the organization of the cerebral cortex, F.Schmitt et al eds., Cambridge, Mass., MIT Press.

Gilbert, P.F.C. and Thach, W.T. (1977). Purkinje cell activity during motor learning. Brain Res., 128:309-328.

Glowinski, J., Tassin, J.P., Thierry, A.M. (1984). The mesocortical-prefrontal dopaminergic neurons . TINS, 48:11.

Goldberg, M.E. and Wurtz, R.H. (1972). Activity of superior colliculus in behaving monkeys. J. Neurophysiol., 35:560-574.

Goldman-Rakic, P.S. (1984). The frontal lobes: unchartered provinces of the brain. TINS, 48:11.

Goldman, P.S. and Nauta, W.J.H. (1977). Columnar distribution of cortico-cortical fibres in the frontal association, limbic and motor cortex of the developing rhesus monkey. Brain Res., 122:393-413.

Goldman-Rakic, P.S. (1981). Development and plasticity of primate frontal association cortex. In "The organization of the cerebral cortex", F.Schmitt et al eds., Cambridge, Mass., MIT Press.

Goldman, B.C. (1974). The hypothalamic-pituitary-gonadal axis and the regulation of ciclicity and sexual behavior. In Neurosciences Third Study Program, F.O. Schmitt, F.G. Worden eds., MIT Press.

Goldstein, M.H., Benson D.A., Heinz, R.D. (1982). Studies of auditory cortex in behaviorally trained monkeys. In Conditionning: representation of involved neural functions, C.D.Woody ed., Plenum.

Goodman, C.S., Raper, J.A., Chang, S., Ho, R. (1983). Grasshopper growth cones: divergent choices and labeled pathways. In " Molecular and cellular interactions underlying higher brain functions" Changeux, J.P., Glowinski, J., Imbert, M., Bloom, F.E. eds. Elsevier Amsterdam.

Gray, E.G. (1959). Axosomatic and axodendritic synapses of the cerebral cortex: an electron microscopy study. J. Anat., 93:420-433.

Graybiel, A.M. and Berson, D.M. (1981). On the relation between trans-thalamic and trans-cortical pathways in the visual system. In "The organization of the cerebral cortex", F.Schmitt et al eds., Cambridge, Mass., MIT Press.

Greenfield, P.M. and Smith, J. (1976). The structure of communication in early language development. Acad. Press, New York.

Grinvald, A., Segal, M. (1984). Optical monitoring of electrical activity: detection of spatiotemporal patterns of activity in hippocampal slices by voltage-sensitive probes.In "Brain slices" R.Dingledine ed. Plenum Press NY.

Gross, C.G., Rocha-Miranda, C.E. and Bender, D.B. (1972). Visual properties of neurons in inferotemporal cortex of the macaque.J. Neurophysiol., 35:96-111.

Hafter, E.R.(1984). Spatial hearing and the duplex theory: how viable is the model?. In "Dynamic aspects of neocortical functions" G.M.Edelman, W.E.Gall, W.M.Cowan eds, John Wiley NY.

Hajdu, F., Somogyi, G.Y. and Tombol, T. (1974). Neuronal and synaptic arrangement in the lateralis posterior-pulvinar complex of the thalamus in the cat. Brain Res., 73:89-104.

Halliday, M. (1975). Learning how to mean. Explorations in the development of language, Arnold, Lond.

Hawkins, R.D., Abrams, T.W., Carew, T.J., Kandel, E.R. (1983). A cellular mechanism of classical conditionning in Aplysia: activity dependant amplification of presynaptic facilitation Science 219: 400, 405.

Hebb, D.O. (1949). The organization of behavior: a neuropsychological theory. Wiley, New York.

Hocaen, H. (1981). Apraxias. In Handbook of clinical neuropsychology, S.D.Filskov et T.J.Bull eds., Wiley and Sons, New York, 257-286.

Hecaen, H. (1981). Neuropsychology of face recognition. In Perceiving and remembering faces, H.D.Ellis, G.Davies and J.Shepherd eds, Acad. Press, Lond., 39-54.

Hecaen, H., Lanteri-Laura, G. (1983). Les fonctions du cerveau. Masson.

Heidmann, T. et Changeux, J.P. (1982). Un modèle moléculaire de régulation d'efficacité au niveau postsynaptique d'une synapse chimique. C. R. Acad. Sc., 295:665-670.

Henderson, C.E. (1983). Role for retrograde factors in synapse formation at the nerve muscle junction. In " Molecular and cellular interactions underlying higher brain functions" Changeux, J.P., Glowinski, J., Imbert, M., Bloom, F F eds. Elsevier Amsterdam.

Henderson, Z. (1981). A projection from acetylcholinesterase-containing neurons in the diagonal band to the occipital cortex of the rat. Neurosci., 6:1081-1088.

Henneman, E. (1980). Organization of the motoneuron pool; the size principle. In Medical physiology, V.B.Mountcastle ed., C.V. Mosby Company.

Hinton, G.E., Anderson. J.A. (1981). Parallel models of associative memory. Hillsdale, NJ: Erlbaum.

Hirsch J.C., Burnod, Y. and Korn, H. (1985). Dorsolateral geniculate neurons in vitro: Reduced postsynaptic excitability following repetitive activation of the optic tract. Neuroscience Letters, 58: 151-156.

Hobson, J.A. (1980). The reticular formation revisited: specifying functions for a non specific system. IBRO 6, Raven Press.

Hobson, J.A. (1984). How does the cortex when to do what? In "Dynamic aspects of neocortical functions" G.M. Edelman, W.E. Gall, W.M. Cowan eds, John Wiley NY.

Hodgkin, A.L. and Huxley, A.F. (1952). A quantitative description of membrane current and its application to conduction and excitation in nerve. J. Physiol., 117:500-544.

Hokfelt, T. and Ljundahl, A. (1972). Autoradiographic identification of cerebral and cerebellar cortical neurons accumulating labeled gamma-aminobutyric acid (3H-GABA). Exp. Brain Res., 14:354-362.

Hopfield, J.J.(1982). Neural networks and physical systems with emergent collective computational abilities, Proc. Natl. Acad. Sci. USA., 79, 2254-2558.

Hotson, J.R. and Prince, D.A. (1980). A calcium activated hyperpolarization follows repetitive firing in hippocampal neurons. J. Neurophysiol., 43:409-419.

Housgarrd, J., Hultborn, H., Kiehn, O. (1986). Transmitter - controlled properties of alpha motoneurons causing long lasting motor discharge to brief excitatory inputs. Progress in Brain Res. Vol 64:39-49.

Hubel, D.H. and Wiesel, T.N. (1962). Receptive fields binocular interaction and functional architecture in the cat's visual cortex. J. Physiol. Lond., 160:106-154.

Hubel, D.H. and Wiesel, T.N. (1972). Laminar and columnar distribution of geniculocortical fibers in the macaque monkey. J. comp Neurol., 146:421-450.

Hubel, D.H. and Wiesel, T. (1977). Functional architecture of macaque monkey visual cortex. Ferrier Lecture Proc. Roy. Soc. Lond.B, 198:1-59.

Hubel, D.H., Wiesel, T.N. and Stryker, M.P. (1978). Anatomical demonstration of orientation columns in macaque monkey. J. comp. Neurol., 177:361-380.

Hyvarinen, J. and Poranen, A. (1974). Function of the parietal associative area 7 as revealed from cellular discharges in alert monkeys. Brain, 97:673-692.

Hyvarinen, J., Poranen, A., Jokinen, Y. (1974). Central sensory activities between sensory input and motor output. In Neurosciences Third Study Program, F.O. Schmitt, F.G. Worden eds., MIT Press.

Hyvarinen, J., Hyvarinen, L., Farkkila, M., Carlson, S. and Leinonen, L. (1978). Modification of visual functions of the parietal lobe at early age in the monkey. Medical Biology, 56:103-109.

Imbert, M., Fregnac, Y. (1983). Specification of cortical neurons by visual experience. In " Molecular and cellular interactions underlying higher brain functions" Changeux, J.P., Glowinski, J., Imbert, M., Bloom, F.E. eds. Elsevier Amsterdam.

Imig, T.J. and Brugge, J.F. (1978). Sources and terminations of callosal axons related to binaural and frequency maps in primary auditory cortex of the cat. J. comp. Neurol., 182:637-660.

Ingram, T.T.S. (1975). Speech disorders in childhood. In E.H. Lenneberg et E. Lenneberg eds, Foundations of language development. A multidisciplinary approach (vol.2), The Unesco Press, Paris.

Ingvar, D. (1977). L'idéogramme cérébral. Encéphale, 3:5-33.

Inhelder, B. et Piaget, J. (1967). La génèse des structures logiques élémentaires, classifications et sériations. Delachaux et Niestlé, Neuchatel.

Isaacson, R.L. and Pribram, K.H. eds. (1975). The Hippocampus. Vol.II, Neurophysiology and Behavior, New York and Lond., Plenum Press.

Ito, M., Sakurai, M. and Tongroach, P. (1982). Climbing fibre induced depression of both mossy fibre responsiveness and glutamate sensitivity of cerebellar purkinje cells. J. Physiol., 324:113-134.

Ito, M. (1982 b). Synaptic plasticity underlying the cerebellar motor learning investigated in rabbit's flocculus. In Advances in behavioral biology, vol. 26, C.D.Woody ed., New York, Plenum Press.

Ito, M. (1982). Mechanisms of motor learning, in Competition and Cooperation in Neural nets, Lectures in Biomathematics, Vol 45, Springer-Verlag.

Jack, J.J.B., Noble, D., Tsien, R.W. (1975). Electric current flow in excitable cells. Oxford University Press.

Jacob, F. (1970). La logique du vivant. Gallimard, Paris.

Jacobsen, C. (1931). A study of cerebral function in learning: the frontal lobes. J. comp. Neurol., 52:271-340.

Jacobsen, S. and Trojanowski, J.Q. (1977). Prefrontal cortex of the rhesus monkey. II. Interhemispheric cortical afferents. Brain Res., 132:235-246.

Jakobson, R. and Halle, M. (1956). Fundamentals of language. The Hague, Mouton.

Jakobson, R. (1969). Langage enfantin et aphasie. Editions de Minuit.

Jankowska, E., Padel, Y. and Tanaka, R. (1975 a). The mode of activation of pyramidal tract cells by intracortical stimuli. J. Physiol. 249:617-636.

Jankowska, E., Padel, Y. and Tanaka, R. (1975). Projections of pyramidal tract cells to motoneurones innervating hind-limb muscles in the monkey. J. Physiol., 249:637-667.

Jasper, H.H., Ricci, G.F. and Doane, B. (1958). Patterns of cortical neuronal discharge during conditioned responses in monkeys. In G. Wolstenholme and C. O'Connor eds., Neurological Basis of Behavior, Boston, Little Brown.

Jasper, H.H., Khan, R.T. and Elliot, K.A.C. (1965). Amino acids released from cerebral cortex in relation to its state of activation. Science, 147:1448-1449.

Jeannerod, M. and Hecaen, H. (1979). Adaptation et restauration des fonctions nerveuses. Villeurbanne, Slmep.

Jeannerod M., Prablanc C., Organisation et plasticité de la coordination oeil-main. In "Du contrôle moteur à l'organisation du geste" H. Hecaen, M. Jeannerod eds. Masson, Paris.

Johnston, D., Brown, D.H. (1984). Biophysics and microphysiology of synaptic transmission in hippocampus. In "Brain slices" R. Dingledine ed. Plenum Press NY.

Jones, E.J., Hendry, S.H.C. (1984). Basket cells. In "Cerebral cortex Vol(1): cellular components of the cerebral cortex " A. Peters and E.G. Jones eds. Plenum Press NY.

Jones E.G. (1984). Laminar distribution of cortical efferent cells. In "Cerebral cortex Vol(1): cellular components of the cerebral cortex " A. Peters and E.G. Jones eds. Plenum Press NY.

Jones, E.G. (1984). Identification and classification of intrinsic circuit elements in the neocortex. In "Dynamic aspects of neocortical functions" G.M. Edelman, W.E. Gall, W.M. Cowan eds, John Wiley NY.

Jones, E.G. (1975). Lamination and differential distribution of thalamic afferents within the sensory-motor cortex of the squirrel monkey. J. comp. Neurol. 160:167-204.

Jones, E.G. (1975). Varieties and distribution of the non-pyramidal cells in the somatic sensory cortex of the squirrel monkey. J. comp. Neurol., 160:205-267.

Jones, E.G., Burton, H. and Porter, R. (1975). Commissural and cortico-cortical "columns" in the somatic sensory cortex of primates. Science, 190:572-574.

Jones, E.G. and Wise, S.P. (1977). Size, laminar and columnar distribution of efferent cells in the sensory-motor cortex of monkeys. J. comp. Neurol., 175:391-438.

Jones, E.G., Coulter, J.D. and Hendry, S.H.C. (1978). Intracortical connectivity of architectonic fields in the somatic sensory, motor and parietal cortex of monkeys. J. comp. Neurol., 181:292-348.

Jones, E.G. (1981). Anatomy of cerebral cortex: columnar input-output organization. In The organization of the cerebral cortex, F. Schmitt et al. eds., Cambridge, Mass., MIT Press, pp. 199-235.

Jones, E. and Powell, P.S. (1970). Anatomical study of converging sensory pathways within the cerebral cortex of the monkey. Brain, 93:793-820.

Jouvet, M. (1974). Monoaminergic regulation of the sleep waking cycle in the cat. In Neurosciences, Third Study Program, F.O. Schmitt, F.G. Worden eds., MIT Press.

Julesz, B. (1984). Toward an axiomatic theory of preattentive vision. In "Dynamic aspects of neocortical functions" G.M. Edelman, W.E. Gall, W.M. Cowan eds, John Wiley NY.

Kaas, J., Nelson, R., Sur, M. and Merzenich, M. (1979). Multiple representation of the body within the primary somatosensory cortex of primates. Science, 204:521-523.

Kaas, J.H., Nelson, R.J., Sur, M. and Merzenich, M.M. (1981). Organization of somatosensory cortex in primates. In the organization of the cerebral cortex, F. Schmitt et al eds., Cambridge, Mass., MIT Press.

Kandel, E.R. (1977 b). Neuronal plasticity and the modification of behaviour. In Handbook of Neurophysiology, Section I, Vol.1, Part. 2, J.M. Brookhart and V.B. Mountcastle eds., Williams and Wilkins, Baltimore.

Kandel, E. and Schwartz, J. (1981). Principles of neural science. Amsterdam, Elsevier, North-Holland.

Katz, B. (1969). The Release of Neural Transmitter Substances. Liverpool, Liverpool University.

Katz, B. and Miledi, R. (1972). The statistical nature of the acetylcholine potential and its molecular components. J. Physiol. Lond., 224:665-699.

Kebabian, J.W., Clement-Cormier, Y.C., Petzold, G.L., Greengard, P. (1975). Chemistry of dopamine receptors. Adv. Neurol., 9:13-24.

Kelly, J.P. and Van Essen, D.C. (1974). Cell structure and function in the visual cortex of the cat. J. Physiol., 238:515-547.

Kemp, J.M. and Powell, T.P.S. (1971). The connexions of the striatum and globus pallidus: synthesis and speculation. Proc. Roy. Soc. B, 262:441-457.

Kimura, D. (1961 b). Cerebral dominance and the perception of verbal stimuli. Canadian Journal of Psychology, 15:166-171.

Kimura, D. (1963). Speech lateralization in young children as determined by an auditory test. Journal of Comparative and Physiological Psychology, 56:899-902.

Kirscfield, K. (1979). The visual system of the fly: physiological optics and functional anatomy as related to behavior. In The Neurosciences, Fourth Study Program, F.O. Schmitt, W.G. Worden eds., MIT Press.

Kitai, S.T., Kita, H. (1984). Electrophysiological study of the neostriatum in brain slice preparation. In "Brain slices" R.Dingledine ed. Plenum Press NY.

Kitzes, L.M., Farley, G.R., Starr, A. (1978). Modulation of auditory cortex unit activity during the performance of a conditioned response. Exp. Neurol., 62:678-697.

Klein, M., Kandel, E.R. (1978). Presynaptic modulation of voltage dependant Ca current: mechanism for behavioral sensitization in Aplysia californica. Proc. Natl. Acad. Sci., 75:3512.

Knudsen, E.I. (1984). Synthesis of a neural map of auditory space in the owl. In "Dynamic aspects of neocortical functions" G.M. Edelman, W.E. Gall, W.M. Cowan eds, John Wiley NY.

Koch, C., Poggio, T., Torre, V. (1983). Non linear interactions in a dendritic tree: localization, timing, role in information processing. Proc. Natl. Acad. Sci., 75:3512.

Kohonen, T. (1977). Associative memory. Springer Verlag, New York.

Kohonen, T. (1984). Self-organization and associative memory. Berlin, Springer-Verlag.

Korn, H., Triller, A., Mallet, A. and Faber, D. (1981). Fluctuating responses ar a central synapse: n of binomial fit predicts number of stained presynaptic boutons. Science, 213:898-1201.

Korn, H., Faber, D.S., Burnod, Y., and Triller, A. (1984). Regulation of efficacy at central synapses. J. Neurosc. 4:125-130.

Korn, H., Burnod, Y., and Faber, D.S. (1987). Spontaneous quantal currents in a central neuron match predictions from binomial analysis, P.N.A.S, USA, 24, 5981-5985.

Kornhuber, H.H. (1974). Cerebral cortex, cerebellum and basal ganglia: an introduction to their motor functions. In the Neurosciences, Third Study Program, F.O. Schmitt and F.G. Worden eds. Cambridge, MIT, 267-280.

Koshland, D.E. Jr. (1979). A model regulatory system: bacterial chemotaxis. Physiological Reviews, 4:812-855.

Krieg, W.J. (1949). Connections of the cerebral cortex. J. Comp. Neur., 91:1-38.

Krnjevic, K. (1973). Chemical nature of synaptic transmission in vertebrates. Physiol. Rev., 53, 674-723.

Krnjevic, K. and Whittaker, V.P. (1965). Excitation and depression of cortical neurons by brain fractions released from micro-pipettes. J. Physiol., 179:298-322.

Kubota, K. and Mikami, A. (1980). Neuronal activity in the monkey dorso-lateral prefrontal cortex during a discrimination task with delay. Brain Res., 183:29-42.

Kubota, K. (1982). Prefrontal neuron activities, reversal and error performance. In " Conditioning: representation of involved neural functions", C.D.Woody ed., Plenum Press.

Kuffler, J. and Nicholls, J. (1976). From neuron to brain: a cellular approach to the function of the nervous system. Sunderland, Mass., Sinauer Ass.

Kuno, M. (1964). Mechanism of facilitation and depression of the excitatory synaptic potential in spinal motoneurons. J. Physiol. Lond. 175:100-112.

Kwan, H.C., MacKay, W.A., Murphy, J.T. and Wong, Y.C. (1978). Spatial organization of precentral cortex in awake primates. II. Motor outputs. J. Neurophysiol., 41:1120-1131.

Lamarre, Y., Bioulac, B. and Jacks, B. (1978). Activity of precentral neurons in conscious monkeys: effects of deafferentation and cerebellar ablation. J. Physiol., Paris, 74:253-264.

Landry, P. and Deschenes, M. (1981). Intracortical arborizations and receptive fields of identified ventrobasal thalamocortical afferents to the primary somatic sensory cortex in the cat. J. comp. Neurol., 199:345-371.

Langley, P. (1981). Data-driven discovery of spatial laws. Cognitive Science 5.

Laurière, J.L. (1978). A language and a program for stating and solving combinatorial problems. Artificial Intelligence, 10,1.

Le Brun Kemper, T., Galaburda A.M. (1984). Principles of cytoarchitectonics. In "Cerebral cortex Vol(1): cellular components of the cerebral cortex" A.Peters and E.G.Jones eds. Plenum Press NY.

Le Doux, J.E., Wilson, D.H. and Gazzaniga, M.S. (1977). Manipulo-spatial aspects of cerebral lateralization: clues to the origin of lateralization. Neuropsychologia, 15:743-750.

Lehninger, A.L. (1972). Biochemistry, the molecular basis of cell structure and function. Worth Publishers Inc.

Lenat D.B. (1977). The ubiquity of discovery. Artificial intelligence. Vol 9,3.

Lenneberg, E. (1967). Biological foundations of language. Wiley, New York.

Le Vay, S. (1973). Synaptic patterns in the visual cortex of the cat and monkey. Electron microscopy of Golgi preparations. J. comp. Neurol., 150:53-86.

Le Vay, S., Hubel, D.H. and Wiesel, T.N. (1975). The pattern of ocular dominance columns in macaque visual cortex revealed by a reduced silver stain. J. comp. Neurol., 159:559-576.

Le Vay, S., Wiesel, T.N. and Hubel, D.H. (1981). The postnatal development and plasticity of ocular-dominance columns in the monkey.In the organization of the cerebral cortex, F.Schmitt et al eds., Cambridge, Mass., MIT Press.

Levi-Montalcini, R. (1964). The nerve growth factor. Ann. N.Y. Acad.Sci, 118:149-170.

Lev-Tov, A., Miller, J.P., Burke, R.E. and Rall, W. (1983). Factors that control amplitude of EPSPs in dendritic neurons. J. Neurophysiology, vol. 50, no. 2, printed in USA.

Levitan, I.B., Adams, W.B., Lemos, J.R., Novak-Hofer, I. (1983). A role for protein phosphorylation in thre regulation of electrical activity of an identified nerve cell. In " Molecular and cellular interactions underlying higher brain functions" Changeux, J.P., Glowinski, J., Imbert, M., Bloom, F.E. eds. Elsevier Amsterdam.

Levy, J. (1974). Psychobiological implications of bilateral asymmetry. In S.J. Dimond and J.G. Beaumont eds., Hemisphere Function in the Human Brain, Lond., Paul Elek.

Levy, W.B., Steward, O. (1979). Synapses as associative memory elements in the hippocampal formation. Brain Res., 175:233-245.

Lewis, D.V. and Wilson, W.A. (1982). Calcium Influx and Poststimulus Current During Early Adaptation in Aplysia Giant Neurons. J. Neurophysiol., vol.48, no.1, Printed in USA.

Lhermitte, F., Derouesne, J. and Signoret, J.L. (1972). Analyse neuropsychologique du syndrome frontal. Revue Neurologique, 127:415-440.

Lindsay, P.H., Norman, D.A. (1972). Human information processing: an introduction to psychology. New York, Acad. Press.

Lieberman, P. (1973). On the evolution of language: a unified view. Cognition, 2:59-94.

Livingston, K.E. and Escobar, A. (1973). Tentative limbic system models for certain patterns of psychiatric disorders. In L.V. Laitinen and K.E. Livingston eds., Surgical Approaches in Psychiatry, Baltimore: University Park Press, p.245.

Llinas, R. and Sugimori, M. (1980 a). Electrophysiological properties of in vitro Purkinje cell somata in mammalian cerebellar slices. J. Physiol., Lond., 305:171-195.

Llinas, R.R. (1984). Comparative electrobiology of mammalian central neurons. In "Brain slices" R. Dingledine ed. Plenum Press NY.

Llinas, R., Greenfield, S.A., Jahnsen, H. (1984). Electrophysiology of pars compacta in the in vitro substantia nigra: a possible mechanism of dendritic release. Brain Res. 294:127-132.

Lohrman, R., Orgel, L.E. (1968). Prebiotic synthesis: phosphorylation in aquaeous solution. Science, 161:64-66.

Lorente de No, R. (1938). The cerebral cortex: architecture, intracortical connections and motor projections. In Physiology of the nervous system, J. Fulton, ed., Lond., Oxford University Press, pp. 291-325.

Lorente de No, R. (1943). Cerebral cortex: architecture, intracortical connections, motor projections. In Physiology of the nervous system, J. Fulton, ed., Lond., Oxford University Press, pp. 274-301.

Lund, J.S. and Boothe, R.G. (1975). Interlaminar connections and pyramidal neuron organization in the visual cortex, area 17, of the macaque monkey. J. comp. Neurol., 159:305-334.

Lund, J.S. (1984). Spiny stellate neurons. In "Cerebral cortex Vol(1): cellular components of the cerebral cortex " A.Peters and E.G.Jones eds. Plenum Press NY.

Lund, J.S., Boothe, R.G. and Lund, R.D. (1977). Development of neurons in the visual cortex (area 17) of the monkey (Macaca nemestrina): a Golgi study from fetal day 127 to postnatal maturity. J. comp. Neurol., 176:149-188.

Lund, J.S. (1981). Intrinsic organization of the primate visual cortex, area 17, as seen in Golgi preparations.In the organization of the cerebral cortex, F.Schmitt et al eds., Cambridge, Mass., MIT Press.

Lynch, G., Kessler, M., Baudry, M. (1984). Correlated electrophysiological and biochemical studies of hippocampal slices. In "Brain slices" R. Dingledine ed. Plenum Press NY.

Luria, A.R. (1966 a). Higher cortical functions in Man. New York, Basic Books.

Luria, A.R. (1973 a). The working brain. New York, Basic Books.

Luria, A. (1978). Les fonctions corticales superieures de l'homme. Presses Universitaires de France, Paris.

Luscher, H.R., Ruenzel, P. and Henneman, E. (1983). Composite EPSPs in motoneurons of different sizes before and during PTP: implications for transmission failure and its relief in la projections. J.Neurophysiology, vol.49, no 1, printed in USA.

Lynch, J.C., Mountcastle, V.B., Talbot, W.H. and Yin, T.C.T. (1977). Parietal lobe mechanisms for directed visual attention. J. Neurophysiol., 40:362-389.

von der Malsburg, C. (1981). The correlation theory of brain function. Internal Report 81-2 Max-Planck Institute for Diophysical Chemistry, Department of Neurobiology, D-3400, Gottingen, West-Germany.

Marin-Padilla M. (1984). Neurons of layer I: a developmental analysis. In "Cerebral cortex Vol(1): cellular components of the cerebral cortex " A.Peters and E.G.Jones eds. Plenum Press NY.

Marin-Padilla, M. (1974). Three-dimensional reconstruction of the pericellular nests (baskets of the motor -area 4- and visual-area 17- areas of the human cerebral cortex). A Golgi study.Z. Anat. Entwickl.-Gesch., 144:123-135.

Marr, D. (1970). A theory for cerebral neocortex. Proc. R. Soc. B., 176:161-234.

Marr, D. (1969). A theory of cerebellar cortex. J. Physiol., 202:437-470.

Marr, D. (1982). Vision. Freeman, NY.

Martin, A.R. (1966). Quantal nature of synaptic transmission. Physiol.Rev., 46:51-66.

Martin, A.R. (1977). Junctional transmission. Presynaptic mechanisms. In Handbook of Physiology, J.M. Brookhart, V.B. Mountcastle eds., Williams and Wilkins, Baltimore.

Martin, K.A.C., Perry, V.H. (1983). The role of fiber ordering and axon collateralization in the formation of topographic projections. In " Molecular and cellular interactions underlying higher brain functions" Changeux, J.P., Glowinski, J., Imbert, M., Bloom, F.E. eds. Elsevier Amsterdam.

Martin, K.A.C, Somogyi, P. and Whitteridge, D. (1983). Physiological and morphological properties of identified basket cells in the cat's visual cortex. Exp. Brain Res., 50:193-200.

Mates, S.L. and Lund, J.S. (1983). Spine Formation and Maturation of Type 1 Synapses on Spiny Stellate Neurons in Primate Visual Cortex. J. comp. Neurol., 221:91-97.

Mc Culloch, W.S., Pitts, W. (1943). A logical calculus of the ideas immanent in nervous activity. Bull. Math. Biophys., 5:115-133.

Mc Kenna, T.M., Whitsel, B.L. and Dreyer, D.A. (1982). Anterior Parietal Cortical Topographic Organization in Macaque Monkey: a Reevaluation. J. Neurophysiol., vol.48, no.2, Printed in USA.

Mc Kinney, M., Coyle, J.T. and Heldreen, J.C. (1983). Topographic Analysis of the Innervation of the Rat Neocortex and Hippocampus by the Basal Forebrain Cholinergic System. J. comp.Neurol., 217:103-121.

Mc Lean, P. (1970). The triune brain, emotions and scientific bias. In The Neurosciences, Second Study Program, F.Schmitt ed., New York, Rockefeller University Press, 336-349.

McClelland J.L., Rumelhart D.E. (1986). Parallel Distributed Processing Explorations in the microstructure of cognition. Vol 2 : Psychological and biological models. MIT Press. Cambridge.

Mc Naughton, B.L., Barnes, C.A. (1977). Physiological identification and analysis of dentate granule cell responses to stimulation of the medial and lateral perforant pathways in the rat. J. comp. Neurol., 175:439-453.

Mc Naughton, B.L., Douglas, R.M., Goddard, G.V. (1978). Synaptic enhancement in fascia dentata: cooperativity among coactive afferents. Brain Res., 157:277-293.

Meech, R. (1979). Membrane potential oscillations in molluscan.

Menyuk, P. (1971). The acquisition and development of language. Englewood cliffs, N.J., Prentice-Hall.

Merzenich, N.M., Nelson, R.J., Styker, M.P., Cyhnader, M., Schoppmann, A., Zook, J.M. (1984). Somato-sensory cortical maps changes following digit amputation in adult monkeys. J.Comp.Neur., 224:591-604.

Merzenich, M.M., Jenkins, W.M., Middlebrooks J.C. (1984). Observations and hypothesis on special organisational features of the central auditory nervous system. In "Dynamic aspects of neocortical functions" G.M. Edelman, W.E. Gall, W.M.Cowan eds, John Wiley NY.

Mesulam, M.M. and Mufson, E.J. (1982). Insula of the Old World Monkey.III: Efferent Cortical Output and Comments on Function.J. comp. Neurol., 212:38-52.

Miller, J.M., Beaton, R.D., O'Connor, T. and Pfingst, B.E. (1974). Response pattern complexity of auditory cells in the cortex of unanesthetized monkeys. Brain Res., 69:101-113.

Miller, J.P. and Selverston, A.I. (1982). Mechanisms Underlying Pattern Generation in Lobster Stomatogastric Ganglion as Determined by Selective Inactivation of Identified Neurons. IV. Network Properties of Pyloric System. J. Neurophysiol., vol.48, no.6, Printed in USA.

Milner, B. (1974 a). Hemispheric specialization: scope and limits. In F.O.Schmitt and F.G.Worden eds., The Neurosciences, Third Study Program, Cambridge, Mass., MIT Press, 75-88.

Milner, B., Petrides, M. (1984). Behevioral effects of frontal lobe lesions in man. TINS, 48:11.

Minsky, M., Papert, S. (1972). Perceptrons. Cambridge, Mass., MIT Press.

Mountcastle, V.B., Motter, B.C., Steinmetz, M.A., Duffy.C.J. (1984). Looking and seeing: the visual functions of the parietal lobe.In "Dynamic aspects of neocortical functions" G.M.Edelman, W.E. Gall, W.M. Cowan eds, John Wiley NY.

Mountcastle, V.B., Lynch, J.C., Georgopoulos, A., Sakata, H. and Acuna, A. (1975). Posterior parietal association cortex of the monkey:command functions for operation within extrapersonal space. J. Neurophysiol., 38:871-908.

Mountcastle, V.B. (1978). An organizing principle for cerebral function: the unit module and the distributed system. In The mindful brain, F.O.Schmitt ed., MIT Press, Cambridge, Mass. pp. 7-50.

Mountcastle, V.B. (1980). Sleep, wakefulness and the conscious state. In Medical physiology, V.B.Mouncastle ed., C.V. Mosby Company.

Mountcastle, V.B., Andersen, R.A. and Motter, B.C. (1981). Tho influence of attentive fixation upon the excitability of the light-sensitive neurons of the posterior parietal cortex. J. Neurosci., 1:1218-1235.

Nauta, W.J.H. (1962). Neural associations of the amygdaloid complex in the monkey. Brain, 85:505.

Nauta, W.J.H. and Karten, H.J. (1970). A general profile of the vertebrate brain, with sidelights on the ancestry of cerebral cortex In The Neurosciences, Second Study Program, F.O.Schmitt, ed., New York, Rockefeller, pp. 7-25.

Nauta, W.J.H. (1971). The problem of the frontal lobe: a reinterpretation. Journal of Psychiatric Research, 8:167-187.

Neher, E., Stevens, C.F. (1979). Voltage driven conformational changes in intrinsic membrane proteins. In The Neurosciences, Fourth Study Program, F.O.Schmitt, W.G.Worden eds., MIT Press.

Neher, E., Marty, A., Fenwick, E. (1983). Ionic channels for signal transmission and propagation. In " Molecular and cellular interactions underlying higher brain functions" Changeux, J.P., Glowinski, J., Imbert, M., Bloom, F.E. eds. Elsevier Amsterdam.

Newell, A. and Simon, H.A. (1972). Human problem solving. Englewood Cliffs, N.J., Prentice-Hall.

Niouellon, A., Cheramy, A., Glowinski, J. (1977). Release of dopamine in vivo from cat substantia nigra. Nature, 266, 375-377.

Nishizawa, Y., Skyhojolsen, T., Larsen, B. and Lassen, N.A. (1982). Left-Right Cortical Asymmetries of Regional Cerebral Blood Flow During Listening to Words. J. Neurophysiol., vol.48, no.2, Printed in USA.

Ojemann, G.A., Fedio, P. and Buren, J.M. (1968). Anomia from pulvinar and subcortical parietal stimulation. Brain, 91:99-116.

Ojemann, G. and Mateer, C. (1979). Human language cortex: localization of memory, syntax and sequential motor-phenomene identifcation systems. Science, 205:1401-1403.

O'Hara, P.T., Liebermann, A.R., Hund, S.P., Wu, J.Y. (1983). Neuronal element containing glutamic acid decarboxylase (GAD) in the dorsal lateral geniculate nucleus of the rat: immunohistochemical studies by light and electron microscopy. Neurosciences 8: 189-211.

O'Keefe, J. (1983). Two spatial learning systems in the rat brain - implications for the neural basis of learning and memory. In " Molecular and cellular interactions underlying higher brain functions" Changeux, J.P., Glowinski, J., Imbert, M., Bloom, F.E. eds. Elsevier Amsterdam.

O'Keefe, J. and Nadel, L. (1978). The hippocampus as a cognitive map. Oxford University Press, Lond.

O'Kusky, J. and Colonnier, M. (1982). A Laminar Analysis of the Number of Neurons, Glia and Synapses in the Visual Cortex (Area 17) of Adult Macaque Monkeys. J. comp. Neurol., 210:278-290.

Olds, J. and Milner, P. (1954). Positive reinforcement produced by electrical stimulation of septal area and other regions of rat brain. J. comp. Physiol. Psychol., 47:419-427.

Olds, J., Disterhoft, J.F., Segal, M., Kornblith, C.L. and Hirsch, R. (1972). Learning centers of rat brain mapped by measuring latencies of conditioned unit responses. J. Neurophysiol., 35:202.

Oleron, P. (1976). L'acquisition du langage. In H. Gratiot-Alphandery et R. Zazzo eds., Traité de psychologie de l'enfant, vol 6, PUF, Paris, 71-208.

Olson, G.M. (1973). Developmental changes in memory and the acquisition of language. In T.E. Moore ed., Cognitive development and the acquisition of language, New York, Acad. Press.

Oscarsson, O. (1976). Spatial distribution of climbing and mossy fibre inputs into the cerebellar cortex. Exp. Brain Res., 1:36-42.

Osgood, L.E., Sebeok, T.A. eds. (1954). Psycholinguistics. A survey of theory and research problems. Baltimore.

Oshima, T. (1969). Studies of pyramidal tract cells. In Basic Mechanisms of the Epilepsies, H.H. Jasper, A.A. Ward and A. Pope, eds., Boston, Little Brown, pp. 253-262.

Paillard J., Beaubaton D. (1978). De la coordination visuo-motrice a l'organisation de la saisie manuelle. In "Du contrôle moteur a l'organisation du geste" H. Hecaen, M. Jeannerod eds., Masson, Paris.

Palay, S. (1978). The Meynert cell, an unusual cortical pyramidal cell. In Architectonics of the cerebral cortex, M.Brazier and H.Petsche eds., New York, Raven Press, pp. 31-42.

Pandya, D.N. and Kuypers, H.G.J.M. (1969). Cortico-cortical connections in the rhesus monkey. Brain Research, 13:13.

Pandya, D.N., Dye, P. and Butters, N. (1971). Efferent cortico-cortical projections of the pre-frontal cortex in the rhesus monkey. Brain Res., 31:35-46.

Papez, J.W. (1937). A proposed mechanism of emotion. Archives of Neurological Psychiatry, 38:725.

Patterson, P.H. (1978). Environmental determination of autonomic transmitter functions. Ann. Rew. Neurosc., 1:1-17.

Pavlov, I. (1949). Oeuvres complètes, Moscou.

Pellionisz, A. and Llinas, R. (1982). Tensor theory of brain function: the cerebellum as a space-time metric. In Competition and cooperation in neural nets, S.Amari and M.Arbib eds., Berlin, Springer Verlag, pp. 294-417.

Penfield, W. and Rasmussen, T. (1950). The cerebral cortex of man.Mc Millan, New York, 11-65.

Penfield, W. and Jasper, H. (1954). Epilepsy and the functionnal anatomy of the human brain. Boston, Little Brown.

Perret, E. (1974). The left frontal lobe of man and the suppression of habitual responses in verbal categorical behavior.Neuropsychologia, 12:323-330.

Peters, A., Jones, E.G. (1984). Classification of cortical neurons. In "Cerebral cortex Vol(1): cellular components of the cerebral cortex " A. Peters and E.G. Jones eds. Plenum Press NY.

Peters A. (1984). Chandelier cells. In "Cerebral cortex Vol(1): cellular components of the cerebral cortex " A. Peters and E.G. Jones eds. Plenum Press NY.

Peters A.(1984). Bipolar cells. In "Cerebral cortex Vol(1): cellular components of the cerebral cortex " A. Peters and E.G. Jones eds. Plenum Press NY.

Phelps, M.E., Kuhl, D. and Mazziotta, J. (1981). Metabolic mapping of the brain's response to visual stimulation: studies in humans. Science, 211:1445-1447.

Phillips, C.G. and Porter, R. (1977). Corticospinal Neurons. Their Role in Movement. Lond., Academic.

Piaget, J. et Inhelder, B. (1948). La représentation de l'espace chez l'enfant. PUF, Paris.

Piaget, J. (1950). La construction du réel chez l'enfant. Neuchatel, Delachaux et Niestlé.

Piaget, J. (1964). La formation du symbole chez l'enfant. Paris, Delachaux et Niestlé.

Piaget, J. (1968). La naissance de l'intelligence chez l'enfant. Neuchatel et Paris, Delachaux et Niestlé (9e édition).

Piaget, J. (1975 b). L'équilibration des structures cognitives, problème central du développement. PUF, Paris.

Pierce, J.E. (1974). The phonological structure of infant language: year one. Bulletin d'audio-phonologie, Prelangage, 2:337 363.

Pitrat, J. (1977). A chess combination program which uses plans. Journal of artificial Intelligence, Vol.8(3).

Poggio, G.F. and Fisher, B. (1977). Binocular interaction and depth sensitivity of striate and prestriate cortical neurons of the behaving rhesus monkey. J. Neurophysiol., 40:1392-1405.

Poggio, G.F. (1984). Processing of stereoscopic information in primate visual cortex. In "Dynamic aspects of neocortical functions" G.M Edelman, W.E. Gall, W.M. Cowan eds, John Wiley NY.

Pottier, B. (1973). Les langues dans le monde. In "Le langage" B. Pottier ed. CEPL, Paris.

Powell, T.P.S., Guillery, R.W. and Cowan, W.M. (1957). A quantitative study of the fornix-mammillo-thalamic system. J. Anat.91:419-437.

Premack, D. (1971). Language in chimpanzee? Science, 172:808-822.

Premack, D. (1976 a). Mechanisms of intelligence: preconditions for language. Annals of the New York Academy of Sciences, 280:544-561.

Prosser, C.L. (1973). Central nervous sytem. In Comparative animal physiology, W.B. Saunders.

Purpura, D.P., Shofer, R.J. and Musgrave, F.S. (1964). Cortical intracellular potentials during augmenting and recruiting responses. II. Patterns of synaptic activities in pyramidal and nonpyramidal tract neurons. J. Neurophysiol., 27:133-151.

Rabinowicz, T. (1974). Some aspects of the maturation of the human cerebral cortex. In Pre and postnatal development of the human brain, Karger, Basel.

Rakic, P. (1971). Guidance of neurons migrating to the fetal monkey neocortex. Brain Res., 33:471-476.

Rakic, P. (1974). Neurons in rhesus monkey visual cortex: systematic relation between time of origin and eventual disposition. Science, 183:425-427.

Rakic, P. (1981). Developmental events leading to laminar and areal organization of the neocortex. In the organization of the cerebral cortex, F. Schmitt et al eds., Cambridge, Mass., MIT Press.

Rakic, P. and Goldman-Rakic, P. (1982). Development and modifiability of the cerebral cortex. Neurosci. Res. Prog. Bull., 20:429-611.

Rakic, P. (1983). Geniculo-cortical connections in primates: normal and experimentally altered development. In " Molecular and cellular interactions underlying higher brain functions" Changeux, J.P., Glowinski, J., Imbert, M., Bloom, F.E. eds. Elsevier Amsterdam.

Rall, W. (1964). Theoretical significance of dendritic trees for neuronal input-output relations. In Neural Theory and Modelling, R.F. Reiss ed., Palo Alto, Stanford University Press, pp. 73-97.

Rall, W. and Rinzel, J. (1971). Dendritic spine function and synaptic attenuation calculations. Soc. Neurosci. Abstr., 64.

Ramier, A.M. and Hecaen, H. (1970). Rôle respectif des atteintes frontales et de la latéralisation lésionnelle dans les déficits de la "fluence verbale". Revue Neurologique, 123:17-22.

Rasmussen (1984). Calcium messenger system: an integrated view. Physiological reviews 64(3).

Reich, P. (1976). The early acquisition of word meaning. Journal of Child Language, 3:117-123.

Ribak, C.E. (1978). Aspinous and sparsely-spinous stellate neurons in the visual cortex of rats contain glutamic acid decarboxylase. J. Neurocytol., 7:461-478.

Richelle, M. (1971). L'acquisition du langage. Dessart et Mardaga, Bruxelles.

Richmond, B.J., Wurtz, R.H., Sato, T., (1983). Visual responses of IT neurons in the awake monkey. J. Neurophysiol. 50:1415-32.

Rizzolatti, G., Scando-Lara, C., Matelli, M. and Gentilucci, M. (1981). Afferent properties of periarcuate neurons in macaque monkeys. I. Somato-sensory responses. Behav. Brain Research, 2:125-146.

Robinson, D.L., Goldberg, M.E. and Stanton, G.B. (1975). Parietal association cortex in the primate: sensory mechanisms and behavioral modulations. J. Neurophysiol., 41:910-932.

Robson, J.A. and Hall, W.C. (1977). The organization of the pulvinar in the grey squirrel (sciurus carolinensis). II synaptic organization and comparisons with the dorsal lateral geniculate nucleus. J. comp. Neurol., 173:389-416.

Rockel, A.J., Hiorns, R.W. and Powell, T.P.S. (1974). Numbers of neurons through full depth of neocortex. Proc. Anat. Soc. Gr.Br.Ire., 118:371.

Rockell, A. Hiorns, R. and Powell, T. (1980). The basic uniformity in structure of the neocortex. Brain, 103:221-224.

Rockland, K.S. and Lund, J.S. (1983). Intrinsic Laminar Lattice Connections in Primate Visual Cortex. J. comp. Neurol., 216:303-318.

Rockland, K.S. Lund, J.S. (1982): Widespread periodic intrisic connections in the tree-shrew visual cortex. Science 215:1532-34.

Roland, P.E. (1984). Metabolic measurement of the working frontal cortex in man. TINS, 48:11.

Roland, P.E. (1982). Cortical Regulation of Selective Attention in Man. A Regional Cerebral Blood Flow Study. J. Neurophysiol., vol.48, no.5, Printed in USA.

Rolls, E.T. (1982). Neural mechanisms underlying the formation and disconnections of associations between visual stimuli and reinforcement in primates. In Conditioning: representations of involved neural functions, C.D.Woody ed., Plenum Press.

Rondal, J.A. (1978 a). Langage et éducation. Dessart et Mardaga, Bruxelles.

Rosenblatt, F. (1958). The perception: a probabilistic model for information storage and organization in the brain. Psych. Rev., 65:386-408.

Rumelhart D.E., McClelland J.L. (1986). Parallel Distributed Processing Explorations in the microstructure of cognition. Vol 1 : Foundations. MIT Press. Cambridge.

Ruwet, N. (1967). Introduction à la grammaire générative. Plon Paris.

Saltz, E. (1971). The cognitive bases of human learning. Homewood III, Dorsey Press.

Sakai, M., Hamada, I. (1981). Intracellular activity and morphology of the precentral neurons related to visual attention tasks in behaving monkeys. Exp. Brain. Res., 41:195-198.

Sakata, H., Takaska, Y., Karasawak, A. and Shubitani, H. (1973). Somatosensory properties of neurons in the superior parietal cortex (Area 5) of the rhesus monkey. Brain Res., 64:85.

Sandell, J.H., Sciller, P.H. (1982). Effects of cooling area 18 on stiate cortex cells in the squirrel monkey. J. Neurophysiol. 84.

Sauer, B., Kammradt, G., Krauthausen, I. Kretschmann, H.J., Lange, H.W. and Wingert, F. (1983). Qualitative and Quantitative Development of the Visual Cortex in Man. J. comp. Neurol., 214:441-450.

Schank, R.C. (1975). Conceptual information processing. NY North Holland.

Schank, R.C., Abelson R (1977). Scripts, plans, goals and understanding. Lawrence Erlbaum Ass. N.J.

Schwartzkroin, P.A. and Stafstrom, C.E. (1980). Effects of EGTA on the calcium-activated after hyperpolarization in hippocampal CA3 pyramidal cells. Science, 210:1125-1126.

Shepherd, G.M. (1979). The synaptic organization of the brain. New-York, Oxford University Press.

Shinoda, Y., Yokata, J., Futami, T. (1982). Morphology of physiologically identified rubrospinal axons in the spinal cord. Brain Res. 242:231-235.

Siegel, J.M. (1979). Behavioral functions of the reticular formation. Brain Res Rew., I:69-105.

Sillito, A.M. (1975). The contribution of inhibitory mechanisms to the receptive field properties of neurons in the striate cortex of the cat. J. Physiol. Lond., 250:305-329.

Sillito, A.M. (1977). Inhibitory processes underlying the directional specificity of simple, complex and hypercomplex cells in the cat's visual cortex. J. Physiol., 271:699-720.

Simon, J.-C. La reconnaissance des formes par algorithmes ; Masson, Paris.

Sinclair, H. and Bronckart, J.P. (1972). S.V.O. A linguistic universal? A study in developmental psycholinguistics. Journal of Experimental Child Psychology, 14:329-348.

Smith, M. (1926). An investigation of the development of sentence and the extent of vocabulary in children. University of Iowa Studies in Welfare, 3, no.5.

Smith, A.M. (1979). The activity of supplementary motor area neurons during a maintained precision grip. Brain Res., 172:315-327.

Somogyi, P. (1977). A specific "axo-axonal" interneuron in the visual cortex of the rat. Brain Res., 136:345-350.

Somogyi, P., Cowey, A. (1984). Double bouquet cells. In "Cerebral cortex Vol(1): cellular components of the cerebral cortex " A. Peters and E.G. Jones eds. Plenum Press NY.

Somogyi, P. and Cowey, A. (1980). The synapses formed by Cajal's cellules a double bouquet dendritique in the visual cortex of the cat and monkey. A combined Golgi and electron microscopy study. Neuroscience Letters, Suppl.5, 118.

Spencer, W.A. and Kandel, E.R. (1961). Electrophysiology of hippocampal neurons. J. Neurophysiol., 24:272-285.

Spencer, W.A. (1977). The physiology of supraspinal neurons. In Handbook of Physiology, J.M. Brookhart, V.B. Mountcastle eds., Williams and Wilkins.

Sperry, R.W. and Gazzaniga, M.S. (1967). Language following surgical disconnection of the hemisphere. In C.H. Millikan and F. Darley eds., Brain Mechanisms Underlying Speech and Language, New York, Grune and Stratton.

Sperry, R.W. (1974). Lateral specialization in the surgically hemispheres. In F.O. Schmitt ed., The neurosciences, Third Study Program, Cambridge, MIT Press.

Stafstrom, C.E., Schwindt, P.C., Chubb, M.C., Crill, W.E. (1985).Properties of persistant sodium conductance and calcium conductance of layer V neurons from cat sensorimotor cortex in vitro. J. Neuphysiol. Vol 53.

Stefanis, C. and Jasper, H. (1964). Intracellular microelectrode studies of antidromic responses in cortical pyramidal tract neurons. J. Neurophysiol., 27:828-854.

Stefanis, C. and Jasper, H. (1964). Recurrent collateral inhibition in pyramidal tract neurons. J. Neurophysiol., 27:855-877.

Stent, G., Kristian, W., Friesen, W., Ort, C., Poon, M. and Calabrese, R.(1978). Neuronal generation of the leech swimming movement.Science, 200:1348-1357.

Stent, G.S. (1983). Rhythm generator circuit in a simple nervous system. In " Molecular and cellular interactions underlying higher brain functions" Changeux, J.P., Glowinski, J., Imbert, M., Bloom, F.E. eds. Elsevier, Amsterdam.

Steriade, M. (1984). The excitatory-Inhibitory response sequence in thalamic and neocortical cells: state -related changes and regulatory systems. In "Dynamic aspects of neocortical functions" G.M. Edelman, W.E. Gall, W.M. Cowan eds, John Wiley NY.

Stone, J. and Dreher, B. (1973). Projection of X- and Y- cells of the cat's lateral geniculate nucleus to areas 17 and 18 of visual cortex. J. Neurophysiol., 36:551-567.

Stone, T.W. (1976). Blockade by amino-acid antagonists of neuronal excitation mediated by the pyramidal tract. J. Physiol., 257:187-198.

Strick, P.L. and Preston, J.B. (1982). Two Representations of the Hand in Area 4 of a Primate. I. Motor Output Organization. J. Neurophysiol., vol.48, no.1, Printed in USA.

Suga, N. (1984). The extent to which binaural information is represented in the bat auditory cortex. In "Dynamic aspects of neocortical functions" G.M.Edelman, W.E.Gall, W.M.Cowan eds, John Wiley NY.

Szentagothai, J. (1970). Glomerular synapses, complex synaptic arrangements, and their operational significance. In the Neurosciences, Second Study Program F.O.Schmitt, ed., New York, Rockefeller, pp. 427-443.

Szentagothai, J. (1975). The "module concept" in cerebral cortex architecture. Brain Res., 95:475-496.

Szentagothai, J. (1979). Local neuron circuits of the neocortex. In The Neurosciences, Fourth Study Program, F.O.Schmitt and F.G.Worden eds., MIT Press, Cambridge, Mass., pp. 399-415.

Takahashi, K., Kubota, K. and Uno, M. (1967). Recurrent facilitation in cat pyramidal tract cells. J. Neurophysiol., 30:22-34.

Takeuchi, A. (1977). Junctional transmission. Postsynaptic mechanisms In Handbook of physiology, J.M.Brookhart, V.B.Mountcastle eds., Williams and Wilkins, Baltimore.

Tanji, J. and Evarts, E.V. (1976). Anticipatory activity of motor cortex neurons in relation to direction of an intended movement. J. Neurophysiol., 39:1062-1068.

Taylor, D.A. and Stone, T.W. (1981). Neurotransmodulatory control of cerebral cortical neuron activity. In the organization of the cerebral cortex, F. Schmitt et al eds., Cambridge, Mass., MIT Press.

Thach, W.T. (1978). Correlation of neural discharge with pattern and force of muscular activity, joint position and direction of intended movement in motor cortex and cerebellum. J. Neurophysiol., 41:650-676.

Thierry, A.M., Blanc, G., Sobel, A., Stinus, L. and Glowinski, J. (1973). Dopamine terminals in the rat cortex. Science, 182:499-501.

Thorpe (1963). Learning and instinct in animals. Methuen, Lond.

Tombol, T. (1984). Layer VI cells. In "Cerebral cortex Vol(1): cellular components of the cerebral cortex " A.Potors and E.G.Jones eds. Plenum Press NY.

Toyama, K., Tanaka, K. (1984). Visual cortical functions studied by cross-correlations analysis. In "Dynamic aspects of neocortical functions" G.M. Edelman, W.E. Gall, W.M. Cowan eds, John Wiley NY

Traub, R.D. and Llinas, R. (1979). Hippocampal pyramidal cells: significance of dendritic ionic conductances for neuronal function and epileptogenesis. J. Neurophysiol., 42:476-498.

Tsukahara, N. (1981). Synaptic plasticity in the mammalian central nervous system. Ann. Rev. Neurosci., 4:351-379.

Tsukahara, N. (1982). Classical conditioning mediated by the red nucleus. In Conditioning: representations of involved neural functions, C.D. Woody ed., Plenum Press.

Tsumoto, T., Eckart, W. and Creutzfeldt, O.D. (1979). Modification of orientation sensitivity of cat visual cortex neurons by removal of GABA-mediated inhibition. Ex. Brain Res., 34:351-363.

Ungerleider, L.G., Desimone, R. (1986). Projections to the Superior Temporal sulcus from he central and peripheral representation of V1 and V2. J. Comp. Neur 248:164-189.

Turner, D.A. and Schwartzkroin, P.A. (1980). Steady-state electronic analysis of intracellularly stained hippocampal neurons. J. Neurophysiol., 44:184-199.

Turner, D.A., Schwartzkroin, P.A. (1984). Passive electotonic structure and dendritic properties of hippocampal neurons.In "Brain slices" R.Dingledine ed. Plenum Press NY.

Turner, J. (1975). Cognitive development. Lond., Methuen.

Ullman, S., (1984). On the measurement and use of visual motion. In "Dynamic aspects of neocortical functions" G.M.Edelman, W.E.Gall, W.M.Cowan eds, John Wiley NY.

Van Essen, D.C. and Zeki, S.M. (1978). The topographic organization of rhesus monkey prestriate cortex. J. Physiol., Lond., 277:273-290.

Van Essen, D.C. (1979). Visual areas of the mammalian cerebral cortex. Ann. Rev. Neurosci., 2:227-263.

Van Essen, D.C., Maunsell, J.H.R. (1983). Hierarchical organization and functional streams in the visual cortex. Trends in neurosciences. 6.9.

Vogt, B.A. and Gorman, L.F. (1982). Responses of Cortical Neurons to Stimulation of Corpus Callosum in Vitro. J. Neurophysiol., vol.48, no.6, Printed in USA.

Von Economo, C. (1929). The cytoarchitectonics of the human cerebral cortex. Lond., Oxford University Press.

Vurpillot, E. (1972 b). Les perceptions du nourrisson. PUF, Paris.

Walter, W.G. (1973). Human frontal lobe fuction in sensory motor association. In K.H.Pribman and A.R.Luria eds., Psychophysiology of the Frontal Lobes, New York, Acad. Press, 109-122.

Weisblat, D. (1983). Cell lineage development of the leech nervous system. In " Molecular and cellular interactions underlying higher brain functions" Changeux, J.P., Glowinski, J., Imbert, M., Bloom, F.E. eds. Elsevier Amsterdam.

Weiskrantz, L. (1956). Behavioral changes associated with ablation of the amygdaloid complex in monkeys. Journal of Comparative and Physiological Psychology, 49:381-391.

Wernicke, C. (1874). Der aphasische Symptomencomplex. Breslau, M. Cohn et Weigert, 72pp.

White, E.L. (1979). Thalamocortical synaptic relations: a review with emphasis on the projections of specific thalamic nuclei to the primary sensory areas of the cortex. Br. Res. Rev., 1:275-311.

White, E. (1981). Thalamocortical synaptic relations. In the organization of the cerebral cortex, F. Schmitt et al. eds., Cambridge, Mass., MIT Press, pp. 153-162.

Whitsel, B.L., Ropollo, J.R. and Werner, G. (1972). Cortical information processing of stimulus motion on primate skin. J. Neurophysiol., 32:170-183.

Widrow, G., Hoff, M.E. (1960). Adaptive switching circuits. Institute of Radio Engineers, Western Electronic Show and Convention, Convention Record, Part 4, 96-104.

Winfield, D.A., Brook, D.L.N., Sloper, J.J., Powell, T.P.S. (1981). A combined Golgi-electron microscopic study of the synapses made by the proximal axon and recurent collaterals of a proximal cells in the somatosensory cortex of the monkey Neurosci. 6:1217-30.

Wise, S.P., Strick, P.L. (1984). Anatomical and physiological organisation of the non-primary motor cortex. TINS, 48:11.

Wise, S.P. (1984). The non-primary cerebral cortex and its role in the cerebral control of mouvement. In "Dynamic aspects of neocortical functions" G.M.Edelman, W.E.Gall, W.M.Cowan eds, John Wiley NY.

Wong, J.T.F. (1981). Coevolution of genetic code and aminoacid biosynthesis. Trends Bioch. Sci., 6:33.

Woody, C.D. and Black-Cleworth, P. (1973). Differences in excitability of cortical neurons as a function of motor projection in conditioned cats. J. Neurophysiol., 36:1104-1116.

Woody, C.D., Knispel, J.D., Crow, J.J. and Black-Cleworth, P.A. (1976). Activity and excitability of electrical current of cortical auditory receptive neurons of awake cats as effected by stimulus association. J. Neurophysiol., 39:1045-1061.

Woody, C.D. and Engel, J. (1979). Changes in unit activity and thresholds to electrical microstimulation at coronal-pericruciate cortex of cat with classical conditioning of different facial movements. J. Neurophysiol., 35:230-241.

Woolsey, C.N., Settlage, P.H., Meyer, D.R., Spencer, W., Hamuy, T.P. and Travis, A.M. (1950 b). Patterns of localization in precentral and concept of a premotor area. Annual Research of Nervous and Mental Disease, Proceedings, 30:238-264.

Woolsey, C.N. (1958). Organization of somatic sensory and motor areas of the cerebral cortex. In Biological and Biochemical Bases of Behavior, H.F. Harlow and C.N. Woolsey eds., University Wisconsin Press, Madison, 63-81.

Woolsey, T.A. and Van Der Loos, H. (1970). The structural organization of layer IV in the somatosensory region (SI) of mouse cerebral cortex. The description of a cortical field composed of discrete cytoarchitectural units. Brain Res., 17:205-242.

Wurtz, R.H., Richmond, B.J., Newsome, W.T. (1984). Modulation of cortical visual processing by attention, perception and movement. In "Dynamic aspects of neocortical functions" G.M.Edelman, W.E.Gall, W.M.Cowan eds, John Wiley NY.

Yakolev, P.I. (1948). Motility, behavior and the brain: stereodynamic organization and neural coordinates of behavior. Journal of Nervous Mental Diseases, 107:313.

Yin, T.C.T., Kuwada, S. (1984). Neuronal mechanisms of binaural interaction. In "Dynamic aspects of neocortical functions" G.M. Edelman, W.E. Gall, W.M. Cowan eds, John Wiley NY.

Zeki, S. (1983). The relationship between wavelength and color studied in single cells of monkey striate cortex. In " Molecular and cellular interactions underlying higher brain functions" Changeux, J.P., Glowinski, J., Imbert, M., Bloom, F.E. eds. Elsevier, Amsterdam.

Zeki, S.M. (1978). Uniformity and diversity of structure and function in rhesus monkey prestriate visual cortex. J. Physiol., Lond., 277:273-292.

Zipser, D., Andersen, R.A. (1988). A back-propagation programmed network that simulates response properties of a subset of posterior parietal neurons. Nature, Vol.331: 679-684.

Index